MEI STRUCTURED MATHEMATI

THIRD EDITION

Statistics 4

Michael Davies
Bob Francis
Bill Gibson
Gerald Goodall

Series Editor: Roger Porkess

AN HACHETTE UK COMPANY

The Publishers would like to thank the following for permission to reproduce copyright material:
Photo credits Life File/David Kampfner (page 1); John Reader/Science Photo Library (page 20); Life File/Emma Lee (page 113).

Acknowledgements
OCR and AQA accept no responsibility whatsoever for the accuracy or method of working in the answers given.

Please note that the AQA (AEB) and AQA (NEAB) questions used on pages 89, 198, 199, 204 and 205 are *not* from the live examinations for the current specification. For GCE Advanced Level Mathematics, new specifications are being introduced in 2005.

Every effort has been made to trace all copyright holders, but if any have been inadvertently overlooked the Publishers will be pleased to make the necessary arrangements at the first opportunity.

Although every effort has been made to ensure that website addresses are correct at time of going to press, Hodder Murray cannot be held responsible for the content of any website mentioned in this book. It is sometimes possible to find a relocated web page by typing in the address of the home page for a website in the URL window of your browser.

Hodder Headline's policy is to use papers that are natural, renewable and recyclable products and made from wood grown in sustainable forests. The logging and manufacturing processes are expected to conform to the environmental regulations of the country of origin.

Orders: please contact Bookpoint Ltd, 130 Milton Park, Abingdon, Oxon OX14 4SB.
Telephone: (44) 01235 827720. Fax: (44) 01235 400454. Lines are open 9 am to 6 pm, Monday to Saturday, with a 24-hour message-answering service. Visit our website at www.hoddereducation.co.uk

© Michael Davies, Bob Francis, Bill Gibson, Gerald Goodall 2005
First published in 1997
Second Edition published in 2003
Third Edition published in 2005 by
Hodder Education,
an Hachette UK Company,
338 Euston Road
London NW1 3BH

Impression number   10 9 8 7 6 5 4
Year   2016 2015

All rights reserved. Apart from any use permitted under UK copyright law, no part of this publication may be reproduced or transmitted in any form or by any means, electronic or mechanical, including photocopying and recording, or held within any information storage and retrieval system, without permission in writing from the publisher or under licence from the Copyright Licensing Agency Limited. Further details of such licences (for reprographic reproduction) may be obtained from the Copyright Licensing Agency Limited, 90 Tottenham Court Road, London W1T 4LP.

Typeset in 10.5/14 pt Minion by Tech-Set, Gateshead, Tyne & Wear.
Printed and bound by CPI Group (UK) Ltd, Croydon, CR0 4YY

A catalogue record for this title is available from the British Library.

ISBN-10: 0340 905 263
ISBN-13: 978 0340 905 265

MEI Structured Mathematics

Mathematics is not only a beautiful and exciting subject in its own right but also one that underpins many other branches of learning. It is consequently fundamental to the success of a modern economy.

MEI Structured Mathematics is designed to increase substantially the number of people taking the subject post-GCSE, by making it accessible, interesting and relevant to a wide range of students.

It is a credit accumulation scheme based on 45 hour units which may be taken individually or aggregated to give Advanced Subsidiary (AS) and Advanced GCE (A Level) qualifications in Mathematics and Further Mathematics. The units may also be used to obtain credit towards other types of qualification.

The course is examined by OCR (previously the Oxford and Cambridge Schools Examination Board) with examinations held in January and June each year.

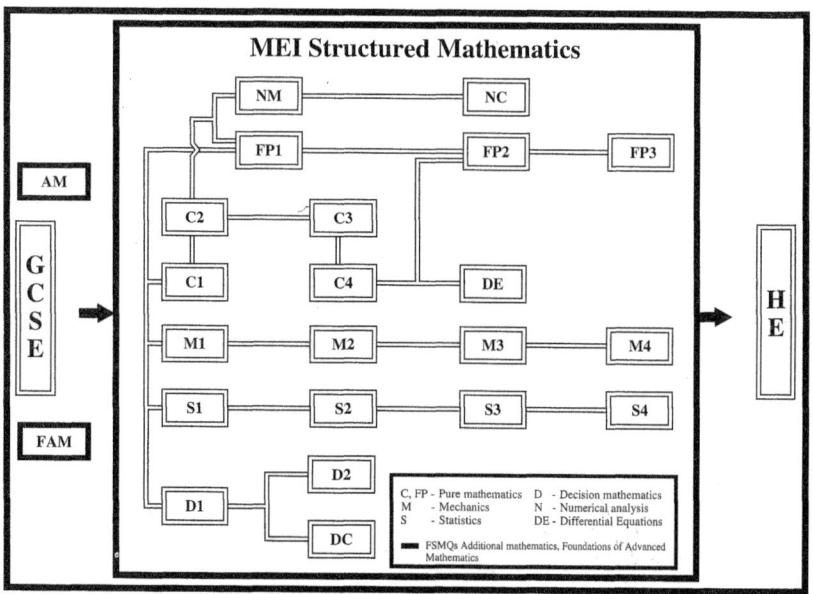

This is one of the series of books written to support the course. Its position within the whole scheme can be seen in the diagram above.

Mathematics in Education and Industry (MEI) is an independent curriculum development body which aims to promote links between education and industry in mathematics. MEI produce relevant examination specifications at GCSE, AS and A Level (including Further Mathematics) and for Free Standing Mathematics Qualifications (FSMQs); these are examined by OCR.

In partnership with Hodder Education, MEI are responsible for three major series of textbooks: Formula One Maths for Key Stage 3, Hodder Mathematics for GCSE and the MEI Structured Mathematics series, including this book, for AS and A Level.

As well as textbooks, MEI take a leading role in the development of on-line resources to support mathematics. The books in this series are complemented by a major MEI website providing full solutions to the exercises, extra questions including on-line multiple choice tests, interactive demonstrations of the mathematics, schemes of work, and much more.

In recent years MEI have worked hard to promote Further Mathematics and, in conjunction with the DfES, they are now establishing the national network of Further Mathematics Centres.

MEI are committed to supporting the professional development of teachers. In addition to a programme of Continual Professional Development, MEI, in partnership with several universities, co-ordinate the Teaching Advanced Mathematics programme, a course designed to give teachers the skills and confidence to teach A Level mathematics successfully.

Much of the work of MEI is supported by the Gatsby Charitable Foundation.

MEI is a registered charity and a charitable company.

MEI's website and email addresses are www.mei.org.uk *and* office@mei.org.uk.

Introduction

This is the fourth and last in a series of books written to support the statistics modules in MEI Structured Mathematics. The material in this book lies within Further Mathematics A level but, taken as a whole, the series is suitable for use on a wide variety of statistics courses.

By the time you reach this book you will have met several of the fundamental ideas of statistics and be ready to take them further; you will also be ready for some more advanced concepts. The book is divided into four sections, each covering an option in the MEI specification. The sections on estimation and generating functions introduce major new concepts, that on inference takes earlier work on hypothesis testing further and the final section, on experimental design, extends the ideas of sampling into new territory. By the time that you finish this book, you will be acquainted with many of the ideas that are used every day by working statisticians and be in a position to follow many of the statistical methods and arguments used in fields such as archaeology, psychology and biology.

This is the third edition of *Statistics 4* in this series. It is quite different from the two earlier books, reflecting a new module structure consequent upon changes to the regulations governing AS and A level Mathematics and Further Mathematics. While much of the material in this book was in the earlier editions of *Statistics 4*, some of it has also been drawn from other modules. Thanks are due to Michael Davies for his work in preparing this new edition.

Readers who are interested in a possible career in mathematics may wish to visit *www.mathscareers.org.uk*. Readers who are interested in a possible career involving statistics may wish to consult the Royal Statistical Society's career website, *www.rss.org.uk/careers* for further information.

Roger Porkess,
Series Editor

Key to symbols in this book

? This symbol means that you may want to discuss a point with your teacher. If you are working on your own there are answers in the back of the book. It is important, however, that you have a go at answering the questions before looking up the answers if you are to understand the mathematics fully.

⚠ This is a warning sign. It is used where a common mistake, misunderstanding or tricky point is being described.

🖥 This is the ICT icon. It indicates where you should use a graphic calculator or a computer.

e This symbol and a dotted line down the right-hand side of the page indicates material which is beyond the criteria for the unit but which is included for completeness.

☆
☆ Harder questions are indicated with stars. Many of these go beyond the usual examination standard.

Contents

1 Modelling — 1
- Sample statistics — 4
- Distributions of functions of random variables — 5
- Distributions of linear combinations of random variables — 10
- Maximum and minimum — 11

2 Estimation — 20
- Estimates for m — 21
- Estimators as random variables — 21
- Good estimators — 24
- Are M_1 and M_2 unbiased? — 25
- Estimators for population mean and variance — 34
- Estimators based on pooled samples — 36
- Methods for comparing estimators — 41
- The sampling distribution of G — 41
- Mean square error — 45
- An alternative formula for the mean square error — 45
- Efficiency — 47
- Consistency — 48

3 Maximum likelihood estimators — 54
- Likelihood — 55
- Logarithmic differentiation — 57
- Properties of maximum likelihood estimators — 60
- Continuous distributions — 61

4 Probability generating functions — 67
- Basic properties — 69
- Expectation and variance — 72
- The sum of independent random variables — 77
- The p.g.f. of a linear transformation — 80
- Extension to three or more random variables — 82
- The p.g.f.s for some standard discrete probability distributions — 85

5 Moment generating functions — 91

- Moments — 92
- Moment generating functions — 97
- Properties of moment generating functions — 103

6 Hypothesis tests on unpaired samples — 113

- The test statistic and its distribution — 115
- Carrying out the t test for an unpaired sample — 117
- Assumptions for the unpaired t test — 118
- The underlying logic of hypothesis testing — 119
- Comparison between paired and unpaired t tests — 121
- Using paired and unpaired t tests — 122
- Testing for a non-zero value of the difference of two means — 125
- Hypothesis tests and confidence intervals — 128
- Confidence intervals for the difference of two means from unpaired samples — 129

7 Large sample tests and confidence intervals — 134

- Tests and confidence intervals when the variances are known — 141
- Different known variances for the two samples — 143
- Tests with large samples — 147
- General procedure for large samples — 149

8 The Wilcoxon rank sum test — 160

- Formal procedure for the Wilcoxon rank sum test — 163
- The Mann–Whitney test — 164
- Critical values for the Wilcoxon rank sum test — 168
- Normal approximation — 169

9 Errors in hypothesis testing — 176

- Types of errors in hypothesis testing — 176
- Normal hypothesis testing — 182
- A simple alternative hypothesis — 186

10 Analysis of variance — 192

The *within groups* estimate s_w^2 — 194
The *between groups* estimate s_b^2 — 194
Carrying out the hypothesis test — 195
The *total* estimate s^2 — 199
The ANOVA model — 202

11 Design of experiments — 209

Principles of experimental design — 210
Terminology — 212
Dealing with subjective measurements — 213
Fitting and checking models — 215
Completely randomised design — 216
Paired design — 222
Comparing several treatments — 225
Randomised block design — 228
Median polish — 233
Latin squares — 239

Appendix — 246

Proof that s_b^2 is an unbiased estimate of σ^2 — 246

Answers — 248

Chapter 1 — 248
Chapter 2 — 248
Chapter 3 — 250
Chapter 4 — 251
Chapter 5 — 252
Chapter 6 — 253
Chapter 7 — 254
Chapter 8 — 256
Chapter 9 — 257
Chapter 10 — 259
Chapter 11 — 260

Index — 267

1 Modelling

To understand God's purpose we must study statistics for these are the measure of his purpose.

Florence Nightingale

Does the gender of a criminal affect the severity of the sentence imposed?

How might a statistician investigate this question?

The first stage would be to model the situation mathematically. You might suggest that for each convicted offender there is a constant probability of probation, suspended sentence or imprisonment, but that these probabilities differ for men and women.

Secondly, you would want to collect some data. You would need to decide how to select a sample of convicted men and women and the sentences imposed on them.

Then, you could use the data to investigate the question asked. You could estimate the probabilities in the suggested model by the relative frequencies with which the three types of sentence are imposed on men and women. A χ^2 test might then be appropriate, testing the hypothesis that the severity of the sentence is independent of the sex of the offender.

Finally, as with all mathematical modelling, you would check whether the model is adequate for your purposes or whether it needs revising. Does the sampling method justify the assumptions made in the χ^2 test? Is there a confounding variable (such as the fact that men are more likely to have previous convictions) which will produce a spurious association? Is the sample size adequate to average out the other effects on severity of sentence?

Statisticians are interested in investigating *data generating processes*, the actual mechanisms by which outcomes arise in the real world. For example:

- all the information brought out at the trial, the prejudices of the judge and the current climate of public opinion which influence the severity of the sentence

- the operator inattention, machine wear or inadequate servicing which lead to faulty devices appearing from a production line

- the combination of genetic endowment, maternal fitness and infant nurture which govern the state of development of a four-month-old puppy

- the angle and height of the roll, the nature of the table surface and the air currents in the room, which determine the position in which a die lands.

Notice that no mention has been made of randomness, and this is deliberate. Actual events do not occur by chance: they occur as a consequence of the state the world is in, and of the actions and decisions taken in this state. They are unpredictable because our knowledge of the world is insufficiently complete to enable us to decide what exactly is going to happen and it is impractical, or too costly, to find the necessary information.

Note

The physical theory of quantum mechanics suggests that in some very small-scale aspects of the universe, such as radioactive beta decay, chance is genuinely involved. This will not be relevant in any of the situations studied in this Statistics course.

The job of the statistician, like that of any applied mathematician, is to provide a useful model of the real world. All mathematical models are simplified representations of reality, ignoring complexities which will have unimportant effects on the final outcome. The unique feature of statistical modelling is that it uses randomness to model those parts of a situation where the details of the process which generate the outcome are unknown, assigning probabilities to possible outcomes, rather than predicting definitely which will occur.

Modelling a situation statistically rather than practically or by calculation is a choice. It is not correct to say that a situation is modelled statistically 'when it involves random chance': the decision to assign probabilities to outcomes is part of the modelling process. For instance, if you wanted to model the position at which a dart struck a dartboard, you could consider the mechanical equations governing the motion of a complex projectile, perhaps ignoring air resistance, and arrive at an equation linking the striking point to the initial speed and angle of projection. Alternatively, you could suggest the probabilities with which the dart would land in the various sectors of the board, given the sector at which it was aimed. Which of these would be a better model would depend on the reason for your interest in the outcomes, on how much trouble you were prepared to go to for a given level of accuracy in prediction, and on which factors most affect the striking point of the dart. It does not depend on whether or not there 'really is' a random aspect to the motion of the dart.

The construction of a statistical model involves:

A Focusing attention on a particular aspect of the outcome of the data generating process which is of interest and assigning a numerical value to different possible outcomes. For example:

- the number of years (to the nearest whole number) of imprisonment imposed
- a 0 or 1 is assigned, depending on whether a device is faulty or not
- the mass of a puppy at four months
- the score on a die.

B Introducing a random variable which will represent this numerical value and assigning probabilities to each possible outcome (or a probability density function in the case of a continuous variable). For example:

- Y has a geometric distribution with

$$P(y \text{ years in prison}) = \frac{3}{4}\left(\frac{1}{4}\right)^y \quad (y = 0, 1, \ldots)$$

- F takes values 0 or 1, with $P(0) = 0.0002$, $P(1) = 0.9998$
- M is Normally distributed with mean 4.2 kg, standard deviation of 0.6 kg
- N takes values 1 to 6, each with probability $\frac{1}{6}$.

The aim is to ensure that the model is an adequate representation of those aspects of the data generating process in which you are interested. The information that enables you to do this is usually obtained from *sampling* the outcomes of the data generating process.

A *sampling process* is the way in which some of the outcomes are selected for consideration and recorded. For example:

- the selection of one week's convictions at each Crown Court in England, noting the gender of the defendant, the offence and the sentence
- the testing of every 100th device appearing from the production line and the recording of the result and time of testing
- the selection from a breeder's records of one puppy from each litter produced by her bitches over the past five years and its mass at four months
- the decision to roll a die 60 times and observe the score each time.

Before this information can be related to the model of the data-generating process, you must make a mathematical model of the sampling process. For complicated sampling processes, such as the 'puppy' example above or for stratified sampling, this is beyond the scope of this book, but there is one important special case which can be modelled reasonably simply.

If the outcome of the data-generating processes is modelled by the random variable X, then the process of taking an *independent random sample* of size n is modelled by the set of n random variables $X_1, X_2, \ldots, X_n$, each of which has a distribution identical to that of X, and all of which are independent of each other.

In the case of a finite population, for instance all the fish in a particular lake, when members of the population are not replaced after sampling, the random variables representing successive members of the sample are not strictly independent. However, if the size of the population is large then the independent random sampling model is still likely to be adequate for most purposes.

Sample statistics

You have already seen examples of the three main ways in which statisticians use the information in a sample to try to ensure that their model is an adequate representation of the data-generating process.

1 *Estimating a parameter*

Given that, when a greengrocer buys pears from a wholesaler he does not know the details of how some come to be bruised (the data-generating process), he could model this by a random variable which takes the values 1 (bruised) and 0 (unbruised) with constant probability. Then, given a sample of fruit, some of which is bruised, he could estimate this probability by finding the fraction of the sample which is bruised. The process of estimation will be considered in detail in Chapter 2.

2 *Testing a hypothesis*

Given that you do not know the details of what determines how many eggs are laid by a given jellyfish (the data-generating process), you could model this by a random variable which has a Normal distribution for which the mean and standard deviation have been reliably estimated for a particular species. Then, given the numbers of eggs laid by a sample of jellyfish living on a polluted beach, you could test the hypothesis that the reproduction rate of these jellyfish is lower than average, by calculating the mean number of eggs laid per jellyfish in the sample.

3 *Checking goodness of fit*

Given that you do not know the details of what determines how many road accidents there will be on the M21 on a given day (the data-generating process), you could model this by a random variable which has a Poisson distribution. Then, given the numbers of accidents on a sample of days this year you could determine the χ^2 value which measures how well the data fit the claimed distribution.

In all these examples, some of the details of the sample were discarded, and only a single figure calculated from the sample was used by the statistical investigator. In **1**, no account was taken of which pears were bruised and only the total number of bruised pears was used. In **2**, the number of eggs laid by each jellyfish was known, but only the single figure of their mean was used. In **3**, the actual numbers of accidents on all the sample days were known but only the single χ^2 value was used to summarise them.

It is standard statistical practice to discard much of the information in the sample, either because it is not relevant to the aspect of the model being investigated or just in order to simplify the analysis. When the values of a random variable in a sample are used to calculate a single figure which summarises these values in some way, this figure is called a *sample statistic*.

Distributions of functions of random variables

In more advanced statistical work, it is often essential to know the distribution, or at least the mean and perhaps variance, of a sample statistic, given the distribution of the random variable modelling the data-generating process. This section discusses two ideas which are often useful in this.

Note that in earlier books in the series we used r to denote a discrete random variable and x to denote a continuous random variables. This distinction is often not made in higher level statistics and so we shall use x to denote both a discrete and a continuous random variable here.

Suppose that the random variable X has the probability distribution

x	-2	-1	0	1	2
$P(x = x)$	0.08	0.24	0.36	0.24	0.08

What is the distribution of X^2?

The possible values of X^2 are the squares of the possible values of X, that is: 0, 1, 4.

The value of X^2 will be 0 precisely when the value of X is 0, so:

$$P(X^2 = 0) = P(X = 0) = 0.36$$

but the value of X^2 will be 1 when the value of X is 1 or -1, so:

$$P(X^2 = 1) = P(X = 1) + P(X = -1) = 0.48$$

and similarly with $P(X^2 = 4)$. Thus the complete distribution of X^2 is:

x	0	1	2
$y = x^2$	0	1	4
$P(Y = y) = P(X^2 = y)$	0.36	0.48	0.16

Notice that $Y = X^2$. In general, if X is a random variable and $Y = g(X)$ is a function of X, then the probability that $g(X)$ takes a particular value y is the sum of the probabilities of all the x values with $g(x) = y$. Formally:

$$P(Y = y) = P(g(X) = y) = \sum_{g(x)=y} P(X = x).$$

The expected value of a function of X can be calculated in two ways. In the example:

$$E[X^2] = E[Y] = \sum_{y=0,1,4} y \times P(Y = y)$$
$$= 0 \times 0.36 + 1 \times 0.48 + 4 \times 0.16 = 1.12$$

by definition of the expectation. However, this is the same thing as:

$$E[X^2] = E(Y) = \sum_{x=-2,-1,0,1,2} x^2 \times P(X = x)$$
$$= (-2)^2 \times 0.08 + (-1)^2 \times 0.24 + 0^2 \times 0.36 + 1^2 \times 0.24 + 2^2 \times 0.08$$

because, for instance, $(-2)^2 = 2^2 = 4$ and $P(X = -2) + P(X = 2) = P(X^2 = 4)$.

In general, if X is a random variable and $Y = g(X)$ is a function of X, then the expectation of $g(X)$ is, by definition:

$$E[g(X)] = E[Y] = \sum_{y} y \times P(Y = y)$$

Because of the result for $P(g(X) = y)$ above, however, this can be rewritten:

$$E[g(X)] = \sum_{y} y \times \sum_{g(x)=y} P(X = x) = \sum_{x} g(x) \times P(X = x).$$

This second form is often easier to calculate.

For a continuous random variable, the situation is less straightforward, as the distribution is given as a *probability density function* (p.d.f.), rather than a set of probabilities. In this case, the route from the p.d.f. of a random variable to the p.d.f. of a function of this variable is usually via the cumulative distribution function.

Suppose that the random variable X has the p.d.f.:

$$f(x) = \begin{cases} 0 & x < 1 \\ \dfrac{3}{x^4} & x \geq 1 \end{cases}$$

What is the p.d.f. of $Y = X^2$?

The cumulative distribution function of X is, by definition

$$F_X(x) = P(X \leqslant x) = \begin{cases} 0 & x < 1 \\ \int_1^x \dfrac{3}{t^4} \, dt & x \geqslant 1 \end{cases}$$

which is the same as

$$F_X(x) = P(X \leqslant x) = \begin{cases} 0 & x < 1 \\ 1 - \dfrac{1}{x^3} & x \geqslant 1 \end{cases}$$

The definition of the cumulative distribution function of $Y = X^2$ is

$$F_Y(y) = P(Y \leqslant y)$$

or

$$F_{X^2}(y) = P(Y^2 \leqslant y)$$

$$F_{X^2}(y) = P(X \leqslant \sqrt{y})$$

Writing this with x rather than y as the variable gives

$$F_{X^2}(x) = P(X \leqslant \sqrt{x}) \qquad \text{since } x > 0.$$

$$= F_X(\sqrt{x})$$

$$= \begin{cases} 0 & x < 1 \\ 1 - x^{-\frac{3}{2}} & x \geqslant 1 \end{cases}$$

Finally, use the relationship $f(x) = \dfrac{d}{dx} F(x)$ between the density function and cumulative distribution function to give the density function of X^2

$$f_{X^2}(x) = \begin{cases} 0 & x < 1 \\ \dfrac{3}{2} x^{-\frac{5}{2}} & x \geqslant 1 \end{cases}$$

The expectation of X^2 can be calculated, as in the discrete case, in two ways.

First, by definition:

$$E[X^2] = \int x f_{X^2}(x) \, dx$$

$$= \int_1^\infty \frac{3}{2} x^{-\frac{3}{2}} \, dx = \left[-3x^{-\frac{1}{2}} \right]_1^\infty = 0 - (-3) = 3$$

But the same result is obtained from the integral:

$$E[X^2] = \int x^2 f_X(x) \, dx$$

$$= \int_1^\infty 3x^{-2} \, dx$$

$$= \left[-3x^{-1} \right]_1^\infty = 0 - (-3) = 3$$

In general, if X is a continuous random variable and $Y = g(X)$ is a function of X, then the expectation of $g(X)]$ is, by definition:

$$E[g(X)] = \int y f_{g(X)}(y) \, dy$$

where $f_{g(X)}(y)$ is the density function of $g(X)$.

However, this can be rewritten:

$$E[g(X)] = \int g(x) f_X(x) \, dx$$

using the density function, $f_X(x)$, of X itself. Again, this second form is often easier to calculate.

The formulae for the variance of a function of a random variable follow automatically from those for the expectation because, by definition, $\text{Var}[X] = E[X - E[X]^2] = E[X^2] - E[X]^2$.

For a discrete variable, then:

$$\text{Var}[g(X)] = \sum_x \{g(x) - E[g(X)]\}^2 \times P(X = x)$$
$$= \sum_x \{g(x)\}^2 \times P(X = x) - E[g(X)]^2$$

while in the continuous case:

$$\text{Var}[g(X)] = \int \{g(x) - E[g(X)]\}^2 \times f_X(x) \, dx$$
$$= \int \{g(x)\}^2 \times f_X(x) \, dx - E[g(X)]^2.$$

EXAMPLE 1.1

The distribution of magnitudes M of a particular type of star is given by the probability density function:

$$f(m) = \tfrac{1}{4} m e^{-\frac{m}{2}}.$$

The magnitude of a star is related to its luminosity (brightness), L, by:

$$L = 10^{-\frac{2}{5}m} = e^{-\frac{2}{5} m \ln 10}.$$

Find the expected brightness of this type of star and the variance of the brightness.

SOLUTION

Use the result $\displaystyle\int_0^\infty t e^{-at} \, dt = a^{-2}$.

$$E[L] = \int L(m) f(m) \, dm$$

$$= \int_0^\infty e^{-\frac{2}{5} m \ln 10} \times \frac{1}{4} m e^{-\frac{1}{2}m} \, dm$$

$$= \frac{1}{4} \int_0^\infty m e^{-\left(\frac{2}{5} \ln 10 + \frac{1}{2}\right)m} \, dm$$

$$= \frac{1}{4} \left(\frac{2}{5} \ln 10 + \frac{1}{2} \right)^{-2} \approx 0.124$$

$$\text{Var}[L] = \int \{L(m)\}^2 f(m)\, dm - \{E[L]\}^2$$

$$= \int_0^\infty \left\{e^{-\frac{2}{5}m\ln 10}\right\}^2 \times \frac{1}{4} m e^{-\frac{1}{2}m}\, dm - \{E[L]\}^2$$

$$= \frac{1}{4}\int_0^\infty m e^{-(\frac{4}{5}\ln 10+\frac{1}{2})m}\, dm - \{E[L]\}^2$$

$$= \frac{1}{4}\left\{\frac{4}{5}\ln 10 + \frac{1}{2}\right\}^{-2} - \{E[L]\}^2 \approx 0.0302$$

EXAMPLE 1.2

When R users are logged on to the Internet via a particular server, the average speed (in kilobytes per second) at which each person's data are transferred is $T = 30\left(\frac{8}{9}\right)^R$.

If the number of users logged on at any one time has a binomial distribution with $n = 20$ and $p = \frac{1}{4}$, find the expectation and variance of the average speed at which data is transferred.

SOLUTION

Use the result (binomial expansion) $\sum_{r=0}^{n} {}^nC_r p^r q^{n-r} = (p+q)^n$.

$$E[T] = \sum_r T(r) \times P(R = r) = \sum_{r=0}^{20} 30\left(\frac{8}{9}\right)^r \times P(R = r)$$

$$= \sum_{r=0}^{20} 30\left(\frac{8}{9}\right)^r \binom{20}{r}\left(\frac{1}{4}\right)^r \left(\frac{3}{4}\right)^{20-r}$$

$$= 30 \sum_{r=0}^{20} \binom{20}{r}\left(\frac{8}{9}\times\frac{1}{4}\right)^r \left(\frac{3}{4}\right)^{20-r} = 30 \sum_{r=0}^{20} \binom{20}{r}\left(\frac{2}{9}\right)^r \left(\frac{3}{4}\right)^{20-r}$$

$$= 30\left(\frac{2}{9} + \frac{3}{4}\right)^{20} = 30\left(\frac{35}{36}\right)^{20} = 17.08$$

$$E[T^2] = \sum_r \{T(r)\}^2 \times P(R = r) = \sum_{r=0}^{20}\left\{30\left(\frac{8}{9}\right)^r\right\}^2 \times P(R = r)$$

$$= \sum_{r=0}^{20} 900\left(\left(\frac{8}{9}\right)^2\right)^r \binom{20}{r}\left(\frac{1}{4}\right)^r \left(\frac{3}{4}\right)^{20-r}$$

$$= 900 \sum_{r=0}^{20} \binom{20}{r}\left(\frac{64}{81}\times\frac{1}{4}\right)^r \left(\frac{3}{4}\right)^{20-r} = 900 \sum_{r=0}^{20} \binom{20}{r}\left(\frac{16}{81}\right)^r \left(\frac{3}{4}\right)^{20-r}$$

$$= 900\left(\frac{16}{81} + \frac{3}{4}\right)^{20} = 900\left(\frac{307}{324}\right)^{20} = 306.27$$

so $\text{Var}[T] = 306.27 - (17.08)^2 = 14.54$

Distributions of linear combinations of random variables

You have modelled a sample as n independent random variables, with identical distributions. You already know some results about distributions of combinations of such sets of random variables, which will be revised and extended here.

A *linear combination of a set of n random variables X_i is a sum*

$$a_1X_1 + a_2X_2 + \ldots + a_nX_n = \sum_{i=1}^{n} a_iX_i$$

where the a_i are any set of constants.

A In general, the distribution of a linear combination of random variables is not simply related to the distribution of the variables being combined, but you saw in *Statistics 3* that, if the X_i are all Normal, the linear combination will also be Normal.

B It is true for any linear combination of random variables that:

$$E[a_1X_1 + a_2X_2 + \ldots + a_nX_n] = a_1E[X_1] + a_2E[X_2] + \ldots + a_nE[X_n]$$

or

$$E\left[\sum_{i=1}^{n} a_iX_i\right] = \sum_{i=1}^{n} a_iE[X_i].$$

If the random variables are identically distributed, then each X_i has the same expectation, say $E[X_i] = \mu$, and then:

$$E\left[\sum_{i=1}^{n} a_iX_i\right] = \mu\left(\sum_{i=1}^{n} a_i\right)$$

C It is true for any linear combination of *independent* random variables that:

$$\mathrm{Var}[a_1X_1 + a_2X_2 + \ldots + a_nX_n] = a_1^2\mathrm{Var}[X_1] + a_2^2\mathrm{Var}[X_2] + \ldots + a_n^2\mathrm{Var}[X_n]$$

or

$$\mathrm{Var}\left[\sum_{i=1}^{n} a_i^2X_i\right] = \sum_{i=1}^{n} a_i^2\mathrm{Var}[X_i].$$

If the random variables are identically distributed, then each X_i has the same variance, say $E[X_i] = \sigma^2$, and then:

$$\mathrm{Var}\left[\sum_{i=1}^{n} a_iX_i\right] = \sigma^2\left(\sum_{i=1}^{n} a_i^2\right)$$

D An important special case is the situation where each $a_i = \dfrac{1}{n}$. Then we define the combination:

$$\overline{X} = \frac{X_1 + X_2 + \ldots + X_n}{n} = \frac{1}{n}\sum_{i=1}^{n} X_i$$

called the *sample mean*. In this case, if the X_i are identically distributed and independent, then the results in **B** and **C** above reduce to:

$$E[\overline{X}] = \mu, \quad \text{Var}[\overline{X}] = \frac{\sigma^2}{n}.$$

EXAMPLE 1.3

When a 'ready-meal' curry is being assembled, the number of grams of chicken per portion is Normally distributed with mean 80 and variance 230. The number of grams of sauce added is also Normally distributed with mean 55 and variance 140 and is independent of the amount of chicken added. The portion is then made up to exactly 350 grams with rice.

Chicken contains 1.8 kilocalories per gram, the sauce 4.5 kilocalories per gram and the rice 2.6 kilocalories per gram. What is the distribution of the random variable K which gives the calorific value of the portion? If the testing process involves determining the mean calorific value of random samples of twelve portions, what will be the distribution of this sample mean?

SOLUTION

The variables are $C \sim N(80, 230)$, for the weight of chicken and $S \sim N(55, 140)$ for the weight of sauce. Then:

$$K = 1.8C + 4.5S + 2.6(350 - C - S) = 910 - 0.8C + 1.9S.$$

K is Normally distributed, because C and S are, and:

$$E[K] = 910 - 0.8E[C] + 1.9E[S] = 950.5$$

$$\text{Var}[K] = (-0.8)^2 \text{Var}[C] + (1.9)^2 \text{Var}[S] = 652.6$$

The variable $\overline{K}$, which is the mean calorific value of a sample of twelve portions, is also normally distributed with:

$$E[\overline{K}] = E[K] = 950.5$$

$$\text{Var}[\overline{K}] = \frac{\text{Var}[K]}{12} = 54.38.$$

Maximum and minimum

Given a set of n random variables $X_1, X_2, \ldots, X_n$ constituting a sample, the largest of the n values taken, is itself a random variable, the *sample maximum L*.

When X is a continuous variable, the distribution of L can be found by noting that:

- if all n of a set of numbers are less than the value ℓ, then the largest of them is also less than ℓ

- if the largest of a set of n numbers is less than a value ℓ, then all of them are less than ℓ.

Thus, the states of affairs $\{L \leqslant \ell\}$ and $\{X_1 \text{ and } X_2 \text{ and } \ldots \text{ and } X_n \leqslant \ell\}$ are identical.

So, because the X_i are independent:

$$P(L \leqslant \ell) = P(X_1 \text{ and } X_2 \text{ and} \ldots \text{and } X_n \leqslant \ell)$$
$$= P(X_1 \leqslant \ell) \times P(X_2 \leqslant \ell) \times \ldots \times P(X_n \leqslant \ell)$$

and because $X_1, X_2, \ldots, X_n$ are identically distributed, with the same distribution as the random variable X which models the data-generating process, this reduces to

$$P(L \leqslant \ell) = \{P(X \leqslant \ell)\}^n.$$

But the left-hand side of this is just, by definition, the cumulative distribution function for L and the right-hand side can similarly be written in terms of the cumulative distribution function of X

$$F_L(\ell) = \{F_X(\ell)\}^n.$$

Finally, the probability density function for L is obtained by differentiating the cumulative distribution function.

EXAMPLE 1.4

The time T (in minutes) for which a passenger must wait for a train each morning has an exponential distribution with mean 8, that is:

$$f_T(x) = \frac{1}{8} e^{-\frac{1}{8}x} \quad (0 \leqslant x < \infty)$$

Find the distribution of the maximum wait in a sample of three mornings, and determine its mean.

SOLUTION

The cumulative distribution function of T is:

$$F_T(x) = \int_0^x \frac{1}{8} e^{-\frac{1}{8}t} \, dt = 1 - e^{-\frac{1}{8}x}$$

so the cumulative distribution function of L, the longest of the three waits, is:

$$F_L(x) = \left(1 - e^{-\frac{1}{8}x}\right)^3$$

and so its density function is:

$$f_L(x) = \frac{d}{dx} F_L(x) = \frac{3}{8} e^{-\frac{1}{8}x} \left(1 - e^{-\frac{1}{8}x}\right)^2 = \frac{3}{8} \left(e^{-\frac{1}{8}x} - 2e^{-\frac{1}{4}x} + e^{-\frac{3}{8}x}\right).$$

The expectation can then be calculated, using the result $\int_0^\infty xe^{-ax}\,dx = a^{-2}$, as

$$E[L] = \int_0^\infty xf_L(x)\,dx = \int_0^\infty \frac{3}{8}x\left(e^{-\frac{1}{8}x} - 2e^{-\frac{1}{4}x} + e^{-\frac{3}{8}x}\right)dx$$

$$= \frac{3}{8}\left(64 - 2 \times 16 + \frac{64}{9}\right) = \frac{44}{3}$$

A similar technique is applicable in the case of discrete distributions, but here the formal method is unnecessarily complicated. It is easier to understand the idea from examples.

EXAMPLE 1.5

The probability of winning in a one-armed bandit game is $\frac{1}{4}$. This means that the number W of wins in five games has a binomial distribution with:

$$P(W = w) = \binom{5}{w}\left(\frac{1}{4}\right)^w\left(\frac{3}{4}\right)^{5-w} \qquad (0 \leqslant w \leqslant 5).$$

If seven people play the game, find the distribution of the maximum number of wins any of them achieves and the expectation of this number.

SOLUTION

The table shows the probability of each possible value of W and the cumulative distribution function for this variable.

w	0	1	2	3	4	5
$P(W = w)$	0.2373	0.3955	0.2637	0.0879	0.0146	0.0010
$P(W \leqslant w)$	0.2373	0.6328	0.8965	0.9844	0.9990	1.0000

As in the continuous case, the probability that the greatest of seven numbers is less than or equal to m is just the probability that each of them is less than or equal to m. So, if M is the maximum number of wins, you can construct the cumulative distribution function for M as

$$P(M \leqslant m) = (P(W \leqslant m))^7.$$

m	0	1	2	3	4	5
$P(M = m)$	0.0000	0.0406	0.4654	0.8956	0.9932	1.0000

Finally, notice, for example, that the difference between '3 or fewer wins' and '2 or fewer wins' is 'exactly 3 wins'. In general

$$P(M = m) = P(M \leqslant m) - P(M \leqslant m - 1)$$

so that the distribution of M is:

m	0	1	2	3	4	5
$P(M = m)$	0.0000	0.0406	0.4248	0.4302	0.0976	0.0068

and its expectation is:

$$E[M] = \sum_{m=0}^{5} m \times P(M = m) = 2.605.$$

EXAMPLE 1.6   The probability of winning in a scratchcard game is $\frac{1}{12}$.

This means that the number S of scratchcards bought before the first win has a geometric distribution with:

$$P(S = s) = \frac{1}{12}\left(\frac{11}{12}\right)^{s-1} \quad (1 \leqslant s < \infty).$$

If three people buy scratchcards, find the distribution of the number of scratchcards bought before they have all won at least once and the expectation of this number.

SOLUTION

The cumulative distribution function of S is:

$$P(S \leqslant s) = \sum_{i=1}^{s} \frac{1}{12}\left(\frac{11}{12}\right)^{i-1} = 1 - \left(\frac{11}{12}\right)^{s}$$

Again, the probability that the longest of three waits is less than or equal to s is just the probability that each of the waits is less than or equal to s. So, if L is the longest wait:

$$P(L \leqslant \ell) = \left(1 - \left(\frac{11}{12}\right)^{\ell}\right)^{3}$$

You can use the same method as before to find the distribution of L, because:

$$P(L = \ell) = P(L \leqslant \ell) - P(L \leqslant \ell - 1)$$

$$= \left(1 - \left(\frac{11}{12}\right)^{\ell}\right)^{3} - \left(1 - \left(\frac{11}{12}\right)^{\ell-1}\right)^{3}$$

$$= 3\left(1 - \left(\frac{11}{12}\right)\right)\left(\frac{11}{12}\right)^{\ell-1} - 3\left(1 - \left(\frac{11}{12}\right)^{2}\right)\left(\left(\frac{11}{12}\right)^{2}\right)^{\ell-1}$$

$$+ \left(1 - \left(\frac{11}{12}\right)^{3}\right)\left(\left(\frac{11}{12}\right)^{3}\right)^{\ell-1}$$

A graph of this probability distribution is shown in Figure 1.1.

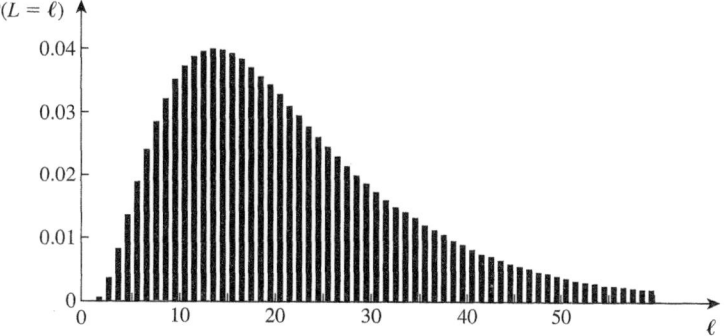

Figure 1.1

The expectation of L is, by definition

$$E[L] = \sum_{\ell=1}^{\infty} \ell \times P(L = \ell)$$

$$= 3\sum_{\ell=1}^{\infty} \ell\left(1 - \left(\frac{11}{12}\right)\right)\left(\frac{11}{12}\right)^{\ell-1} - 3\sum_{\ell=1}^{\infty} \ell\left(1 - \left(\frac{11}{12}\right)^2\right)\left(\left(\frac{11}{12}\right)^2\right)^{\ell-1}$$

$$+ \sum_{\ell=1}^{\infty} \ell\left(1 - \left(\frac{11}{12}\right)^3\right)\left(\left(\frac{11}{12}\right)^3\right)^{\ell-1}$$

which can be evaluated using the result

$$\sum_{\ell=1}^{\infty} \ell(1-p)p^{\ell-1} = \frac{1}{1-p}$$

to give:

$$E[L] = \frac{3}{1 - \left(\frac{11}{12}\right)} - \frac{3}{1 - \left(\frac{11}{12}\right)^2} + \frac{1}{1 - \left(\frac{11}{12}\right)^3} = 21.57.$$

ACTIVITY

1 Decide how to find the distribution of the least value taken by a random variable in a sample.
Apply your method to Examples 1.3, 1.4 and 1.5.

2 Look back at the work you have done in earlier Statistics components. Discuss how this fits into the general pattern of statistical analysis outlined above.

EXERCISE 1A

1 The random variable X has a uniform (rectangular) distribution on $[0, 1]$.

  (i) Find the mean and variance of the variable $P = 4\sqrt{1 - X^2}$.

  (ii) If $X_1, X_2, \ldots, X_n$ are a sample of n random numbers on $[0, 1]$, find the mean and variance of
  $$\overline{P} = \frac{1}{n}(P_1 + P_2 + \ldots + P_n)$$
  in terms of n.

  (iii) Explain how to use a sample of n random numbers on $[0, 1]$ to estimate π, and calculate how large n would have to be before you could expect accuracy to 3 decimal places.

2 A jar contains a large number of mixed black and white peppercorns. When ten of these are removed at random and the number W of white peppercorns removed is counted, you might use $\frac{W}{10}$ as an estimate of the proportion p of white peppercorns in the jar. If the jar is large enough to ignore the fact that you are sampling without replacement, W will have an approximately binomial distribution $B(10, p)$ with variance $10p(1 - p)$, so you might use:
$$S = \sqrt{10\frac{W}{10}\left(1 - \frac{W}{10}\right)} = \sqrt{\frac{W(10 - W)}{10}}$$
as an estimate of the standard deviation of W. Find the distribution of S if $p = \frac{1}{3}$ and find its mean and variance.

3 The dyadic size $|n|_2$ of an integer n is the reciprocal of the largest power of 2 that divides the number. For instance, $|56|_2 = \frac{1}{8}$, because 8 is the highest power of 2 to divide 56, and $|55|_2 = 1$, because $1 = 2^0$ is the highest power of 2 to divide 55. If N is a random variable uniformly distributed on the integers from 1 to 100, find the distribution of $|N|_2$. Find also the mean and variance of $|N|_2$.

If N is instead uniformly distributed on the integers from 1 to a large number L, investigate what happens to the mean of $|N|_2$ as $L \to \infty$.

4 When a ball is thrown vertically upwards from ground level, the height H (in metres) that it reaches is a function:
$$H = \frac{1}{20}U^2$$
of the speed U (in metres per second) with which it is thrown.

The ball is thrown in such a way that U has a distribution with probability density function:
$$f(x) = \frac{1}{4}\left(1 - \left(\frac{x - 20}{3}\right)^2\right) \quad (17 \leqslant x \leqslant 23)$$

  (i) Find the density function for the variable L which is the larger of the two initial speeds of two balls thrown independently in this way. Find the mean of L.

  (ii) Find the mean and variance of H.

  (iii) When a sample of five balls are thrown independently in this way, the mean of their heights is M. Find the mean and variance of M.

5 (i) Find the expectation and variance of the score on a single tetrahedral die, with sides numbered 1, 2, 3, 4.

Three such dice are thrown.

  (ii) Find the distribution of the largest score obtained and calculate its expectation and variance.

  (iii) Find the distribution of the sum of the three scores.

Hence calculate explicitly the expectation and variance of the mean of the three scores, and show that they are related as you expect to your answers to part (i).

6 An A level component has a written paper marked out of 70 and a coursework task marked out of 14. The final mark must be out of 60, with the written paper counting for 80% and the coursework task 20%. For a particular candidate, the written mark is modelled as a Normal random variable $W \sim N(46, 49)$ and the coursework mark is modelled as an independent Normal random variable $C \sim N(9, 4)$.
   (i) Explain why the variable T which records the candidate's final mark out of 60 is given by:
   $$T = \frac{24}{35}W + \frac{6}{7}C.$$
   (ii) Find the mean and variance of T, and hence find the probability that the candidate gains an A grade, if she must achieve a final mark of 47 or more out of 60 to do this.

7 In a game, each player throws four ordinary six-sided dice. The random variable X is the largest number showing on the dice.
   (i) Find the probability that $X = 1$.
   (ii) Find the probability that $X \leqslant 2$ and deduce that the probability that $X = 2$ is $\frac{5}{432}$.
   (iii) Find the probability that $X = 3$.
   (iv) Find the probability that $X = 6$, and explain without further calculation why 6 is the most likely value of X.

8 The continuous random variable X has a uniform (or rectangular) distribution on the interval $0 \leqslant x \leqslant 4$.
   (i) Write down the probability density function for X, and sketch its graph.
   (ii) Find the cumulative distribution function $F(x) = P(X \leqslant x)$.

A second random variable, Y, is related to X by the equation $Y = \sqrt{X}$.

   (iii) Show that
   $$P(Y \leqslant y) = P(X \leqslant y^2) = \frac{1}{4}y^2.$$
   Using this, the cumulative distribution function for Y, find the probability density function for Y. State the range of values which Y takes.
   iv Show that the median value of Y is the square root of the median value of X.

9 A secretary types letters on to sheets of paper 30 cm long and then folds the letters as shown.

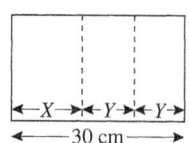 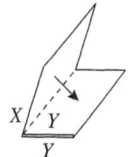 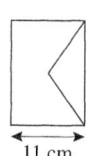

The first fold is X cm from one edge of the paper and the second, Y cm from the other edge, is exactly in the middle of the remainder of the paper, so that
$$Y = \frac{1}{2}(30 - X).$$
The distance X cm is Normally distributed with mean 10.2 cm and standard deviation 1.2 cm.
   (i) Obtain the distribution of Y.
   (ii) The letters have to fit into envelopes 11 cm wide. Find
      (a) $P(X > 11)$
      (b) $P(Y > 11)$
      (c) the proportion of folded letters which *will* fit into the envelope.
   (iii) The 'overlap' is $X - Y$. Show that
   $$X - Y = \frac{3}{2}(X - 10)$$
   and hence verify that $\mathrm{Var}(X - Y)$ is *not* equal to $\mathrm{Var}(X) + \mathrm{Var}(Y)$.
   (iv) Explain why the rule
   $$\mathrm{Var}(aX + bY) = a^2\mathrm{Var}(X) + b^2\mathrm{Var}(Y)$$
   does not apply in this case.

10 For a positive integer r, the rth moment of the distribution of the random variable X about its mean μ is denoted by μ_r and defined by

$$\mu_r = E[(X - \mu)^r].$$

(i) Show that $\mu_1 = 0$ for any X.

(ii) What is the familiar interpretation of μ_2?

(iii) μ_3 is often interpreted as a measure of the *skewness* of a distribution. What will be the value of μ_3 for a symmetrical distribution?

(iv) Prove the results

(a) $\mu_2 = E[X^2] - (E[X])^2$

(b) $\mu_3 = E[X^3] - 3E[X]E[X^2] + 2(E[X])^3.$

(v) Using the results of part (iv), or otherwise, find the values of μ_2 and μ_3 for the continuous random variable Y with probability density function

$$f(y) = \begin{cases} 3y^2 & 0 < y < 1 \\ 0 & \text{elsewhere} \end{cases}$$

State whether this is a symmetrical distribution.

(vi) The discrete random variable T has

$$P(T = 3) = \frac{1}{10}, P(T = 1) = \frac{1}{2},$$

$$P(T = -2) = \frac{2}{5}.$$

Find the value of μ_3 for T. Is this a symmetrical distribution?

KEY POINTS

1 If a random variable Y is a function $Y = g(X)$ of a random variable X then

- if X, Y are discrete

$$E[Y] = \sum_x g(x) \times P(X = x)$$

$$\text{Var}[Y] = \sum_x (g(x))^2 \times P(X = x) - E[Y]^2$$

- if X, Y are continuous, and X has density function $f(x)$

$$E[Y] = \int g(x) \times f(x) \, dx$$

$$\text{Var}[Y] = \int (g(x))^2 \times f(x) \, dx - E[Y]^2$$

2 If a random variable Y is a linear combination $Y = \sum_{i=1}^{n} a_i X_i$ of the n random variables X_i then

- if the X_i are Normally distributed then so is Y

- in general

$$E[Y] = \sum_{i=1}^{n} a_i E[X_i]$$

- if the X_i are independent then

$$\text{Var}[Y] = \sum_{i=1}^{n} a_i^2 \text{Var}[X_i]$$

- in the case where the X_i are identically distributed with mean μ and variance σ^2, the specific linear combination $\overline{X} = \frac{1}{n} \sum_{i=1}^{n} X_i$,

  has

$$E[\overline{X}] = \mu, \quad \text{Var}[\overline{X}] = \frac{\sigma^2}{n}.$$

3 If a random variable Y is the largest of the n random variables X_i, which are identically distributed with cumulative distribution function $F_X(x)$, then the cumulative distribution function of Y is

$$F_Y(x) = (F_X(x))^n.$$

Estimation

Depend upon it, a lucky guess is never merely luck — there's always some talent in it.

Jane Austen

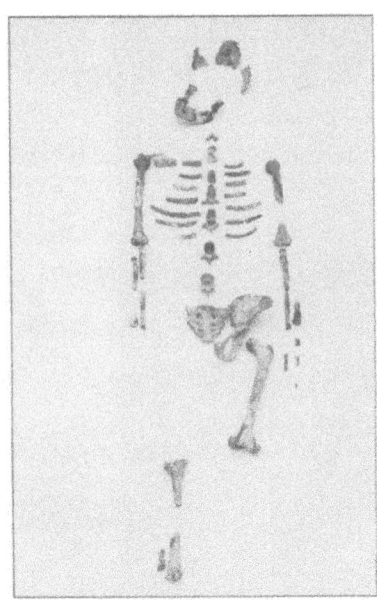

This fossil, known as Lucy, was discovered in Ethiopia between 1973 and 1977 and is widely accepted as the earliest link in the human record. It is 3.3 million years old.

Recently, the remains of a primitive human were found in the Great Rift Valley of Africa. It was the third specimen of its particular subspecies of human. The three specimens found so far are calculated to have been aged 9, 16 and 35 at the times of their deaths.

What can be said about the distribution of ages at death in the population of this species of human, from the sample available?

The obvious answer to this question is 'not much': there is a very small sample to work with, and a very large amount of information is needed to determine the details of a distribution. You need to start by making an heroic assumption about the general shape of the distribution of ages at death. The easiest assumption to start with is that it is a uniform (rectangular) distribution: humans from this species were equally likely to die at every age up to some maximum. Formally, if X is the random variable 'age at death', then you are assuming that X is uniformly distributed on $[0, m]$, where m is the maximum age to which these humans lived.

The task is now dramatically simplified. You need to use the sample merely to *estimate the parameter m* of the distribution of ages at death.

 What estimate would you make of the parameter *m*, the maximum age at death, from the sample given?

Estimates for *m*

Two *possible* methods for estimating *m* are given below, but if you have thought of others, you could follow the work through with your method.

Method 1: Take the largest age in the sample and multiply by $\frac{6}{5}$.

Rationale: The largest age in the sample ought to be in the middle of the highest third of the distribution, i.e. at about $\frac{5}{6}$ of the maximum age.

Method 2: Find the mean of the sample and double it.

Rationale: The mean age at death ought to be about half of the maximum.

Note that the relationships these methods establish between the experimental outcome and the numerical value produced are referred to as *estimators* for *m*: the numerical values that the methods produce in particular cases are the *estimates*.

For this sample, these methods give the following estimates.

Method 1: $m_1 = \frac{6}{5} \times 35 = 42$

Method 2: $m_2 = 2 \times \left(\frac{9 + 16 + 35}{3}\right) = 40$

Estimators as random variables

It is important to realise that an estimator is a random variable – it gives a method for determining a numerical value which cannot be predicted in advance, and which will depend on the sample which happens to be chosen.

In the example above, if you assume that the three sets of remains found were a random sample from the entire population of this subspecies of human, then the ages at death of the three individuals are the values of the three random variables X_1, X_2 and X_3 each of which comes from a population with a uniform (rectangular) distribution on $[0, m]$.

The variables M_1 and M_2, which are the estimators described by Methods 1 and 2 respectively, are then given by:

$$M_1 = \frac{6}{5} \max\{X_1, X_2, X_3\}$$

and

$$M_2 = \frac{2}{3}(X_1 + X_2 + X_3).$$

As a random variable, an estimator has a distribution. If it is a discrete random variable, the distribution will be the set of possible values which it might take, together with the probability with which each value arises. If it is a continuous random variable, the distribution is given by a density function. The uncertainty involved arises from the process of taking samples at random from the population as a whole, and therefore this distribution is called the *sampling distribution* of the estimator.

In the example, you can derive the sampling distribution of M_1 and M_2 from the distribution of the X_i: this is done below in the case of M_1.

The sampling distribution of M_1

The probability density function for X is:

$$f(x) = \begin{cases} \dfrac{1}{m} & 0 \leq x \leq m \\ 0 & \text{otherwise} \end{cases}$$

The graph of this function for $m = 40$ is sketched in figure 2.1.

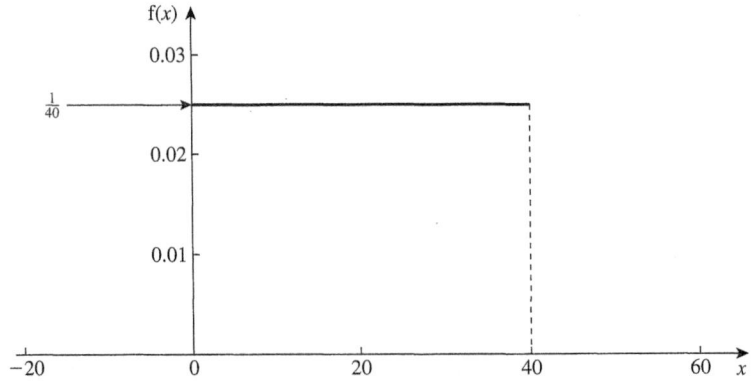

Figure 2.1

The cumulative distribution function for X is obtained by integration.

$$F(x) = P(X \leq x) = \int_0^x f(t')\,dt' = \begin{cases} 0 & x \leq 0 \\ \dfrac{x}{m} & 0 \leq x \leq m \\ 1 & x \geq m \end{cases}$$

The cumulative distribution function for the estimator M_1 is found by noting that the largest of three numbers will be less than a value x if and only if all three of them are less than x. Thus the probability that the largest of the three sample values is less than x is the same as the probability that all three sample values are less than x.

So you can find the cumulative distribution function of M_1 from the cumulative distribution function of X as follows.

$$F(x) = P(M_1 \leq x) = P\left(\max\{X_1, X_2, X_3\} \leq \frac{5}{6}x\right) \quad \text{by definition}$$

$$= P\left(X_1 \leq \frac{5}{6}x \text{ and } X_2 \leq \frac{5}{6}x \text{ and } X_3 \leq \frac{5}{6}x\right) \quad \text{by the argument above}$$

$$= P\left(X_1 \leq \frac{5}{6}x\right) \times P\left(X_2 \leq \frac{5}{6}x\right) \times P\left(X_3 \leq \frac{5}{6}x\right) \quad \text{because the } X_i \text{ are independant}$$

$$= \begin{cases} 0 & x \leq 0 \\ \left(\dfrac{5x}{6m}\right)^3 & 0 \leq x \leq \dfrac{6}{5}m \\ 1 & x \geq \dfrac{6}{5}m \end{cases}$$

Then the probability density function of M_1, which is found by differentiating the cumulative distribution function, is

$$f(x) = \frac{d}{dx}F(x) = \begin{cases} 3\left(\dfrac{5}{6m}\right)^3 x^2 & 0 \leq x \leq \dfrac{6}{5}m \\ 0 & \text{otherwise} \end{cases}$$

A graph of this density function is sketched in figure 2.2

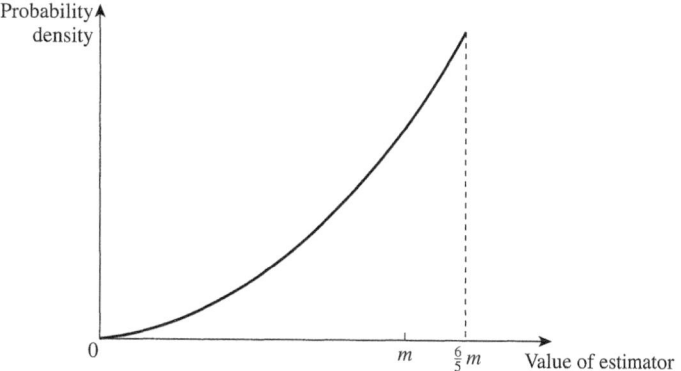

Figure 2.2

This graph illustrates the following points.

- Since each of the X_i is restricted to the range 0 to m, so is the largest of them. Thus the estimator M_1 cannot take values greater than $\dfrac{6}{5}m$.

- The distribution is strongly negatively skewed: this should not be surprising, since the largest of the X_i is relatively unlikely to be in the lower part of the range 0 to *m*.

ACTIVITY

Using a spreadsheet (or a calculator which produces random numbers in the range 0 to 1) you can simulate, for the case $m = 1$, the sampling process used here.

1. Find three random numbers between 0 and 1. ⟵ Simulates measuring X_1, X_2 and X_3
2. Choose the largest. ⟵ Simulates finding max $\{X_1, X_2, X_3\}$
3. Multiply this by $\frac{6}{5}$. ⟵ Simulates finding M_1
4. Repeat steps **1**, **2** and **3** 200 times.
5. Plot a histogram showing the simulated sampling distribution of M_1.

It should resemble the probability density function shown in figure 2.2, with $m = 1$.

Good estimators

 What makes a good estimator?

Ideally, whatever the true value of the population parameter, the value taken by the estimator on *every sample* should be *exactly equal* to this value. However, this is unlikely to be possible, because the values in a finite sample could usually arise from more than one possible value of the population parameter, so no calculation with these values can determine the precise value of the parameter.

One way of relaxing this ideal is to ask that, whatever the true value of the population parameter, the value taken by the estimator on *most samples* should be *reasonably near* to this value.

An alternative is to ask that, whatever the true value of the population parameter, the *average value* taken by the estimator over all samples should be *exactly equal* to this value.

Formally, this second criterion means that the expected value of the estimator should be equal to the population parameter: an estimator which has this property is called *unbiased*; other estimators are *biased*.

The motivation behind this criterion comes from considering what happens if the estimator is used repeatedly. In the example, this would mean using it to estimate the lifespans of different subspecies of humans, each time using three specimens of the subspecies. You might expect that a good estimator would sometimes give a value above the true lifespan, and sometimes a value below, but that there should be no average tendency for one of these to predominate. This is what unbiasedness requires. However, you are in fact only going to use this estimator once, so it is not obvious that this criterion is the most sensible one.

In everyday English, to describe something as unbiased is usually to express approval of it: beware of assuming that this is also true in statistics.

For example, consider the estimator, M, for m which is calculated using the method 'pick one of the three specimens at random, and double its age'.

Because the age at death has a uniform distribution, the specimen picked is equally likely to have any age at death between 0 and m, so that its expected age at death is $\frac{1}{2}m$.

The expected value of M, which is double this, is therefore just m. This means that M is unbiased. However, it should strike you as a rather unsatisfactory way of estimating m from the data.

Are M_1 and M_2 unbiased?

The expected value of M_1 is:

$$E[M_1] = \int_{-\infty}^{\infty} xf(x)\, dx = \int_0^{\frac{6}{5}m} 3\left(\frac{5}{6m}\right)^3 x^3\, dx$$

$$= \left[3\left(\frac{5}{6m}\right)^3 \frac{x^4}{4}\right]_0^{\frac{6}{5}m} = \frac{9m}{10}.$$

This shows that M_1 is biased. It does not, on average over all possible samples, give the true value of the population parameter.

You can see that M_2 is unbiased even though you have not calculated its full sampling distribution. Each of the X_i has a uniform distribution on $[0, m]$ and hence $E[X_i] = \frac{1}{2}m$.

Therefore

$$E[M_2] = E\left[\frac{2}{3}(X_1 + X_2 + X_3)\right]$$

$$= E\left[\frac{2}{3}(X_1)\right] + E\left[\frac{2}{3}(X_2)\right] + E\left[\frac{2}{3}(X_3)\right]$$

$$= \frac{2}{3}(E[X_1] + E[X_2] + E[X_3])$$

$$= \frac{2}{3}\left(\frac{m}{2} + \frac{m}{2} + \frac{m}{2}\right) = m.$$

You have found that M_1 is biased, but the estimator:

$$M_3 = \frac{10}{9} M_1 = \frac{4}{3} \max\{X_1, X_2, X_3\}$$

is unbiased, because:

$$E[M_3] = E\left[\frac{10}{9} M_1\right] = \frac{10}{9} E[M_1] = \frac{10}{9} \times \frac{9m}{10} = m.$$

Note

You cannot always create an unbiased estimator from a biased one by multiplying by a constant. It was only possible to do so in this case because the expected value of the biased estimator, although not equal to the population parameter, was just a constant multiple of it.

For the original sample, the value of M_3 is:

$$m_3 = \frac{4}{3} \times 35 = 46\frac{2}{3}.$$

Bias

The *bias* of an estimator for some parameter is simply defined to be the amount by which it is expected to over- or under-estimate that parameter.

That is, if T is an estimator for a parameter τ, the bias of T is

$$\text{bias}(T) = E[T] - \tau$$

so that the bias is positive for an estimator which overestimates on average, and negative if, on average, it underestimates. An unbiased estimator is therefore just one with zero bias.

INVESTIGATION

You made the assumption at the start of the analysis that the age at death had a uniform distribution, but this is not very realistic. In fact, it seems likely that primitive humans were much more likely to die younger. A better model for the distribution of the age at death in such a species might therefore be the triangular distribution with density function:

$$f(x) = \begin{cases} \frac{2}{m^2}(m-x) & 0 \leqslant x \leqslant m \\ 0 & \text{otherwise} \end{cases}$$

The graph of this density function is sketched in figure 2.3.

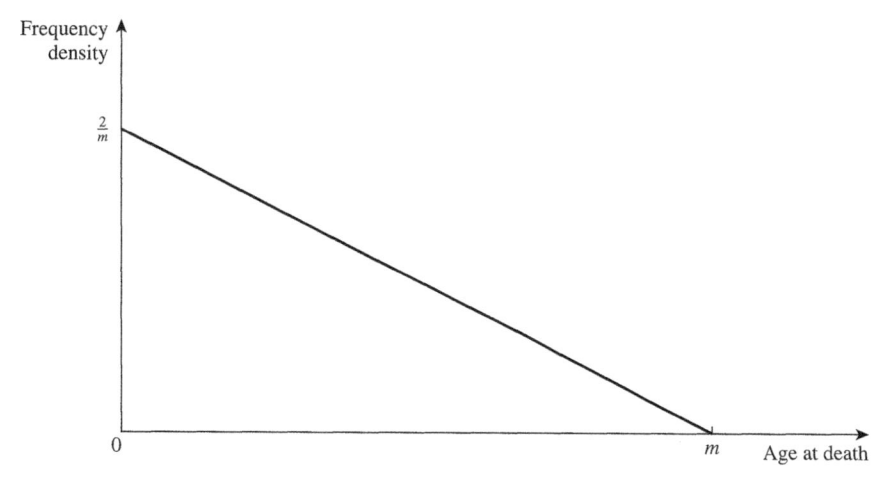

Figure 2.3

Using the same estimators M_1 and M_2 for m and assuming X to have this new distribution, find:

(i) the sampling distribution of M_1

(ii) the expectation of M_1, using your sampling distribution

(iii) the expectation of M_2

and so determine whether M_1 and M_2 are biased or unbiased. If either estimator is biased, find a multiple of it which is unbiased.

Note

In both the original example and in this investigation, the population distribution has been assumed to have a very definite form, so that the determination of the exact population distribution has required the estimation of only one parameter. In general, you may want to make less restrictive assumptions about the form of the population distribution, in which case you may need to estimate two or more parameters. For instance, if you assume that the population distribution is Normal, you will want to estimate both its mean and its variance. This example is dealt with in detail later in the chapter.

INVESTIGATION

Use the original (uniform) distribution for X, but suppose that a sample of size n is available. The estimators M_4 and M_5 are extensions of M_3 and M_2 to this situation.

$$M_4 = \frac{n+1}{n} \max\{X_1, X_2, \ldots, X_n\}$$

and:

$$M_5 = \frac{2}{n}(X_1 + X_2 + \ldots + X_n).$$

Determine:

(i) the sampling distribution for M_4

(ii) the expected value of M_4, using your sampling distribution

(iii) the expected value for M_5

and so decide whether M_4 and M_5 are biased or unbiased.

EXAMPLE 2.1   Suppose that you buy scratchcards until you have won three times. The number of cards you have purchased by then is recorded as the value of the random variable N. Calculate the sampling distribution of N and show that $\Pi = \dfrac{2}{N-1}$ is an unbiased estimator of p, the probability that a scratchcard is a winning card.

SOLUTION

The probability that N has the value n is the probability that the third win will occur with the nth card.

That is:

the nth card is a winner

and:

there have been exactly two winners in the first $n-1$ cards

so

P(third win with nth card) = P(nth card wins) $\times$ P(2 wins in first $n-1$ cards).

The nth card wins with probability p, and the binomial distribution gives the probability that two of the first $n-1$ cards are winners (and so $(n-3)$ are not winners) as:

$$\binom{n-1}{2} p^2 (1-p)^{(n-3)}.$$

Therefore:
$$\text{P(third win with } n\text{th card)} = p \times \binom{n-1}{2} p^2 (1-p)^{(n-3)}$$
$$= \binom{n-1}{2} p^3 (1-p)^{(n-3)}.$$

Note that: $\binom{n-1}{2} = \dfrac{(n-1)(n-2)}{2}.$

Hence the sampling distribution of N is:

$$P(N = n) = \frac{1}{2}(n-1)(n-2) p^3 (1-p)^{n-3} \quad (n \geq 3).$$

(Note that $n < 3$ is impossible: the third win cannot occur before the third card.)

To determine whether $\Pi = \dfrac{2}{N-1}$ is unbiased, you must calculate $E[\Pi]$.

Because Π is a function of N, you can use the result:
$$E[f(N)] = \sum_{\text{all } n} f(n) \times P(N = n)$$
to obtain:
$$E[\Pi] = \sum_{n=3}^{\infty} \frac{2}{n-1} \times \frac{1}{2}(n-1)(n-2)p^3(1-p)^{n-3}$$
$$= p^3 \sum_{n=3}^{\infty} (n-2)(1-p)^{n-3}.$$

Now substitute $n - 3 = r$. This gives also $n - 2 = r + 1$, and means that $n = 3$ corresponds to $r = 0$ while $n = \infty$ corresponds to $r = \infty$, so $E[\Pi]$ becomes
$$E[\Pi] = p^3 \sum_{r=0}^{\infty} (r+1)(1-p)^r.$$

But this is just a binomial series:
$$(1-a)^{-2} = 1 + (-2)(-a) + \frac{(-2)(-3)}{2!}(-a)^2 + \ldots$$
$$+ \frac{(-2)(-3)\ldots(-[r+1])}{r!}(-a)^r + \ldots$$
$$= 1 + 2a + 3a^2 + \ldots + (r+1)a^r + \ldots$$
$$= \sum_{r=0}^{\infty} (r+1)a^r.$$

So
$$E[\Pi] = p^3(1 - [1-p])^{-2} = p^3 p^{-2}$$
$$= p$$

and Π is unbiased, as required.

EXERCISE 2A

1 A coin is tossed n times and the number of heads, H is counted. The probability of a head is p.

(i) Show that $\Pi = \dfrac{H}{n}$ is an unbiased estimator of p.

(ii) The variance of the underlying binomial distribution is given by $np(1-p)$. Show that $V = n\Pi(1 - \Pi)$ is not an unbiased estimate of the variance of the distribution. What multiple of V is unbiased?

Hint:
You may find the binomial sum:
$$\sum_{r=0}^{n} r^2 \binom{n}{r} p^r (1-p)^{n-r} = n(n-1)p^2 + np$$
helpful.

2 A typist makes errors at a rate of r per minute. The number of errors, N, he makes in t minutes is counted. Assuming that N is a Poisson variable, write $E[N]$ in terms of r and t.

Show that $R = \dfrac{N}{t}$ is an unbiased estimator of r.

3

An experimenter places six balls, numbered from 1 to 6, in a bag. Three balls are to be drawn from this bag, the largest, L, of the three numbers and the median, M, of the three numbers being noted.

(i) Assume that the balls are drawn without replacement.

   (a) Write down all 20 possible samples of size three, and hence calculate the probability distributions for L and M.

   (b) Use these distributions to calculate the expected values of L and M.

A subject, who knows that the bag contains n balls numbered 1 to n, but does not know the value of n, is asked to draw three balls from the bag. He uses L and $2M - 1$ as estimates for the value of n.

   (c) Explain why $2M - 1$ is unbiased as an estimator for n, but L is not.

(ii) Repeat part (i) for the case where the three balls are drawn with replacement. (There are 56 distinct samples, not all equally likely.)

4

A fairground game requires players to attempt to throw ping-pong balls into pots; the game is so difficult that balls land essentially at random. The pot that wins £1 has twice the area of the pot that wins a teddy-bear, so that, if p is the probability that a ball lands in the teddy-bear pot, $2p$ is the probability that it lands in the £1 pot and $(1 - 3p)$ is the probability that a ball misses the prize pots altogether. To obtain an estimator Π of p, throw two ping-pong balls and see where they land; then record the value of Π, as in this table.

If balls land:	Value of Π
both in one of the prize pots	$\frac{1}{3}$
exactly one in one of the prize pots	$\frac{1}{6}$
both missing the prize pots	0

(i) Calculate, in terms of p, the probability of each of these outcomes.

(ii) Hence show that Π is an unbiased estimator of p.

(iii) I suspect that the true value of p is about 0.01. How can estimating probabilities as in the table give an unbiased estimate – are they not much too large? Is this a sensible estimation scheme? Can you find a better one based on two balls, or is the crude scheme above the best you can do with so little evidence?

5

The manufacturer of my breakfast cereal is giving away little plastic dinosaurs. One dinosaur is supposed to be included in each packet of cereal but in fact, because of packing difficulties, a certain proportion of packets have – very disappointingly – had their little dinosaurs missed out. I am hoping to estimate the proportion, p, of packets without dinosaurs by waiting until the first packet without a dinosaur turns up. If I have, by then, bought and opened N packets of cereal,

I might use the estimator $\Pi = \dfrac{1}{N}$ for p.

(i) Explain why (provided $p \neq 0$ or 1) the distribution of N is geometric:
$$P(N = n) = (1 - p)^{n-1} p.$$

(ii) Check that $E[N] = \dfrac{1}{p}$ so that N is an unbiased estimator for $\dfrac{1}{p}$ ($p \neq 0$ or 1).

(iii) Show, using the logarithm series
$$\sum_{r=1}^{\infty} \frac{x^r}{r} = -\ln(1 - x) \quad (0 \leq x < 1),$$
that:
$$E[\Pi] = \frac{p}{1-p} \sum_{n=1}^{\infty} \frac{(1-p)^n}{n} = \frac{p}{1-p} \ln\left(\frac{1}{p}\right)$$
$(p \neq 0$ or 1)
so that Π is not, in general, unbiased.

(iv) Sketch a graph of $E[\Pi]$ against p $(0 < p < 1)$.
Compare $E[\Pi]$ with p. How bad is the bias? Are there values of p for which this estimate is unbiased?

(v) What happens if $p = 0$ or 1?

6 A coin is tossed repeatedly until h heads have appeared, and the number, N, of tosses required to do this is recorded.

(i) Explain why, if p is the probability of a head: $P(N = n) = P(\text{exactly } h - 1 \text{ heads in the first } n - 1 \text{ tosses and a head on the } n\text{th toss})$ and hence show that:

$$P(N = n) = \binom{n-1}{h-1} p^h (1-p)^{n-h}$$

$(n = h, h+1, \ldots)$ is the distribution of N.

(ii) Show that $\Pi = \dfrac{h-1}{N-1}$ is an unbiased estimator of p.

(*Hint*: You will need to recognise a binomial sum.)

7 Faced with 100 square kilometres of forest, you are asked to estimate the proportion of diseased trees in the forest. Devise a sampling method and an appropriate estimator, based on the sample. You should bear in mind that some parts of the forest may be less healthy than others.

8 (i) If the n random variables $X_1, X_2, \ldots, X_n$, represent independent drawings from a population whose distribution has mean μ, show that the sample mean:

$$\overline{X} = \frac{1}{n}\sum_{i=1}^{n} X_i$$

is an unbiased estimator of μ.

(ii) More generally, show that if $\alpha_1, \alpha_2, \ldots, \alpha_n$ are any n numbers with the property that:

$$\sum_{i=1}^{n} \alpha_i = 1$$

then the weighted mean

$$\overline{X}_\alpha = \sum_{i=1}^{n} \alpha_i X_i$$

is an unbiased estimator of μ.

(iii) The results above show that, given a random sample of size n drawn from a population of which the distribution has mean μ, then:

$$T_1 = X_1$$
$$T_2 = \frac{1}{5}(4X_1 - 2X_2 + 3X_3)$$
$$T_3 = \frac{1}{n}(X_1 + X_2 + \ldots + X_n)$$

are all unbiased estimators for μ. Which of them is preferable and why? (You might try a computer simulation.)

9 $X_1, X_2, \ldots, X_n$ $(n > 1)$ are independent random variables all having the same Normal distribution; σ^2 denotes the common variance. The random variable Y is defined by

$$Y = \sum_{i=1}^{n}(X_i - \overline{X}^2) \text{ where } \overline{X} = \frac{1}{n}\sum_{i=1}^{n} X_i.$$

You may in this question assume the results

$$E[Y] = (n-1)\sigma^2$$
$$\text{Var}(Y) = 2(n-1)\sigma^4.$$

(i) It is proposed to estimate σ^2 by an estimator of the form $T = kY$ where k is a constant to be determined. Write down the mean and variance of T.

(ii) The bias of T is defined to be $E[T] - \sigma^2$. Deduce that T will have a zero bias if and only if, $k = \dfrac{1}{(n-1)}$.

The mean square error of T, $\text{mse}(T)$, is given by $\text{mse}(T) = \text{Var}(T) + (\text{bias of } T)^2$. This is one way of assessing how 'good' T is as an estimator of σ^2, and it is desirable for it to be as small as possible.

(iii) Show that
$$\mathrm{mse}(T) = \sigma^4(n^2-1)k^2 - 2\sigma^4(n-1)k + \sigma^4$$

(iv) Hence use calculus to show that the value of k that minimises $\mathrm{mse}(T)$ is
$$\frac{1}{(n+1)}.$$

10 A library has been given three books belonging to a very rare set. These books carry volume numbers $X_1, X_2,$ and X_3 (where $X_1 < X_2 < X_3$), but it is not known how many volumes there are altogether in the set.

Suppose that there are n volumes, numbered $1, 2, \ldots, n$, in the set and that the three books in the library are regarded as a random sample from this total of n. Two estimators of n are proposed.

$Y = X_3 +$ average gap between the observed numbers $= \frac{1}{2}(3X_3 - X_1)$
$Z =$ twice sample median $- 1 = 2X_2 - 1$

(i) Consider the case where n is in fact 3. Show that the value of Y is certain to be 4 and that the value of Z is certain to be 3.

(ii) Consider the case where n is in fact 4. Show that the possible values of Y are 4, 5 and $5\frac{1}{2}$.

Show that the mean of Y is 5 and that the variance of Y is $\frac{3}{8}$.

(iii) Still considering the case where n is in fact 4, find the possible values of Z and the mean and variance of Z.

(iv) If n is in fact 5, the following results may be derived:

mean of $Y = 6$ variance of $Y = 0.9$
mean of $Z = 5$ variance of $Z = 2.4$

(You are *not* required to verify these results.)

Using this information and the results you have obtained in parts (i), (ii) and (iii), discuss, with reasons, whether either Y or Z is preferable as an estimator of n, for the values of n considered in this question.

11 The continuous random variable X has a uniform distribution on $[0, \theta]$. The following facts may be used without proof in this question:

(A) The p.d.f. of X is $f(x) = \frac{1}{\theta}$ for $0 \leqslant x \leqslant \theta$.

(B) The cumulative distribution function of X, i.e. $P(X < x)$, is $f(x) = \frac{x}{\theta}$ for $0 \leqslant x < \theta$.

(C) The mean of X is $\frac{\theta}{2}$.

(D) The variance of X is $\frac{\theta^2}{12}$.

$X_1, X_2, \ldots, X_n$ are independent random variables each distributed as X. The random variable $\overline{X}$ is defined by
$$\overline{X} = \frac{1}{n}\sum_{i=1}^{n} X_i$$
and the random variable Y is defined to be the maximum of $X_1, X_2, \ldots, X_n$.

(i) Use (C) and (D) above to show that $2\overline{X}$ is an unbiased estimator of θ with variance
$$\frac{\theta^2}{3n}.$$

(ii) Deduce from (B) that the cumulative distribution function of Y, i.e.
$$P(Y \leqslant y), \text{ is } \left(\frac{y}{\theta}\right)^n \text{ for } 0 \leqslant y \leqslant \theta.$$

(iii) Hence deduce that the p.d.f. of
$$Y \text{ is } \frac{ny^{n-1}}{\theta^n} \text{ for } 0 \leqslant y \leqslant \theta.$$

(iv) Obtain the mean and variance of Y.

(v) Deduce that $Z = \left(1 + \frac{1}{n}\right)Y$ is an unbiased estimator of θ and find its variance.

(vi) Would you prefer $2\overline{X}$ or Z as an estimator of θ? Justify your answer.

12 X_1 and X_2 are independent random variables. They both have the same mean μ. Their variances are σ_1^2 and σ_2^2, respectively, where σ_1^2 and σ_2^2 are assumed to be known constants.

It is proposed to estimate μ by an estimator T having the form
$$T = c_1 X_1 + c_2 X_2$$
where c_1 and c_2 are constants to be determined.

(i) Show that T will be an unbiased estimator of μ if $c_1 + c_2 = 1$. For the remainder of the question, assume this condition holds.

(ii) Find an expression for Var(T) in terms of c_1, σ_1^2 and σ_2^2.

Hence obtain the value of c_1 that minimises Var(T). Write down the corresponding value of c_2. Find the minimum of Var(T).

(iii) Summarise the desirable properties possessed by T (with the obtained values of c_1 and c_2) as an estimator of μ. In practice, what difficulty would arise in estimating μ in this way?

13 $X_1, X_2, \ldots, X_n$ are independent random variables each of which takes value 1 with probability p $(0 < p < 1)$ and value 0 with probability $1 - p$. Let $Y = \sum_{i=1}^{n} X_i$ so that $\overline{X} = \frac{1}{n}\sum_{i=1}^{n} X_i = \frac{1}{n}Y$. Using the fact that Y is a B(n, p) random variable,

(i) show that $\overline{X}$ is an unbiased estimator of p

(ii) show that $\text{Var}(\overline{X}) = \frac{p(1-p)}{n}$

(iii) show that
$$E\left[\frac{\overline{X}(1-\overline{X})}{n}\right] = \frac{n-1}{n} \cdot \frac{p(1-p)}{n}$$

(iv) deduce the constant k such that $k\overline{X}(1-\overline{X})$ is an unbiased estimator of Var($\overline{X}$).

[MEI]

14 The number of breakdowns per week on a computer network is a random variable Y having the Poisson distribution with parameter θ. State the mean and variance of Y, and hence find $E[Y^2]$.

The random variables $Y_1, Y_2, \ldots, Y_n$ represent a random sample of observations of the weekly number of breakdowns. Show that $\overline{Y}$ is an unbiased estimator of θ and state its variance.

Find the function of θ for which $\dfrac{1}{n}\sum Y_i^2$ is an unbiased estimator.

The weekly cost of repairing the breakdowns is modelled by
$$C = 4Y + 2Y^2.$$
Show that $E[C] = 6\theta + 2\theta^2$. Find constants a and b such that $a\overline{Y} + \dfrac{b}{n}\sum Y_i^2$ is an unbiased estimator of $E[C]$.

[MEI]

15 A sequence of independent trials, each of which has two outcomes (success or failure), is carried out. On each trial, the probability of a success is p $(0 < p < 1)$ and that of a failure is $q = 1 - p$. The random variable X counts the number of trials up to and including the first success.

(i) Explain why $P(X = x) = q^{x-1}p$ for $x = 1, 2, \ldots$.

(ii) Show that $E[X] = \dfrac{1}{p}$.

(iii) Deduce that a reasonable estimator of p is $\dfrac{1}{X}$.

(iv) Find $E\left[\dfrac{1}{X}\right]$. Determine whether or not $\dfrac{1}{X}$ is an unbiased estimator of p.

(v) Given that $\text{Var}(X) = \dfrac{1-p}{p^2}$, find $E[X^2]$ and hence find constants a and b such that $aX^2 + bX$ is an unbiased estimator of Var(X).

(You may find it helpful to use the results
$(1-q)^{-2} = 1 + 2q + 3q^2 + \ldots$
$\ln(1-q) = -q - \dfrac{1}{2}q^2 - \dfrac{1}{3}q^3 - \ldots$
for $0 < q < 1$.)

Estimators for the population mean and variance

In *Statistics 3*, you saw how to estimate the mean and variance of a population from a sample. Now that you have looked at the idea of an estimator, you can derive these results more formally.

Consider the following model. You take a random sample of size n from a population which is very large (so that you can consider sampling with or without replacement to be identical). You measure, for each element of the sample, a variable, X, for which the distribution in the population has mean μ and variance σ^2, which are unknown parameters. Taking the sample can be considered as measuring the values of the n random variables $X_1, X_2, \ldots, X_n$ each of which has mean μ and variance σ^2 and which are all independent of one another, because of the assumption that the population is very large. The problem is to use $X_1, X_2, \ldots, X_n$ to construct random variables which are estimators for μ and σ^2.

An unbiased estimator for μ

An obvious candidate for an estimator for μ is:

$$M = \frac{X_1 + X_2 + \ldots + X_n}{n}$$

the sample mean. To show that M is unbiased, calculate its expectation.

$$E[M] = E\left[\frac{X_1 + X_2 + \ldots + X_n}{n}\right] = E\left[\frac{1}{n}\{X_1 + X_2 + \ldots + X_n\}\right]$$

$$= \frac{1}{n} E[X_1 + X_2 + \ldots + X_n]$$

because $E[tA] = tE[A]$ for constant t

$$= \frac{1}{n}\{E[X_1] + E[X_2] + \ldots + E[X_n]\}$$

because $E[A + B + \ldots] = E[A] + E[B] + \ldots$

$$= \frac{1}{n}\{\mu + \mu + \ldots + \mu\} = \mu$$

So M is an unbiased estimator of μ.

An estimator for σ^2

You might naturally try, as an estimator of σ^2, the variance of the n elements of the sample. Define V as:

$$V = \frac{S}{n-1}$$

where

$$S = (X_1 - M)^2 + (X_2 - M)^2 + \ldots + (X_n - M)^2.$$

then, multiplying out all the brackets and collecting the similar terms:

$$S = (X_1^2 - 2X_1M + M^2) + (X_2^2 - 2X_2M + M^2) + \ldots + (X_n^2 - 2X_nM + M^2)$$

$$= (X_1^2 + X_2^2 + \ldots + X_n^2) - 2M(X_1 + X_2 + \ldots + X_n) + nM^2$$

$$= (X_1^2 + X_2^2 + \ldots + X_n^2) - 2nM^2 + nM^2 \quad \text{(because } X_1 + X_2 + \ldots + X_n = nM\text{)}$$

$$= (X_1^2 + X_2^2 + \ldots X_n^2) - nM^2.$$

So, again using the results $E[tA] = tE[A]$ and $E[A + B + \ldots] E[A] + E[B] + \ldots$,

$$E[S] = (E[X_1^2] + E[X_2^2] + \ldots + E[X_n^2]) - nE[M^2]$$

$$= n(E[X^2] - E[M^2])$$

and

$$E[V] = \frac{n}{n-1}(E[X^2] - E[M^2]) \quad \text{(because } E[X_1^2] = E[X_2^2] = \ldots = E[X^2]\text{)}$$

But you know that

$$\text{Var}[R] = E[R^2] - (E[R])^2$$

for any random variable R, and so, turning this around:

$$E[R^2] = \text{Var}[R] + (E[R])^2.$$

Hence

$$E[V] = \frac{n}{n-1}(\text{Var}[X] + \mu^2 - (\text{Var}[M] + \mu^2))$$

$$= \frac{n}{n-1}(\text{Var}[X] - \text{Var}[M]).$$

You can also obtain the familiar result

$$\text{Var}[M] = \text{Var}\left[\frac{1}{n}\{X_1 + X_2 + \ldots + X_n\}\right] \quad \text{(because Var}[tA] = t^2\text{Var}[A]\text{ for constant } t\text{)}$$

$$= \frac{1}{n^2}\text{Var}[X_1 + X_2 + \ldots + X_n]$$

$$= \frac{1}{n^2}\{\text{Var}[X_1] + \text{Var}[X_2] + \ldots + \text{Var}[X_n]\}$$

(because $\text{Var}[A + B + \ldots] = \text{Var}[A] + \text{Var}[B] + \ldots$ for independant $A, B, \ldots$)

$$= \frac{1}{n^2}\{\sigma^2 + \sigma^2 + \ldots + \sigma^2\} = \frac{\sigma^2}{n}.$$

Thus:
$$E[V] = \frac{n}{n-1}(\text{Var}[X] - \text{Var}[M])$$
$$= \frac{n}{n-1}\left(\sigma^2 - \frac{\sigma^2}{n}\right)$$
$$= \sigma^2.$$

Therefore, V is an unbiased estimator of σ^2. In fact, this explains why you have been using a denominator of $n-1$ for the sample variance since you first met the idea in *Statistics 1*, which may not then have seemed the obvious choice.

Remember that the sample estimate of the population variance
$$s^2 = \frac{\sum_{i=1}^{n}(x_i - \bar{x})^2}{n-1}$$
can also be written in the form
$$s^2 = \frac{\sum_{i=1}^{n}x_i^2 - n \cdot \bar{x}^2}{n-1}$$
which is sometimes more convenient.

> Note
>
> This estimate of the variance is said to have (n – 1) *degrees of freedom*. Intuitively this is because one of the *n* independent sources of variability in the sample is 'used up' in estimating the mean – you are calculating the variance of the sample data about the sample mean, which is the value which minimises this variance, rather than about the true mean.

Estimators based on pooled samples

My local grocer has a set of scales to which he gives a quick check every morning by weighing one packet from that morning's delivery of butter from the dairy, which he reckons varies in weight only a little. Over eight days, the weights (in grams) recorded by his scales are:

$$407, 417, 416, 402, 409, 411, 409, 413$$

with mean, 410.5 g.

From these eight readings you can estimate:

$$s_1^2 = \frac{\sum_{i=1}^{8} x_i^2 - 8\bar{x}^2}{8 - 1} = \frac{1\,348\,250 - 8 \times (410.5)^2}{7} = 24.$$

Last week, the service engineer from the company which leases him his scales came in to reset them, which he does every three months. Over the next five days, the weights (in grams) of his checking packets of butter are recorded as:

$$423, \ 415, \ 418, \ 423, \ 427$$

which seem to be higher. They have mean 421.2 g.

From these five readings you can estimate:

$$s_2^2 = \frac{\sum_{i=1}^{5} y_i^2 - 5\bar{y}^2}{5 - 1} = \frac{887\,136 - 5 \times (421.2)^2}{4} = 22.2.$$

You can take it that there has been a shift in the measured weights of the butter because of the adjustment of the scales, but that the variance of the measurements, presumably caused by the small daily variation in the butter weights, will have stayed the same. How could you estimate this common variance?

The statistical model of the grocer's sampling process is that he has taken a sample of size $n_1 = 8$ from a population of butter packets with unknown mean μ_1 and unknown variance σ^2; then a sample of size $n_2 = 5$ from a population of butter packets with unknown and (possibly) different mean μ_2 and unknown but identical variance σ^2.

In this case, an appropriate unbiased estimate of σ^2 is given by:

$$s^2 = \frac{\sum_{i=1}^{n_1}(x_i - \bar{x})^2 + \sum_{i=1}^{n_2}(y_i - \bar{y})^2}{(n_1 + n_2 - 2)} = \frac{(n_1 - 1)s_1^2 + (n_2 - 1)s_2^2}{(n_1 + n_2 - 2)}.$$

Before you prove this, make sure you can see why it is intuitively sensible. Figure 2.4 shows what the underlying distributions of butter weights before and after adjustment might look like: you are trying to find the common spread of these distributions, so that it makes sense to look at how far each weight is from the centre of the appropriate distribution (which you estimate by the separate sample means), not how far it is from some common mean value somewhere in between the two distributions.

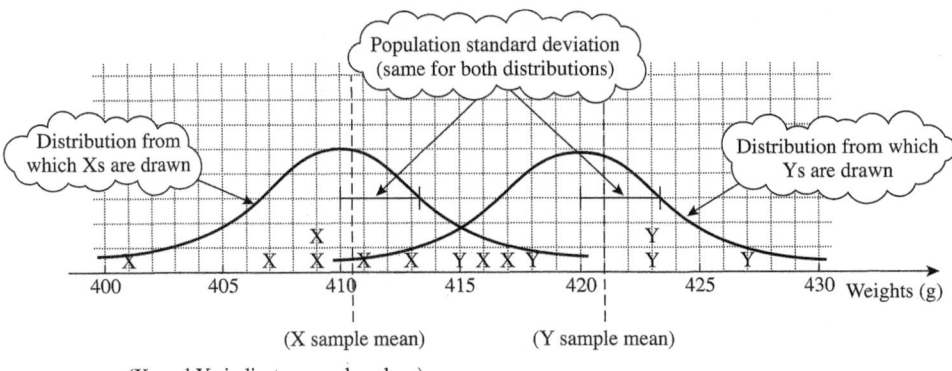

Figure 2.4

This explains the numerator; the denominator fits what was said about degrees of freedom above – two of the $n_1 + n_2$ independent pieces of information in the sample are contained in the two sample means and the remaining $n_1 + n_2 - 2$ independent pieces of information are used to determine the variance.

Proof

Let S^2, S_1^2, S_2^2 denote the estimators of which s^2, s_1^2, s_2^2, are particular values. Then:

$$E[S^2] = E\left[\frac{(n_1 - 1)S_1^2 + (n_2 - 1)S_2^2}{(n_1 + n_2 - 2)}\right]$$

$$= E\left[\frac{(n_1 - 1)}{(n_1 + n_2 - 2)}S_1^2 + \frac{(n_2 - 1)}{(n_1 + n_2 - 2)}S_2^2\right].$$

But $E[aX + bY] = aE[X] + bE[Y]$ for constant a and b so

$$E[S^2] = \frac{(n_1 - 1)}{(n_1 + n_2 - 2)}E[S_1^2] + \frac{(n_2 - 1)}{(n_1 + n_2 - 2)}E[S_2^2]$$

$$= \frac{(n_1 - 1)}{(n_1 + n_2 - 2)}\sigma^2 + \frac{(n_2 - 1)}{(n_1 + n_2 - 2)}\sigma^2$$

because both S_1^2 and S_2^2 are unbiased estimates of σ^2, so:

$$E[S^2] = \frac{(n_1 - 1) + (n_2 - 1)}{n_1 + n_2 - 2}\sigma^2 = \sigma^2.$$

An unbiased estimate of the variance of the weights of butter packs is therefore:

$$s^2 = \frac{7 \times 24 + 4 \times 22.2}{8 + 5 - 2} = \frac{256.8}{11} = 23.3.$$

In general, the process of calculating a pooled estimate of the variance is used where a statistical model identifies two samples as coming from populations with different means but the same variance: the pooled-sample estimate is then an unbiased estimate of that common variance.

EXERCISE 2B

1 Use the data below to calculate unbiased estimates of the population variance.
  (i) A single random sample
    (a) 12.3, 17.1, 5.7, 12.1, 10.3, 14.2, 6.9, 7.1, 10.7
    (b) $n = 23$, $\sum_{i=1}^{23} x_i = 1782.4$, $\sum_{i=1}^{23} x_i^2 = 141\,328.6$
  (ii) Two random samples drawn from populations with the same variance, but possibly different means
    (a) **First sample:** 23.2, 31.6, 28.4, 27.9, 29.0, 33.1, 27.6, 30.2
        Second sample: 33.2, 31.4, 35.7, 36.8, 33.2
    (b) **First sample:** $n = 17$,
        $\sum_{i=1}^{17} x_i = 451.88$, $\sum_{i=1}^{17} x_i^2 = 12\,186.34$
        Second sample: $n = 14$,
        $\sum_{i=1}^{14} y_i = 439.72$, $\sum_{i=1}^{14} y_i^2 = 14\,204.67$
    (c) **First sample:**
        $n = 11$, $\bar{x} = 250.4$, $s_x^2 = 17.340$
        Second sample:
        $n = 7$, $\bar{y} = 213.2$, $s_y^2 = 26.031$

2 An experiment requires a balloon to be dropped from three different heights and the time of descent from each height to be measured. A student conducting this experiment decides to time the descent from each height several times to get a more accurate result. The error made in each time measurement can be modelled as Normally distributed with a mean which may have a different non-zero value for each height but a constant variance. His times, in seconds, are listed below.

First height: 7.23, 7.18, 7.19, 7.25, 7.13
Second height: 5.61, 5.71, 5.70, 5.58, 5.61, 5.63
Third height: 3.82, 3.66, 3.83, 3.86

Calculate an unbiased estimate of the variance of the error from these data. (You will have to extend the ideas in the text to three samples.)

3 Two samples are taken from distributions with the same variance but with means which may differ. Unbiased estimates of the variance are derived as follows:

From the first sample: 28.375
From the second sample: 30.86
From the combined sample: 30.15

Given that the combined sample had 16 elements, calculate the sizes of the two smaller samples.

4 Suppose two separate samples $x_1, x_2, \ldots, x_{n_1}$ and $y_1, y_2, \ldots, y_{n_2}$ have been taken from the *same population*, and you want to pool the samples for the purposes of estimating the population variance. There is no problem, of course, if you have all the data available to you, but suppose the information you have is limited to the estimates of the population mean and variance derived separately from the two samples. That is, you know $\bar{x}, s_x^2, n_1$ and $\bar{y}, s_y^2, n_2$ and you need to determine s^2.

  (i) Calculate $\sum x$ and $\sum x^2$ in terms of $\bar{x}, s_x^2$ and n_1 and $\sum y$ and $\sum y^2$ in terms of $\bar{y}, s_y^2$ and n_2. Let $z_1, z_2, \ldots, z_{n_1 + n_2}$ describe the pooled sample so that:
  $\sum z = \sum x + \sum y;$
  $\sum z^2 = \sum x^2 + \sum y^2.$
  (ii) Hence calculate s^2.
  (iii) Explain how this process differs from that by which a pooled variance estimate was derived in the text.

5 The random variables $X_1, X_2, \ldots, X_n$ (where $n > 1$) are independent and they all have the same distribution with mean μ and variance σ^2. The random variable $\overline{X}$ is defined by
$$\overline{X} = \frac{1}{n}\sum_{i=1}^{n} X_i.$$

(i) Show that
$$\sum_{i=1}^{n}(X_i - \overline{X})^2 = \sum_{i=1}^{n}(X_i - \mu)^2 - n(\overline{X} - \mu)^2.$$

(ii) Write down the expected value of
$$\sum_{i=1}^{n}(X_i - \mu)^2.$$
You are reminded that, if the random variable U has mean θ,
$$\text{Var}(U) = E[(U - \theta)^2].$$

(iii) State the variance of $\overline{X}$ and hence write down the expected value of $n(\overline{X} - \mu)^2$.

(iv) Deduce that
$$Y = \frac{1}{n-1}\sum(X_i - \overline{X})^2$$
is an unbiased estimator of σ^2.

(v) You are given the result that if the common distribution of the X_i is $N(\mu, \sigma^2)$, then Y has variance $\dfrac{2\sigma^4}{n-1}$ and, if n is large, is approximately Normally distributed. Using this result explain why, in large samples, an approximate 95% confidence interval for σ^2 is given by
$$s^2\left(1 \pm 1.96\sqrt{\frac{2}{n-1}}\right)$$
where s^2 is the observed value of
$$\frac{1}{n-1}\sum(X_1 - \overline{X}^2).$$

6 You may in this question *use* the result that
$$\int_0^\infty y^m e^{-y}\,dy = m!$$
for non-negative integer m.

(i) The probability density function of the continuous random variable X is
$$f(x) = \begin{cases} k(x - \theta)^{v-1}e^{-(x-\theta)} & 0 < x < \infty \\ 0 & \text{elsewhere} \end{cases}$$
where the parameters θ and v are both positive and v is an integer. Show, by using the substitution $y = x - \theta$, that
$$k = \frac{1}{(v-1)!}$$

(ii) Show that the mean of X is $\theta + v$.

(iii) Find $E[X^2]$ and hence show that the variance of X is v.

(iv) Deduce that plausible estimators of θ and v are $\overline{X} - S^2$ and S^2, where $\overline{X}$ and S^2 are defined as usual by
$$\overline{X} = \frac{1}{n}\sum_{i=1}^{n} X_i$$
$$S^2 = \frac{1}{n-1}\sum_{i=1}^{n}(X_i - \overline{X})^2$$
and $\{X_1, X_2, \ldots, X_n\}$ is a random sample of observations on X.

(v) State, with *brief* justifications, whether or not S^2 is an unbiased estimator of v and whether or not $\overline{X} - S^2$ is an unbiased estimator of θ.

7 (i) The random variable Y has mean α. The variance of Y is defined by $\text{Var}(Y) = E[(Y - \alpha)^2]$; prove from this definition that $\text{Var}(Y) = E[Y^2] - \alpha^2$.

(ii) Deduce that $E[Y^2] = \text{Var}(Y) + (E[Y])^2$.

(iii) The random variable X has a distribution with mean μ and variance σ^2, where μ is known. Use the result in part (ii) to *write down* an expression for $E[X^2]$ in terms of μ and σ^2.

(iv) $X_1, X_2, \ldots, X_n$ are independent random variables each with the same distribution X in part (iii). Using the definition of variance in part (i), or otherwise, show that
$$\frac{1}{n}\sum_{i=1}^{n}(X_i - \mu)^2$$
is an unbiased estimator of σ^2.

(v) The random variable $\overline{X}$ is defined by $\overline{X} = \frac{1}{n}\sum_{i=1}^{n} X_i$. Use the result in part (ii) to *write down* an expression for $\mathrm{E}[\overline{X}^2]$ in terms of μ, σ^2 and n.

(vi) The random variable T is defined by

$$T = \frac{1}{n}\sum_{i=1}^{n}(X_i - \overline{X})^2.$$

Show that

$$T = \frac{1}{n}\sum_{i=1}^{n} X_i^2 - \overline{X}^2.$$

(vii) Deduce that T is not an unbiased estimator of σ^2.

[MEI]

Methods for comparing estimators

Earlier, you considered what can be said about the distribution of ages at death in the population of this subspecies of human, from the sample available. It was assumed there that the distribution of ages at death is a uniform distribution: humans from this subspecies were equally likely to die at every age up to some maximum. Formally, if the random variable X is age at death, then it was assumed that X has a uniform distribution on $[0, m]$, where m is the maximum age to which these humans lived. The sample was then used to estimate the parameter m of the distribution of ages at death.

This section will extend this earlier work, and consider an alternative method of comparing estimators.

The estimator you will consider is

$$G = \alpha \times \max\{X_1, X_2, X_3\}$$

for different values of α where X_1, X_2, and X_3 are the random variables representing the three elements of the sample.

The sampling distribution of G

The probability density function for X is the uniform distribution

$$f(x) = \begin{cases} \frac{1}{m} & 0 \leqslant x \leqslant m \\ 0 & \text{otherwise.} \end{cases}$$

The cumulative distribution function for X is obtained by integration

$$F(x) = P(X \leqslant x) = \int_{-\infty}^{x} f(t)\, dt = \begin{cases} 0 & x \leqslant 0 \\ \frac{x}{m} & 0 < x \leqslant m \\ 1 & x > m \end{cases}$$

The cumulative distribution function for the estimator G is found by noting that the largest of three numbers will be less than a value x if, and only if, all three of them are less than x.

So, the probability that the largest of the three sample values is less than x is the same as the probability that all three sample values are less than x.

You can find the cumulative distribution function of G from the cumulative distribution function of X as follows:

$$F(x) = P(G \leqslant x) = P\left(\max\{X_1, X_2, X_3\} \leqslant \frac{x}{\alpha}\right)$$

$$= P\left(X_1 \leqslant \frac{x}{\alpha} \text{ and } X_2 \leqslant \frac{x}{\alpha} \text{ and } X_3 \leqslant \frac{x}{\alpha}\right)$$

$$= P\left(X_1 \leqslant \frac{x}{\alpha}\right) \times P\left(X_2 \leqslant \frac{x}{\alpha}\right) \times P\left(X_3 \leqslant \frac{x}{\alpha}\right)$$

$$= \begin{cases} 0 & x \leqslant 0 \\ \left(\dfrac{x}{\alpha m}\right)^3 & 0 < x \leqslant \alpha m \\ 1 & x > \alpha m. \end{cases}$$

Therefore, the probability density function of G, which is found by differentiating the cumulative distribution function, is

$$f(x) = \frac{d}{dx} F(x) = \begin{cases} \dfrac{3x^2}{(\alpha m)^3} & 0 \leqslant x \leqslant \alpha m \\ 0 & \text{otherwise.} \end{cases}$$

A graph of this density function is plotted in figure 2.5 for $m = 50$ and three different values of α.

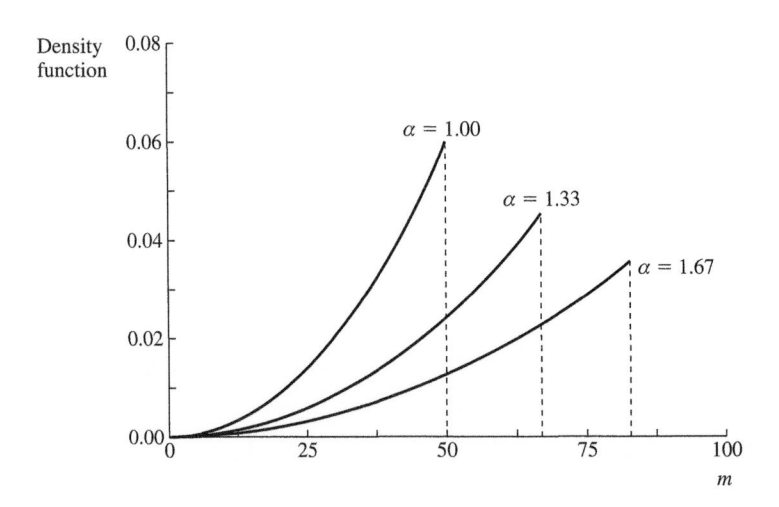

Figure 2.5

You can also use the distribution of G to calculate its mean and variance.

$$E[G] = \int_0^{\alpha m} x f(x)\, dx = \int_0^{\alpha m} x \frac{3x^2}{(\alpha m)^3}\, dx = \left[\frac{3x^4}{4(\alpha m)^3}\right]_0^{\alpha m} = \frac{3\alpha m}{4}$$

and

$$E[G^2] = \int_0^{\alpha m} x^2 f(x)\, dx = \int_0^{\alpha m} x^2 \frac{3x^2}{(\alpha m)^3}\, dx = \left[\frac{3x^5}{5(\alpha m)^3}\right]_0^{\alpha m} = \frac{3(\alpha m)^2}{5}$$

so

$$\text{Var}[G] = E[G^2] - (E[G])^2 = \frac{3(\alpha m)^2}{5} - \left(\frac{3\alpha m}{4}\right)^2 = \frac{3(\alpha m)^2}{80}.$$

The estimator G will be unbiased if α has the value $\frac{4}{3}$, since in this case $E[G] = m$, which is the definition of unbiasedness: the expected value of an estimator is equal to the parameter being estimated. Remember that the intuitive meaning of unbiasedness is that if the estimator G with $\alpha = \frac{4}{3}$, is used many times on samples of size 3 to find the parameter m in situations modelled by the uniform distribution, it will give the correct result on average.

The bias of G in the cases of $\alpha = 1$ and $\alpha = \frac{5}{3}$ is of the same magnitude (though with opposite sign).

$$\alpha = 1: \quad \text{bias}[G] = E[G] - m = \frac{3m}{4} - m = -\frac{m}{4}$$

$$\alpha = \frac{5}{3}: \quad \text{bias}[G] = E[G] - m = \frac{5m}{4} - m = \frac{m}{4}$$

However, looking at the density functions in figure 2.5 which correspond to these two cases, the estimator with $\alpha = 1$ seems intuitively more satisfactory because, although estimates will be consistently too small, they will only rarely be very far from the true value of 50.

The estimator with $\alpha = \frac{5}{3}$, although only as far from the true value on average, is spread much more widely about this mean and can therefore be expected to take values far from the true value much more frequently. The formal way that you have seen for describing this is that the estimator G has a much larger standard deviation in the $\alpha = \frac{5}{3}$ case than in the $\alpha = 1$ case.

In general, when investigating how good an estimator is, you will want to consider its bias, that is how far its mean is from the true parameter value, but also its standard deviation as a measure of its spread about this mean value. The term *standard error* is usually used to refer to the standard deviation of an estimator.

EXAMPLE 2.2 The variable X has a Normal distribution with unknown mean μ and standard deviation σ.

(i) A sample $X_1, X_2, \ldots, X_n$ of size n is taken and the sample mean $\overline{X}$ is used to estimate μ.

(ii) A sample of size 3 is taken, and the estimator $L = \frac{1}{3}(7X_1 - 8X_2 + 4X_3)$ is used to estimate μ.

In each case, show that the estimator is unbiased and find its standard error.

SOLUTION

(i) You know that $E[\overline{X}] = \mu$ and that $Var[\overline{X}] = \frac{\sigma^2}{n}$ so that the standard error of $\overline{X}_n$ is $\frac{\sigma}{\sqrt{n}}$.

Note that the standard error decreases with sample size.

(ii) $E[L] = \frac{1}{3}(7E[X_1] - 8E[X_2] + 4E[X_3])$

$= \frac{1}{3}(7\mu - 8\mu + 4\mu) = \mu$

$Var[L] = \frac{1}{3^2}(7^2 Var[X_1] + 8^2 Var[X_2] + 4^2 Var[X_3])$

$= \frac{1}{9}(49\sigma^2 + 64\sigma^2 + 16\sigma^2) = \frac{43\sigma^2}{3}$

so that the standard error of L is $\sqrt{43}\frac{\sigma}{\sqrt{3}}$: that is, about 6.5 times as large as that of $\overline{X}$, in the case $n = 3$.

In practice, you would not normally know the value of σ and so you could only estimate the standard error of the sample mean, by making a sample estimate of the variance.

EXAMPLE 2.3 Given that 11, 12, 17, 22, 35 and 47 are six values sampled from a Normal distribution with unknown mean μ and unknown standard deviation σ, find an estimate of μ and of the standard error of this estimate.

SOLUTION

From these data: $\overline{x} = \frac{1}{6}(11 + 12 + 17 + 22 + 35 + 47) = 24$

$s^2 = \frac{6}{5} \times \left(\frac{1}{6}(11^2 + 12^2 + 17^2 + 22^2 + 35^2 + 47^2) - 24^2\right) = 203.2$

so an (unbiased) estimate of μ is 24, and the standard error (se) of this sample mean is estimated as $se(\overline{x}) = \sqrt{\frac{203.2}{6}} = 5.82$.

Mean square error

In trying to capture what you want from a good estimator, you might sum it up as 'not being too far away from the true value too often'. The *mean square error* is the expected squared difference between the estimator and the true value of the parameter being estimated. Asking for an estimator to have a small mean square error then translates this idea of a good estimator fairly directly into formal language. If T is an estimator for parameter τ, then the mean square error is

$$\mathrm{mse}(T) = \mathrm{E}[(T - \tau)^2].$$

For the estimator G in the example on page 42 you can calculate the mean square error directly.

$$\mathrm{mse}(G) = \mathrm{E}[(G - m)^2] = \int_0^{\alpha m} (x - m)^2 \times \mathrm{f}(x) \, \mathrm{d}x$$

$$= \int_0^{\alpha m} (x - m)^2 \frac{3x^2}{(\alpha m)^3} \, \mathrm{d}x$$

$$= \frac{3}{(\alpha m)^3} \left[\frac{x^5}{5} - 2m \frac{x^4}{4} + m^2 \frac{x^3}{3} \right]_0^{\alpha m} = \frac{m^2}{10} (6\alpha^2 - 15\alpha + 10)$$

The minimum value of this expression occurs when $\alpha = \frac{5}{4}$ (by differentiation or completing the square). Note that this is not the value of α which makes G unbiased.

You should be clear that the mean square error is not a unique measure of how good an estimator is. An alternative measure would be the *mean absolute error (mae)*, for instance: $\mathrm{mae}(T) = \mathrm{E}[|T - \tau|]$.

To choose the mean square error as a criterion is to make a choice about the relative weighting of prospective large and small errors in estimation: the mean square error weights large errors relatively more highly than the mean absolute error would. In the end, the problem comes down to one you have met before: what makes a good estimator depends on what it is to be used for, and how expensive it will be to make mistakes of various sizes or types.

An alternative formula for the mean square error

In the calculation above, the mse for G was relatively easy to find, but in more complex cases an alternative formula is useful.

$$\text{mse}(T) = \text{E}[(T-\tau)^2] \qquad \text{(by definition)}$$

$$= \text{E}[T^2] - \text{E}[2\tau T] + \text{E}[\tau^2] \qquad \text{(expanding and using } \text{E}[X \pm Y] = \text{E}[X] \pm \text{E}[Y]\text{)}$$

$$= \text{E}[T^2] - 2\tau\text{E}[T] + \tau^2 \qquad \text{(since } \tau \text{ is a non-random)}$$

$$= \text{E}[T^2] - \text{E}[T]^2 + \text{E}[T]^2 - 2\tau\text{E}[T] + \tau^2$$

$$= \text{Var}[T] + (\text{E}[T] - \tau)^2 \qquad \text{(using Var }[T] = \text{E}[T^2] - \text{E}[T]^2\text{)}$$

Noting that $(\text{E}[T] - \tau)$ measures the bias of T, the extent to which $\text{E}[T]$ is not equal to the true value of the parameter τ, you can summarise this as

$$\text{mse}(T) = \text{Var}[T] + (\text{bias}(T))^2 = (\text{standard error}(T))^2 + (\text{bias}(T))^2.$$

This shows that to have a small mean square error requires a small spread in the values given by the estimator (standard error is small) about a mean which is not too far from the true value (bias is small): this corresponds neatly to the intuitive idea of what constitutes a good estimator.

As an example, look at how the mean square error in G is made up, for the values $\alpha = 1, \frac{5}{4}, \frac{4}{3}$ and with $m = 50$.

α	E[G]	Bias[G] = E[G]−50	Var[G]	mse[G] = Var[G] + (Bias [G])²	Comment
1	37.5	−12.5	93.75	250.00	a small spread, but about a mean value which is far from the true perimeter
$\frac{5}{4}$	46.875	−3.125	146.48	156.25	a compromise between the two effects: a moderate spread about a mean not to far from the true parameter value
$\frac{4}{3}$	50.0	0.0	166.67	166.67	a mean equal to the true parameter value but a large spread about the mean

Efficiency

If one estimator of a particular parameter has a smaller mean square error than another for all possible values of the parameter, then the first estimator is said to be a more *efficient* estimator of this parameter. If the two estimators are both unbiased, then the formula above shows that one estimator is more efficient than the other, if it has the smaller standard error for all values of the parameter.

You saw above that the value of α which makes G as efficient as possible is $\alpha = \frac{5}{4}$.

EXAMPLE 2.4

The variable X has a distribution with unknown mean μ and standard deviation s.

A sample X_1, X_2, X_3 of size 3 is taken and the estimator $L = aX_1 + bX_2 + cX_3$ used to estimate μ.

(i) If L is required to be unbiased, find the values of a, b and c which make L as efficient as possible, and state the mean square error in this case.

(ii) Find the mean square error in the case $a = b = c = \frac{1}{4}$. Compare this estimator with the one found in part (i).

SOLUTION

(i) $E[L] = E[aX_1 + bX_2 + cX_3] = aE[X_1] + bE[X_2] + cE[X_3] = (a+b+c)\mu$.

For L to be unbiased this must equal μ, so that $(a+b+c) = 1$.

Since L is unbiased,

$$\begin{aligned}\text{mse}(L) &= \text{Var}[L] \\ &= \text{Var}[aX_1 + bX_2 + cX_3] \\ &= a^2\text{Var}[X_1] + b^2\text{Var}[X_2] + c^2\text{Var}[X_3] \\ &= (a^2 + b^2 + c^2)\sigma^2\end{aligned}$$

so that the question is asking for the minimum value of $(a^2 + b^2 + c^2)$, given that $(a+b+c) = 1$. Because

$$(a^2 + b^2 + c^2) = \frac{1}{3}\{(a+b+c)^2 + (a-b)^2 + (b-c)^2 + (c-a)^2\},$$

this minimum value occurs when the last three terms of the expression in curly brackets are all equal to zero, i.e. when $a = b = c = \frac{1}{3}$ (so that $(a+b+c) = 1$). In this case, the mean square error is

$$\frac{1}{3}(a+b+c)^2\sigma^2 = \frac{1}{3}\sigma^2.$$

(ii) In the case $a = b = c = \frac{1}{4}$,

$$\text{Var}[L] = (a^2 + b^2 + c^2)\sigma^2 = \frac{3}{16}\sigma^2$$

and

$$E[L] = (a + b + c)\mu = \frac{3}{4}\mu,$$

so

$$\text{mse}[L] = \frac{3}{16}\sigma^2 + \left(\frac{3}{4}\mu - \mu\right)^2 = \frac{3}{16}\sigma^2 + \frac{1}{16}\mu^2.$$

This will be less than the mean square error of the unbiased estimator if $\frac{3}{16}\sigma^2 + \frac{1}{16}\mu^2 < \frac{1}{3}\sigma^2$ that is, if $\mu^2 < \frac{7}{3}\sigma^2$, and greater otherwise. Because neither estimator has a smaller mse than the other for all values of the parameter μ, you cannot describe either as being more efficient than the other.

Consistency

As you have seen above, it is not necessary for an estimator to be unbiased. However, you would normally expect that an estimator based on a larger sample will come closer to, and be more certain of, identifying the true parameter value. You would hope that it would be more nearly correct on average, and that the spread about that average would decrease.

That is, if T_n is an estimator for τ based on a sample size of n, you would expect that as n gets larger,

- $E[T_n]$ would tend towards τ
- $\text{Var}[T_n]$ would tend towards zero.

An estimator with these properties is said to be *consistent*, and an equivalent definition is that the mean square error of the estimator tends to zero as n gets larger.

EXAMPLE 2.5 Show that if $X_1, X_2, \ldots, X_n$ is an independent random sample from a distribution with mean μ and variance σ^2, the estimator

$$M_n = \frac{1}{n+1}(X_1 + X_2 + \ldots + X_n)$$

is a consistent estimator of the mean.

SOLUTION

$$E[M_n] = \frac{1}{n+1}(E[X_1] + E[X_2] + \ldots + E[X_n]) = \frac{1}{n+1}n\mu$$

$$= \left(1 - \frac{1}{n+1}\right)\mu$$

which tends towards μ as n gets larger, and

$$\text{Var}[M_n] = \left(\frac{1}{n+1}\right)^2(\text{Var}[X_1] + \text{Var}[X_2] + \ldots + \text{Var}[X_n])$$

$$= \frac{n}{(n+1)^2}\sigma^2$$

which tends towards zero as n gets larger.
Equivalently, the mean square error of M_n is

$$\text{mse}[M_n] = \text{Var}[M]_n + (E[M_n] - \mu)^2 = \frac{n}{(n+1)^2}\sigma^2 + \left(-\frac{\mu}{n+1}\right)^2$$

$$= \frac{n\sigma^2 + \mu^2}{(n+1)^2}$$

which tends towards zero as n gets larger.

EXERCISE 2C

1 A coin is tossed n times and the number of heads, H, is counted.

The probability of a head is p.

(i) Show that $\Pi_1 = \dfrac{H}{n}$ is an unbiased estimator of p, and find its standard error as a function of n and p.

(ii) Sketch a graph of the standard error as a function of p, for fixed n and show that the standard error obeys s.e. $\leq \dfrac{1}{2\sqrt{n}}$.

(iii) Roughly, what value of n is required to estimate p correct to 3 decimal places.

2 Errors are made by a typist at a rate of r per minute.

(i) The number of errors, N, he makes in t minutes is counted.
Assuming that N is a Poisson variable, write $E[N]$ and $\text{Var}[N]$ in terms of r and t. Show that $R_1 = \dfrac{N}{t}$ is an unbiased estimator of r and find its standard error.

(ii) The number of minutes, T, he takes before making his nth mistake is counted.

Assuming that T is a random variable with density function

$$f(t) = \frac{r^n t^{n-1} e^{-rt}}{(n-1)!} \quad (0 \leq t < \infty)$$

write $E[T]$ and $\text{Var}[T]$ in terms of r and n. (You may find the integral

$$\int_0^\infty t^s e^{-kt}\, dt = \frac{s!}{k^{s+1}} \text{ helpful.})$$

Show that the estimator $R_2 = \dfrac{n}{T}$ of r is not unbiased and find its standard error.

Suggest an estimator similar to R_2, which is unbiased. Compare the mean square errors of R_2 and your estimator.

3 A bus comes every t minutes to my nearest stop. I use the bus rarely and my time of arrival at the stop when I do use it is independent of the bus timetable, so that the random variable W which records the time I have to wait for the bus on a particular occasion has a uniform distribution on $[0, t]$.

(i) Calculate the mean and variance of W.

I am going to estimate t by recording the value of W on the next six occasions on which I use the bus (call these values $W_1, W_2, \ldots, W_6$) and finding twice their mean, that is

$$T = \frac{W_1 + W_2 + \ldots + W_6}{3}$$

will be my estimate of the value of t.

(ii) Find $E[T]$ and $Var[T]$ (notice that $W_1, W_2, \ldots, W_6$ are independent), and hence show that T is unbiased and find its standard error.

The variable S is defined as the largest of my next six waiting times. The cumulative distribution function of S is

$$F(s) = P(S < s) = P(\text{all six } W_i < s)$$
$$= \{P(W < s)\}^6.$$

(iii) Calculate $F(s)$ and hence find $f(s)$, the p.d.f. of S.

(iv) Use the p.d.f. to calculate $E[S]$ and $Var[S]$.

Now consider the estimator $T_a = aS$.

(v) Find $E[T_a]$ and $Var[T_a]$ as functions of a and t.

(vi) For which value of a is T_a unbiased? What is the mean square error of T_a for this value of a?

(vii) Find an expression for the mean square error of T_a in terms of a, and hence determine the value of a which minimises the mean square error. What is the mean square error of T_a for this value of a?

(viii) Which estimator would you use?

4 When a random sample of size $(2r + 1)$ is taken from a random variable X, whose distribution has density function $f(x)$, and cumulative distribution function $F(x)$, the median of the sample has density function

$$m(x) = \frac{(2r + 1)!}{r!r!} (F(x))^r f(x)(1 - F(x))^r.$$

(i) Explain intuitively why this is the density function for the median.

Suppose X has a uniform distribution on $[0, a]$ and take $r = 1$, i.e. a sample of size 3.

(ii) Find the expectation and variance of

(a) the median of the sample

(b) the mean of the sample.

(iii) Show that the median and the mean are both unbiased estimators of the mid-point of the distribution, and compare their standard errors.

(iv) Consider the variables $L_k = k \times \{\text{the largest of the three elements in the sample}\}$ as estimators of the mid-point of the distribution.

(a) Find expressions in terms of k for the mean and variance of L_k, and hence for its mean square error.

(b) Is there a value of k for which the estimator L_k is unbiased?

(c) Is there a value of k for which L_k is more efficient than the mean or the median?

5 A coin is tossed n times and the number of heads, H, is counted. The probability of a head is p.

(i) Show that $\Pi_2 = \dfrac{H + 0.5}{n + 1}$ is not an unbiased estimate for p, and find an expression for the mean square error of Π_2 as a function of p. Is Π_2 consistent?

(ii) Compare Π_2 with the estimator Π_1 whose mse was determined in question 1. When is Π_2 preferable?

(iii) Even a biased coin is likely to have a value of p near to 0.5, where Π_2 has a smaller mse. Would Π_2 therefore be a better detector of biased coins?

(iv) Consider the estimator Π_3, which is just equal to 0.5, for all samples. Is this estimator consistent? Will this ever be the best estimator?

6 The time T at which an oil seal first fails is a random variable with density function

$$f(t) = \frac{t}{\lambda^2} e^{-\frac{t}{\lambda}} \quad (0 \leqslant t < \infty)$$

where λ is an unknown parameter.

(i) Find $E[T]$ and $Var[T]$.

A sample of n oil seals is tested until they fail. The times of failure are $T_1, T_2, \ldots, T_n$. Consider, as estimators of λ, the variables

$$S_c = c \sum_{i=1}^{n} T_i.$$

(ii) Determine the mean and variance of S_c and hence its bias and mean square error.

(iii) For what value of c is S_c unbiased?

(iv) For what value of c does S_c have minimum mean square error?

(v) Is S_c consistent for the values of c in parts (iii) and (iv)?

7 The independent random variables $X_1, X_2, \ldots, X_n$ represent a random sample from the $N(\mu, \sigma^2)$ distribution. The variance σ^2 is to be estimated.

Consider first the estimator $T = \frac{1}{2}(X_1 - X_2)^2$ which involves only X_1 and X_2.

(i) State the distribution of $X_1 - X_2$ and its mean and variance.

(ii) Use the result that $Var(X_1 - X_2) = E[(X_1 - X_2)^2] - \{E[X_1 - X_2]\}^2$ to deduce that $E[T] = \sigma^2$. State what this implies about T as an estimator of σ^2.

(iii) Using the result that $E[Z^4] = 3$ where $Z \sim N(0, 1)$, deduce further that $E[T^2] = 3\sigma^4$ and hence find $Var(T)$.

Now consider the estimator

$$S^2 = \frac{1}{n-1} \sum_{i=1}^{n} (X_i - \overline{X})^2$$

where $\overline{X}$ is the mean of $X_1, X_2, \ldots, X_n$. You are *given* the following results.

(1) The sampling distribution of S^2 is $\frac{\sigma^2}{n-1}\chi^2_{n-1}$.

(2) The mean of a χ^2_{n-1} random variable is $n - 1$.

(3) The variance of a χ^2_{n-1} random variable is $2(n - 1)$.

(You are *not* required to prove these results.)

(iv) Use these results to show that S^2 is an unbiased estimator of σ^2 and that its variance is $\frac{2\sigma^4}{n-1}$.

(v) Find $\frac{Var(T)}{Var(S^2)}$. Hence discuss the efficiency of S^2 relative to T as an estimator of σ^2.

(vi) Suggest possible circumstances when T might be a useful estimator of σ^2.

[MEI]

INVESTIGATIONS

1 A variable X has a Cauchy distribution, that is, its density function is

$$f(x) = \frac{1}{\pi(1 + (x - \alpha)^2)}.$$

Two estimators based on a sample of size n have been suggested for α: the mean and the median.

Conduct a computer simulation to investigate the distributions of these two estimators: choose different sample sizes, and look at the spread of the distributions. Do you think both estimators are unbiased? Do you think both estimators are consistent? Which estimator is preferable?

The calculations are easier if you take $\alpha = 0$. In this case, if RAND is a variable with a uniform distribution on [0, 1] (which is provided by the BASIC language and by most spreadsheets), then

$$X = \tan(\pi(\text{RAND} - 0.5))$$

will have a Cauchy distribution.

2 An art historian, who knows that the signed and numbered copies of a Picasso print were numbered consecutively from 001 upward, has found five surviving copies, numbered 104, 078, 011, 083, 122.

Devise estimators for the number of copies made originally, and investigate their properties. Use the one you consider best to estimate the number of copies made from the data given.

KEY POINTS

1. If the form of the population distribution of a random variable is known or can be assumed, but the value of some parameter, τ, of the distribution is unknown, then a statistic, T, calculated from a random sample of values of the variable can often be found which gives an *estimator* of that parameter. The value of the estimator from a particular sample is an *estimate* of the parameter.

2. The estimator is itself a random variable, and the probability, or probability density, with which each of its possible values arises in random samples from the population is called the *sampling distribution* of the estimator.

3. If the expected value of the estimator is equal to the population parameter, $E[T] = \tau$, the estimator is said to be *unbiased*.
   Otherwise, if $E[T] \neq \tau$ the estimator is *biased* and the *bias* of T is $(E[T] - \tau)$.

4. The *standard error* of T is its standard deviation $\mathrm{se}(T) = \sqrt{\mathrm{Var}[T]}$.

5. The *mean square error* of T is defined as $\mathrm{mse}(T) = E[(T - \tau)^2]$ which can also be calculated from $\mathrm{mse}(T) = \mathrm{Var}(T) + (\mathrm{bias}(T))^2$.

6. One estimator of a parameter τ is more *efficient* than another if it has smaller mean square error for all values of τ.

7. Given a sample of n values $x_1, x_2, \ldots, x_n$ from a distribution with mean μ and variance σ^2, unbiased estimates of μ and σ^2 are given by:

$$\bar{x} = \frac{\sum_{i=1}^{n} x_i}{n}$$

$$s^2 = \frac{\sum_{i=1}^{n}(x_i - \bar{x})^2}{n-1} = \frac{\sum_{i=1}^{n} x_i^2 - n\bar{x}^2}{n-1}.$$

8. Given a sample of n_1 values $x_1, x_2, \ldots, x_{n_1}$ from a distribution with mean μ_1, and variance σ^2, and a sample of n_2 values $y_1, y_2, \ldots, y_{n_2}$ from a distribution with a mean μ_2 (which may be different from μ_1) but the same variance σ^2, an unbiased estimate of σ^2 is given by

$$s^2 = \frac{\sum_{i=1}^{n_1}(x_i - \bar{x})^2 + \sum_{i=1}^{n_2}(y_i - \bar{y})^2}{(n_1 + n_2 - 2)} = \frac{(n_1 - 1)s_1^2 + (n_2 - 1)s_2^2}{(n_1 + n_2 - 2)}$$

where s_1^2 and s_2^2 are the unbiased estimates of σ^2 calculated from the two separate samples.

3 Maximum likelihood estimators

Unless we have complete information, we need thinking in order to make the best use of the information we have.

Edward de Bono

When a beta particle passes through a plastic sheet, the probability that it is absorbed depends only on the thickness of the sheet. When 20 beta particles are passed through two identical plastic sheets, seven are absorbed by the first sheet and nine by the second. How should the probability, p, that a particle is absorbed by a single sheet, be estimated?

Assuming that the passage of each particle is independent of the others, four possible estimates are as follows.

1 When 20 particles were passed through the first sheet, 7 were absorbed; so the probability should be estimated as $p_1 = \frac{7}{20} = 0.35$.

2 When the 13 remaining particles were passed through the second sheet, 9 were absorbed; so the probability should be estimated as $p_2 = \frac{9}{13} = 0.6923$.

3 The probability that a particle is absorbed by the second sheet is $(1-p)p$, and 9 out of 20 were absorbed by the second sheet, so you could try to choose

$$(1-p_3)p_3 = \frac{9}{20}$$

but this has no real solutions.

4 The probability that a particle is not absorbed at all is $(1-p)^2$, and 4 out of 20 were not absorbed at all, so you could choose

$$(1-p_4)^2 = \frac{4}{20} \quad \Rightarrow \quad p_4 = 1 - \frac{1}{\sqrt{5}} = 0.5528.$$

Some of these estimators have nice properties. For instance p_1 is unbiased: but this merely means that *if you repeated the experiment many times*, the average estimate made by this method should approach the true value – and here there is substantial evidence (9 out of 13 remaining particles absorbed by the second sheet) that *in this case* the method has given too low a value for p.

How can you take all the information available into account in settling on a good estimate for p?

Likelihood

The *likelihood* of the set of observations in a sample is simply the probability that this particular sample occurs. In a context where a parameter is unknown, the likelihood will be a function of this unknown parameter.

Here, for example, the probability that, of 20 particles, seven will be stopped by the first sheet, nine by the second and four will pass through will depend on p, so you can calculate the likelihood, $L(p)$, as follows. Any particular sample of this type, whatever the order in which those particles stopped by the first sheet, the second sheet or neither sheet are observed, has probability (as the fats of the particles are independent)

$$P(\text{stopped by first sheet})^7 \times P(\text{stopped by second sheet})^9 \times P(\text{not stopped})^4$$

How many samples of this sort are there? In other words, in how many different orders can the particles stopped by the first sheet, the second sheet or neither sheet be observed? Equivalently, how many ways are there of arranging seven Fs (stopped by first sheet), nine Ss (stopped by second sheet) and four Ns (not stopped) in a row? Twenty letters can be arranged in 20! ways, but this overcounts the distinct arrangements by factors of 7! (the Fs rearranged among themselves), 9! (the Ss) and 4! (the Ns), so that, in fact, there are $\dfrac{20!}{7!9!4!}$ such samples.

Thus:

$$L(p) = \frac{20!}{7!9!4!} \times P(\text{stopped by first sheet})^7 \times P(\text{stopped by second sheet})^9 \\ \times P(\text{not stopped})^4$$

but, in terms of the unknown parameter, p:

$$P(\text{stopped by first sheet}) = p$$
$$P(\text{stopped by second sheet}) = (1-p)p$$
$$P(\text{not stopped}) = (1-p)^2$$

so, finally:

$$L(p) = \frac{20!}{7!9!4!} \times [p]^7 \times [(1-p)p]^9 \times [(1-p)^2]^4$$
$$= 55\,426\,800 \times p^{16} \times (1-p)^{17}$$

The three estimates obtained above and the likelihood of the sample results if each was correct, are:

$p_1 = 0.35$ $L(p_1) = 0.001\,855$
$p_2 = 0.6923$ $L(p_2) = 0.000\,307$
$p_4 = 0.5528$ $L(p_4) = 0.004\,824$

You can see that, for instance, if p were equal to estimate p_2 the sample obtained would have a rather small probability of occurring, whereas if p were equal to estimate p_4, the probability of the sample actually obtained would be much higher – about 16 times as great. This makes estimate p_4 seem intuitively more sensible than estimate p_2.

You can follow this argument further: if you think that estimate p_4 is better than estimate p_2 because it makes the probability of the sample actually obtained greater, then an even better estimate of p would be the value which makes the probability of the sample actually obtained as great as possible. That is, you should choose the estimate, $\hat{p}$ which makes $L(\hat{p})$ a maximum.

A graph of $L(p)$ against p is shown in figure 3.1.

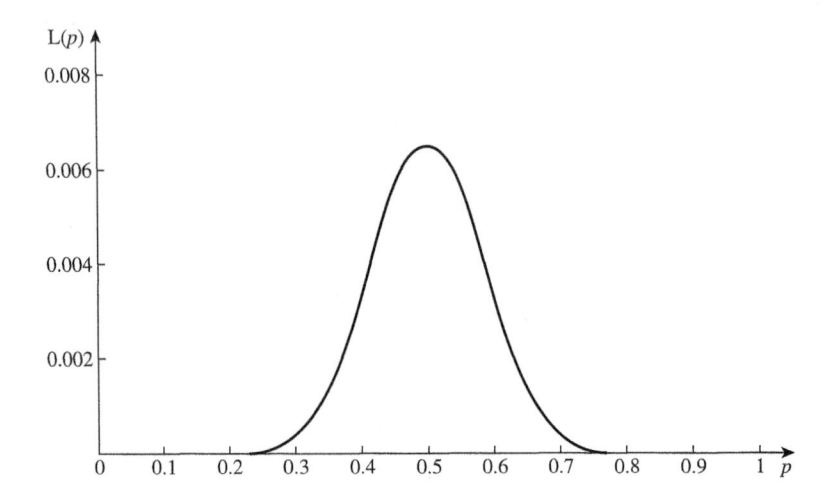

Figure 3.1

The value of p which makes $L(p)$ a maximum is just under 0.5. You can determine the exact value by differentiation.

$$L(p) = 55\,426\,800 \times p^{16} \times (1-p)^{17}$$

so

$$\frac{dL}{dp} = 55\,426\,800 \times [16p^{15} \times (1-p)^{17} + p^{16} \times -17(1-p)^{16}]$$

$$= 55\,426\,800 \times p^{15} \times (1-p)^{16} \times [16(1-p) - 17p]$$

$$= 55\,426\,800 \times p^{15} \times (1-p)^{16} \times (16 - 33p)$$

The maximum occurs when this expression is equal to zero, i.e. when $p = \frac{16}{33} = 0.485$, as you can see from figure 3.1 that the other two turning points, $p = 0$ and $p = 1$, are minima of L. Note that, having found this estimate by maximising the likelihood, you can see that it makes sense. The fraction is just

$$\frac{\text{total number of particles stopped by a sheet}}{\text{total number of particles approaching a sheet}}$$

This method for deriving an estimate for a parameter from a set of data is called the *maximum likelihood method*. It is conventional to refer to the maximum likelihood estimate of a parameter by placing a caret (^) over the letter, so a maximum likelihood estimate of λ would be called $\hat{\lambda}$.

ACTIVITY

You can use the same method to produce a complete estimator for this problem. Suppose that, in an experiment, a particles were stopped by the first sheet, b by the second sheet and c were not stopped. $N = a + b + c$ is the total number of particles passed through the sheets.

(i) Show that
$$L(p) = K \times p^{a+b} \times (1-p)^{b+2c}$$
where K stands for the combinatorial constant $\dfrac{(a+b+c)!}{a!b!c!}$

(ii) Find $\dfrac{dL}{dp}$ and from this show that the maximum likelihood estimator for p is
$$\hat{p} = \frac{a+b}{a+2b+2c}$$

(iii) The general form of estimator p_1 – using only the data from the first sheet – is
$$p_1 = \frac{a}{a+b+c}$$
and the general form of estimator – using only the data from the second sheet – is
$$p_2 = \frac{b}{b+c}.$$
In fact, the maximum likelihood estimator lies between these two. Prove this.

Summary

The *maximum likelihood criterion for estimation* suggests that if you are trying to estimate a parameter, t, then, given any set of data, you should choose as we estimate the value of t which makes the likelihood of the actual data as great as possible.

Logarithmic differentiation

When finding the maximum likelihood estimate above, you differentiated the expression $L(p)$. This was relatively straightforward in that example, but this is not always the case and the technique of logarithmic differentiation is often useful in maximum likelihood problems. This relies on the observation that as the expression $L(p)$ is a probability, it is always positive and so you can find its natural logarithm $\ln[L(p)]$. Because the graph of the logarithm function has a positive gradient, the largest value of $\ln[L(p)]$ will occur when $L(p)$ itself is largest, so that you can replace the problem of finding the value of p which maximises $L(p)$, with the problem of finding the value of p which maximises $\ln[L(p)]$. The advantage of the method is that this is often much easier!

Formally,

$$\frac{d}{dp} \ln [Lp)] = \frac{1}{L(p)} \frac{dL}{dp}$$

which is equal to zero whenever $\frac{dL}{dp}$ is.

EXAMPLE 3.1

Find the maximum value of $L(p) = \frac{(a+b+c)!}{a!b!c!} \times p^{a+b} \times (1-p)^{b+2c}$.

SOLUTION

$$\ln [L(p)] = \ln \frac{(a+b+c)!}{a!b!c!} + \ln (p^{a+b}) + \ln ((1-p)^{b+2c})$$

(because $\ln (A \times B) = \ln A + \ln B$)

$$= \ln \frac{(a+b+c)!}{a!b!c!} + (a+b) \ln (p) + (b+2c) \ln (1-p)$$

(because $\ln (A^n) = n \ln (A)$)

so:

$$\frac{d}{dp} \ln [L(p)] = \frac{a+b}{p} - \frac{b+2c}{1-p}$$

This must be set equal to zero to determine the value of p giving a maximum.

$$\frac{a+b}{p} - \frac{b+2c}{1-p} = 0 \Rightarrow (a+b)(1-p) - (b+2c)p = 0$$

$$\Rightarrow (a+b) = (a+2b+2c)p \Rightarrow p = \frac{a+b}{a+2b+2c}$$

as before, but with rather less work.

EXAMPLE 3.2

In an investigation of arctic lichen cover, a botanist records, for each of 24 randomly located square metres of tundra, whether it contains no, one or more than one lichen colony.
His results are:

no colonies	11 square metres
one colony	6 square metres
more than one colony	7 square metres

Assuming that the number of colonies of lichen in each square metre of tundra follows a Poisson distribution, find an equation satisfied by the maximum likelihood estimate $\hat{\lambda}$ of λ, the mean number of colonies per square metre, and show that your equation is approximately satisfied by $\hat{\lambda} = 0.94$.

SOLUTION

The assumption of a Poisson distribution with mean λ implies that for each square metre:

$P(\text{no colonies}) = e^{-\lambda}$

$P(\text{one colony}) = \lambda e^{-\lambda}$

$P(\text{more than one colony}) = 1 - [P(\text{no colonies}) + P(\text{one colony})]$
$\qquad = 1 - (1 + \lambda)e^{-\lambda}$

so that the likelihood of these observations is:

$$L(p) = \frac{24!}{11!6!7!} [e^{-\lambda}]^{11} [\lambda e^{-\lambda}]^6 [1 - (1+\lambda)e^{-\lambda}]^7$$

$$= \frac{24!}{11!6!7!} e^{-11\lambda} \times \lambda^6 \times e^{-6\lambda} \times [1 - (1+\lambda)e^{-\lambda}]^7$$

$$= \frac{24!}{11!6!7!} e^{-17\lambda} \times \lambda^6 \times [1 - (1+\lambda)e^{-\lambda}]^7$$

You can use the technique of logarithmic differentiation here.

$$\ln[L(p)] = \ln\left[\frac{24!}{11!6!7!}\right] - 17\lambda + 6\ln\lambda + 7\ln[1 - (1+\lambda)e^{-\lambda}]$$

so: $\quad \dfrac{d}{d\lambda} \ln[L(\lambda)] = -17 + \dfrac{6}{\lambda} + \dfrac{7}{1-(1+\lambda)e^{-\lambda}} \times \lambda e^{-\lambda}$

The maximum likelihood estimator, $\hat{\lambda}$, therefore satisfies the equation

$$-17 + \frac{6}{\hat{\lambda}} + \frac{7}{1-(1+\hat{\lambda})e^{-\hat{\lambda}}} \times \hat{\lambda} e^{-\hat{\lambda}} = 0$$

$\Rightarrow \qquad (6 - 17\hat{\lambda})(1 - (1+\hat{\lambda})e^{-\hat{\lambda}}) + 7\hat{\lambda}^2 e^{-\hat{\lambda}} = 0$

$\Rightarrow \qquad (24\hat{\lambda}^2 + 11\hat{\lambda} - 6)e^{-\hat{\lambda}} + (6 - 17\hat{\lambda}) = 0$

The value $\hat{\lambda} = 0.94$ given is an approximate solution to this equation, correct to two significant figures, because the value of the left-hand side when $\hat{\lambda} = 0.935$ is 0.024, which is positive, and when $\hat{\lambda} = 0.945$ is -0.026, which is negative.

If you do not sketch the likelihood function, as in this case, you need to check that 0.94 gives a maximum of L. You can do this by showing $\dfrac{d^2 L}{d\lambda^2} < 0$, and there is a useful logarithmic technique for this. Note that:

$$\frac{d^2}{d\lambda^2} \ln[L(\lambda)] = \frac{d}{d\lambda}\left\{\frac{1}{L(\lambda)} \frac{dL}{d\lambda}\right\}$$

$$= \frac{1}{L(\lambda)} \frac{d^2 L}{d\lambda^2} - \frac{1}{[L(\lambda)]^2}\left\{\frac{dL}{d\lambda}\right\}^2$$

You are interested in the sign of $\frac{d^2L}{d\lambda^2}$ at $\hat{\lambda}$, the value of λ where $\frac{dL}{d\lambda} = 0$.

Substituting $\frac{dL}{d\lambda} = 0$ in the equation above gives

$$\frac{d^2}{d\lambda^2} \ln[L(\lambda)] = \frac{1}{L(\lambda)} \frac{d^2L}{d\lambda^2} \qquad \text{when } \lambda = \hat{\lambda}.$$

As $L(\lambda)$ is a probability and so positive, the sign of $\frac{d^2L}{d\lambda^2}$ is the same as the sign of $\frac{d^2}{d\lambda^2} \ln[L(\lambda)]$, so the criterion for a maximum of the likelihood is that the second derivative of $\ln L$ is negative at a turning point of $\ln L$.

In this example:

$$\frac{d^2}{d\lambda^2} \ln[L(\lambda)] = \frac{d}{d\lambda} \left\{ -17 + \frac{6}{\lambda} + \frac{7}{1-(1+\lambda)e^{-\lambda}} \times \lambda e^{-\lambda} \right\}$$

$$= -\frac{6}{\lambda^2} + \frac{7e^{-\lambda}\{(1-\lambda) - e^{-\lambda}\}}{[1-(1+\lambda)e^{-\lambda}]^2}$$

$$= -25.7$$

at $\lambda = 0.94$, which confirms that value gives the maximum likelihood.

Properties of maximum likelihood estimators

You should be clear that the maximum likelihood method is *one* way of deciding how to estimate a parameter – but *not necessarily* the best way. In general, there is no guarantee that a maximum likelihood estimator will be efficient, unbiased, have a small mean square error, or, indeed, possess any nice properties, but in practice, these estimators are often among the most satisfactory that can be obtained, particularly in large samples. The following example, however, illustrates a case where the maximum likelihood method produces an intuitively unsatisfactory estimator.

EXAMPLE 3.3

A tub contains a complete set of one each of N different model farm animals where N is unknown. A small boy pulls animals from the tub until he removes the cow, which occurs on his fifth draw. Estimate N using the method of maximum likelihood.

SOLUTION

The probability that the cow is drawn on the fifth draw is zero if there are fewer than five animals and $\frac{1}{N}$ if there are five or more animals. A graph of the likelihood function is shown in figure 3.2. You can see from the graph that the maximum likelihood occurs when $N = 5$.

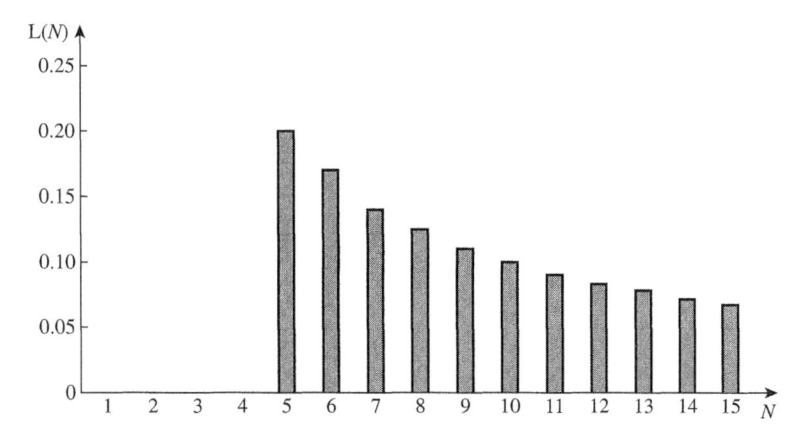

Figure 3.2

The estimate obtained in Example 3.3 is the one required, but it should strike you that there is something rather odd about the estimator $\hat{N} = $ 'the number of the draw on which the cow is drawn'. For example, it is certainly not unbiased because, for a given value of N, the possible draws on which the cow may be drawn are the first, second, ..., Nth and these are all equally likely so that the expected draw for the cow, and therefore $E[\hat{N}]$, is $\dfrac{N+1}{2}$. In general, where the range of possible sample values depends on the parameter being estimated, the maximum likelihood method can give rather unexpected results!

This example shows that the maximum likelihood estimator cannot always be found by differentiating, either because the parameter may be restricted to take a discrete rather than a continuous range of values – here, N must be a positive integer – or because there may be a limited range of permissible parameter values and the maximum likelihood may occur at one end of this range rather than within the permitted interval – here, N must be greater than or equal to 5 and the maximum likelihood, in fact, occurs at the lowest point of this permitted range.

Continuous distributions

The times between successive arrivals of customers in a shop are often taken to have exponential distribution; that is, the probability density of the random variable T which measures the time between successive arrivals is

$$f(t) = \lambda e^{-\lambda t}$$

with parameter λ.

The times, in seconds, between four successive arrivals in one shop were

$$t_1 = 27; \quad t_2 = 19; \quad t_3 = 16; \quad t_4 = 38.$$

Assuming the inter-arrival times are exponentially distributed, how could you estimate the value of λ?

If you try to use the maximum likelihood method here, you meet an immediate problem – with a continuously distributed random variable, the probability of any particular sample value is zero! All is not lost, however. In the examples above, it was not, in fact, important that the likelihood was *equal* to the probability of the sample values obtained: you only needed a likelihood which was *proportional* to the probability of the sample values obtained. If you multiply or divide the likelihood function by any constant of proportionality independent of the parameter, there will always be a maximum at the same value of λ and so the same maximum likelihood estimator will be produced.

For a continuous random variable, the probability densities at two possible values of that variable are proportional to the relative probabilities of those values. Therefore, the relative probabilities of two samples are proportional to the probability densities of the samples, which, in turn, are equal to the products of the densities for each member of the sample, provided these are drawn independently.

This motivates the following definition.

> If a random variable X has a continuous distribution, described by the probability density function $f(x)$ and you draw an independent random sample of size n from this distribution, then the likelihood of the set of sample values $x_1, x_2, \ldots, x_n$ of X is $L = f(x_1) \times f(x_2) \times \ldots \times f(x_n)$.
>
> If the distribution of X has an unknown parameter, then L will be a function of this parameter.

In this example, therefore, L is dependent on λ, and equal to:

$$L(\lambda) = \lambda e^{-27\lambda} \times \lambda e^{-19\lambda} \times \lambda e^{-16\lambda} \times \lambda e^{-38\lambda} = \lambda^4 e^{-\lambda(27+19+16+38)} = \lambda^4 e^{-100\lambda}$$

The maximum value of $L(\lambda)$ occurs at the value of λ for which $\dfrac{dL}{d\lambda} = 0$:

$$\frac{dL}{d\lambda} = 4\lambda^3 e^{-100\lambda} - 100\lambda^4 e^{-100\lambda}$$
$$= \lambda^3 e^{-100\lambda}(4 - 100\lambda) = 0 \quad \Rightarrow \quad \lambda = 0.04 \text{ or } \lambda = 0$$

and

$$\frac{d^2L}{d\lambda^2} = (12\lambda^2 - 400\lambda^3)e^{-100\lambda} - 100(4\lambda^3 - 100\lambda^4)e^{-100\lambda}$$
$$= \lambda^2 e^{-100\lambda}(12 - 800\lambda + 10\,000\lambda^2)$$
$$= (0.04)^2 e^{-4}(12 - 32 + 16) = -0.0064 e^{-4} < 0 \text{ at } \lambda = 0.04$$

so the maximum likelihood estimator of λ is $\hat{\lambda} = 0.04$ (as $\lambda = 0$ gives $L = 0$ which must be a minimum of L as likelihoods are always positive).

EXAMPLE 3.4 X has a Normal distribution with known mean μ and unknown variance σ^2. A sample drawn from X gives the n values $\{x_1, x_2, \ldots, x_n\}$. Estimate the value of σ^2.

SOLUTION

The likelihood of the sample values is

$$L(\sigma^2) = f(x_1)f(x_2) \ldots f(x_n)$$

where $f(x)$ is the density function for the Normal distribution with mean μ and variance σ^2:

$$f(x) = \frac{1}{\sqrt{2\pi}\sigma} e^{-((x-\mu)^2/2\sigma^2)}$$

so that:

$$L(\sigma^2) = \frac{1}{\sqrt{2\pi}\sigma} e^{-((x_1-\mu)^2/2\sigma^2)} \times \frac{1}{\sqrt{2\pi}\sigma} e^{-((x_2-\mu)^2/2\sigma^2)} \times \ldots \times \frac{1}{\sqrt{2\pi}\sigma} e^{-((x_n-\mu)^2/2\sigma^2)}$$

$$= \left(\frac{1}{\sqrt{2\pi}\sigma}\right)^n e^{-((x_1-\mu)^2+(x_2-\mu)^2+\ldots+(x_n-\mu)^2/2\sigma^2)}$$

$$= \left(\frac{1}{\sqrt{2\pi}\sigma}\right)^n e^{-\sum_{i=1}^{n}(x_i-\mu)^2/2\sigma^2}$$

which gives:

$$\ln[L(\sigma^2)] = n\ln\left(\frac{1}{\sqrt{2\pi}}\right) - n\ln\sigma - \frac{\sum_{i=1}^{n}(x_i-\mu)^2}{2\sigma^2}.$$

Differentiating to find the maximum likelihood gives:

$$\frac{d}{d\sigma}\ln[L(\sigma^2)] = -\frac{n}{\sigma} + \frac{\sum_{i=1}^{n}(x_i-\mu)^2}{\sigma^3} = 0$$

$$\Rightarrow \qquad -n\hat{\sigma}^2 + \sum_{i=1}^{n}(x_i-\mu)^2 = 0$$

$$\Rightarrow \qquad \hat{\sigma}^2 = \frac{\sum_{i=1}^{n}(x_i-\mu)^2}{n}.$$

You could check that this is in fact the unbiased estimator of σ^2 in the case where μ is known.

EXERCISE 3A

1 The number of cars passing a point on a road travelling east has mean λ per minute. The number of cars passing the same point travelling west also has mean λ per minute. An observer counts a cars travelling east in a 5-minute period; b cars travelling west in a further 3-minute period; and c cars passing in either direction in a final 6-minute period.

(i) Find an expression in terms of a, b and c for the likelihood of these observations, and determine a maximum likelihood estimate of λ.

(ii) Explain why this estimate is intuitively reasonable.

2 Genetic theory predicts that a characteristic determined by a single gene will occur in the population in three genotypes, called dd, dr and rr, in the proportions

dd	p^2
dr	$2p(1-p)$
rr	$(1-p)^2$

where p is an unknown parameter.

In an experiment, the number of each of genotype found is

dd	a
dr	b
rr	c

where $n = a + b + c$ is the sample size.

Find the maximum likelihood estimator of p.

3 In a plant survey, the number of orchids found in each of 12 fifty-metre squares of downland is counted. It is thought that the numbers can be modelled by the distribution:

P(r orchids found in a square)
$$= \binom{r+2}{2}(1-p)^3 p^r$$

($r = 0, 1, 2, \ldots$)

Given the data

r	0	1	2	3	>3
Frequency	4	5	2	1	0

determine a maximum likelihood estimate for p.

4 Batches of apples are classified on the basis of a sample of size 4. If none of the sample is bruised, the batch is classified 'perfect', if one is bruised the batch is classified 'excellent' and if two or more are bruised then the batch is classified 'good'.

(i) Use a binomial model, with p being the probability that an apple is not bruised, to derive an expression for the likelihood of the observations:

a perfect batches
b excellent batches
c good batches

in $(a + b + c)$ batches.

(ii) Find a cubic equation satisfied by the maximum likelihood estimate of p, and show that if $a = 231$, $b = 156$, $c = 113$, then the maximum likelihood estimate of p is $\frac{4}{5}$.

5 Two types of motherboard which contain a series of integrated circuits are being made. When the boards are constructed, the probability that each integrated circuit is fitted correctly is p, and a board functions correctly only if all the integrated circuits are fitted correctly.

Boards of type 1 contain four integrated circuits and boards of type 2 contain eight integrated circuits.

(i) Find an expression for the likelihood of the observations:
a motherboards of type 1 out of *m* manufactured function correctly and *b* motherboards of type 2 out of *n* manufactured functions correctly and find an equation satisfied by the maximum likelihood estimate $\hat{p}$ of *p*.

(ii) Show that this equation reduces to a quadratic in $\hat{p}$, and from this find $\hat{p}$ if $a = 17$, $m = 28$, $b = 18$, $n = 20$.

6 The number of enquiries received by a travel firm about a particular destination is recorded in the weeks after a television series set in that area is begun. The number of enquiries in the week after the *n*th episode of the series is broadcast is thought to follow a Poisson distribution with mean either

(a) $120 + \mu n$ or (b) $120\lambda^n$

the distribution for the separate weeks being independent.

(i) If the numbers of enquiries in the weeks after the first, second and third episodes of the series are *a*, *b* and *c* respectively, find equations satisfied by the maximum likelihood estimates of:
μ, assuming model (a) is correct and
λ, assuming model (b) is correct.

(ii) Find each of these estimates if $a = 160$, $b = 210$ and $c = 270$.

7 The time for which a light bulb lasts is a random variable with density function

$$f(x) = \frac{1}{2\beta\sqrt{x}} e^{-(\sqrt{x}/\beta)}$$

for some unknown parameter β.

Light bulbs are tested by passing current through *n* bulbs, waiting for time τ and recording the number, *r*, of bulbs which have failed at this time, and the times $t_1, t_2, \ldots, t_r$ at which these failed.

Write down an expression for the likelihood of these results, and from this find an expression for the maximum likelihood estimator of β.

8 The diagram shows a cross-section of a radiating wire, W, an unknown distance, δ, from the flat plate of a scintillation counter. The emissions from wire W are distributed uniformly in angular direction, θ, and, when they strike the plate, the co-ordinate, X, of the point of reception is recorded by the counter.

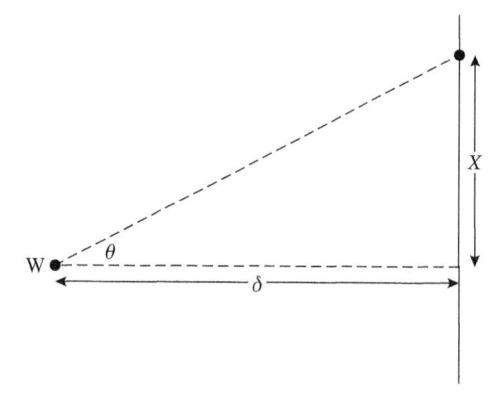

(i) Find the density function of X.

(ii) Find an equation obeyed by the maximum likelihood estimate of δ based on *n* independent observations of X.

(iii) Repeat parts (i) and (ii) when the scintillation counter plate extends only as far as $x = \pm H$, so that the distribution of θ is uniform on

$$\left[-\arctan\left(\frac{H}{\delta}\right), \arctan\left(\frac{H}{\delta}\right) \right] \text{ only.}$$

(iv) If, instead, δ is known, but W is misplaced at a distance, ξ, above the horizontal line $x = 0$, find an equation satisfied by the maximum likelihood estimate of ξ based on *n* independent observations of X.

9 The time, T, of failure of a component has density function:

$$f(t) = \begin{cases} \alpha e^{-\alpha(t-\beta)} & (t > \beta) \\ 0 & (\text{otherwise}) \end{cases}$$

so that failure does not occur until unknown time β.

Seven components fail at times 31, 34, 35, 37, 40, 46, 58.

(i) If α is known, find the maximum likelihood estimate of β.

(ii) Assuming that β has the value you determined in part (i), find the maximum likelihood estimate of α.

10 The distribution of a randomly determined ratio, which can take the values in [0, 1] only, is modelled by the density function

$$f(x) = \kappa(\kappa+1)x^{\kappa-1}(1-x) \quad (0 \leqslant x \leqslant 1)$$

where κ is unknown.

(i) Derive a quadratic equation for the maximum likelihood estimator based on the measured ratios $x_1, x_2, \ldots, x_n$ in a sample of size n.

(ii) Write down the solution to this equation in terms of $s = -\ln(g)$, where g is the geometric mean $(x_1 x_2 \ldots x_n)^{1/n}$ of the sample.

(iii) Find the value of this estimate when the measured ratios are:

0.19, 0.47, 0.68, 0.81, 0.87, 0.92, 0.94, 0.98.

INVESTIGATION

Given that an unknown number β of the n balls in a box are blue, and that in a sample of size s, taken without replacement, B of the balls are blue, investigate the process of finding a maximum likelihood estimate of β.

Hint: Consider the ratio $\dfrac{L(n+1)}{L(n)}$.

KEY POINTS

1 The *likelihood* of a set of observations of a discrete random variable is the probability of that set of observations arising, given the distribution of the random variable. If the distribution contains an unknown parameter, the likelihood will be a function of that parameter.

2 The likelihood of a set of observations $x_1, x_2, \ldots, x_n$ of a continuous random variable is the product of the values of its probability density function at each observation:

$$L = f(x_1) \times f(x_2) \times \ldots \times f(x_n)$$

3 Given a set of observations of a random variable, X, the *maximum likelihood estimation* strategy is to choose as an estimate for parameter τ of the distribution of X that value which makes the likelihood of the observations as great as possible.

Probability generating functions

Expect nothing. Live frugally on surprise.

Alice Walker

During the first season of the FA Premier League, 462 football matches were played. The frequency of the number of goals scored in each game by the *away* team, and associated relative frequencies, were recorded as follows.

Number of goals	0	1	2	3	4	5	> 5
Frequency	149	179	91	37	3	3	0
Relative frequency	0.322...	0.387...	0.196...	0.080...	0.006...	0.006...	0.000...

Assuming that these relative frequencies reflect the general pattern of scoring in FA Premier League matches, they may be used as *empirical* probabilities of 0, 1, 2, ... goals being scored by *away* teams per match.

Let X be the discrete random variable representing the number of goals scored per game by away teams, then one way of storing the probabilities is in the *probability generating function* (p.g.f.):

$$G(t) = 0.322\ldots + 0.387\ldots \times t + 0.196\ldots \times t^2 + 0.080\ldots \times t^3 \\ + 0.006\ldots \times t^4 + 0.006\ldots t^5$$

where the coefficients of t^x are the probabilities $P(X = x)$. The variable t is a *dummy* variable as, in itself, it has no significance. However, it has an important role to play in subsequent analysis, which you will appreciate later on.

Substituting $t = 1$, gives

$$G(1) = 0.322\ldots + 0.387\ldots + 0.196\ldots + 0.080\ldots + 0.006\ldots + 0.006\ldots = 1$$

as the sum of the probabilities has to be 1.

This can be set out in tabular form.

t^x	t^0	t^1	t^2	t^3	t^4	t^5
$P(X = x)$	0.322	0.387	0.197	0.080	0.007	0.007
$t^x P(X = x)$	0.322...	0.387... × t	0.196... × t^2	0.080... × t^3	0.006... × t^4	0.006... × t^5

Thus
$$G(t) = \sum_x t^x P(X=x) = E(t^x),$$

which gives the general definition for a probability generating function.

The way in which G(t) generates probabilities is best seen from a *theoretical* model. From the shape of the probability distribution for goals scored by away teams, it looks as though a Poisson distribution might produce a good fit.

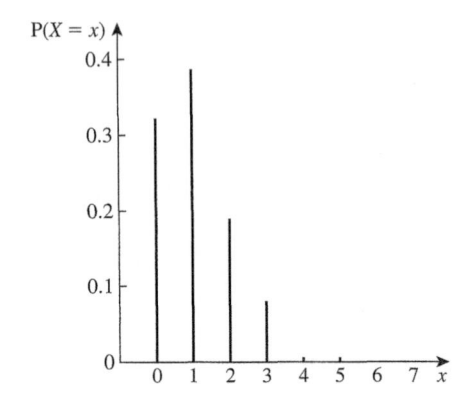

Figure 4.1

Using a suitable χ^2 test you can check that, at the 5% level of significance, a Poisson distribution with mean 1.08... (using the sample mean as an unbiased estimate of the population mean) produces a good fit. The *theoretical* probabilities for a Poisson distribution, with mean $= 1.08\ldots$, are given by

$$P(X=x) = e^{-1.08} \frac{1.08^x}{x!}.$$

Therefore the p.g.f. G(t), given by $E(t^x) = \sum_x t^x P(X=x)$ may be written in a convenient form:

$$G(x) = \sum_{x=0}^{\infty} e^{-1.08} \frac{1.08^x}{x!} t^x$$

$$= e^{-1.08}\left(1 + 1.08t + \frac{1.08^2}{2!}t^2 + \frac{1.08^3}{3!}t^3 + \cdots\right)$$

$$= e^{-1.08} e^{1.08t}$$

$$= e^{1.08(t-1)}$$

This result shows why the p.g.f. can be useful: using a list of probabilities as the coefficients of powers of t in a function does not at first seem like a good idea – and does not seem to do anything that listing the probabilities in a table could not do more easily. The reason that it can be worthwhile is that the function made up by using a list of probabilities as the coefficients of powers of t can sometimes be written in an alternative, simpler way. Here, by recognising an exponential series, the function, which started out as an infinite sum, can be written in a very neat way: this is the beautiful p.g.f. trick at work.

Note

The p.g.f. for a discrete random variable X, where $X \sim$ Poisson (λ), is given by $G(t) = e^{\lambda(t-1)}$. A formal proof is given on page 86.

Basic properties

The example above illustrates some basic properties of probability generating functions (p.g.f.) for any discrete random variable X.

Definition $\quad G(t) = E(t^x) = \sum_x t^x P(X = x)$

$\Rightarrow \quad G(1) = \sum_x 1^x P(X = x) = \sum_x P(X = x) = 1$

If X takes non-negative integral values only, then the probability generating function takes the form of a polynomial in t which is often written as

$$G(t) = \sum_x p_x t^x = p_0 + p_1 t + p_2 t^2 + \ldots + p_n t^n + \ldots$$

where p_x denotes $P(X = x)$, e.g. p_2 denotes $P(X = 2)$. The function $G(t)$ may be either a finite or infinite polynomial, i.e. it may terminate after n terms or continue indefinitely.

EXAMPLE 4.1

Uniform distribution

Let X be the discrete random variable that denotes the score when a fair die is thrown. Find the probability generating function (p.g.f.) for X.

SOLUTION

The probability distribution is given by:

x	1	2	3	4	5	6
$P(X = x)$	$\frac{1}{6}$	$\frac{1}{6}$	$\frac{1}{6}$	$\frac{1}{6}$	$\frac{1}{6}$	$\frac{1}{6}$

The p.g.f. for X is:

$$\begin{aligned} G(t) = E(t^x) &= \tfrac{1}{6}t + \tfrac{1}{6}t^2 + \tfrac{1}{6}t^3 + \tfrac{1}{6}t^4 + \tfrac{1}{6}t^5 + \tfrac{1}{6}t^6 \\ &= \tfrac{1}{6}t(1 + t + t^2 + t^3 + t^4 + t^5) \\ &= \tfrac{1}{6}t \times \frac{1 - t^6}{1 - t} \\ &= \frac{t(1 - t^6)}{6(1 - t)} \end{aligned}$$

The first of six terms of a G.P. with first term 1 and common ratio t.

EXAMPLE 4.2 Binomial distribution

Dan is a keen archer. He has taken part in many competitions. When aiming for the centre of the target, called the gold, he finds that he hits the gold 70% of the time. Find the p.g.f. for X, the number of gold hits in four consecutive shots at the target.

SOLUTION

As $X \sim B(4, 0.7)$, the probabilities are given by $P(X = x) = {}^4C_x 0.3^{4-x} 0.7^x$, which gives the following distribution.

x	0	1	2	3	4
$P(X = x)$	0.3^4	$4 \times 0.3^3 \times 0.7$	$6 \times 0.3^2 \times 0.7^2$	$4 \times 0.3 \times 0.7^3$	0.7^4

The p.g.f. for X is

$$G(t) = E(t^x) = \sum_{x=0}^{4} p_x t^x = \sum_{x=0}^{4} {}^4C_x \times 0.3^{4-x} \times 0.7^x t^x$$

$$= 0.3^4 + 4 + 0.3^3 \times 0.7t + 6 \times 0.3^2 \times 0.7^2 t^2$$
$$\quad + 4 \times 0.3 \times 0.7^3 t^3 + 0.7^4 t^4$$

$$= (0.3 + 0.0.7t)^4.$$

Note

When $X \sim B(n, p)$, i.e. $P(X = x) = {}^nC_x q^{n-x} p^x$, where $q = 1 - p$, the p.g.f. for X is given by $G(t) = (q + pt)^n$. A formal proof is given on page 85.

EXAMPLE 4.3 Geometric distribution

A card is selected at random from a normal pack of 52 playing cards. If it is a heart, the experiment ends, otherwise it is replaced, the pack is shuffled and another card is selected. Let X represent the number of cards selected up to and including the first heart. Find the p.g.f. for X.

SOLUTION

As X follows a geometric distribution, i.e. $X \sim \text{Geometric}\left(\frac{1}{4}\right)$, the probabilities are given by $P(X = x) = \left(\frac{3}{4}\right)^{x-1} \times \frac{1}{4}$, which gives the following distribution.

x	1	2	3	4	5	...
$P(X = x)$	$\frac{1}{4}$	$\frac{3}{4} \times \frac{1}{4}$	$\left(\frac{3}{4}\right)^2 \times \frac{1}{4}$	$\left(\frac{3}{4}\right)^3 \times \frac{1}{4}$	$\left(\frac{3}{4}\right)^4 \times \frac{1}{4}$	...

The p.g.f. for X is

$$G(t) = E(t^x) = \sum_{x=1}^{\infty} p_x t^x = \sum_{x=1}^{\infty} \left(\tfrac{3}{4}\right)^{x-1} \left(\tfrac{1}{4}\right) t^x$$

$$= \left(\tfrac{1}{4}\right)t + \left(\tfrac{3}{4}\right)\left(\tfrac{1}{4}\right)t^2 + \left(\tfrac{3}{4}\right)^2\left(\tfrac{1}{4}\right)t^3 + \left(\tfrac{3}{4}\right)^3\left(\tfrac{1}{4}\right)t^4 + \left(\tfrac{3}{4}\right)^4\left(\tfrac{1}{4}\right)t^5 + \ldots$$

$$= \left(\tfrac{1}{4}\right)t\left[1 + \left(\tfrac{3}{4}t\right) + \left(\tfrac{3}{4}t\right)^2 + \left(\tfrac{3}{4}t\right)^3 + \left(\tfrac{3}{4}t\right)^4 + \ldots\right]$$

$$= \left(\tfrac{1}{4}\right)t\left[\frac{1}{1 - \tfrac{3}{4}t}\right]$$

The sum to infinity of a G.P. with first term 1 and common ratio $\tfrac{3}{4}t$.

$$= \frac{t}{4 - 3t}.$$

Note

When $X \sim \text{Geometric}(p)$, i.e. $P(X = x) = q^{x-1}p$, where $q = 1 - p$, the p.g.f. for X is given by $G(t) = \dfrac{pt}{1 - qt}$. A formal proof is given on page 87.

EXERCISE 4A

1 Let X be the discrete random variable that denotes the sum of the scores when two fair dice are thrown. Construct a table for the probability distribution and so write down the p.g.f.

2 Let X be the discrete random variable that denotes the absolute difference of the scores when two fair dice are thrown ($x = 0, 1, 2, 3, 4, 5$). Construct a table for the probability distribution and so write down the p.g.f.

3 A fair coin is tossed three times and the number of tails appearing is noted as the discrete random variable X ($x = 0, 1, 2, 3$). Construct a table for the probability distribution and so write down the p.g.f.

4 A box contains three red balls and two green balls. They are taken out one at a time, *without* replacement. Let X represent the number of withdrawals until a red ball is chosen. Find its p.g.f.

5 The experiment in question 4 is repeated, but this time *with* replacement. Find the p.g.f. for the number of withdrawals until a red ball is chosen.

6 A random number generator in a computer game produces values which can be modelled by the discrete random variable X with probability distribution given by:
$P(X = r) = kr!$, $r = 1, 2, 3, 4, 5$.
Determine the value of k and so write down $G(t)$, the p.g.f. for X.

7 A mathematics student is shown three graphs. She is also given three equations, one for each graph. If she matches each graph with its equation at random, construct a table for the probability distribution of X, the number of correctly identified graphs. Deduce the p.g.f. for X.

8 Two students are to be chosen to represent a class containing nine boys and six girls. Assuming that the students are chosen at random, find the p.g.f. for X, the number of girls representing the group.

Expectation and variance

For any discrete probability distribution, the *expectation* (mean) and *variance* may be computed, using the shorthand $P(X = x) = p_x$:

$$\mu = E(X) = \sum_x x p_x$$

$$\sigma^2 = \text{Var}(X) = E(X - \mu)^2 = \sum_x (x - \mu)^2 p_x = \sum_x x^2 p_x - \mu^2$$

$$= E(X^2) - \mu^2.$$

By successively differentiating $G(t)$, the probability generating function for X, formulae for the expectation and variance can be derived elegantly. It is here that the power of the p.g.f. as an algebraic tool becomes apparent.

Expectation

This may be obtained from the probability generating function $G(t)$ by differentiating with respect to t and evaluating the expression at $t = 1$.

$$G(t) = E[t^X] = \sum_x p_x t^x$$

$$\Rightarrow \quad G'(t) = \sum_x x p_x t^{x-1} = E[X t^{X-1}]$$

$$\Rightarrow \quad G'(1) = \sum_x x p_x = E[X]$$

Therefore: $\mu = E(X) = G'(1)$.

Variance

This may be obtained by differentiating $G'(t)$ and evaluating the expression at $t = 1$.

$$G'(t) = \sum_x x p_x t^{x-1} = E[X t^{X-1}]$$

$$\Rightarrow \quad G''(t) = \sum_x x(x - 1) p_x t^{x-2} = E[X(X - 1) t^{X-2}]$$

$$\Rightarrow \quad G''(1) = \sum_x x(x - 1) p_x = E[X(X - 1)]$$

$$\Rightarrow \quad G''(1) = \sum_x x^2 p_x - \sum_x x p_x = E[X^2] - E[X]$$

$$\Rightarrow \quad E[X^2] = G''(1) + E[X] = G''(1) + G'(1)$$

Therefore:

$$\sigma^2 = G''(1) + G'(1) - (G'(1))^2 \quad \text{or} \quad \sigma^2 = G''(1) + \mu - \mu^2.$$

Summary

Whenever a p.g.f. is given for discrete random variable, the expectation (mean) and variance may be evaluated using the following definitions.

$$\mu = E(X) = G'(1) \quad \text{and} \quad \sigma^2 = \text{Var}(X) = G''(1) + G'(1) - (G'(1))^2$$

In the following examples, the first one shows how the polynomial form for a probability generating function $G(t)$ may be differentiated twice in order to derive the expectation and variance. You should notice that this just reproduces exactly the usual calculations for mean and variance, and there is no gain from the p.g.f. method. However, the two further examples demonstrate the remarkable power of the p.g.f. method when it is possible to write the function $G(t)$ in a simpler form.

EXAMPLE 4.4

Let X be the discrete random variable that denotes the absolute difference of scores when two fair dice are thrown. Using a p.g.f. confirm that $E(X)$ is just under 2 and determine $\text{Var}(X)$.

SOLUTION

The probability distribution of X was derived in Exercise 4A, question 2, as:

x	0	1	2	3	4	5
$P(X=x)$	$\frac{3}{18}$	$\frac{5}{18}$	$\frac{4}{18}$	$\frac{3}{18}$	$\frac{2}{18}$	$\frac{1}{18}$

The p.g.f. for X is as follows.

$$G(t) = \tfrac{3}{18} + \tfrac{5}{18}t + \tfrac{4}{18}t^2 + \tfrac{3}{18}t^3 + \tfrac{2}{18}t^4 + \tfrac{1}{18}t^5$$

$\Rightarrow \quad G'(t) = \tfrac{5}{18} + \tfrac{8}{18}t + \tfrac{9}{18}t^2 + \tfrac{8}{18}t^3 + \tfrac{5}{18}t^4$

$\Rightarrow \quad G''(t) = \tfrac{8}{18} + \tfrac{18}{18}t + \tfrac{24}{18}t^2 + \tfrac{20}{18}t^3$

Therefore: $\quad G'(1) = \tfrac{5}{18} + \tfrac{8}{18} + \tfrac{9}{18} + \tfrac{8}{18} + \tfrac{5}{18} = \tfrac{35}{18} = 1\tfrac{17}{18}$

and $\quad G''(1) = \tfrac{8}{18} + \tfrac{18}{18} + \tfrac{24}{18} + \tfrac{20}{18} = \tfrac{70}{18} = 3\tfrac{8}{9}$.

$\Rightarrow \quad E(X) = G'(1) = 1\tfrac{17}{18}$

and $\quad \text{Var}(X) = G''(1) + G'(1) - (G'(1))^2$
$\qquad = 3\tfrac{8}{9} + 1\tfrac{17}{18} - \left(1\tfrac{17}{18}\right)^2 = 2\tfrac{17}{324} \approx 2.05$

Confirm that these results may also be derived from first principles, i.e.:

$$\mu = E(X) = \sum_x xp_x \quad \text{and} \quad \sigma^2 = \text{Var}(X) = \sum_x x^2 p_x - \mu^2.$$

EXAMPLE 4.5 Four unbiased coins are tossed and the number of heads (X) is noted. Show that the p.g.f. for X is given by $G(t) = \frac{1}{16}(1+t)^4$. From this calculate the mean and variance of X.

SOLUTION

As $X \sim B(4, \frac{1}{2})$, the probabilities are given by

$$P(X = x) = {}^4C_x \left(\frac{1}{2}\right)^{4-x} \left(\frac{1}{2}\right)^x = {}^4C_x \left(\frac{1}{2}\right)^4 = {}^4C_x \frac{1}{16}.$$

The p.g.f. for X is

$$G(t) = E(t^x) = \sum_{x=0}^{4} p_x t^x = \frac{1}{16} \sum_{x=0}^{4} {}^4C_x t^x$$

$$= \frac{1}{16}(1 + 4t + 6t^2 + 4t^3 + t^4)$$

$$= \frac{1}{16}(1+t)^4$$

From the p.g.f. the mean and variance of X are found by differentiation.

$$G'(t) = 4 \times \frac{1}{16}(1+t)^3 = \frac{1}{4}(1+t)^3 \quad \Rightarrow \quad G'(1) = \frac{1}{4} \times 2^3 = 2$$

$$G''(t) = 3 \times \frac{1}{4}(1+t)^2 = \frac{3}{4}(1+t)^2 \quad \Rightarrow \quad G''(1) = \frac{3}{4} \times 2^2 = 3$$

$\Rightarrow \qquad E(X) = G'(1) = 2$

and $\qquad \text{Var}(X) = G''(1) + G'(1) - (G'(1))^2 = 3 + 2 - 2^2 = 1$

EXAMPLE 4.6 A box contains three red balls and two green balls. They are taken out one at a time, with replacement. Let X represent the number of withdrawals until a red ball is chosen. Calculate the mean and variance of X.

SOLUTION

In this experiment the outcomes follow a geometric distribution. $X \sim$ Geometric (p), where $p = \frac{3}{5}$ and $q = 1 - \frac{3}{5} = \frac{2}{5}$, and so the p.g.f. is:

$$G(t) = \frac{pt}{1-qt} = \frac{\frac{3}{5}t}{1-\frac{2}{5}t} = \frac{3t}{5-2t}.$$

Differentiating with respect to t, using the quotient rule:

$$G'(t) = \frac{(5-2t) \times 3 - 3t \times (-2)}{(5-2t)^2} = \frac{15}{(5-2t)^2} \Rightarrow G'(1) = \frac{15}{9} = 1\frac{2}{3}$$

Differentiating with respect to t, using the chain rule:

$$G''(t) = -2 \times 15 \times (5-2t)^{-3} \times (-2) = \frac{60}{(5-2t)^3} \Rightarrow G''(1) = \frac{60}{27} = 2\frac{2}{9}$$

$\Rightarrow \qquad E(X) = G'(1) = 1\frac{2}{3}$

and $\qquad \text{Var}(X) = G''(1) + G'(1) - (G'(1))^2 = 2\frac{2}{9} + 1\frac{2}{3} - \left(1\frac{2}{3}\right)^2 = 1\frac{1}{9}$

EXAMPLE 4.7

A discrete random variable X ($x = 0, 1, 2$) has p.g.f. given by
$G(t) = a + bt + ct^2$, where a, b and c are constants. If the mean is $1\frac{1}{4}$ and the variance is $\frac{11}{16}$, find the values of a, b and c.

SOLUTION

As $P(X = 0) = a$, $P(X = 1) = b$ and $P(X = 2) = c$:

$$G(t) = a + bt + ct^2 \quad \Rightarrow \quad G(1) = a + b + c = 1 \qquad \text{①}$$

As $\mu = 1\frac{1}{4}$ and $E(X) = G'(1)$:

$$G'(t) = b + 2ct \quad \Rightarrow \quad G'(1) = b + 2c = 1\frac{1}{4} \qquad \text{②}$$

As $\sigma^2 = G''(1) + G'(1) - (G'(1))^2$, so $G''(1) = \sigma^2 - G'(1) + (G'(1))^2 = 1$:

$$G''(t) = 2c \quad \Rightarrow \quad G''(1) = 2c = 1 \qquad \text{③}$$

From equation ③: $\quad 2c = 1 \quad \Rightarrow \quad c = \frac{1}{2}$
From equation ②: $\quad b + 2c = 1\frac{1}{4} \quad \Rightarrow \quad b = 1\frac{1}{4} - 2 \times \frac{1}{2} = \frac{1}{4}$
From equation ①: $\quad a + b + c = 1 \quad \Rightarrow \quad a = 1 - \frac{1}{4} - \frac{1}{2} = \frac{1}{4}$

Therefore: $a = \frac{1}{4}$, $b = \frac{1}{4}$, $c = \frac{1}{2}$.

EXERCISE 4B

1 A random variable has p.g.f. $G(t) = \frac{1}{6} + \frac{1}{3}t + \frac{1}{4}t^3 + \frac{1}{6}t^4 + \frac{1}{12}t^5$. Find its mean and variance.

2 A random variable X has p.g.f. $G(t) = \frac{1}{81}(1 + 2t)^4$. Calculate $E(X)$ and $Var(X)$.

3 Let X be the discrete random variable that denotes the score when a fair die is thrown. Use its p.g.f. to find $E(X)$ and $Var(X)$.

4 A fair coin is tossed three times and the number of tails appearing is noted as the discrete random variable $X(x = 0, 1, 2, 3)$. Use the p.g.f.
$$G(t) = \frac{1}{8}(1 + 3t + 3t^2 + t^3)$$
to calculate the mean and variance of X.

5 The probability generating function of a discrete random variable, X, is
$G(t) = (at + 1 - a)^n$, where a is a constant $(0 \leqslant a \leqslant 1)$ and n is a positive integer.
Prove that $E(X) = na$, and find the variance of X.
[Cambridge]

6 An ordinary pack of playing cards is cut four times. Let X represent the number of aces appearing. Find the probability generating function for X and so find the mean and variance of X.

7 The King and Queen of Muldovia want a son and heir to their kingdom. Let X represent the number of children they have until a boy is born.
   (i) Assuming that each pregnancy results in a single child, and that the probability of a boy is 0.5, show that the p.g.f. for X is given by
   $$G(t) = \frac{t}{2 - t}$$
   (ii) From this show that both $E(X)$ and $Var(X) = 2$.

8 A random variable has p.g.f.
   $G(t) = a + bt + ct^2$. It has mean $\frac{7}{6}$ and variance $\frac{29}{36}$. Find values for a, b and c.

9 Two fair dice are thrown and X represents the larger of the two scores. Find the p.g.f. for X and so find the mean and variance of X.

INVESTIGATION

In a competition, the entrant has to match a number of famous landmarks (A, B, C, etc.) with the country in which it is to be found (1, 2, 3, etc.).

Figure 4.2

Let X represent the number of correct matches which the entrant makes. For the purposes of this investigation, assume that the matching of the landmark to its country is chosen at random.

In each case take the correct matching as $A \leftrightarrow 1, B \leftrightarrow$, $C \leftrightarrow 3$, etc.

(i) For three famous landmarks the possible matchings and values of X are as follows.

A	1	1	2	2	3	3
B	2	3	1	3	1	2
C	3	2	3	1	2	1
X	3	1	1	0	0	1

Find the p.g.f. for X and show that $E(X) = \text{Var}(X) = 1$.

(ii) (a) For *four* famous landmarks explain why there are $4! = 24$ possible matchings, only one of which is a complete matching.

(b) Show that the p.g.f. for X is given by $G(t) = \frac{3}{8} + \frac{1}{3}t + \frac{1}{4}t^2 + \frac{1}{24}t^4$.

(c) Use the p.g.f. to show that $E(X) = \text{Var}(X) = 1$.

(iii) (a) For n ($n > 2$) famous landmarks there are $n!$ possible matchings. Explain why $P(X = n) = \dfrac{1}{n!}$ and $P(X = n - 1) = 0$.

(b) Prove that $P(X = n - 2) = \dfrac{1}{2 \times (n - 2)!}$ and

$$P(X = n - 3) = \dfrac{1}{3 \times (n - 3)!}$$

(c) Verify these results for $n = 3$ and $n = 4$.

(iv) For *five* famous landmarks, use the results from part (iii) and the assumption that $E(X) = 1$ to derive the p.g.f. for X.

(v) For *six* famous landmarks, use the results from part (iii) and the assumptions that $E(X) = 1$ and $Var(X) = 1$ to derive the p.g.f. for X.

(vi) (a) Compare the p.g.f.s in parts (i), (ii), (iv) and (v). How are they related to each other?

(b) How can you use the p.g.f. for n possible matches to derive the p.g.f. for $n - 1$ possible matches and for $n + 1$ possible matches?

The sum of independent random variables

At the beginning of the chapter you saw that, with a mean of 1.08 goals per match, the random variable X, the number of goals scored by the *away* team in each game was distributed approximately Poisson (1.08). Let the probability generating function for X be denoted by $G_X(t)$, then $G_X(t) = e^{1.08(t-1)}$.

Let Y represent the number of goals scored by the *home* team, then, from the data collected for the same season for *home* teams:

Number of goals	Frequency	Relative frequency
0	100	0.216...
1	157	0.339...
2	110	0.238...
3	53	0.114...
4	28	0.060...
5	10	0.021...
6	3	0.006...
7	1	0.002...

the sample mean is 1.56.... Again a Poisson distribution is a good fit to model the number of *home* goals; i.e. $Y \sim$ Poisson (1.56...) with p.g.f. $G_Y(t) = e^{1.56(t-1)}$.

What do the models predict for the distribution of the total number of goals scored by both sides in a match? For instance, what do they predict for $P(X + Y = 3)$?

$$P(X + Y = 3) = P(X = 0 \text{ and } Y = 3) + P(X = 1 \text{ and } Y = 2)$$
$$+ P(X = 2 \text{ and } Y = 1) + (X = 3 \text{ and } Y = 0).$$

The probabilities $P(X = a \text{ and } Y = b)$ are not simply related to the separate probabilities of away and home goals, $P(X = a)$ and $P(Y = b)$ unless you assume that the random variables X and Y are independent. You might not expect this to be the case (if one side plays a lot better and scores a lot of goals, then their opponents do not) but, surprisingly, the figures suggest that it is true to a reasonable approximation.

If X and Y are independent, $P(X = a \text{ and } Y = b) = P(X = a) \times P(Y = b)$, so

$$P(X + Y = 3) = P(X = 0) \times P(Y = 3) + P(X = 1) \times P(Y = 2)$$
$$+ P(X = 2) \times P(Y = 1) + P(X = 3) \times P(Y = 0).$$

This figure can be found very neatly from the p.g.f.s for X and Y, because

$$G_X(t) \times G_Y(t) = (P(X = 0) + P(X = 1)t + P(X = 2)t^2 +$$
$$P(X = 3)t^3 + \ldots) \times (P(Y = 0) + P(Y = 1)t$$
$$+ P(Y = 2)t^2 + P(Y = 3)t^3 + \ldots).$$

Picking out from this product the terms in t^3, you get

$$P(X = 0) \times P(Y = 3)t^3 + P(X = 1)t \times P(Y = 2)t^2 + P(X = 2)t^2 \times$$
$$P(Y = 1)t + P(X = 3)t^3 \times P(Y = 0)$$
$$= P(X + Y = 3) \times t^3$$

The same relationship holds for other values of $X + Y$, and so for other powers of t in the product $G_X(t) \times G_Y(t)$. This means that

$$G_X(t) \times G_Y(t) = P(X + Y = 0) + P(X + Y = 1)t +$$
$$P(X + Y = 2)t^2 + P(X + Y = 3)t^3 + \ldots,$$

but the right-hand side of this equation is just the p.g.f. for the random variable $X + Y$, so that

$$G_X(t) \times G_Y(t) = G_{X+Y}(t)$$

and so

$$G_{X+Y}(t) = e^{1.08\ldots(t-1)} \times e^{1.56\ldots(t-1)} = e^{2.64(t-1)}.$$

This p.g.f. is just that for a Poisson random variable with mean $2.64\ldots$, which is the sum of the means for the two independent random variables which you are adding. This result, that the sum of two independent Poisson variables with means λ and μ is a Poisson variable with mean $\lambda + \mu$, should be familiar to you from your earlier work on the Poisson distribution.

The result derived for these variables in fact holds, by exactly the same argument, for any pair of independent random variables X and Y. A formal proof is given here.

The coefficient of t^r in $(a_0 + a_1 t + a_2 t^2 + \ldots + a_r t^r + \ldots)(b_0 + b_1 t + b_2 t^2 + \ldots + b_r t^r + \ldots)$ is $a_0 b_r + a_1 b_{r-1} + \ldots + a_s b_{r-s} + \ldots a_r b_0$. If the two power series represent $G_X(t)$ and $G_Y(t)$ respectively, then $a_s = P(X = s)$ and $b_s = P(Y = s)$ for each s, so that the coefficient of t^r in $G_X(t) \times G_Y(t)$ can be written as

$$\sum_{s=0}^{r} a_s b_{r-s} = \sum_{s=0}^{r} P(X = s) \times P(Y = r - s)$$

$$= \sum_{s=0}^{r} P(X = s \text{ and } Y = r - s)$$

$$= P(X + Y = r). \quad \text{(Since X and Y are independent)}$$

Therefore

$$G_X(t) \times G_Y(t) = \sum_{r=0}^{\infty} P(X + Y = r) t^r = G_{X+Y}(t).$$

A neater argument is as follows

$$G_{X+Y}(t) \equiv E[t^{X+Y}] = E[t^X t^Y] = E[t^X] \times E[t^Y]$$

$$= G_X(t) \times G_Y(t) \quad \text{(Since X and Y are independent)}$$

However, this relies on the result that if X and Y are independent, then

$$E[f(X) \times g(Y)] = E[f(X)] \times E[g(Y)]$$

for any functions f and g, which is not proved in this course.

If X and Y are two *independent* discrete random variables with p.g.f.s $G_X(t)$ and $G_Y(t)$ then the probability generating function for $X + Y$ is given by

$$G_{X+Y}(t) = G_X(t) \times G_Y(t)$$

i.e. the p.g.f. of the sum $\equiv$ the product of the p.g.f.s.

This is known as the *convolution theorem*.

EXAMPLE 4.8

A discrete random variable X ($x = 0, 1, 2$) has p.g.f. $G_X(t) = \frac{1}{4} + \frac{1}{4}t + \frac{1}{2}t^2$ and another discrete random variable Y ($y = 0, 1$) has p.g.f. $G_Y(t) = \frac{2}{3} + \frac{1}{3}t$. Assume that X and Y are independent.

(i) Find the p.g.f. for $X + Y$, i.e. $G_{X+Y}(t)$
(ii) Show that $E(X + Y) = E(X) + E(Y)$ and $Var(X + Y) = Var(X) + Var(Y)$.

SOLUTION

(i) $G_{X+Y}(t) = G_X(t) \times G_Y(t) = \left(\frac{1}{4} + \frac{1}{4}t + \frac{1}{2}t^2\right)\left(\frac{2}{3} + \frac{1}{3}t\right)$

$= \frac{1}{4} \times \frac{2}{3} + \left(\frac{1}{4} \times \frac{1}{3} + \frac{1}{4} \times \frac{2}{3}\right)t + \left(\frac{1}{4} \times \frac{1}{3} + \frac{1}{2} \times \frac{2}{3}\right)t^2 + \left(\frac{1}{2} \times \frac{1}{3}\right)t^3$

$= \frac{1}{6} + \frac{1}{4}t + \frac{5}{12}t^2 + \frac{1}{6}t^3$

(ii) By differentiation

$$G'_X(t) = \tfrac{1}{4} + t, \; G'_Y(t) = \tfrac{1}{3} \text{ and } G'_{X+Y}(t) = \tfrac{1}{4} + \tfrac{5}{6}t + \tfrac{1}{2}t^2$$

$\Rightarrow \quad E(X) = G'_X(1) = \tfrac{1}{4} + 1 = 1\tfrac{1}{4}$ and $E(Y) = G'_Y(1) = \tfrac{1}{3}$

$$E(X+Y) = G'_{X+Y}(1) = \tfrac{1}{4} + \tfrac{5}{6} + \tfrac{1}{2} = 1\tfrac{7}{12}$$

$\Rightarrow \quad E(X) + E(Y) = 1\tfrac{1}{4} + \tfrac{1}{3} = 1\tfrac{7}{12} = E(X+Y)$

By further differentiation:

$$G''_X(t) = 1, \; G''_Y(t) = 0 \text{ and } G''_{X+Y}(t) = \tfrac{5}{6} + t$$

$\Rightarrow \quad \text{Var}(X) = G''_X(1) + G'_X(1) - (G'_X(1))^2 = 1 + 1\tfrac{1}{4} - \left(1\tfrac{1}{4}\right)^2 = \tfrac{11}{16}$

$\text{Var}(Y) = G''_Y(1) + G'_Y(1) - (G'_Y(1))^2 = 0 + \tfrac{1}{3} - \left(\tfrac{1}{3}\right)^2 = \tfrac{2}{9}$

$\text{Var}(X+Y) = G''_{X+Y}(1) + G'_{X+Y}(1) - (G'_{X+Y}(1))^2$

$= 1\tfrac{5}{6} + 1\tfrac{7}{12} - \left(1\tfrac{7}{12}\right)^2 = \tfrac{131}{144}$

$\Rightarrow \quad \text{Var}(X) = \text{Var}(Y) = \tfrac{11}{16} + \tfrac{2}{9} = \tfrac{131}{144} = \text{Var}(X+Y)$

The p.g.f. of a linear transformation

A special case of the *convolution theorem* provides a useful relationship between probability generating functions for discrete random variables X and Y, where $Y = aX + b$. Let the respective p.g.f.s be $G_X(t)$ and $G_Y(t)$, then

$$G_Y(t) = E[t^Y] = E[t^{aX+b}] = E[t^{aX} t^b] = E[t^{aX}] \times E[t^b]$$

but as b is a constant $E[t^b] = t^b$, and $E[t^{aX}] = E[(t^a)^X]$

$$G_Y(t) = t^b G_X(t^a).$$

From this definition you can deduce the result for the expectation of $G_Y(t)$. Differentiating with respect to t, using the product rule:

$$G'_Y(t) = t^b a t^{a-1} G'_X(t^a) + bt^{b-1} G_X(t^a)$$

$\Rightarrow \quad G'_Y(1) = 1^b a 1^{a-1} G'_X(1^a) + b 1^{b-1} G_X(1^a) \quad \longleftarrow \; G_X(1) = 1$

$\Rightarrow \quad G'_Y(1) = a G'_X(1) + b$

i.e. $\quad E[Y] = a E[X] + b$

By further differentiation it is possible to deduce the equivalent result for the variance of $G_Y(t)$, viz. $\text{Var}[Y] = a^2 \text{Var}[X]$. There are formal proofs, using p.g.f.s, of results which you have met when studying discrete random variables.

EXAMPLE 4.9

In a multiple choice test of 25 questions, each question has five choices of answer, only one of which is correct. The random variable X represents the number of correct answers. Find a variable Y which represents a candidate's score and is a linear transformation of X with the properties that a candidate who gets all the questions correct should have a score of 100 and a candidate who just guesses each answer should have an expected score of 0. Deduce the p.g.f. of Y for a candidate who guesses.

SOLUTION

For a candidate who just guesses, X has a Binomial distribution $B(25, 0.2)$ with expected value 5, so the transformation required is $Y = 5X - 25$. The p.g.f. of X is $(0.8 + 0.2t)^{25}$, so the p.g.f. required is

$$G_Y(t) = t^{-25}(0.8 + 0.2t^5)^{25}$$

$$= \left(\frac{0.8}{t} + 0.2t^4\right)^{25}$$

Notice that this p.g.f. extends the ideas you have met so far because, when it is expanded as a series, there are terms with negative powers of t, corresponding to the fact that it is possible to get a negative score in this test. In fact

$$G_Y(t) = 0.8^{25} t^{-25} + \binom{25}{1} \times 0.8^{24} \times 0.2 \times t^{-20} +$$

$$\binom{25}{2} \times 0.8^{23} \times 0.2^2 \times t^{-15} + \ldots$$

$$\ldots + \binom{25}{5} \times 0.8^{20} \times 0.2^5 \times t^0$$

$$+ \binom{25}{6} \times 0.8^{19} \times 0.2^6 \times t^5 + \ldots + 0.2^{25} \times t^{100}.$$

Generating functions of this type are perfectly legitimate, and useful, but you have to take care with them: for instance, in the examples you met earlier $G_X(0) = P(X = 0)$, but here $G_Y(0)$ is not even defined.

However, $G_Y(1) = 1$, as before,

$$E[Y] = G'_Y(1) \quad \text{and} \quad \text{Var}[Y] = G''_Y(1) + G'_Y(1) - (G'_Y(1))^2.$$

? Consider this problem in the case where there are 20 questions in the test, so that the linear transformation required is $Y = \frac{25}{4}X - 25$. This leads to fractional powers of t in the p.g.f. Check that the derivations for $E(Y)$ and $\text{Var}[Y]$ are still valid.

Extension to three or more random variables

The result, that the p.g.f. of the sum of two independent random variables is the product of the p.g.f.s, can be extended to three or more variables. For example, if X, Y and Z are three independent discrete random variables with p.g.f.s $G_X(t)$, $G_Y(t)$ and $G_Z(t)$ then the probability generating function for $X + Y + Z$ is given by

$$G_{X+Y+Z}(t) = G_X(t) \times G_Y(t) \times G_Z(t).$$

If n independent discrete random variables all have the same p.g.f., $G(t)$, then the probability generating function for their sum is

$$[G(t)]^n.$$

EXAMPLE 4.10   Find the probability generating function for the total number of 6s when five fair dice are thrown. Deduce the mean and variance.

SOLUTION

When *one* die is thrown, a 6 occurs with probability $\frac{1}{6}$, therefore the p.g.f. for the number of sixes is $G(t) = \frac{5}{6} + \frac{1}{6}t$. Therefore, when *five* dice are thrown, the p.g.f. for X, the total number of 6s, is given by

$$G_X(t) = [G(t)]^5 = \left(\tfrac{5}{6} + \tfrac{1}{6}t\right)^5.$$

Applying the results derived earlier.

$$G'_X(t) = 5 \times \left(\tfrac{5}{6} + \tfrac{1}{6}t\right)^4 \times \tfrac{1}{6} = \tfrac{5}{6}\left(\tfrac{5}{6} + \tfrac{1}{6}t\right)^4$$

$$G''_X(t) = 4 \times \tfrac{5}{6}\left(\tfrac{5}{6} + \tfrac{1}{6}t\right)^3 \times \tfrac{1}{6} = \tfrac{5}{9}\left(\tfrac{5}{6} + \tfrac{1}{6}t\right)^3$$

$$\Rightarrow \qquad E(X) = G'(1) = \tfrac{5}{6}\left(\tfrac{5}{6} + \tfrac{1}{6}\right)^4 = \tfrac{5}{6} \qquad \text{(as } \tfrac{5}{6} + \tfrac{1}{6} = 1\text{)}$$

and

$$\operatorname{Var}(X) = G''(1) + G'(1) - (G'(1))^2$$

$$= \tfrac{5}{9}\left(\tfrac{5}{6} + \tfrac{1}{6}\right)^3 + \tfrac{5}{6} - \left(\tfrac{5}{6}\right)^2 = \tfrac{5}{9} + \tfrac{5}{6} - \tfrac{25}{36} = \tfrac{25}{36}$$

Note

As $X \sim B(5, \tfrac{1}{6})$, the results that $E(X) = 5 \times \tfrac{1}{6}$ and $\operatorname{Var}(X) = 5 \times \tfrac{1}{6} \times \tfrac{5}{6}$ have been verified.

The proof for the mean and variance of $X \sim B(n, p)$ is given on page 85.

EXAMPLE 4.11 Gina likes having a go at the coconut shy whenever she goes to the fair. From experience, she knows that the probability of her knocking over a coconut at any throw is $\frac{1}{3}$.

(i) Find the p.g.f. $G(t)$ of the number of throws until she hits her first coconut.

(ii) Show that the p.g.f. of the number of throws until she hits her second coconut is $[G(t)]^2$.

(iii) Explain why the p.g.f. of the number of throws until she hits her kth coconut is $[G(t)]^k$.

SOLUTION

(i) Let X represent the number of throws up to and including Gina's *first* hit, then the random variable X forms a geometric distribution with

$$P(X = r) = \left(\tfrac{2}{3}\right)^{r-1} \tfrac{1}{3}.$$

The p.g.f. for X is

$$G_X(t) = \left(\tfrac{1}{3}\right)t + \left(\tfrac{2}{3}\right)\left(\tfrac{1}{3}\right)t^2 + \left(\tfrac{2}{3}\right)^2\left(\tfrac{1}{3}\right)t^3 + \left(\tfrac{2}{3}\right)^3\left(\tfrac{1}{3}\right)t^4 + \left(\tfrac{2}{3}\right)^4\left(\tfrac{1}{3}\right)t^5 + \cdots$$

$$= \left(\tfrac{1}{3}\right)t\left[1 + \left(\tfrac{2}{3}t\right) + \left(\tfrac{2}{3}t\right)^2 + \left(\tfrac{2}{3}t\right)^3 + \left(\tfrac{2}{3}t\right)^4 + \cdots\right]$$

$$= \left(\tfrac{1}{3}\right)t\left[\frac{1}{1 - \tfrac{2}{3}t}\right]$$

$$= \frac{t}{3 - 2t}.$$

(ii) Let Y represent the number of throws up to and including Gina's *second* hit. This is called a *negative binomial distribution*, given by the formula

$$P(Y = r) = {}^{r-1}C_1 \left(\tfrac{2}{3}\right)^{r-2}\left(\tfrac{1}{3}\right)^2 = (r-1)\left(\tfrac{2}{3}\right)^{r-2}\left(\tfrac{1}{3}\right)^2.$$

The p.g.f. for Y is

$$G_Y(t) = \left(\tfrac{1}{3}\right)^2 t^2 + 2\left(\tfrac{2}{3}\right)\left(\tfrac{1}{3}\right)^2 t^3 + 3\left(\tfrac{2}{3}\right)^2\left(\tfrac{1}{3}\right)^2 t^4 + 4\left(\tfrac{2}{3}\right)^3\left(\tfrac{1}{3}\right)^2 t^5 + \cdots$$

$$= \left(\tfrac{1}{3}t\right)^2\left[1 + 2\left(\tfrac{2}{3}t\right) + 3\left(\tfrac{2}{3}t\right)^2 + 4\left(\tfrac{2}{3}t\right)^3 + \cdots\right]$$

$$= \left(\tfrac{1}{3}t\right)^2\left[\frac{1}{(1 - \tfrac{2}{3}t)^2}\right]$$

$$= \left[\frac{t}{3 - 2t}\right]^2 = [G_X(t)]^2.$$

(iii) The number of throws required until the kth success is equivalent to the sum of k geometric distributions, so the p.g.f. for this sum is the product of the p.g.f.s, i.e. $[G(t)]^k$.

EXERCISE 4C

1 (i) A fair die is thrown repeatedly until a 6 occurs. Show that the p.g.f. for the number of throws required is given by
$$G(t) = \frac{t}{6-5t}$$
(ii) Obtain the p.g.f. for the number of throws required to obtain two 6s (not necessarily consecutively).

(iii) Calculate the expected value and variance of the number of throws required to obtain two 6s.

2 The probability distributions of two independent random variables. X and Y, are as follows.

x	1	2
$P(X = x)$	0.6	0.4

y	1	2	3
$P(Y = y)$	0.2	0.5	0.3

(i) Write down the p.g.f.s for X and Y. Hence show that the p.g.f. for $X + Y$ is given by $G(t) = t^2(0.12 + 0.38t + 0.38t^2 + 0.12t^3)$.

(ii) Show that $E(X + Y) = E(X) + E(Y)$ and $Var(X + Y) = Var(X) + Var(Y)$.

3 The discrete random variable X has p.g.f. $G_X(t)$.

(i) Given that $Y = X + c$, where c is a constant, prove that its p.g.f. $G_Y(t)$ is given by $G_Y(t) = t^c G_X(t)$.

(ii) Show that $E(X + c) = E(X) + c$ and $Var(X + c) = Var(X)$.

4 In a traffic census on a two-way stretch of road, the number of vehicles per minute, X, travelling past a checkpoint in one direction is modelled by a Poisson distribution with parameter 3.4, and the number of vehicles per minute, Y, travelling in the other direction is modelled by a Poisson distribution with parameter 4.6, i.e. $X \sim$ Poisson (3.4) and $Y \sim$ Poisson (4.8).

(i) Find the p.g.f.s for both X and Y.

(ii) Show that $E(X) = Var(X) = 3.4$.

(iii) Find the p.g.f. for $X + Y$, the total number of vehicles passing the checkpoint per minute, assuming X and Y are independent.

(iv) Demonstrate in two ways that $E(X + Y) = Var(X + Y) = 8.2$

5 In a machine game of chance, when a lever is pulled one of the numbers 1, 2, 3 appears in a window. The lever is pulled five times and the total score is recorded. The probabilities associated with the numbers 1, 2, 3 are $\frac{1}{6}, \frac{1}{3}, \frac{1}{2}$, respectively.

(i) Write down the p.g.f. for the numbers appearing in the window and so deduce the p.g.f. for the possible total scores.

(ii) Calculate the expected value and variance of the total score.

6 A game consists of rolling two dice, one six-sided and the other four-sided, and adding the scores together. Both dice are fair, the first is numbered 1 to 6 and the second is numbered 1 to 4.

Show that the p.g.f. of Z, where Z is the sum of the scores on the two dice, is
$$G(t) = \frac{t^2}{24} \times \frac{(1-t^6)(1-t^4)}{(1-t)^2}$$

The p.g.f.s for some standard discrete probability distributions

There are several standard discrete probability distributions which are useful for modelling statistical data. Three of these, the binomial, the Poisson and the geometric distributions, you have met and used before. In this final section you will see how the p.g.f. is derived for each of these discrete distributions and how it is used to provide neat proofs for the expectation, $E(X)$, and variance, $\text{Var}(X)$.

The binomial distribution

Let Y be the discrete random variable with probability distribution:

y	0	1
$P(Y = y)$	q	p

The p.g.f. for Y is therefore $G(t) = q + pt$ and $G(1) = q + p = 1$.

Now let the discrete random variable X be defined by $X = Y_1 + Y_2 + \cdots + Y_n$, where each Y_i has p.g.f. $G(t) = q + pt$, then X has p.g.f. $G_X(t)$, given by

$$G_x(t) = [G(t)]^n = (q + pt)^n.$$

If '1' represents 'success' and '0' represents 'failure', then X represents the number of 'successes' in n independent trials, for which the probability of 'success' is p and the probability of failure is q.

Therefore $X \sim B(n, p)$ with p.g.f. $G_X(t) = (q + pt)^n$.

Having established the p.g.f., the mean and variance may be proved.

Differentiating with respect to t:

$$G'_X(t) = n(q + pt)^{n-1} \times p = np(q + pt)^{n-1}$$

$\Rightarrow \quad G'_X(1) = np(q + p)^{n-1} = np$

and $\quad G''_X(t) = (n-1)np(q + pt)^{n-2} \times p = n(n-1)p^2(q + pt)^{n-2}$

$\Rightarrow \quad G''_X(1) = n(n-1)p^2(q + p)^{n-2} = n(n-1)p^2$

Therefore:

$$E(X) = G'_X(1) = np$$

$$\text{Var}(X) = G''_X(1) + G'_X(1) - (G'_X(1))^2 = n(n-1)p^2 + np - (np)^2$$

$$= n^2 p^2 - np^2 + np - n^2 p^2$$

$$= np(1 - p) = npq$$

i.e. $\quad E(X) = np \quad \text{and} \quad \text{Var}(X) = npq$

The Poisson distribution

Let X be a Poisson random variable with parameter λ, i.e. $X \sim$ Poisson (λ), then the p.g.f. for X is

$$G_X(t) = e^{-\lambda} + e^{-\lambda} \times \lambda t + e^{-\lambda} \times \frac{\lambda^2}{2!}t^2 + \cdots + e^{-\lambda} \times \frac{\lambda^r}{r!}t^r + \cdots$$

$$= e^{-\lambda}\left(1 + \lambda t + \frac{(\lambda t)^2}{2!} + \cdots + \frac{(\lambda t)^r}{r!} + \cdots\right) = e^{-\lambda} \times e^{\lambda t} = e^{\lambda(t-1)}.$$

Having established the p.g.f., the mean and variance may be proved.

Differentiating with respect to t:

$$G'_X(t) = \lambda e^{\lambda(t-1)} \quad \Rightarrow \quad G'_X(1) = \lambda e^0 = \lambda$$

$$G''_X(t) = \lambda^2 e^{\lambda(t-1)} \quad \Rightarrow \quad G''_X(1) = \lambda^2 e^0 = \lambda^2$$

Therefore:

$$E(X) = G'_X(1) = \lambda$$

$$\text{Var}(X) = G''_X(1) + G'_X(1) - (G'_X(1))^2 = \lambda^2 + \lambda - (\lambda)^2 = \lambda$$

i.e. $\quad E(X) = \text{Var}(X) = \lambda$

The Poisson approximation to the binomial

You know that if $X \sim$ Binomial (n, p), where n is large and p is small (e.g. $n = 150$, $p = 0.02$), then a good approximation to the distribution of X is $X \sim$ Poisson (λ), where $\lambda = np$. The p.g.f.s can be used to show that the Poisson distribution is the limit of the binomial distribution as $n \to \infty$, $p \to 0$ and np remains fixed.

For the binomial distribution $G(t) = (q + pt)^n$, where $q = 1 - p$

$$\Rightarrow \quad G(t) = (1 - p + pt)^n = (1 + p(t-1))^n.$$

But $\lambda = np \Rightarrow p = \dfrac{\lambda}{n}$, where λ is fixed

$$\Rightarrow \quad G(t) = \left(1 + \frac{\lambda(t-1)}{n}\right)^n.$$

Using the result that $e^x = \lim\left(1 + \dfrac{x}{n}\right)^n$ as $n \to \infty$, the limit of $G(t)$ $n \to \infty$ is given by

$$G(t) = \lim\left(1 + \frac{\lambda(t-1)}{n}\right)^n \text{ as } n \to \infty = e^{\lambda(t-1)}.$$

The geometric distribution

If a sequence of independent trials is conducted, for each of which the probability of success is p and that of failure q (where $q = 1 - p$), and the random variable X is the number of the trial on which the first success occurs, then X has a geometric distribution with $P(X = r) = pq^{r-1}$, $r \geq 1$.

The corresponding p.g.f. is given by

$$G(t) = pt + pqt^2 + pq^2t^3 + \ldots + pq^{r-1}t^r + \ldots$$
$$= pt[1 + qt + (qt)^2 + \ldots + (qt)^{r-1} + \ldots]$$
$$= pt\left(\frac{1}{1-qt}\right) = \frac{pt}{1-qt}.$$

Differentiating with respect to t, using the quotient rule:

$$G'(t) = \frac{(1-qt) \times p - pt \times (-q)}{(1-qt)^2} = \frac{p}{(1-qt)^2} \quad \Rightarrow \quad G'(1) = \frac{p}{(1-q)^2} = \frac{1}{p}.$$

Differentiating with respect to t, using the chain rule:

$$G''(t) = -2p(1-qt)^{-3} \times (-q) = \frac{2pq}{(1-qt)^3} \quad \Rightarrow \quad G''(1) = \frac{2pq}{(1-q)^3} = \frac{2q}{p^2}$$

$$\Rightarrow \quad E(X) = G'(1) = \frac{1}{p}$$

$$Var(X) = G''(1) + G'(1) - (G'(1))^2$$
$$= \frac{2q}{p^2} + \frac{1}{p} - \left(\frac{1}{p}\right)^2 = \frac{2q+p-1}{p^2} = \frac{q}{p^2}$$

i.e. $\quad E(X) = \dfrac{1}{p} \quad$ and $\quad Var(X) = \dfrac{q}{p^2}$

EXERCISE 4D

1 (i) The random variable X can take values 1, 2, 3, ... and its p.g.f. is $G(t)$. Show that the probability that X is even is given by $\frac{1}{2}[1 + G(-1)]$.

(ii) For each of the following probability distributions, state the p.g.f. and, from this, find the probability that the outcome is even.

(a) The total score when two ordinary dice are thrown

(b) The number of attempts it takes Kerry to pass her driving test, given that the probability of passing at any attempt is $\frac{2}{3}$

2 Two people, A and B, fire alternatively at a target, the winner of the game being the first to hit the target. The probability that A hits the target with any particular shots is $\frac{1}{3}$ and the probability that B hits the target with any particular shot is $\frac{1}{4}$.

Given that A fires first, find
(i) the probability that B wins the game with his first shot
(ii) the probability that A wins the game with his second shot
(iii) the probability that A wins the game.
(iv) If R is the total number of shots fired by A and B, show that the probability generating function of R is given by
$$G(t) = \frac{2t + t^2}{3(2 - t^2)}.$$
Find $E(R)$.

[Cambridge]

3 (i) The variable X has a Poisson distribution with mean λ. Write down the value of $P(X = r)$ and the p.g.f. for X in the form $G_X(t) = \ldots$.

(ii) The variable Y can take only the values 1, 2, 3, ... and is such that $P(Y = r) = kP(X = r)$, where k is a constant and $r > 0$. Find the value of k.

(iii) Show that the p.g.f. of Y is given by
$$G_Y(t) = \frac{e^{\lambda t} - 1}{e^{\lambda} - 1}.$$

(iv) Calculate $E(Y)$ and show that $Var(Y) = \mu(\lambda + 1 - \mu)$, where $\mu = E(Y)$.

[Cambridge]

4 Two duellists take alternate shots at each other until one of them scores a 'hit' on the other. If the probability that the first duellist scores a 'hit' is $\frac{1}{5}$ and the probability that the second scores a 'hit' is $\frac{1}{3}$, find the expected number of shots *before* a hit.

5 Independent trials, on each of which the probability of a 'success' is p $(0 < p < 1)$, are being carried out. The random variable, X, counts the number of trials up to and including that on which the first 'success' is obtained.

(i) Write down an expression for $P(X = x)$ for $x = 1, 2, \ldots$ and show that the probability generating function of X is

$$G(t) = \frac{pt}{1 - qt}$$

where $q = 1 - p$.

(ii) Use $G(t)$ to find the mean and variance of X.

(iii) The random variable Y counts the number of trials up to and including that on which the kth 'success' is obtained. Write down, in terms of p, q and t, an expression for the probability generating function of Y.

[MEI]

6 The independent random variables X and Y have Poisson distributions with parameters θ_1 and θ_2 respectively.

(i) Write down an expression for $P(X = x)$ and an expression for $P(Y = y)$ and, from this, derive an expression for $P(X + Y = z)$, where x, y, z are non-negative integers. Simplify the expression for $P(X + Y = z)$ as far as possible.

(ii) Obtain the probability generating function (p.g.f.) of the random variable X; deduce the p.g.f. of Y and hence obtain the p.g.f of $X + Y$.

(iii) Use this p.g.f. to find
(a) $P(X + Y = z)$, where z is a non-negative integer
(b) the mean of $X + Y$
(c) the variance of $X + Y$.

[MEI]

7 The variable R has probability generating function given by $G(t) = ke^{t^2+t}$, where k is a constant. Find k and obtain

(i) $P(R = 0)$, $P(R = 1)$, $P(R = 2)$, $P(R = 3)$ and $P(R = 4)$
(ii) the mean of R
(iii) the variance of R
(iv) the smallest value r_0 of R for which $P(R > r_0) < 0.4$.

[Cambridge]

8 In a simple model for forecasting the weather at a seaside resort, each day's weather is classified as either dull or fine. The probability that the weather on any one day will be the same as that on the preceding day has a constant value, p, independently of the weather on earlier days. The probability that the first day of the holiday season will be find is θ.

Let P_n denote the probability that the nth day of the holiday season will be fine, so that $P_1 = \theta$.

(i) Show that, for $n \geq 2$,
$$P_n = (2p-1)P_{n-1} + (1-p) \quad (\ast)$$

(ii) Let $H(t)$ denote the generating function for the probabilities P_n, i.e.
$$H(t) = \sum_{n=1}^{\infty} P_n t^n, \text{ for an appropriate range}$$
of values of t. By multiplying each side of $(\ast)$ by t^n and summing from $n=2$ to $n=\infty$, show that
$$H(t) - \theta t = (2p-1)tH(t) + (1-p)\frac{t^2}{1-t}$$
and therefore that $H(t) = \theta t + t^2(1-p-\theta)[1-t]^{-1}[1-(2p-1)t]^{-1}$.

(iii) From this, or otherwise, obtain an expression for P_n

[MEI]

9 Every packet of a well-known brand of cornflakes contains a plastic spaceman, drawn at random from a set of N different spacemen. I am trying to collect a complete set. Suppose that, at the stage when I have managed to collect $j-1$ different spacemen, the variable X_j ($j = 1, 2, \ldots, N$) denotes the number of additional packets I have to buy until I get may jth new spaceman.

(i) Show that the probability that $X_j = k$ (for $k = 1, 2, 3, \ldots$) may be expressed in the form $q_j^{k-1} p_j$, for some suitable p_j, q_j which should be specified.

(ii) Find the generator for these probabilities and use it to find $E(X_j)$.

(iii) Also show that the variance
$$\text{Var}(X_j) = \frac{N(j-1)}{(N-j+1)^2}$$

(iv) Let X be the total number of packets I have to buy, starting from scratch, in order to collect the full set of spacemen. use the relation $X = X_1 + X_2 + \cdots + X_N$ to show that
$$E(X) = N\left(1 + \frac{1}{2} + \frac{1}{3} + \cdots + \frac{1}{N}\right)$$
and find an expression of a similar kind for $\text{Var}(X)$.

[SMP]

10 Three balls, **a**, **b**, **c** are placed at random in three boxes **A**, **B**, **C** (with one ball in each box). The random variable X is defined by $X = 1$ if ball **a** is in box **A**, $X = 0$ otherwise.

(i) Find the probability generator for X.

The variable Y is defined in the table.

	Box			Value
	A	**B**	**C**	of **Y**
Contents	a	b	c	0
	c	a	b	0
	b	c	a	0
	a	c	b	1
	b	a	c	1
	c	b	a	1

(ii) Deduce the probability generator of Y.

(iii) The variable S is defined by $S = X + Y + 1$. Given that X, Y are independent, show that S has generator $\frac{1}{6}(t^3 + 3t^2 + 2t)$ and deduce the mean and variance of S.

[SMP]

KEY POINTS

1. For a discrete probability distribution, the *probability generating function* (*p.g.f.*) is defined by
$$G(t) = E(t^X) = \sum_{x} t^x p_x,$$
where $p_x = P(X = x)$.

2. The sum of probabilities $= 1 \Rightarrow G(1) = 1$.

3. *Expectation:* $E(X) = G'(1) = \mu$

4. *Variance:* $Var(X) = G''(1) + G'(1) - (G'(1))^2 = G''(1) + \mu - \mu^2$

5. Special probability generating functions

Probability distribution	$P(X = r)$	p.g.f. $G_X(t)$	Expectation $E(X)$	Variance $Var(X)$
Binomial	$^nC_r q^{n-r} p^r$	$(q + pt)^n$	np	npq
Poisson	$e^{-\lambda}\dfrac{\lambda^r}{r!}$	$e^{\lambda(t-1)}$	λ	λ
Geometric	$q^{r-1}p$	$\dfrac{pt}{1-qt}$	$\dfrac{1}{p}$	$\dfrac{q}{p^2}$

6. For two *independent* random variables X and Y
$$G_{X+Y}(t) = G_X(t) \times G_Y(t).$$

5 Moment generating functions

The human mind has first to construct forms, independently, before we can find them in things.

Albert Einstein

In Chapter 4, on probability generating functions, you saw how useful the concept of auxiliary functions of this kind can be. One illustration of their usefulness is in obtaining means and variances; for example, it is very much easier to obtain the mean and variance of a binomial distribution using its probability generating function than by using standard algebraic summation techniques.

However, this is only a small part of the value of probability generating functions. Their real worth is in giving an alternative approach to specifying *all* our knowledge about discrete random variables. In most of the examples and questions in Chapter 4, you worked 'forwards' in the sense that you were given a probability distribution and asked to find its probability generating function. However, this process can also be carried out 'backwards' – if you are given a probability generating function, you can, so to speak, 'undo it' and obtain the complete set of probabilities for the underlying random variable. In other words, *all the information about a discrete random variable* is contained in its probability generating function. In the work you have done so far, it has rarely, if ever, been necessary for you to use probability generating functions in this way; it has been more natural, and usually easier, to work with the individual probabilities or the probability function. In more advanced work, however, this is very often not so – it can be much easier to use the probability generating function to obtain results. Indeed, the ease with which the mean and variance of the binomial (or Poisson) distribution can be obtained is, perhaps, a first step in this direction.

There is, however, an obvious drawback in this use of probability generating functions. They only make sense for discrete random variables. This is, of course, because continuous random variables do not have individual probabilities to generate. So all the advantages of the generating functions approach would be restricted to discrete random variables if probability generating functions were the only functions that could be used in this sort of work. Fortunately, however, this is not the case. There is another generating function, called the *moment generating function*, which can sensibly be applied for both discrete and continuous random variables. As its name suggests, it generates quantities called *moments*. It is now necessary to break off the thread of the development of this work in order to introduce the concept of moments.

Moments

Moments are merely expected values of particular functions of a random variable. In a sense, they generalise the very familiar ideas of mean and variance. (If you are studying advanced mechanics, you will also be able to see analogies with the concepts of centre of mass (in *Mechanics 2* and *3*) and moment of inertia (in *Mechanics 4*).)

Given any random variable, X, the mean is simply the expected value of X itself. Using the customary notation of the Greek letter μ, the definition of the mean is

$$\mu = E[X] = \sum_x x \times P(X = x) \quad \text{for a discrete random variable, } X,$$

where the summation is over all the values that x can take

or

$$\mu = E[X] = \int x f(x) \, dx \quad \text{for a continuous random variable, } X, \text{ where f}(x) \text{ is the p.d.f.}$$

Similarly, the variance σ^2 is defined as $E[(X - \mu)^2]$. This expected value has a similar definition as a sum for a discrete random variable or an integral for a continuous one. In most expressions of this type from now on, only the integral giving the continuous definition will be displayed; you will need to understand that for discrete random variables an analogous expression involving a summation is required. Thus the variance is given by

$$\sigma^2 = \int (x - \mu)^2 f(x) \, dx.$$

Notice that both the mean and the variance are defined as the expected value of a *power* of a deviation of X from a specified *point*. The point is zero in the case of the mean, and the mean μ itself in the case of the variance. The power is 1 in the case of the mean and 2 in the case of the variance. This idea can be generalised by considering the expected value of any power of the deviation of X from any point as follows.

$$E[(X - a)^r]$$

This quantity is called the *rth moment of the distribution of X about the point a* (the words 'the distribution of' and 'the point' are sometimes omitted). Usually the power, r, is limited to positive integers. The point, a, in the definition can be any point but is usually taken to be either zero (giving what are called 'moments about zero' or 'moments about the origin') or the mean μ (giving what are called 'moments about the mean', or sometimes 'central moments' on the (somewhat misleading!) basis that the mean can be considered as the 'centre' of the distribution).

Note

Sometimes it is also convenient to include the case $r = 0$, giving what is sometimes called the 'zeroth moment' or the 'moment of zero order'. This is *always* equal to 1, no matter what the point, a, in the definition is. This is because any quantity raised to power zero is 1; thus $E[(X - a)^0] = E[1] = 1$.

If you consider the mean and the variance in terms of this generalised definition, you can see that the mean is the first moment about zero and the variance is the second moment about the mean. Thus moments about zero can be thought of, in a sense, as a sort of generalisation of the idea of the mean; and, similarly, moments about the mean are a sort of generalisation of the idea of variance.

A special notation is often used for moments about zero and about the mean. The rth moment about zero is denoted by μ'_r (read this as '$\mu\, r$ dash') and the rth moment about the mean as μ_r (without the dash; read it as '$\mu\, r$'). So, in this general moments notation, the mean would be written as μ'_1 and the variance as μ_2.

You already know, of course, that the mean and variance give important summaries of a distribution – its 'location' and 'spread', respectively. Some higher moments also have helpful geometrical interpretations concerning the shape of the distribution.

Thus the third moment gives a measure of *skewness*. For a distribution that is symmetrical, $\mu_3 = 0$. Unfortunately this is not true in reverse – asymmetrical distributions can be constructed which have $\mu_3 = 0$ (a very simple case is shown in Exercise 5A, question 1). Usually, however, distributions that are skewed to the left have $\mu_3 > 0$ and are therefore called 'positively skew', while distributions that are skewed to the right have $\mu_3 < 0$ and are called 'negatively skew'. (Simple examples of this are also shown in Exercise 5A.) You may have worked out skewness measures for data. What is being done here is to find the corresponding measures for the whole distribution.

Proceeding onwards, the fourth moment gives a measure of how flat-topped or otherwise the 'peak' that typically occurs in the centre of a distribution is. This is sometimes referred to as a measure of the *kurtosis* of a distribution, 'kurtosis' being a Greek word that means 'flatness'. Further geometrical interpretations can be found for yet higher moments, although they quickly become rather obscure.

You can obtain moments for any distribution by working out the sum or integral that gives the expected value. Sometimes this is easy and sometimes, of course it can be very difficult! Sometimes it turns out that the moments arre given by a fairly simple formula, an example of which follows.

EXAMPLE 5.1

Exponential distribution

Find a formula for the rth moment about the origin for the exponential distribution and from this find the mean and variance of this distribution.

SOLUTION

The exponential distribution (sometimes called the negative exponential distribution) with parameter λ (where $\lambda > 0$) has probability density function

$$f(x) = \lambda e^{-\lambda x} \quad \text{for } x \geq 0.$$

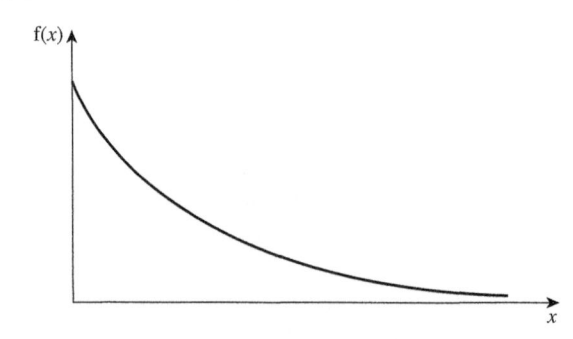

Figure 5.1

This distribution provides a useful model for many situations such as waiting times in queues. The rth moment about the origin is

$$\mu'_r = E[X^r] = \int_0^\infty x^r \times \lambda e^{-\lambda x}\, dx$$

$$= \lambda \int_0^\infty x^r e^{-\lambda x}\, dx.$$

Repeated integration by parts gives

$$\mu'_r = \frac{r!}{\lambda^r}.$$

This is valid for any positive integer r (and also for the trivial case $r = 0$).

You can now quickly write down the mean and variance using this general formula. The mean is simply μ'_1 which is $\frac{1}{\lambda}$. To obtain the variance, use the familiar expression $\mathrm{Var}(X) = E[X^2] - \{E[X]\}^2$ which, in general moments notation, becomes

$$\mathrm{Var}(X) = \mu'_2 - \{\mu'_1\}^2$$

$$= \frac{2!}{\lambda^2} - \left(\frac{1}{\lambda}\right)^2 = \frac{1}{\lambda^2}$$

You have seen in this section that moments give a sort of generalisation of the ideas of mean and variance and can have useful geometrical interpretations. This, however, is not the real point of introducing and studying the general idea of moments. Their real power is that they give *an alternative way of specifying all the information about a distribution.* In the example above, about the negative exponential distribution, and in Exercise 5A, you start with a distribution whose probabilities or probability density function are known, from which you can find some moments. However, this process can also be done *in reverse*. If you know all the moments of a distribution, you can 'undo' them and discover the probabilities or probability density function for the distribution. It will not be obvious to you how to do this (and sometimes it is very difficult!) but the point is that it *can* be done. It also may not be obvious to you *why* you should want to do this! Certainly there has been no need to do it in any of the work you have studied so far. In more advanced statistical theory, however, it is actually very often useful and more convenient to work with moments of distribution rather than directly with the underlying probabilities; the fact that this *can be done* makes moments very important in statistics.

You will remember that in the introduction to this chapter much the same thing was said about probability generating functions. As you move on to study moment generating functions, you will see the ideas come together – the moment generating function will give you another way of specifying all the information about a distribution, and it will do this in a way that is often very convenient to use in advanced work.

You should note, however, that there is a problem when working with moments. Sometimes, in obtaining a moment by working out a sum or integral, the answer comes to ∞ or to $-\infty$, or, even worse, does not converge to a sensible answer (even to $\pm\infty$) at all. In such cases, all that can be said is that the moment concerned does not exist. Fortunately, this does not happen with most of the everyday distributions that are useful models and which are met in usual statistical practice. Nevertheless, it can happen, and this introduces considerable complications in the full advanced theory connected with moments. These complications are a long way beyond the scope of this book and you need not be concerned about them, but you should know that they exist.

EXERCISE 5A

1 The discrete random variable, X, takes values -2, 1 or 3 with the following probabilities.

$$P(X = -2) = \tfrac{2}{5}$$
$$P(X = 1) = \tfrac{1}{2}$$
$$P(X = 3) = \tfrac{1}{10}$$

Find the value of μ_3 for this distribution.

Hint: Notice that the mean of the distribution is 0, so μ_3 is simple $E[X^3]$.

Note: You should find $\mu_3 = 0$ – yet this is clearly an *asymmetrical* distribution.

2 Prove the following results.
  (i) $\mu_2 = \mu_2' - \{\mu_1'\}^2$
  (ii) $\mu_3 = \mu_3' - 3\mu_1'\mu_2' + 2\{\mu_1'\}^3$

Note: Notice that the first of these results expresses the familiar formula $\text{Var}(X) = E[X^2] - \{E[X]\}^2$ in general moments notation, and shows how the second moment about the mean can be worked out form moments about the origin. Similarly, the second result expresses the third moment about the mean in terms of moments about the origin. Similar results can be found for fourth and higher moments. These results are often useful when trying to work out moments about the mean.

3 The continuous random variable, X, has the following probability density function.

$$f(x) = \begin{cases} 3x^2 & 0 < x < 1 \\ 0 & \text{elsewhere} \end{cases}$$

  (i) Sketch the graph of $f(x)$ and notice that it is skewed to the right.
  (ii) Using the results of question 2, or otherwise, find μ_3.

4 Repeat question 3 for the random variable with probability density function:

$$f(x) = \begin{cases} 3(1-x)^2 & 0 < x < 1 \\ 0 & \text{elsewhere} \end{cases}$$

noticing that this graph is skewed to the left.

INVESTIGATION

Investigate the third moment about the mean, μ_3, for some continuous distributions. Work out the value of μ_3 for some symmetrical distributions, confirming that it is always zero. (You will probably find the second result in Exercise 5A, question 2 helpful. The simplest case to work with is the uniform (rectangular) distribution, but you should try some others as well.) Now work out the value of μ_3 for some assymmetrical distributions (you could start with the exponential distribution – remember that a general formula for its moments about the origin was found in Example 5.1); you will nearly always find it to be non-zero (as happened in Exercise 5A, questions 3 and 4).

Now try to create some continuous distributions that are symmetrical and yet have $\mu_3 = 0$. You will probably find it best to make sure the mean is zero, and then try probability density functions which are a different shape for negative x than for positive x. Distributions that you create in this way are likely to be somewhat artificial and not particularly useful models, but you should begin to get a good appeciation of shape.

Moment generating functions

The moment generating function for a discrete or a continuous random variable, X, is defined in the following way. (You will see a little later on how this function generates the moments.) First, recall again that for the probability generating function, the definition is given by $E[t^X]$. For the moment generating function, often abbreviated to m.g.f. and often denoted by $M_X(\theta)$, the definition is

$$M_X(\theta) = E[e^{\theta X}] = \sum_x e^{\theta x} \times P(X = x)$$ for a discrete random variable, X, where the summation is over all the values, x, that it can take

or $$M_X(\theta) = E[e^{\theta X}] = \int e^{\theta x} f(x)\, dx$$ for a continuous random variable, X, where $f(x)$ is the p.d.f.

The θ in this definition is a 'dummy variable', just like the t in the definition of the probability generating function. You can, of course, use any letter you like for this; t, θ and z are commonly used.

You will next see several worked examples of obtaining moment generating functions using this definition. In the first few examples, you will see cases where the m.g.f. is easy to obtain; but gradually it will become more difficult and you will see examples where it cannot be obtained at all because the sum or integral in the definition does not come out to a sensible finite answer. This is, in fact, another aspect of the problem referred to at the end of the section on moments, that moments sometimes do not exist. In the same way, moment generating functions sometimes do not exist. As with moments themselves, this (fortunately!) does not happen for distributions that commonly turn up in statistical work. However it can happen and this complicates the general theory of generating functions. Nevertheless, moment generating functions are *extremely* useful in statistics.

Note

Just to give you a look ahead to yet more advanced work, well beyond the scope of this book, there is another auxillary function, called the *characteristic function*, which is similar to the moment generating function but which is defined using a *complex* variable instead of the real variable θ. By going to this higher level of mathematical sophistication, it turns out that you get a function which *always* exists and so can be used in a completely general way in statistical theory.

After you have looked at the examples, you will learn about the general properties of moment generating functions, including how they can be used to generate the moments. You will also see some of the many other uses of moment generating functions.

One of the uses that you will see is in proving results about sums of random variables. To help you to follow the thread of the development of m.g.f. work, one very important result about sums will gradually be built up for you as you come to various stages of the work. This is the result that says, roughly speaking, 'Normal distributions add up'. Strictly speaking, the result is that if

$$X_1 \sim N(\mu_1, \sigma_1^2), \qquad X_2 \sim N(\mu_2, \sigma_2^2), \qquad \ldots, \qquad X_n \sim N(\mu_n, \sigma_n^2)$$

and all these random variables are independent, then:

$$X_1 + X_2 + \ldots + X_n \sim N(\mu_1 + \mu_2 + \ldots + \mu_n, \sigma_1^2 + \sigma_2^2 + \ldots + \sigma_n^2).$$

You will already have used this result a large number of times and are probably quite familiar with proving that the mean and variance of the sum are as stated. However, you will not have proved that the distribution of the sum is Normal. You will see how to do this using moment generating functions. It would be very much more difficult to do it otherwise!

Questions 1 and 2 in Exercise 5B at the end of this chapter ask you to prove similar results for the binomial and Poisson distributions.

EXAMPLE 5.2

Binomial distribution

Find the m.g.f. for the $B(n, p)$ distribution.

SOLUTION

Here the probability is

$$P(X = x) = \binom{n}{x} p^x q^{n-x}$$

> You may have learnt this using r rather than x as is used here.

for $x = 0, 1, 2, \ldots, n$
so the m.g.f. is

$$M_X(\theta) = E[e^{\theta X}] = \sum_{x=0}^{n} e^{\theta x} \binom{n}{x} p^x q^{n-x}$$

> Notice $e^{\theta x} p^x = (pe^\theta)^x$.

$$= \sum_{x=0}^{n} \binom{n}{x} (pe^\theta)^x q^{n-x}.$$

You ought to recognise this as a binomial expansion but, in case you don't, you can write out a few terms of it as follows (this shows the terms for $x = 0, 1, 2$ and n).

$$q^n + \binom{n}{1}(pe^\theta)q^{n-1} + \binom{n}{2}(pe^\theta)^2 q^{n-2} + \ldots + (pe^\theta)^n$$

You can now see this to be the binomial expansion of

$$(q + pe^\theta)^n$$

and so this is the moment generating function for $B(n, p)$.

Before proceeding to the next example, recall the probability generating function for B(n, p). Using θ as the dummy variable, this is $(q + p\theta)^n$. You should now notice that the moment generating function is *exactly the same functional form* as the probability generating function except that e^θ has replaced θ. You will see this happen again in the next example.

Another point you should notice is that there is no problem at all here of the m.g.f. not existing. It is a simple finite sum of finite terms and is therefore bound to come out to a finite answer.

EXAMPLE 5.3

Poisson distribution

Find the m.g.f. for the Poisson (m) distribution.

SOLUTION

In this example, the letter m is used as the Poisson parameter to avoid any possible confusion with the θ that is the dummy variable of the m.g.f. The probability function is

$$P(X = x) = \frac{e^{-m} m^x}{x!} \quad \text{for } x = 0, 1, 2, \ldots$$

so the m.g.f.

$$M_X(\theta) = E[e^{\theta X}] = \sum_{x=0}^{\infty} e^{\theta x} \frac{e^{-m} m^x}{x!}$$

$$= e^{-m} \sum_{x=0}^{\infty} \frac{(me^\theta)^x}{x!}.$$

As in the previous example, you ought to recognise the form of the summation here, but, again, if you don't recognise it, write out a few terms to see what is happening.

$$M_X(\theta) = e^{-m} \left\{ 1 + me^\theta + \frac{(me^\theta)^2}{2!} + \frac{(me^\theta)^3}{3!} + \cdots \right\}$$

$$= e^{-m} e^{me^\theta}$$

This, then, is the moment generating function for Poisson (m).

As with the B(n, p) example, recall now the probability generating function for Poisson (m). Using θ as the dummy variable, this is $e^{-m} e^{m\theta}$. Notice again that the moment generating function is *exactly the same functional form* as the probability generating functions except that e^θ has replaced θ.

Another point to notice is that there is no problem of the m.g.f. not existing. Although in this case it is an infinite sum, it comes out to a finite answer.

EXAMPLE 5.4

Standard Normal distribution

Find the m.g.f. for the N(0, 1) distribution.

SOLUTION

The probability density function is

$$f(x) = \frac{1}{\sqrt{2\pi}} e^{-\frac{x^2}{2}}$$

and the m.g.f. is

$$M_X(\theta) = E[e^{\theta X}] = \frac{1}{\sqrt{2\pi}} \int_{-\infty}^{\infty} e^{\theta x - \frac{x^2}{2}} dx.$$

This integral can be found by completing the square in the exponent

$$\theta x - \frac{x^2}{2} = \frac{\theta^2}{2} - \frac{1}{2}(x - \theta)^2$$

and so

$$M_X(\theta) = \frac{1}{\sqrt{2\pi}} e^{\frac{\theta^2}{2}} \int_{-\infty}^{\infty} e^{-\frac{(x-\theta)^2}{2}} dx$$

This integral may appear daunting but, in fact, it is trivial once you spot the fact that you don't really need to work it out at all! For, taking the $\frac{1}{\sqrt{2\pi}}$ with the integrand, you will see that you have created the probability density function of N(θ, 1) which *simply* integrates to 1. So the moment generating function of N(0, 1) is

$$M_X(\theta) = e^{\frac{\theta^2}{2}}.$$

This is a result you should try to remember.

It is also the first intermediate result that you will need in proving the result about 'Normal distribution adding up'. Recall that it is the m.g.f. for N(0, 1). You will see later how to obtain the m.g.f. for the general Normal distribution N(μ, σ^2) from this m.g.f.

As N(0, 1) is a continuous random variable, there is no probability generating function here with which to compare the moment generating function but the m.g.f is clearly well-defined. You had to evaluate an integral, both of whose limits were infinite – but it came out to a simple finite answer.

EXAMPLE 5.5

Exponential distribution

Find the m.g.f. for the exponential distribution.

SOLUTION

The probability density function is

$$f(x) = \lambda e^{-\lambda x} \quad \text{for } x \geqslant 0, \text{ where } \lambda \text{ is a parameter } (\lambda > 0)$$

and the m.g.f. is

$$M_X(\theta) = E[e^{\theta X}] = \int_0^\infty e^{\theta x} \times \lambda e^{-\lambda x}\, dx$$

$$= \lambda \int_0^\infty e^{-(\lambda - \theta)x}\, dx$$

$$= \lambda \left[\frac{e^{-(\lambda - \theta)x}}{-(\lambda - \theta)} \right]_{x=0}^{x=\infty}$$

$$= [0] - \left[\lambda \frac{1}{\theta - \lambda} \right]$$

$$= \frac{\lambda}{\lambda - \theta} = \left(1 - \frac{\theta}{\lambda}\right)^{-1}$$

You might have noticed some problems in working out this integral. Remember that θ is simply a real variable which, at first sight, may take any value. On the other hand, λ is a (positive) parameter whose value is fixed for any particular exponential distribution. You should be able to see immediately that you cannot allow θ to equal λ, for this would give rise to division by zero.

Rather more subtly, you also cannot allow θ to be greater than λ. This is because, in evaluating the upper limit of the integral, you have to take $x = \infty$ in the expression $e^{-(\lambda - \theta)x}$. If $\lambda - \theta$ is itself negative, you will get $e^{+\infty}$ which is, of course, infinite; so you cannot allow θ to be greater than λ. Provided $\lambda - \theta$ is positive, there is no difficulty – you simply get $e^{-\infty}$ which is zero, as is shown in the derivation above.

This means that the exponential distribution is a case where the moment generating function can only sensibly be defined for a *limited range* of values of the dummy real variable θ – you have to limit it to $\theta < \lambda$. Recalling that λ is a positive parameter, you can see that this means that θ is restricted to only some positive values, although it can be allowed to take any negative value. This is in contrast with the binomial, Poisson and Normal distributions in Examples 5.2, 5.3 and 5.4, where θ can take any value at all.

In the next two examples, you will meet cases where the required restrictions on θ get progressively worse.

You need not worry if you do not understand the technical details in the next two examples. They are included merely to show cases of 'things going wrong'. If you want to, you could ignore these next examples and pick up the thread of the work again on page 103.

EXAMPLE 5.6

Investigate the m.g.f. of the discrete random variable, X, which takes values 1, 2, 3, ... and for which the probability function is

$$P(X = x) = \frac{6}{\pi^2 x^2} \quad \text{for } x = 1, 2, 3, \ldots.$$

SOLUTION

Although it is artificial, you can show that it is a well-defined random variable – all the probabilities are positive and less than one, and the sum of them all comes to one. However, the moment generating function would be

$$E[e^{\theta X}] = \sum_{x=1}^{\infty} \frac{6 e^{\theta x}}{\pi^2 x^2}.$$

You should be able to see that if θ is positive then, as x increases, the terms in the numerator are going to get larger more quickly (*much* more quickly!) than the terms in the denominator, so that the sum cannot possibly converge to any finite answer. On the other hand, if θ is negative then the terms in the numerator are all negative powers of e, which become smaller and smaller (i.e. tend to zero) as x increases, so the sum will converge to a finite answer. There remains the special case $\theta = 0$. This is trivial for, in this case, the numerator is simply 6 (because $e^0 = 1$), so the sum is simply the same as the sum of the individual probabilities and is therefore equal to one.

This example provides a case where the moment generating function could not be defined for any positive values of θ, although it would be all right for all negative values (and for zero).

The next example is even worse – you will see that the moment generating function in it cannot be defined for any non-zero values of θ.

EXAMPLE 5.7

Cauchy distribution

The continuous random variable, X, is said to have a Cauchy distribution if its probability density function is

$$f(x) = \frac{1}{\pi(1 + x^2)}$$

for all values of x (i.e. for $-\infty < x < \infty$). Investigate its m.g.f.

SOLUTION

It is trivial to show that this is a well-defined random variable – the density function is positive everywhere and the integral of it over the full range of x is 1. You might wish to spend a few minutes sketching the graph of the density function – notice that it is very similar to the Normal distribution in it s general shape, but slightly 'flatter in the middle' and 'thicker in the tails'.

However, the moment generating function would be

$$E[e^{\theta x}] = \int_{-\infty}^{\infty} \frac{e^{\theta x}}{\pi(1+x^2)} \, dx.$$

Without going to details, you should be able to see that this integral must give an infinite answer, at the upper limit if θ is positive or at the lower limit if θ is negative. The only value of θ for which the integral gives a finite answer is $\theta = 0$, for in this case it reduces trivially to the integral of the density function itself, which, of course, is one.

It is usual to regard the moment generating function as existing only if the sum or integral defining it converges to a finite answer for, *at least*, all values of θ in some finite interval *around* the origin – that is, *at least* for *some positive AND* for *some negative* values of θ. Thus the binomial, Poisson and Normal distributions immediately qualify, for with these the answer is finite for all positive and all negative values of θ. The exponential distribution also qualifies, for the answer is finite for some positive and all negative values of θ. The artificial distribution in Example 5.6 does not qualify, for these are *no* positive values of θ that give a finite answer. Nor does the Cauchy distribution do so, for there are no non-zero values of θ at all that give a finite answer.

As was stated before the examples, this problem of non-existence does limit the theoretical usefulness of moment generating functions but, nevertheless, they are very useful because for the routine 'everyday' distributions the problem of non-existence does not arise.

You saw that, even in the 'awkward' examples, the moment generating function came out to a simple finite answer (1) in the special case $\theta = 0$. This is, in fact, trivial to prove in general. By definition, the moment generating function is $E[e^{\theta X}]$ which, in the case $\theta = 0$, reduces the $E[e^0]$ which is, immediately, $E[1] = 1$.

Properties of moment generating functions

Relationship with probability generating functions

In Examples 5.2 and 5.3 (the binomial and Poisson distributions), you saw that the functional form of the moment generating function was exactly the same as that of the probability generating function except that the dummy variable, θ, in the p.g.f. was replaced by e^θ in the m.g.f. This is true in general and can very easily be seen from the basic definitions.

The general result is as follows: if a discrete random variable has p.g.f. $G(\theta)$, then its m.g.f. is $G(e^\theta)$. This follows because the m.g.f. is $E[e^{\theta X}]$ by definition, and the p.g.f. is $E[\theta^X]$ by definition – so you can see straight away in the definitions that all that has happened is the θ in the p.g.f. has become e^θ in the m.g.f.

'Linear transformation' result

You can easily obtain the moment generating function of a random variable that is a linear transformation of another random variable whose m.g.f. in known. Suppose a random variable, X, has m.g.f., $M(\theta)$, which is known, and a random variable, Y, is given by $Y = aX + b$ where a and b are known constants. Then the m.g.f. of Y is, by definition

$$E[e^{\theta Y}] = E[e^{\theta(aX+b)}]$$

$$= E[e^{b\theta} \times e^{a\theta X}] \quad \text{(remember now that } \theta \text{ is not a random variable; the expectation is with respect to } X\text{)}$$

$$= e^{b\theta} E[e^{(a\theta)X}] \quad \text{(now notice that } E[e^{(a\theta)X}] \text{ is simply the m.g.f. of } X \text{ with } \theta \text{ replaced by } a\theta\text{)}$$

$$= e^{b\theta} M(a\theta)$$

This result is often useful. Two examples of how to apply it follow. The first is somewhat artificial but gives a simple illustration of the technique; the second is more important, showing how the m.g.f. of the general Normal disribution can be obtained from the m.g.f. of the standard Normal distribution which you saw in Example 5.4.

EXAMPLE 5.8

Suppose X is the binomial random variable $B(n, p)$ and $Y = 7X - 4$. Find the m.g.f. for Y.

SOLUTION

You saw in Example 5.2 that the m.g.f., $M(\theta)$, for the random variable $X \sim B(n, p)$ is $(q + pe^\theta)^n$. Now you have $Y = 7X - 4$ which is a linear transformation of X: $Y = aX + b$ with $a = 7$ and $b = -4$. So you can immediately write down the m.g.f. of Y. It is

$$e^{-4\theta}(q + pe^{7\theta})^n.$$

EXAMPLE 5.9 Find the m.g.f. for the general Normal random variable $Y \sim N(\mu, \sigma^2)$.

SOLUTION

In Example 5.4, you saw that the m.g.f. for the standard Normal random variable $X \sim N(0, 1)$ is

$$e^{\frac{\theta^2}{2}}$$

You now have that Y is a linear transformation of X: $Y = \sigma X + \mu$. So you can write down that the m.g.f. of Y is

$$e^{\mu\theta} e^{\frac{(\sigma\theta)^2}{2}} = e^{\mu\theta + \frac{\sigma^2\theta^2}{2}}.$$

You can, incidentally, obtain this by explicit integration using the probability density function of $N(\mu, \sigma^2)$ but, as you have already obtained the m.g.f. of $N(0, 1)$, it is much easier to use the linear transformation result as shown here.

The result in this example is the next stage in proving the result about 'Normal distributions adding up'. You now have the m.g.f. for the general Normal distribution $N(\mu, \sigma^2)$. You can apply this for each of the Normal random variables $X_1, X_2, \ldots, X_n$ in the result by putting the appropriate subscript $1, 2, \ldots, n$ on each of μ and σ^2.

You may remember that there is similar 'linear transformation' result for probability generating functions. This is also true for the next result – most aspects of probability and moment generating functions are very similar.

Convolution theorem

This is a *very important* result. It is also very simple, both to state and to prove. It simply says that the moment generating function for a *sum* of *independent* random variables is the *product* of their separate moment generating functions.

To prove the result, consider the case of two independent random variables, X and Y, both of whose moment generating functions are known, and let Z be their sum, $Z = X + Y$. Then the m.g.f. of Z is, by definition

$$E[e^{\theta Z}] = E[e^{\theta(X+Y)}] = E[e^{\theta X} \times e^{\theta Y}].$$

You now need to use the theorem that the expected value of a product involving independent random variables is the product of the separate expected values. Using the theorem, you get

$$E[e^{\theta Z} \times e^{\theta Y}] = E[e^{\theta X}] \times E[e^{\theta Y}]$$

which, immediately, is the product of the two separate moment generating functions. Obviously, this proof can be extended to a sum of any number of independent random variables.

The convolution theorem often provides the easiest way of handling problems involving sums of (independent) random variables.

Continuing with the result about 'Normal distributions adding up', you can now write down the m.g.f. for the sum of the independent Normal random variables – it is simply the product of their individual moment generating functions. So it is

$$e^{\mu_1\theta+\frac{\sigma_1^2\theta^2}{2}} \times e^{\mu_2\theta+\frac{\sigma_2^2\theta^2}{2}} \times \ldots \times e^{\mu_n\theta+\frac{\sigma_n^2\theta^2}{2}}$$

$$= e^{(\mu_1+\mu_2+\ldots+\mu_n)\theta+\frac{(\sigma_1^2+\sigma_2^2+\ldots+\sigma_n^2)\theta^2}{2}}$$

To complete the result, you now need to know how to show that the distribution underlying this new m.g.f. is $N(\mu_1 + \mu_2 + \ldots + \mu_n, \sigma_1^2 + \sigma_2^2 + \ldots + \sigma_n^2)$. You will see how to do this a little later on.

Generation of moments

There are two ways in which you can obtain moments from a moment generating function.

First, consider expanding the m.g.f. in a power series. Letting $M(\theta)$ denote a general m.g.f. for a random variable X, you get

$$M(\theta) = E[e^{\theta X}]$$

$$= \left[1 + \theta X + \frac{\theta^2 X^2}{2!} + \frac{\theta^3 X^3}{3!} + \ldots\right] \quad \text{(now take expected values term by term)}$$

$$= 1 + \theta E[X] + \frac{\theta^2}{2!}E[X^2] + \frac{\theta^3}{3!}E[X^3] + \ldots \quad \text{(now write this in general moments notation)}$$

$$= 1 + \theta\mu_1' + \frac{\theta^2}{2!}\mu_2' + \frac{\theta^3}{3!}\mu_3' + \ldots.$$

So the rth moment about the origin, μ_r', appears as the coefficient of $\frac{\theta^r}{r!}$ in this expansion; that is μ_r' is $r!$ multiplied by the coefficient of θ^r in the m.g.f.

EXAMPLE 5.10 Use the power series expansion method to obtain the moments of the $N(0, 1)$ distribution.

SOLUTION

$$M(\theta) = e^{\frac{\theta^2}{2}}$$

$$= 1 + \frac{\theta^2}{2} + \frac{1}{2!}\left(\frac{\theta^2}{2}\right)^2 + \frac{1}{3!}\left(\frac{\theta^2}{2}\right)^3$$

$$= 1 + 0 \times \theta + \frac{\theta^2}{2!} \times 1 + 0 \times \theta^3 + \frac{\theta^4}{4!} \times 3 + 0 \times \theta^5 + \frac{\theta^6}{6!} \times 15 + \ldots.$$

So, picking out the coefficients, you can see that

$$\mu_1' = 0, \mu_2' = 1, \mu_3' = 0, \mu_4' = 3, \mu_5' = 0 \quad \text{and so on.}$$

Note

One feature of the N(0, 1) distribution that you can see straight away from this expansion is that all the odd-order moments are zero.

The second method is to differentiate the moment generating function with respect to θ and then set $\theta = 0$. To see how and why this works, look at the power series on page 106 and differentiate it term by term. Letting $M'(\theta)$ denote differentiation of the m.g.f. with respect to θ, you get

$$M'(\theta) = \mu'_1 + \theta\mu'_2 + \frac{\theta^2}{2!}\mu'_3 + \ldots$$

and now setting $\theta = 0$ gives

$$M'(0) = \mu'_1.$$

Differentiating a second time gives

$$M''(0) = \mu'_2 + \theta\mu'_3 + \ldots$$

and so

$$M''(0) = \mu'_2$$

Continuing in this way, you can obtain μ'_r as $M^{(r)}(0)$, i.e. the rth derivative of the m.g.f. with respect to θ evaluated at $\theta = 0$.

EXAMPLE 5.11 Use the differentiation method to obtain the moments of the N(0, 1) distribution.

SOLUTION

From

$$M(\theta) = e^{\frac{\theta^2}{2}}$$

you get

$$M'(\theta) = e^{\frac{\theta^2}{2}} \times \theta$$

and so

$$\mu'_1 = M'(0) = 0.$$

Differentiating a second time gives

$$M''(\theta) = e^{\frac{\theta^2}{2}} \times 1 + \theta \times e^{\frac{\theta^2}{2}} \times \theta$$

and so

$$\mu'_2 = M''(0) = 1 + 0 = 1$$

You can continue this process to find higher moments.

From this you can see that moment generating functions do indeed generate moments. (Moments about the origin are the ones that appear immediately from the m.f.g. but moments about other points can be found by a little algebraic manipulation.) This is useful in itself, for the m.g.f. is often the easiest way to find means and variances. However, it also opens the door to the real point of moment generating functions, to their central importance in much of statistical theory. You will remember that, at the end of the section on moments, it was pointed out that moments do, in fact, specify all the information about a distribution. You can now see that the moment generating function specifies the moments. So it must necessarily follow that *the moment generating function specifies **all** the information about a distribution.*

In the examples, you were always given the underlying distribution, either by specifying the probability function if it was a discrete distribution, or by specifying the probability density function if it was continuous. You worked 'forwards' from there to find the moment generating function. However, this process can also be done 'backwards'. You can start from a moment generating function and 'undo' it to find the probability function or probability density function of the underlying distribution. This is a unique one-to-one process. Any given distribution has only one m.g.f.; and any given m.g.f. has only one distribution underlying it.

You will remember that this ability to work 'backwards' has already been pointed out for probability generating functions. The advantage of using moment generating functions is that they can be applied to continuous as well as discrete random variables.

The techniques for 'undoing' (the proper technical word is 'inverting') a moment generating function are quite advanced and certainly beyond the scope of this book. However, in many applications of this work, you do not actually need explicitly to 'undo' a moment generating function to find the underlying distribution. You might well be able to recognise the m.g.f. as being one you have met before, i.e. the m.g.f. of a distribution with which you are familiar. Then, because the relationship between a distribution and its m.g.f. is unique, you can at once conclude that the underlying distribution must be this one.

You can now complete the proof of the result that 'Normal distribution add up'.

First recall that the m.g.f. of the general Normal distribution $N(\mu, \sigma^2)$ is $e^{\mu\theta + \frac{\sigma^2\theta^2}{2}}$. Think of this as being:

$$e^{(\text{something})\theta + (\text{something else})\frac{\theta^2}{2}}$$

where the 'something' is the mean and the 'something else' is the variance.

Now recall that you have found the m.g.f. of the sum to be

$$= e^{(\mu_1 + \mu_2 + \ldots + \mu_n)\theta + \frac{(\sigma_1^2 + \sigma_2^2 + \ldots + \sigma_n^2)\theta^2}{2}}$$

and notice that this is exactly of the form:

$$e^{(\text{something})\theta + (\text{something else})\frac{\theta^2}{2}}$$

which implies that you can deduce straight away that the underlying distribution must be Normal and that its mean is $\mu_1 + \mu_2 + \ldots + \mu_n$ and its variance is $\sigma_1^2 + \sigma_2^2 + \ldots + \sigma_n^2$.

Many results about sequences or sums of random variables are proved in this way, and so is the Central Limit Theorem. To give you a flavour of how the work goes, you might like to consider the result that the B(n, p) distribution is well approximated by the Normal distribution with parameters np and npq if n is large. You will have used this result many times in your earlier work in statistics. You will know that the approximation works best if p is fairly near $\frac{1}{2}$, but it eventually becomes good, if n is large enough, whatever the value of p. It is really a result about a sequence of B(n, p) random variables, investigating what happens to this sequence as n increases. The method of proving the result is to consider the moment generating function of B(n, p) and investigate what happens to this function as n increases. The technical mathematical details of doing this are not straightforward, but it turns out that, as n increases, the function approaches the mathematical form of the m.g.f. of the Normal distribution. Because of the uniqueness of moment generating functions, it therefore follows that the distribution itself approaches the Normal form as n increases.

Generating functions are very important in handlng results of this kind, which would be extremely difficult to deal with in any other way. The further you go in more advanced statistical work, the more useful you are likely to find the generating function approach.

EXERCISE 5B

1 State the moment generating function for the B(n, p) distribution.

Independent random variables $X_1, X_2, \ldots, X_k$ have binomial distributions $X_1 \sim$ B(n, p), $X_2 \sim$ B(n_2, p), $\ldots$, $X_k \sim$ B(n_k, p).

(i) Use the convolution theorem to find the moment generating function of the random variable

$$Y = X_1 + X_2 + \ldots + X_k.$$

(ii) By considering the functional form of this moment generating function, deduce that the distribution of Y is

$$\text{B}(n_1 + n_2 + \ldots + n_k, p)$$

Note: Notice that this would not work if p was not the same for each of the original binomial distributions.

2 State the moment generating function for the Poisson (m) distribution.

Independent random variables $X_1, X_2, \ldots, X_n$ have Poisson distributions $X_1 \sim$ Poisson (m_1), $X_2 \sim$ Poisson (m_2), $\ldots$, $X_n \sim$ Poisson (m_n).

(i) Use the convolution theorem to find the moment generating function of the random variable

$$Y = X_1 + X_2 + \ldots + X_n.$$

(ii) Deduce the distribution of Y.

3 Obtain the mean and variance of the B(n, p) distribution from its m.g.f.

4 Hint: In this question, you may use the result that $\int_0^\infty u^m e^{-u} du = m!$ for any non-negative integer m.

The random variable, X, has probability density function

$$f(x) = \begin{cases} \dfrac{\lambda^{k+1} x^k e^{-\lambda x}}{k!} & x > 0 \\ 0 & \text{elsewhere} \end{cases}$$

where $\lambda > 0$ and k is a non-negative integer.

(i) Show that the moment generating function of X is $\left(\dfrac{\lambda}{\lambda - t}\right)^{k+1}$, explaining why this is valid for $t < \lambda$.

(ii) The random variable, Y, is the sum of n independent random variables each distributed as X. Find the moment generating function of Y and hence find the mean and variance of Y.

(iii) Write down the probability density function of Y.

[MEI]

5 (i) The moment generating function (m.g.f.) of the random variable, X, is denoted by $M_X(t)$. Prove that the m.g.f. of the random variable, $Y = aX + b$, where a and b are constants, is $e^{bt} M_X(at)$.

(ii) Derive the m.g.f. of the N(0, 1) random variable.

(iii) Using the results of parts (i) and (ii), derive the m.g.f. of the N(μ, σ^2) random variable.

(iv) X_1 and X_2 are independent Normal random variables with the same mean μ and the same variance σ^2. Use moment generating functions to show that $X_1 + X_2$ and $X_1 - X_2$ are both Normal random variables and to obtain their means and variances.

[MEI]

6 (i) Show that h(t), the generating function for moments about the mean μ of a probability distribution, is given by
$$\text{h}(t) = e^{-\mu t} \text{g}(t)$$
where g(t) is the generating function for moments about the origin.

(ii) Hence, or otherwise, show that the generating function for moments about the mean μ of a Poisson distribution is
$$\exp(\mu e^t - \mu - \mu t).$$

(iii) Find μ_2, μ_3 and μ_4, respectively the second, third and fourth moments about the mean.

(iv) Find also the value of:
$$\dfrac{\mu_4}{\mu_2^2} - \dfrac{\mu_3^2}{\mu_2^3}$$

[O & C]

7 The probability density function of the random variable, X, having the χ_n^2 distribution is
$$f(x) = K x^{\frac{n-2}{2}} e^{-\frac{x}{2}} \quad x \geqslant 0$$
where K is a constant (dependent on n), for any positive integer n.

(i) By making the substitution $x(\tfrac{1}{2} - \theta) = \tfrac{1}{2} u$ and reconsidering the form of f(x), or otherwise, obtain the moment generating function M(θ) of X.

(ii) Using arguments based on moment generating functions

(a) show that the sum of n independent random variables each having the χ_1^2 distribution is the random variable having the χ_n^2 distribution

(b) prove the additive property of χ^2 distributions, namely that the sum of a random variable having the χ_m^2 distribution and an independent random variable having the χ_n^2 distribution is a random variable having the χ_{m+n}^2 distribution.

[MEI]

8 The number of breakdowns per hour of a small firm's photocopier has a Poisson distribution with mean 0.001. Breakdowns are independent of each other. Whenever the machine breaks down, it is repaired immediately and put back into use.

(i) If X hours is the time which elapses between the photocopier being repaired and the next breakdown, you may assume that $P(X > x) = e^{-0.001x}$.

Find the distribution function and the probability density function of X.

(ii) Prove that $G(t)$, the moment generating function of X, is given by
$$G(t) = \frac{1}{1 - 1000} \quad (t < 0.001).$$

(iii) Use this function to show that the mean time between failures is 1000 hours.

(iv) The repair company offers the firm a choice of two payment arrangements to guarantee the immediate repair service. They are:

Option 1: an immediate payment of £P to cover call-out charges for the next 9 months.

Option 2: an immediate payment of £P to cover call-out charges for the next ten breakdowns.

By considering the expected time to the tenth consecutive breakdown, use the moment generating function to decide which option you would advise the firm to choose.

[O & C]

9 (i) The random variable, V, has the exponential distribution with parameter λ, i.e. its probability density function is
$$f(v) = \begin{cases} \lambda e^{-\lambda v} & v \geq 0 \\ 0 & v < 0 \end{cases}$$
where $\lambda > 0$.

Show that the moment generating function of V is
$$M(\theta) = \frac{\lambda}{\lambda - \theta} \text{ for } \theta < \lambda$$

(ii) Independent random variables, X and Y, have exponential distributions with parameters α and β respectively ($\alpha \neq \beta$; α and β both greater than zero). Write down the moment generating function of $X + Y$.

(iii) By finding the moment generating function of the random variable, Z, whose probability density function is
$$\begin{cases} \dfrac{\alpha \beta}{\beta - \alpha}(e^{-\alpha z} - e^{-\beta z}) & z \geq 0 \\ 0 & z < 0 \end{cases}$$
show that $X + Y$ has the same distribution as Z.

(iv) Using the moment generating function, or otherwise, find the mean of Z.

[MEI]

10 (i) The time between arrivals of cars at a checkpoint is a random variable, X, with probability density function
$$f(x) = \begin{cases} \lambda e^{-\lambda x} & x > 0 \\ 0 & \text{elsewhere} \end{cases}$$
where $\lambda > 0$. Obtain the moment generating function of X and hence find the mean and variance of X.

(ii) The checkpoint is set up at time $x = 0$ and the first car arrives at time X_1. The time between the arrival of car $i - 1$ and the arrival of car i is X_i, $i = 2, 3, \ldots$ The X_i may be taken to be independent, identically distributed random variables each with the same probability density function f(x) as defined in part (i). Interpret the random variable $S_n = X_1 + X_2 + \ldots + X_n$ and write down its moment generating function.

(iii) Verify that the function

$$g(y) = \begin{cases} \dfrac{\lambda^n y^{n-1} e^{-\lambda y}}{(n-1)!} & y > 0 \\ 0 & \text{elsewhere} \end{cases}$$

is a probability density function for some random variable Y. Obtain the moment generating function of Y.

Hint: You may use the result that, if

$$I_m = \int_0^\infty y^m e^{-\lambda y}\,dy, \text{ then } I_m = \frac{m}{\lambda} I_{m-1}$$

for any positive integer m.

(iv) State the probability density function of S_n. Justify your answer.

[MEI]

KEY POINTS

1. For a probability distribution, the *moment generating function* (m.g.f.) is defined by

   $$M(\theta) = E(e^{\theta X}) = \sum_x e^{\theta x} P(X = x) \text{ for } \textit{discrete} \text{ random variables}$$

   $$= \int_x e^{\theta x} f(x)\,dx \qquad \text{for } \textit{continuous} \text{ random variables.}$$

2. The kth moment about zero $= \mu'_k = E(X^k)$.

3. The kth moment about the mean $= \mu_k = E[(X - \mu)^k]$.

4. $M(\theta) = E(e^{\theta X}) = 1 + \dfrac{\theta}{1!} E(X) + \dfrac{\theta^2}{2!} E(X^2) + \dfrac{\theta^3}{3!} E(X^3) + \dfrac{\theta^4}{4!} E(X^4) + \ldots$

5. *Expectation:* $E(X) = M'(0)$ *or* the coefficient of θ in expansion of $M(\theta)$

   $E(X^2) = M''(0)$ *or* the coefficient of $\dfrac{\theta^2}{2!}$ in expansion of $M(\theta)$

   $E(X^3) = M'''(0)$ *or* the coefficient of $\dfrac{\theta^3}{3!}$ in expansion of $M(\theta)$

6. *Variance:* $\text{Var}(X) = E(X - \mu)^2$
   $= E(X^2) - \mu^2$
   $= M''(0) - [M'(0)]^2$

7. *Linear transformation:* $Y = aX + b$
   $M_Y(\theta) = e^{b\theta} M_X(a\theta)$

8. *Convolution theorem:* $Z = X + Y$
   $M_Z(\theta) = M_X(\theta) M_Y(\theta)$

6 Hypothesis tests on unpaired samples

Let not thy left hand know what thy right hand doeth.

St Matthew 6

When he returned to the office at two o'clock, his desk was clear. Until the afternoon post arrived, he had nothing to do. A ray of sunlight shone through a high window and he watched the specks of dust fall gently through it. With one finger, he pushed a paperclip around his blotter. The only sound was the distant tapping of a typewriter in a room down the corridor. For what seemed like hours he sat, sunk in a deep reverie. Then he lowered his eyes and glanced at his watch. It was five past two.

Have you noticed how time often seems to pass more slowly after lunch?

If time passes more slowly, one minute of real time should seem longer, so if you ask people to estimate when a minute appears to have elapsed, the real time elapsed will be less.

You could ask the question: 'Will the mean real time elapsed when one minute appears to have elapsed be less after lunch than before?'

In this example you are interested, not in what the mean value of a random variable is, but in what the difference between the mean values is in two different situations. Statistical problems giving rise to different versions of this general question are the topic of this chapter.

INVESTIGATION

Find a group of volunteers and approach them before lunch. Give each of them a starting signal and ask them to say when one minute has elapsed. Record the real time elapsed. You will then need to find a second group of volunteers to approach after lunch. You will need reasonably large groups to get useful results.

? What are the advantages and disadvantages of using separate groups of people for the before-lunch and after-lunch times? What are the advantages and disadvantages of instead conducting an experiment in which the same people are asked before and after lunch and only the difference in their real times recorded.

The volunteers in research projects are called *subjects* and 'before lunch' and 'after lunch' are the two *conditions* in which testing occurs. An experiment such as the one described above, where a different group of subjects is tested in each of the two conditions is called an *unpaired design*; this is in contrast to the *paired design* you met in *Statistics 3*, where the same set of subjects is tested in both conditions.

The members of a maths class were asked one morning to check the time shown by their watches, then look away and, when they estimated that a minute had elapsed, to check their watches again to see how long had in fact elapsed.

The same procedure was followed with another class, from the same year group, that afternoon. The back-to-back stem-and-leaf diagram below shows the results.

Morning class		Afternoon class
(24 students)		(22 students)
	2	8
2	3	1
5 5 6	3	6
	4	4 4 0
7 8	4	9 9 9 6 6 5
1 1 3 3 3 3 4 4	5	2 2 1 1 1
5 5 5 7 7 7 7	5	8 7 7 5
1 4 4	6	3

| 6 | 3   represents 63 seconds

Figure 6.1

This experiment gives a set of data with which you could investigate the question asked at the start of the chapter. This experiment has an *unpaired design*: two separate groups of subjects are used in the two conditions.

This section uses the data given in figure 6.1 to work through the process of hypothesis testing in the context of an unpaired design. If you have carried out your own investigation, you might find it helpful to repeat the calculations using your data.

You cannot look here at the difference between a before-lunch and an after-lunch time for a particular person but you can look at the difference between the mean before-lunch time and the mean after-lunch time. In fact, you can make the hypotheses:

H_0: There is no difference between the mean of people's estimates of one minute before and after lunch.

H_1: After lunch, the mean of people's estimates of one minute tends to be shorter than before lunch.

You can then use as your sample statistic the difference between the before-lunch sample mean and the after-lunch sample mean. You need to calculate the distribution of this sample statistic on the assumption that the null hypothesis is true.

The test statistic and its distribution

Assume that each before-lunch estimate is an independent random variable X_i ($i = 1, \ldots 24$) with the Normal distribution $N(\mu_b, \sigma_b^2)$ and each after-lunch estimate is an independent random variable Y_j ($j = 1, \ldots, 22$) with Normal distribution $N(\mu_a, \sigma_a^2)$. You are also making the assumption that each X is independent of each Y. This is a plausible assumption; it merely requires the independence of the two samples taken.

Recall that the mean of a sample of size n from a Normal distribution $N(\mu, \sigma^2)$ has distribution

$$N\left(\mu, \frac{\sigma^2}{n}\right).$$

In this case, therefore, the mean of the 24 before-lunch estimates has distribution

$$\overline{X} \sim N\left(\mu_b, \frac{\sigma_b^2}{24}\right)$$

and the mean of the 22 after-lunch estimates has distribution

$$\overline{Y} \sim N\left(\mu_a, \frac{\sigma_a^2}{22}\right).$$

Next you need a result that if X has distribution $N(\mu_X, \sigma_X^2)$ and Y has distribution $N(\mu_Y, \sigma_Y^2)$ then $(X - Y)$ has distribution

$$N(\mu_X - \mu_Y, \sigma_X^2 + \sigma_Y^2).$$

Here, the distribution of the differences of the two sample means is therefore

$$\overline{X} - \overline{Y} \sim N\left(\mu_b - \mu_a, \frac{\sigma_b^2}{24} + \frac{\sigma_a^2}{22}\right).$$

The null hypothesis then states that both means are equal, i.e. $\mu_b = \mu_a$ and so, if the null hypothesis is true

$$\overline{X} - \overline{Y} \sim N\left(0, \frac{\sigma_b^2}{24} + \frac{\sigma_a^2}{22}\right).$$

Unfortunately, you do not know σ_b^2 or σ_a^2, so you will want, as you have in earlier work, to replace these unknown values with sample estimates. It might seem most natural to use separate estimates for the two unknown variances, but in fact it turns out that it is then hard to make any progress in calculating the distribution. This chapter, therefore, only deals with the case where you can assume that the variances in the two conditions are equal: here, this means that $\sigma_b^2 = \sigma_a^2 = \sigma^2$; that is, the before- and after-lunch estimates have the same variance. In this case

$$\overline{X} - \overline{Y} \sim N\left(0, \sigma^2\left(\frac{1}{24} + \frac{1}{22}\right)\right).$$

So that

$$\frac{\overline{X} - \overline{Y}}{\sqrt{\sigma^2\left(\frac{1}{24} + \frac{1}{22}\right)}} = \frac{\overline{X} - \overline{Y}}{\sigma\sqrt{\frac{1}{24} + \frac{1}{22}}} \sim N(0, 1). \qquad \text{①}$$

To estimate σ^2, you can use the pooled variance estimator from the two samples,

$$S^2 = \frac{(24-1)S_b^2 + (22-1)S_a^2}{(24+22-2)}$$

where S_b^2 and S_a^2 are the usual unbiased sample estimators of the population variance given by

$$S_b^2 = \frac{\sum_{i=1}^{24}(X_i - \overline{X})^2}{23} = \frac{\sum_{i=1}^{24}X_i^2 - 24\overline{X}^2}{23} \quad \text{and} \quad S_a^2 = \frac{\sum_{i=1}^{22}(Y_i - \overline{Y})^2}{21} = \frac{\sum_{i=1}^{22}Y_i^2 - 22\overline{Y}^2}{21}$$

The test statistic,

$$\frac{\overline{X} - \overline{Y}}{S\sqrt{\frac{1}{24} + \frac{1}{22}}}$$

which is obtained from ① by replacing the value of σ^2 with its estimator S^2, then has a t distribution, with degrees of freedom equal to that in the pooled variance estimate: $(24 + 22 - 2) = 44$.

Carrying out the *t* test for an unpaired sample

In the example:
$$\bar{x} = 51.542,\ s_b = 8.797;\ \bar{y} = 47.909,\ s_a = 8.574$$

so
$$s = \sqrt{\frac{23 \times 8.797^2 + 21 \times 8.574^2}{44}} = 8.691$$

and the value of the test statistic is:
$$\frac{51.542 - 47.909}{8.691 \times \sqrt{\frac{1}{24} + \frac{1}{22}}} = 1.416.$$

The critical region for a one-tailed test, in the case of 44 degrees of freedom, at the 5% significance level is $t > 1.680$ (this value does not appear in the tables, but can be obtained by interpolation for the values given for 30 and 50 degrees of freedom). Since $1.416 < 1.680$, the results lead you to accept the null hypothesis at this significance level: there is no good evidence that the before-lunch mean and the after-lunch mean of the population as a whole are different.

The process described is a *t test for the difference of two means with unpaired samples*.

EXPERIMENTS

Carry out at least one of the experiments below, and test the hypothesis given using an unpaired sample *t* test.

1 Use a reaction timer to decide whether males and females have the same mean reaction times, or whether older people have slower reactions than young people (you can choose the definition of 'older' to suit the samples you have available) or whether squash players have quicker reactions than non-players.

You can use a 30 cm ruler as a reaction timer: hold the ruler vertically with the zero mark downwards, while the subject holds his thumb and forefinger 2 cm apart at the zero mark of the ruler. You drop the ruler without warning and your subject tries to catch it between thumb and forefinger. The distance, *d*, in millimetres, through which the ruler has fallen before it is caught can be used to measure the reaction time, *t*, in seconds, using the formula

$$t = \frac{\sqrt{d}}{70}.$$

2 Are students studying A-level maths better at mental arithmetic than those taking other A-levels? You will need to devise a mental arithmetic test (Do you want to test speed or accuracy?) and administer it to a group of A-level maths students and a group of students taking other A-levels. *Do not be disappointed by the results!* You can adapt this test to suit your prejudices: are A-level geography students better at naming capitals of foreign countries? Are A-level English students better at spelling?

3 Two groups of subjects are each given lists of 25 words. Both groups must run down the list as quickly as possible. Those in the first group tick the words that are in capital letters. (You should make sure that about half of the words, placed randomly in the list, are in capital letters.) The second group ticks the words which rhyme with a target word which you give them. (Make sure that about half of the words, placed randomly in the list, do rhyme with this word.) You then ask the subjects each to write down as many words as they can remember from the list: do not tell the subjects in advance that they will have to do this. Test the hypothesis that the subjects who have looked for rhymes remember more of the words than those who looked for capital letters. Why would it be difficult to run this experiment with a paired design?

Assumptions for the unpaired *t* test

The assumptions needed for the unpaired *t* test are quite severe.

1 The two samples must be independent random samples of the populations involved.

Strictly, this requires every possible sample to have an equal probability of being chosen. If you simply picked a group of volunteers, therefore, it would probably not be a random sample. However, this method is very close to the method often used by academic psychologists when choosing their samples. The hope in choosing a random sample is that the effects of all the irrelevant differences between members of the population which influence the variables you are testing will average out.

2 The random variables measured in the two conditions must
  • be normally distributed
  • have equal variances in the two conditions.

Are these assumptions justified? The only information you have to help you decide is the two samples: the stem-and-leaf diagram for the data of the example is shown again below.

```
        Morning class           Afternoon class
        (24 students)            (22 students)

                          | 2 | 8
                        2 | 3 | 1
                    5 5 6 | 3 | 6
                          | 4 | 4 4 0
                      7 8 | 4 | 9 9 9 6 6 5
          1 1 3 3 3 3 4 4 | 5 | 2 2 1 1 1
            5 5 5 7 7 7 7 | 5 | 8 7 7 5
                    1 4 4 | 6 | 3

                          | 6 | 3   represents 63 seconds
```

Figure 6.2

At first sight, the distributions here do not look much like samples from a Normal distribution: they are rather obviously negatively skewed. Neither is it clear that they would have come from populations of the same variance. However, these are relatively small samples and it would be unwise to draw any firm conclusions from them about the population distribution from which they are drawn.

You do not look further at these problems here, but there is a test for equality of variances, the F test (see Chapter 10); in Chapter 8 you will meet a test for a difference in location between two conditions which does not require the Normality assumption.

Do you think the assumptions made in the unpaired t test are justified in the case of the experiment you carried out?

The underlying logic of hypothesis testing

When you construct the sampling distribution of a test statistic you use:

1 a model for the distribution of the random variables involved in the statistic

2 the value given to a parameter of this distribution by the null hypothesis.

In the time-estimation example, the construction of the sampling distribution depends on:

1 people's estimates of one minute before and after lunch being independent and distributed Normally, with a common variance

2 the null hypothesis that the difference between the means of their estimates before and after lunch is zero.

The alternative hypothesis, that the difference between these means is greater than zero, gives an alternative range of possible values for the parameter of the distribution, but assumes the same model for the random variables involved.

In the example it was determined (by using pre-calculated tables, in fact), that if

- the model for the random variables was correct

and

- the null hypothesis were true

then a test statistic greater than 1.680 would only arise in a random sample 5% of the time. (The significance level is 5%.)

In the example earlier in the chapter you obtained a value of 1.416 and, since this is less than 1.680, the null hypothesis was accepted. Suppose, instead, that you had obtained a value greater than 1.680, say for example, 1.832. In that case there would be three possible explanations.

Explanation A

1 The model is correct.

2 The null hypothesis is false, because the mean difference in before- and after-lunch times is greater than zero.

Explanation B

1 The model is correct.

2 The null hypothesis is true (or false because the mean difference in before- and after-lunch times is actually less than zero).

However the sample selected happens to give a value of the test statistic greater than 1.680. The probability of this happening is 0.05 (the significance level) if the null hypothesis is true, or less if the mean difference in before- and after-lunch times is actually less than zero.

Explanation C

1 The model is incorrect, because the sampling method does not produce independent estimates for each subject, or because the estimates are not distributed Normally in the population, or do not have a common variance.

2 The null hypothesis is true or false.

In this case you have no idea how likely it is that the test statistic will have any value at all.

The hypothesis testing methodology is

- to assume that explanation C is not the case
- to observe that if explanation B was the case then the results obtained would be very unlikely
- and therefore to accept that explanation A is the case.

Thus you reject the null hypothesis and accept the alternative.

However, you should always be aware that the logic which leads you to this conclusion on the basis of the evidence in the sample depends on the correctness of your sampling and distributional assumptions.

Comparison between paired and unpaired *t* tests

The table below shows summarised data from the experiment you have just been analysing, together with data gathered from a paired experiment using a single sample of twelve people. Each was asked, both before and after lunch, to estimate one minute in the same way as described for the unpaired design.

	Data from paired experiment	Data from unpaired experiment
Before-lunch time	$\bar{x} = 51.250$, $s_b = 8.237$, $n = 12$	$\bar{x} = 51.542$, $s_b = 8.797$, $n = 24$
After-lunch time	$\bar{y} = 47.583$, $s_a = 9.258$, $n = 12$	$\bar{y} = 47.909$, $s_a = 8.574$, $n = 22$

The test statistic for the paired experiment is 1.829, with 11 degrees of freedom and a critical value of 1.796, so that here the null hypothesis is rejected.

Why do you reject the null hypothesis in the paired case where the sample size is considerably smaller which, all other things being equal, would usually lead to a less decisive test, as reflected in the larger critical value?

You can see why the opposite appears to have happened if you look at how the test statistics for the two cases are calculated.

Test statistic for paired experiment	Test statistic for unpaired experiment
$\dfrac{51.250 - 47.583}{6.946\sqrt{\tfrac{1}{12}}} = 1.829$	$\dfrac{51.542 - 47.909}{8.691\sqrt{\tfrac{1}{24} + \tfrac{1}{22}}} = 1.416$

The test statistics for the paired and unpaired calculations have very similar numerators, but the standard error in the denominator is considerably larger in the unpaired calculation, despite the larger sample size in that case.

The crucial point is that there is, for all sorts of reasons, considerable variation amongst people in their reaction times and lunch is only one, relatively small, effect amongst many. Some people will tend to make short estimates in both conditions and some long estimates in both conditions, though in both cases the effect of lunch may be the same.

The paired design enables you to take this into account in a way which the unpaired design cannot because of the way the standard error is estimated.

- The standard error for the paired experiment estimates how much variation to expect in the average difference between *a particular person's* before- and after-lunch times. It is calculated from the standard deviation of these differences in the sample and is therefore based only on the variation in the effect of lunch on different people, not on the values s_b and s_a which describe the very considerable variation in reaction times between people for all the other reasons.

- The standard error for the unpaired experiment estimates how much variation to expect in the average difference between *a random before-lunch time and a random after-lunch time*. It is calculated from the values s_b and s_a which take into account the very considerable variation between people for all sorts of reasons, including the relatively small variation associated with lunch.

Using paired and unpaired *t* tests

It is a characteristic of research by social scientists that they are looking for a small average difference between the values of a particular variable in two different conditions, but that subjects show very substantial variation in the values of this variable within both conditions. In these situations, an unpaired *t* test is not usually very helpful, as it will require a very large sample size to discriminate between the null hypothesis of no difference between the means in the two conditions and the true situation where there is a small difference. In Chapter 9 you will see that this is saying that the unpaired test is not very powerful.

Considerable ingenuity is therefore employed in attempting to match subjects so that a paired test can be used to eliminate some of the variation between them and the small difference between the two experimental conditions is not swamped.

In the paired experiment you used the same subject in each of two conditions, but this is not necessary. In fact, having taken part in one experimental condition sometimes makes it impossible to take part in the second.

For example, if you wish to test the effect on children's intelligence of an upbringing in families from two different social classes you could not use the same child and bring it up twice, nor would an unpaired *t* test be suitable in this case: the variation in intelligence caused by other factors would swamp the effect you are looking for.

One possibility is to find pairs of identical twins who are being adopted at birth and are assigned to adoptive parents of different social classes: these constitute matched pairs of subjects and you could use a *t* test on the differences between the intelligences of the twins from the two types of family. Notice that here the matching is perfect in the sense that both children have identical genetic endowments: the belief implicit in this experiment is that heredity is a major cause of variation in intelligence and this effect will be cancelled out by the matching process. Of course, there will be many differences between the adoptive families other than class, and it is possible that the variations in intelligence induced by these differences in upbringing will still swamp the effect being examined. Ideally, you would want to find identical twins being assigned to families differing only in their social class, but it is unlikely that you would find enough, if any, examples of this to conduct the test!

EXERCISE 6A

In this exercise, you are expected to make a sensible choice of significance level for the hypothesis tests involved. Remember that the 5% level is conventional in scientific contexts.

1 A species of finch has subspecies on two different Galapagos Islands.

The weights of a sample of finches from each island are listed below.

Weights from Daphne Major (grams)
64 67 64 61 68 61 61 67 70 62 66 63

Weights from Daphne Minor (grams)
63 61 65 65 61 63 63

(i) Is there evidence that the finches on Daphne Major are heavier on average than those on Daphne Minor?

(ii) What assumptions do you need to make? Are they reasonable?

2 Two different varieties of sprout being grown around the country, on a variety of different plots with different soil types and weather conditions, are monitored by a crop-testing station.

(i) Test, using an unpaired *t* test, the hypothesis that the two varieties have the same average yield. The yields of sprouts per square metre in kilograms are as follows.

Yields of 'Old Cobby' (kg/m^2)
18 15 14 21 21 19 9 20 26 27
21 12 15 14 27 22 23 18 10 19

Yields of 'Early Yellow' (kg/m^2)
12 20 18 14 15 13 17 15 20 26
17 14 8 29 24 16 20 20 18 23
20 23 23 18 9

(ii) Plot the data on a back-to-back stem-and-leaf diagram. State and comment on the assumptions you are making in carrying out the test. Do you think the assumptions are justified?

(iii) Devise an experiment to test this hypothesis which would use a paired *t* test. Would this be an improvement, do you think?

3. Two groups of subjects are asked to volunteer for a psychology experiment. One group is told that they will be paid £1 for participating, the other that they will be paid £20. The experiment consists of a rather dull task which must be repeated for one hour: subjects are then asked to rate how interesting the task was, on a scale from 1 to 10; 10 being the most interesting.

   (i) Test, using an unpaired t test, the hypothesis that the task was found more interesting by those who were paid less.

   The ratings of the two groups were:

Paid £1	4	2	6	3	5	1	6	4
	3	5	5	3	2	2	6	
	1	7	2	4	5	4	5	

Paid £20	3	5	2	1	3	4	5
	2	1	1	3	4	4	4
	5	2	3	2	1	3	

   (ii) State and comment on the assumptions you are making in order to carry out this test.

   (iii) Could you devise a paired design for this experiment?

4. Some personality theorists classify people into 'introverts', or quiet personalities, and 'extroverts', or outgoing personalities. In an attempt to find physical correlates of these personality types, the heights of a group of 17 extroverts and a group of 17 introverts were measured.

   (i) Show that an unpaired t test with the data below accepts, at the 5% level, the hypothesis that extroverts are taller on average than introverts, stating carefully the assumptions you are making.

   Heights of extroverts (cm)

179	174	166	170	170	168
173	170	173	173	168	174
163	156	157	162	169	

   Heights of introverts (cm)

159	172	167	168	163	155
164	163	166	164	175	155
165	168	164	166	162	

   (ii) The scientist who made these measurements concluded that taller people tend to be more confident and hence extroverted. Is this conclusion justified?

5. A college careers officer investigates the income at age 24 of a group of students who left school at 16, and a group who stayed on to take A-levels.

   The results he finds (measuring incomes in £ per week) are summarised by this table.

	16-year-old leavers	A-levels leavers
Mean	156	164
Sample estimate of variance	673	593
Sample size	37	28

   (i) Show, using an unpaired t test, that the hypothesis that those staying on at school have higher incomes at age 24 is rejected, on the evidence of this sample. What assumptions are you making for an unpaired t test to be appropriate? How plausible are they?

   (ii) What other difference between the two groups inevitably exists that might explain this unexpected result? How could you design an experiment to eliminate this effect?

6 My sister is worried that the office in which she works suffers from 'sick building' syndrome. She has noticed that those who work on her floor, which is air-conditioned, seem to suffer from colds more often than those on the non-air-conditioned floor below. She uses the sick-leave records to discover the number of days of absence with colds in the last year.

(i) Use an unpaired t test to test the hypothesis that staff on the air-conditioned floor have more absences with colds, using the following data.

Absence of staff:

on her floor	6	5	11	2	7	13	8
	10	6	1	0	8	3	2
on the floor below	2	0	5	5	7	1	
	0	3	8	2	4		

(ii) What assumptions are necessary for the t test to be appropriate? Which of them are not justified here?

Testing for a non-zero value of the difference of two means

You have now used the t test to examine the null hypothesis that two different conditions produce the same mean value of some random variable. The method can also be used in a more general way to test null hypotheses which suggest that the mean of a random variable, X, differs by a given amount in the two conditions.

Hypothesis: for some given value of δ

H_0: The difference between the mean values of X in condition 1 and condition 2 is δ.

Sample: Two sets of observations of X, one set in each condition.

Let X_1 and X_2 be the random variables in the two conditions and n_1 and n_2 be the number of observations under each condition.

Use these values to calculate the sample means $\overline{X}_1$ and $\overline{X}_2$ and the unbiased pooled-sample estimator S^2 of the population variance.

Then

$$\frac{(\overline{X}_1 - \overline{X}_2) - \delta}{S\sqrt{\dfrac{1}{n_1} + \dfrac{1}{n_2}}} \sim t_{n_1+n_2-2}$$

provided that the random variable X is distributed normally in the population, with the same variance in each condition, and that the null hypothesis is true.

EXAMPLE 6.1

The manufacturers of a dieting compound 'Slimplan', claim that the use of their product as part of a calorie-counting diet leads to an average extra weight loss of at least five pounds in a fortnight. An experiment has been carried out by a consumers' group which doubts this claim.

The hypotheses are:

H_0: The mean extra weight loss in a fortnight from adding 'Slimplan' to a calorie-counting diet is five pounds.

H_1: The mean extra weight loss in a fortnight from adding 'Slimplan' to a calorie-counting diet is less than five pounds.

The assumptions are that the weight loss in a fortnight from a calorie-counting diet, with or without 'Slimplan', is a Normally distributed random variable and that the addition of 'Slimplan' to the diet does not affect the variance of this random variable.

Thirty-six dieters used 'Slimplan' with their diets; their weight losses x_i ($i = 1, \ldots, 36$) in pounds are summarised by the figures

$$\sum_{i=1}^{36} x_i = 409.32 \qquad \sum_{i=1}^{36} x_i^2 = 6102.39.$$

Sixty-two dieters followed the same calorie-counting procedure, but did not use 'Slimplan'; their weight losses y_j ($j = 1, \ldots, 62$) in pounds are summarised by the figures

$$\sum_{j=1}^{62} y_j = 571.64 \qquad \sum_{j=1}^{62} y_j^2 = 5618.40.$$

SOLUTION

These data give: $\bar{x} = 11.37$, $s_x = 6.433$, $\bar{y} = 9.22$ and $s_y = 2.388$

so that

$$s = \sqrt{\frac{35 \times 6.433^2 + 61 \times 2.388^2}{36 + 62 - 2}} = 4.326$$

The test statistic is

$$\frac{(11.37 - 9.22) - 5}{4.326 \times \sqrt{\frac{1}{36} + \frac{1}{62}}} = -3.144$$

and there are (size of sample 1 + size of sample 2 − 2) = (36 + 62 − 2) = 96 degrees of freedom.

The critical region for a one-tailed test with 96 degrees of freedom at the 5% significance level is $t < -1.661$ and so, since $-3.144 < -1.661$ the null hypothesis is rejected in favour of the alternative that the average extra weight loss is not as great as five pounds.

EXERCISE 6B

In this exercise you need to decide whether the data are from an experiment with a paired or an unpaired design. You are expected to make a sensible choice of significance level for the hypothesis tests involved. Remember that the 5% level is conventional in scientific contexts.

1. Amongst all praying mantises, females are on average 7 cm longer than males. A new variety of mantis has been bred, the insects of which are supposed to be more nearly equal in size.

   Test the hypothesis that the difference between male and female average lengths is less than 7 centimetres, using the lengths in centimetres of the sample of twelve males and twelve females shown below. State clearly the assumptions you are making in your test.

Males	18.4	15.1	11.9	16.3	8.7	13.0
	10.1	20.2	14.2	6.2	16.9	8.8
Females	28.2	24.2	12.4	23.4	13.2	21.4
	10.3	23.5	16.8	11.9	15.5	13.2

2. In fact, the data given in question 1 are paired: each male mantis is paired with its mate in the following way.

Pair	1	2	3	4	5	6
Male	18.4	15.1	11.9	16.3	8.7	13.0
Female	28.2	24.2	12.4	23.4	13.2	21.4
Pair	7	8	9	10	11	12
Male	10.1	20.2	14.2	6.2	16.9	8.8
Female	10.3	23.5	16.8	11.9	15.5	13.2

   (i) Test the hypothesis that male mantises are on average less than 7 centimetres smaller than their mates.

   (ii) Explain clearly what assumptions you make in this case, and how these assumptions differ from those you made in question 1.

   (iii) Why are the results you obtain different in this case from those you found in question 1?

3. It is known from many studies that the best current post-operative treatment reduces stays in hospital after major operations, compared with untreated patients, by an average of 6.2 days. A new treatment is proposed, with the hypothesis that this new treatment will reduce stays in hospital by more than 6.2 days on average, and a trial is conducted on two groups of patients who have just undergone major operations. The results are shown below.

   Days stayed in hospital by untreated patients

35	33	27	27	25	31	27
36	46	32	27	16	28	

   Days stayed in hospital by patients given new treatment

18	18	23	24	22	14	28
29	24	16	18			

   Test the hypothesis given, stating the assumptions you are making clearly.

4. Sergio has developed a climate change model which predicts a global temperature change of 2° between 1965 and 2005. He collects data from weather stations in seven countries around the world for the month of January.

Country	Temperature 1965 (°C)	Temperature 2005 (°C)
Australia	29.4	30.5
Italy	4.8	11.2
Japan	3.8	7.8
Spain	15.6	15.6
UK	0.6	5.2
USA	10.5	12.7
Zambia	24.1	25.5

   (i) Test the hypothesis that the temperature in January rose by 2° between 1965 and 2005.

   (ii) State carefully the assumptions you are making. What is a random sample in this context?

5 Given a list of 30 three-letter 'words' to learn, an adult can recall an average of 10.3 more 'words' if they are genuine English words than if they are random 'nonsense' combinations of three letters. It is thought that in dyslexic adults, however, there is a larger difference in recall ability between real and nonsense 'words'. An experiment to test this is carried out. Ten dyslexic adults are given lists of real and nonsense 'words', and their recall tested. The results are listed in the table below.

Initials	TP	CS	AD	JM	MC
Real words recalled	17	19	24	19	16
Nonsense words recalled	4	5	6	6	12

Initials	AB	RS	PT	LL	MR
Real words recalled	20	25	29	22	15
Nonsense words recalled	3	15	18	10	1

Test the hypothesis that these dyslexic adults recall more than 10.3 fewer nonsense 'words' on average than real words, stating the assumptions you are making.

6 When learning real words, dyslexic adults recall on average 5.1 fewer of a list of 30 words than adults who are non-dyslexic. In an experiment to decide whether this is true also of nonsense words, a group of dyslexic and a group of non-dyslexic adults are given a list of nonsense 'words' to learn. When their recall is tested the numbers of nonsense words recalled were as follows.

	By dyslexic adults	By non-dislexic adults
Mean	5.2	12.8
Sample estimate of variance	36.7	45.1
Sample size	28	41

(i) Test the hypothesis that dyslexic adults recall on average 5.1 fewer nonsense 'words' than those who are non-dyslexic.

(ii) State carefully the assumptions necessary, and explain how these differ from the assumptions of question 5.

(iii) State clearly the relation between this hypothesis and the hypothesis of question 5. Are they related at all? If so, how?

Hypothesis tests and confidence intervals

There is a very close relationship between hypothesis tests and confidence intervals, which should be clearly understood.

A *hypothesis test* suggests a value for an unknown population parameter (the null hypothesis), and then accepts this value if a test statistic lies in a particular range (that is, it lies outside the critical region). However, the critical region depends on the hypothesised population parameter, so you can reverse this process. Thus for a given value of the test statistic, you can determine the range of values for the population parameter which would be accepted by the test if they were offered as null hypotheses. This is called the *confidence interval* for the population parameter.

For instance, in the case where you take an independent random sample of size n from a Normal distribution to test the hypotheses:

H_0: Population mean $= \mu$

H_1: **(a)** Population mean $\neq \mu$

or **(b)** population mean $> \mu$

or **(c)** population mean $< \mu$

The test statistic is

$$\frac{\bar{x} - \mu}{\frac{s}{\sqrt{n}}}$$

and you accept the null hypothesis at the $p\%$ significance level if

(a) $-\tau_2 < \frac{\bar{x} - \mu}{\frac{s}{\sqrt{n}}} < \tau_2$ or **(b)** $\frac{\bar{x} - \mu}{\frac{s}{\sqrt{n}}} < \tau_1$ or **(c)** $\frac{\bar{x} - \mu}{\frac{s}{\sqrt{n}}} > -\tau_1$

where τ_1, τ_2 are the one- and two-tailed critical values respectively for the t distribution with $n - 1$ degrees of freedom at the $a\%$ level.

Alternatively, for a given value of $\bar{x}$ you can view these inequalities as constraining the range of values of μ which would be accepted by the test if they were offered as null hypotheses, and rearranging them gives the $(100 - a)\%$ confidence intervals.

(a) $\bar{x} - \tau_2 \frac{s}{\sqrt{n}} < \mu < \bar{x} + \tau_2 \frac{s}{\sqrt{n}}$ or **(b)** $\bar{x} - \tau_1 \frac{s}{\sqrt{n}} < \mu$ or **(c)** $\bar{x} + \tau_1 \frac{s}{\sqrt{n}} > \mu$

Note

As with the estimators that appear in Chapter 2 the lower and upper bounds of a confidence interval are both random variables: the values they take depend on the sample that happens to be selected. This means that these bounds have sampling distributions with properties that will be of interest to statisticians, though they are not considered further here.

Confidence intervals for the difference of two means from unpaired samples

Two runners are being considered for a place in a team. They have each recently competed in several races, though not against each other. Their times (in seconds) were as shown in the table below.

Runner 1	47.2	51.8	48.1	47.9	49.0	48.2	48.1
Runner 2	49.5	47.4	48.3	49.1	47.6		

You can model the first and second runners' times with variables T_1 and T_2 with distributions $N(\mu_1, \sigma^2)$ and $N(\mu_2, \sigma^2)$, respectively. You are describing their running times as Normally distributed with different means and a common variance. The different means reflect differences in the runners' underlying ability; the random variability comes from factors such as the influence of other runners and weather conditions for which the effects in the different races are independent.

Because you are interested in the difference in the runners' underlying abilities, you are looking for a confidence interval for the difference between μ_1 and μ_2.

The sample means of the runners' times have distributions

$$\overline{T}_1 \sim N\left(\mu_1, \frac{1}{7}\sigma^2\right) \quad \text{and} \quad \overline{T}_2 \sim N\left(\mu_2, \frac{1}{5}\sigma^2\right)$$

so that the distribution of their difference is:

$$(\overline{T}_1 - \overline{T}_2) \sim N\left(\mu_1 - \mu_2, \sigma^2\left(\frac{1}{7} + \frac{1}{5}\right)\right).$$

The standardised variable

$$\frac{(\overline{T}_1 - \overline{T}_2) - (\mu_1 - \mu_2)}{\sigma\sqrt{\left(\frac{1}{7} + \frac{1}{5}\right)}}$$

then has an $N(0, 1)$ distribution.

If you replace σ^2 with its unbiased sample estimator, $S^2 = \dfrac{(7-1)S_1^2 + (5-1)S_2^2}{(7+5-2)}$ where S_1^2 and S_2^2 are the unbiased sample estimators of the variance from the two separate samples, then, finally:

$$D = \frac{(\overline{T}_1 - \overline{T}_2) - (\mu_1 - \mu_2)}{S\sqrt{\left(\frac{1}{7} + \frac{1}{5}\right)}}$$

has distribution $t_{7+5-2} = t_{10}$.

The critical value for the t distribution with ten degrees of freedom at the 5% significance level is 2.228, so that D lies between -2.228 and $+2.228$ in 95% of samples. That is, a 95% confidence interval for $(\mu_1 - \mu_2)$ is defined by:

$$-2.228 < \frac{(\overline{t}_1 - \overline{t}_2) - (\mu_1 - \mu_2)}{s\sqrt{\left(\frac{1}{7} + \frac{1}{5}\right)}} < +2.228.$$

This can be rearranged as:

$$(\overline{t}_1 - \overline{t}_2) - 2.228s\sqrt{\left(\frac{1}{7} + \frac{1}{5}\right)} < (\mu_1 - \mu_2) < (\overline{t}_1 - \overline{t}_2) + 2.228s\sqrt{\left(\frac{1}{7} + \frac{1}{5}\right)}.$$

For the data here,
$$\bar{t}_1 = 48.614, \quad s_1^2 = 2.2514$$
$$\bar{t}_2 = 48.380, \quad s_2^2 = 0.8370$$
so that
$$s^2 = \frac{(7-1)s_1^2 + (5-1)s_2^2}{(7+5-2)} = 1.6857.$$

Thus the 95% confidence interval is
$$-1.4595 < (\mu_1 - \mu_2) < 1.9281.$$

Note the considerable width of this confidence interval. In fact you would not be very surprised to discover that Runner 2 was intrinsically slower than Runner 1. You do not have sufficient data to find a very narrow band for the difference in underlying ability – though in practice the selection of one athlete over another for a team often depends on evidence of this type.

A general method

Suppose that values of two random variables, X_1 and X_2, are measured on random samples of sizes n_1 and n_2. Let

- X_1 and X_2 be distributed Normally in the population with a common variance
- X_1 and X_2 be independent of each other in the population
- s^2 be the pooled-sample estimate of the common population variance of X_1 and X_2
- τ_a be the two-sided a% critical value for the t distribution with $(n_1 + n_2 - 2)$ degrees of freedom.

Then a $(100 - a)$% confidence interval for the difference in the means μ_1 and μ_2 of X_1 and X_2 is given by:

$$(\bar{x}_1 - \bar{x}_2) - \tau_a s \sqrt{\frac{1}{n_1} + \frac{1}{n_2}} < (\mu_1 - \mu_2) < (\bar{x}_1 - \bar{x}_2) + \tau_a s \sqrt{\frac{1}{n_1} + \frac{1}{n_2}}.$$

EXERCISE 6C

In this exercise you need to decide whether the data are from an experiment with a paired or an unpaired design.

1 The masses, in grams, of nine hens' eggs and eight ducks' eggs are recorded below.

Hens	42	47	45	41	48
	39	46	45	48	
Ducks	45	47	51	46	49
	53	53	48		

(i) Construct a 95% confidence interval for the difference in mean masses of hens' eggs and ducks' eggs.

(ii) State the assumptions you are making in constructing this confidence interval.

2 Nineteen pairs of fraternal twins, one male and one female, have their salaries at age 28 recorded (in thousands of pounds, to the nearest thousand pounds).

M	F	M	F
33	17	35	12
24	19	28	27
25	25	27	29
21	35	19	19
20	23	23	18
47	38	15	13
19	16	17	23
41	38	18	17
20	19	24	24
36	30		

(i) Use these data to determine a 90% confidence interval for the mean amount by which the male twin's salary exceeds the female's at age 28.

(ii) What assumptions are you making in constructing your confidence interval?

3 The table below shows the times, in seconds, that 13 rats took to run a maze on the first and second times they performed this task.

First run	Second run	First run	Second run
43	29	56	55
29	11	23	20
50	42	39	15
17	21	31	17
28	12	55	22
41	17	48	40
		36	19

Find a 98% confidence interval for the mean reduction in time between the first and second run.

4 A group of rowers and a group of chess players have their resting pulse rates measured. These data are shown below.

Rowers	65	73	71	80	61
	77	83	70	76	
Chess players	117	93	68	92	73
	102	85			

Construct a one-sided 95% confidence interval, giving an upper limit for the extent to which the mean rest pulse rate of chess players exceeds that of rowers.

5 The amount, p, of infestation of turnip fields by root borers, in grams of the pest per square metre, is measured in randomly chosen square metre areas on 33 turnip farms. Some of the farms have sprayed the crops with a new pesticide. The measurements are summarised in the table below.

	Using new pesticides	Not using new pesticides
Number of farms	14	19
Σp	8831	16 573
Σp^2	5 692 287	14 908 662

Construct a 90% confidence interval for the difference in mean infestation between the sprayed and unsprayed crops.

KEY POINTS

1 Given an experiment which produces sets of values of two random variables X and Y, each of which is normally distributed with the same variance, to conduct an *unpaired t test* with null hypothesis:

$$H_0: E(X) = E(Y) + \delta$$

using as data m values x_i and n values y_i which constitute independent random samples of X and Y, respectively:

- find the means $\bar{x}, \bar{y}$ of the data sets
- calculate the unbiased estimate of the common variance s^2 from the pooled samples
- calculate the test statistic

$$\frac{\bar{x} - \bar{y} - \delta}{s\sqrt{\dfrac{1}{m} + \dfrac{1}{n}}}$$

- compare with the appropriate critical value of the t distribution with $(m + n - 2)$ degrees of freedom.

2 Given an experiment which produces pairs of values of two random variables X and Y, each of which is Normally distributed with the same variance, to construct a *confidence interval* for the mean difference

$$E[X] - E[Y]$$

using as data m values x_i and n values y_j which constitute independent random samples of X and Y, respectively:

- find the means $\bar{x}, \bar{y}$ of the data sets
- calculate the unbiased estimate of the common variance s^2 from the pooled samples
- select the appropriate critical value τ of the t distribution with $(m + n - 2)$ degrees of freedom.
- The confidence interval is

$$\bar{x} - \bar{y} - \tau s\sqrt{\frac{1}{m} + \frac{1}{n}} < E[X] - E[Y] < \bar{x} - \bar{y} + \tau s\sqrt{\frac{1}{m} + \frac{1}{n}}.$$

7 Large sample tests and confidence intervals

Experience isn't interesting till it begins to repeat itself – in fact, till it does that, it hardly is experience.

Elizabeth Brown

In a charity trivia game, players must pay £1.50 for a card and then match the words on the card to their definitions.

> MATCH THE WORD TO THE DEFINITION
> **A:** *Peen* **B:** *Pigsney* **C:** *Noyade*
> **1:** A term of endearment
> **2:** The thin end of a hammer-head
> **3:** Mass execution by drowning

The prize to be won is £1.00 for each correct match.

How much can the charity expect to make per card and how predictable is the actual amount they will make per card, if the charity sells many cards?

On the card shown, the correct matches are A to 2, B to 1 and C to 3. This would win £3.00. There are three ways of winning £1.00 (A1, B2, C3; A2, B3, C1; A3, B1, C2). The two remaining possible matchings (A1, B3, C2; A3, B2, C1) win nothing.

Since the words are not well known, you can assume that players guess at random. For such a player, the probability distribution of the random variable W, the amount won per card, is

Amount won in £	Probability
0	$\frac{2}{6} = \frac{1}{3}$
1	$\frac{3}{6} = \frac{1}{2}$
3	$\frac{1}{6}$

This distribution is illustrated graphically in figure 7.1.

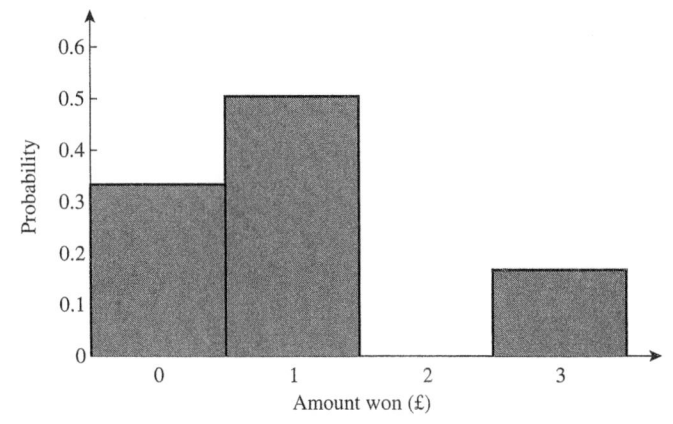

[Figure 7.1: histogram with probability ~1/3 at 0, ~1/2 at 1, ~1/6 at 3]

Figure 7.1

The expected win per card is therefore:

$$E[W] = 0 \times \frac{1}{3} + 1 \times \frac{1}{2} + 3 \times \frac{1}{6} = 1,$$

so that players who guess will lose on average 50p per card.

The variance of the win per card is

$$\text{Var}[W] = 0^2 \times \frac{1}{3} + 1^2 \times \frac{1}{2} + 3^2 \times \frac{1}{6} - 1^2 = 1$$

If a player buys four cards, what could his average win per card be and how likely is each possible value? His total win must be an integer between 0 and 12, so his average win (total divided by 4) must be a multiple of $\frac{1}{4}$ between 0 and 3.

$$P(\text{player's average win per card over four cards} = 0)$$
$$= P(\text{zero matches on each of four cards})$$
$$= \left(\frac{1}{3}\right)^4 = \frac{1}{81}$$

$$P(\text{player's average win per card over four cards} = 0.25)$$
$$P(\text{one match on one card, zero on the other three})$$
$$= \binom{4}{1} \times \frac{1}{2} \times \left(\frac{1}{3}\right)^3 = \frac{2}{27}$$

$$P(\text{player's average win per card over four cards} = 0.5)$$
$$= P(\text{one match on two cards, zero on the other two})$$
$$= \binom{4}{2} \times \left(\frac{1}{2}\right)^2 \times \left(\frac{1}{3}\right)^2 = \frac{1}{6}$$

P(player's average win per card over four cards = 0.75)

= P(one match on three cards, zero on the other three or three matches on one card, zero on the other three)

$$= \binom{4}{3} \times \left(\frac{1}{2}\right)^3 \times \frac{1}{3} + \binom{4}{1} \times \frac{1}{6} \times \left(\frac{1}{3}\right)^3 = \frac{31}{162}$$

Calculations continue in this way, until the distribution tabulated below and illustrated in figure 7.2 is built up.

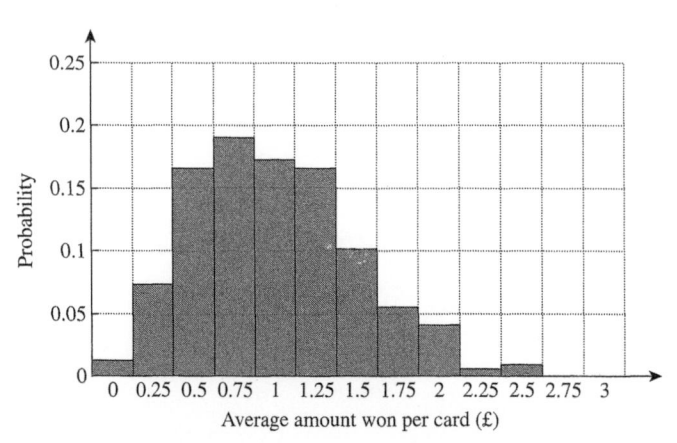

Average amount won per card	Probability
0	$\frac{1}{81}$
0.25	$\frac{2}{27}$
0.5	$\frac{1}{6}$
0.75	$\frac{31}{162}$
1	$\frac{25}{144}$
1.25	$\frac{1}{6}$
1.5	$\frac{11}{108}$
1.75	$\frac{1}{18}$
2	$\frac{1}{24}$
2.25	$\frac{1}{162}$
2.5	$\frac{1}{108}$
2.75	0
3	$\frac{1}{1296}$

Figure 7.2

Imagine many people buying four cards, playing the game with each, and calculating their average win per card over the four cards. The distribution constructed above represents the theoretical proportions with which the different possible results would come up. You can think of each person as taking a sample of size four from the distribution of W and finding the mean of their sample. The distribution constructed above is that of $\overline{W}$, the random variable which represents the mean win per card in a sample of four cards.

How does the distribution of $\overline{W}$ compare with that of W?

- The two distributions have the same range; it is possible to win £3 or £0 on each card, hence have a mean win of £3 or £0 over four cards.
- Both distributions have the same expectation:

$$\begin{aligned} \mathrm{E}[\,\overline{W}\,] &= \mathrm{E}\left[\frac{1}{4}(W_1 + W_2 + W_3 + W_4)\right] \\ &= \frac{1}{4}\left(\mathrm{E}[W_1] + \mathrm{E}[W_2] + \mathrm{E}[W_3] + \mathrm{E}[W_4]\right) \\ &= 1. \end{aligned}$$

($W_1, W_2, \ldots$ are the random variables representing the amounts won on the 1st, 2nd, ... card.)

- The distribution of $\overline{W}$ is more peaked near to its mean than that of W: in fact, the variance of $\overline{W}$ is

$$\begin{aligned} \mathrm{Var}[\,\overline{W}\,] &= \mathrm{Var}\left[\frac{1}{4}(W_1 + W_2 + W_3 + W_4)\right] \\ &= \frac{1}{16}\left(\mathrm{Var}[W_1] + \mathrm{Var}[W_2] + \mathrm{Var}[W_3] + \mathrm{Var}[W_4]\right) \\ &= \frac{1}{4} \end{aligned}$$

so the standard deviation of $\overline{W}$ is half that of W.

- The distribution of $\overline{W}$ is more symmetrical and less skewed, than that of W.

You can repeat the calculations shown above (a computer is very useful) to find the distribution of the mean win per card in larger samples. For instance, the cases where each player buys 16 and 64 cards and calculates the mean win per card are illustrated in figure 7.3 and figure 7.4. (The tables are rather long.)

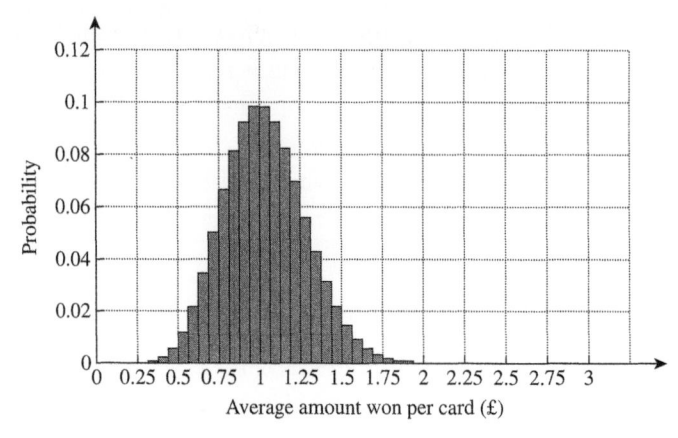

Figure 7.3 Mean win per card in a sample of 16 cards

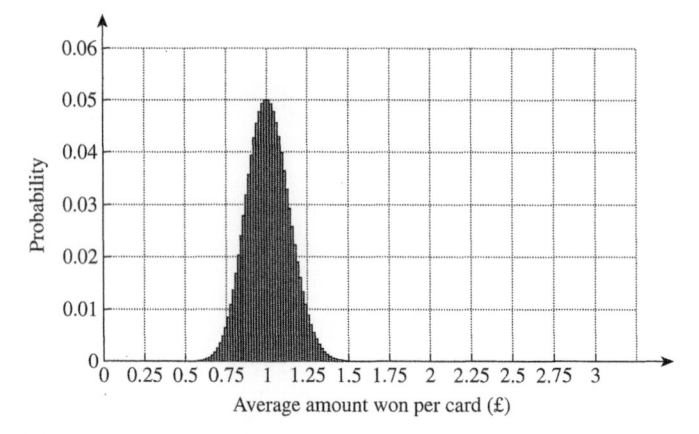

Figure 7.4 Mean win per card in a sample of 64 cards

You know the general results, for a sample of size n,

$$\mathrm{E}[\overline{W}] = \mathrm{E}[W]$$

$$\mathrm{Var}[\overline{W}] = \frac{\mathrm{Var}[W]}{n}$$

so that you would expect,

- for samples of size 16, $\overline{W}$ will have mean 1 and standard deviation $\frac{1}{4}$
- for samples of size 64, $\overline{W}$ will have mean 1 and standard deviation $\frac{1}{8}$.

This explains why the peak of the distribution of the sample mean remains near 1 whatever the sample size. It also explains why, although in principle the distributions of the sample mean for larger sample sizes continue to have the same range, from 0 to 3, the distribution becomes more peaked near to its mean as the sample size increases.

The final feature of the distribution of $\overline{W}$ noted above was that it is more symmetrical and less skewed, than that of W: this continues as the sample size increases. In fact a stronger statement can be made: for large sample sizes, the shape of the distribution appears to be approaching that of the Normal distribution. Figure 7.5 and figure 7.6 show again the distributions of $\overline{W}$ with sample sizes 16 and 64: superimposed are the Normal distribution curves with the same mean and variance as $\overline{W}$ in each case.

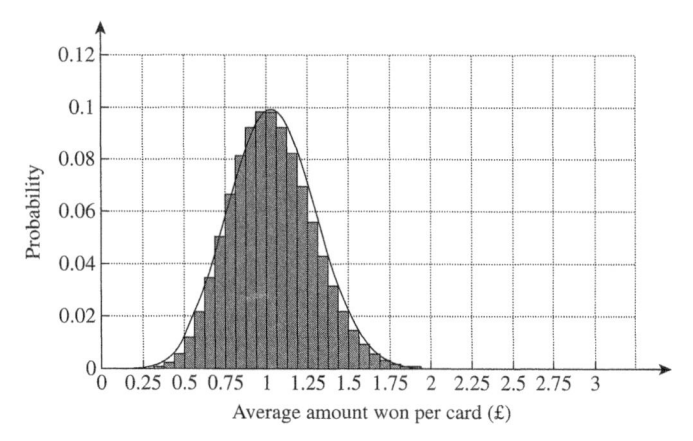

Figure 7.5

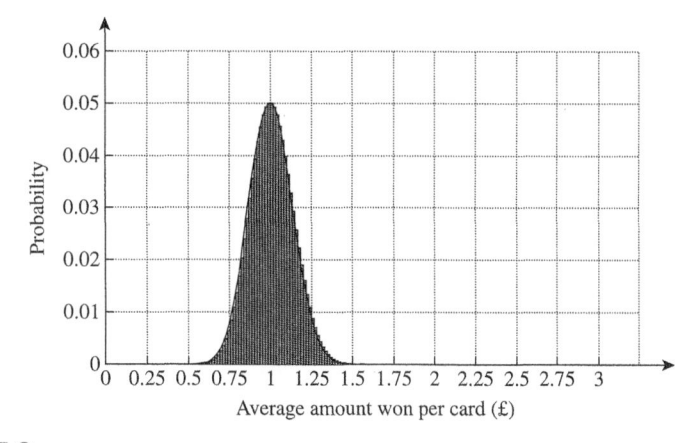

Figure 7.6

Visually, it appears that for a sample size of 64, the Normal curve is an excellent fit. It is surprisingly good even for a sample size of 16. Of course the distribution of $\overline{W}$ remains discrete, while the Normal distribution is continuous, so the two distributions do not become 'the same', but for the purposes of hypothesis testing and constructing confidence intervals, your interest in the distribution of $\overline{W}$ will be to enable you to calculate tail probabilities. For instance, you may wish to find its lower critical value at the 5% level, that is the value of a for which $P(\overline{W} < a) = 0.05$.

The table on page 140 shows part of the exact distribution (to 6 decimal places) of $\overline{W}$ for samples of size 64, together with cumulative probabilities.

a	$P(\overline{W}=a)$	$P(\overline{W}\leqslant a)$	a	$P(\overline{W}=a)$	$P(\overline{W}\leqslant a)$
0.125	0.000 000	0.000 000	0.484 375	0.000 010	0.000 024
0.140 625	0.000 000	0.000 000	0.5	0.000 017	0.000 041
0.156 25	0.000 000	0.000 000	0.515 625	0.000 028	0.000 069
0.171 875	0.000 000	0.000 000	0.531 25	0.000 044	0.000 113
0.187 5	0.000 000	0.000 000	0.546 875	0.000 070	0.000 184
0.203 125	0.000 000	0.000 000	0.562 5	0.000 110	0.000 294
0.218 75	0.000 000	0.000 000	0.578 125	0.000 169	0.000 462
0.234 375	0.000 000	0.000 000	0.593 75	0.000 255	0.000 718
0.25	0.000 000	0.000 000	0.609 375	0.000 380	0.001 098
0.265 625	0.000 000	0.000 000	0.625	0.000 557	0.001 654
0.281 25	0.000 000	0.000 000	0.640 625	0.000 804	0.002 458
0.296 875	0.000 000	0.000 000	0.656 25	0.001 142	0.003 600
0.312 5	0.000 000	0.000 000	0.671 875	0.001 597	0.005 196
0.328 125	0.000 000	0.000 000	0.687 5	0.002 199	0.007 395
0.343 75	0.000 000	0.000 000	0.703 125	0.002 980	0.010 375
0.359 375	0.000 000	0.000 000	0.718 75	0.003 978	0.014 353
0.375	0.000 000	0.000 000	0.734 375	0.005 227	0.019 580
0.390 625	0.000 000	0.000 001	0.75	0.006 762	0.026 342
0.406 25	0.000 001	0.000 001	0.765 625	0.008 612	0.034 954
0.421 875	0.000 001	0.000 003	0.781 25	0.010 799	0.045 754
0.437 5	0.000 002	0.000 005	0.796 875	0.013 332	0.059 085
0.453 125	0.000 004	0.000 008	0.812 5	0.016 203	0.075 288
0.468 75	0.000 006	0.000 014	0.828 125	0.019 388	0.094 676

From this the critical value can be read off:
$$P(\overline{W} \leqslant 0.78125) \leqslant 0.05 \text{ (and } P(\overline{W} \leqslant 0.796875) > 0.05).$$

Using the Normal approximation $\overline{W} \approx N(1, \frac{1}{64})$, the critical value is given by (using 1.645 as the 5% one-tailed critical value for the standard Normal distribution)
$$1 - 1.645 \times \frac{1}{8} = 0.794375$$
which gives precisely the same set of samples in the critical region as the exact critical value, since the sample value of $\overline{W}$ can take only the values listed in the table above and
$$0.78125 < 0.794375 < 0.796875.$$

This example illustrates the claim of *The Central Limit Theorem*:

> Assume random samples of size n are drawn from a distribution, which need not be Normal, with mean μ and variance σ^2.
>
> For large n, the probability of the sample mean being in a given range can be well-approximated by the corresponding area under the Normal density function $N\left(\mu, \frac{\sigma^2}{n}\right)$.

The organisers of the trivia game could ask how much money they are likely to make if they sell more than 2500 cards (and none of their customers has an absurdly large vocabulary). The number of cards they sell is their sample size so, if they sell more than 2500 cards, the average win per card has variance less than $\frac{1}{2500}$ and therefore a standard deviation less than $\frac{1}{50}$. The probability that the average win per card will be outside the range
$$1 - 2.576 \times \frac{1}{50} \approx 0.95 \text{ to } 1 + 2.576 \times \frac{1}{50} \approx 1.05$$
is less than 1%, since 2.576 is the two-tailed 1% critical value for the standard Normal distribution.

The organisers' profit is therefore very unlikely to be outside the range of 45p to 55p per card they sell and, if they sell a lot more than 2500 cards, this range could be narrowed.

Tests and confidence intervals when the variances are known

In studying unpaired t tests, you had to make the assumption that the variance in the population of the random variable you were sampling was the same in both conditions. You then estimated this common variance from the two samples. However, there are some situations in which you know the variance of the whole population and you can use this information in a hypothesis test or in constructing confidence intervals.

For instance, it may be that, before the ability of the maths class to estimate one minute was tested (see page 114), extensive tests were conducted which determined that, in the school population as a whole, students' estimated minutes are Normally distributed and have a standard deviation of 7.42 seconds. You are testing the hypotheses:

H_0: There is no difference between the mean of people's estimates of one minute before and after lunch.

H_1: After lunch, the mean of people's estimates of one minute tends to be shorter than before lunch.

But you can now make the assumption that people's estimates of one minute are Normally distributed with standard deviation 7.42.

The null hypothesis implies that before-lunch and after-lunch estimates have distributions $N(\mu, 7.42^2)$ where μ is the common mean asserted by the null hypothesis. With this assumption, the mean of the 24 before-lunch estimates has distribution

$$\overline{X} \sim N\left(\mu, \frac{7.42^2}{24}\right)$$

and the mean of the 22 after-lunch estimates has distribution

$$\overline{Y} \sim N\left(\mu, \frac{7.42^2}{22}\right)$$

The distribution of the difference of the two sample means is therefore

$$\overline{X} - \overline{Y} \sim N\left(0, \frac{7.42^2}{24} + \frac{7.42^2}{22}\right).$$

In *Statistics 2* you considered hypothesis tests with the Normal distribution: if X has distribution $N(0, \sigma^2)$, where the variance σ^2 is known, then the test statistic $\dfrac{X}{\sigma}$ has the standard Normal distribution, $N(0, 1)$. The test statistic here is

$$\frac{\overline{X} - \overline{Y}}{\sqrt{\dfrac{7.42^2}{24} + \dfrac{7.42^2}{22}}} = \frac{\overline{X} - \overline{Y}}{7.42\sqrt{\dfrac{1}{24} + \dfrac{1}{22}}}$$

With the data used in the example on page 114, $\overline{x} = 51.542$ and $\overline{y} = 47.909$, so the test statistic has the value

$$\frac{51.542 - 47.909}{7.42\sqrt{\dfrac{1}{24} + \dfrac{1}{22}}} = 1.659.$$

The critical region for a one-tailed test at the 5% significance level for the standard Normal distribution is $z > 1.645$. In this case, since $1.659 > 1.645$, you reject the null hypothesis and accept the alternative, that the after-lunch times are shorter than the before-lunch times.

Different known variances for the two samples

Alternatively, you might know separately the variances of the populations from which each sample was drawn, where these need not be the same.

Suppose there are two machines in a factory. The first is a high-accuracy machine, which produces bolts with radii which are Normally distributed with standard deviation 0.052 mm. The second is a lower-accuracy machine, producing washers with internal radii which are Normally distributed with standard deviation 0.172 mm. Both machines are adjustable to produce components with different radii, but today they are supposed to be set so that the high-accuracy machine produces bolts with radii 2 mm smaller than the internal radii of the washers produced by the low-accuracy machine.

To check whether the setting is correct, a sample of components is taken from each machine, and the radius of each measured. The results are shown in the following table.

Radii of bolts from high-accuracy machine (mm)
8.42,   8.21,   8.29,   8.31,   8.25,   8.38,   8.29

Internal radii of washers from low-accuracy machine (mm)
10.32,   10.12,   9.98,   10.09,   10.57,   10.49,   10.10,   10.28,   10.35

You are testing the hypotheses:

H_0: The mean radius of the bolts being produced is 2 mm less than the mean internal radius of the washers being produced.

H_1: The mean radius of the bolts and the mean internal radius of the washers being produced do not differ by 2 mm.

You can assume that the radii of the components being produced by each machine are Normally distributed with the standard deviations given above.

If X_W denotes the internal radius of a washer, and X_B the radius of a bolt, what is the distribution of the sample statistic $\overline{X}_W - \overline{X}_B$?

With the assumptions stated, the mean internal radius of nine washers from the low-accuracy machine has distribution

$$\overline{X}_W \sim N\left(\mu_W, \frac{0.172^2}{9}\right)$$

where μ_W is the mean internal radius of the washers.

Similarly, the mean radius of seven bolts from the high-accuracy machine has distribution

$$\overline{X}_B \sim N\left(\mu_B, \frac{0.052^2}{7}\right)$$

where μ_B is the mean radius of the bolts.

The distribution of the difference of the two sample means is therefore

$$\overline{X}_W - \overline{X}_B \sim N\left(\mu_W - \mu_B, \frac{0.172^2}{9} + \frac{0.052^2}{7}\right).$$

The null hypothesis then states that $\mu_W - \mu_B = 2$ and so, if the null hypothesis is true

$$\overline{X}_W - \overline{X}_B \sim N\left(2, \frac{0.172^2}{9} + \frac{0.052^2}{7}\right).$$

Therefore, the test statistic

$$\frac{\overline{X}_W - \overline{X}_B - 2}{\sqrt{\frac{0.172^2}{9} + \frac{0.052^2}{7}}}.$$

has a standard Normal distribution.

In this case $\bar{x}_W = 10.256$ and $\bar{x}_B = 8.307$, so the test statistic is

$$\frac{10.256 - 8.307 - 2}{\sqrt{\frac{0.172^2}{9} + \frac{0.052^2}{7}}} = -0.84.$$

The critical region for a two-tailed test with the standard Normal distribution at the 5% significance level is $z > 1.96$ or $z < -1.96$, and so here, since $-1.96 < -0.84 < 1.96$, you accept the null hypothesis that the machines are correctly set.

You can use the same data to construct a 95% confidence interval for the difference in mean radii being produced by the two machines. You saw above that the distribution of the difference of the two sample means is

$$\overline{X}_W - \overline{X}_B \sim N\left(\mu_W - \mu_B, \frac{0.172^2}{9} + \frac{0.052^2}{7}\right)$$

so that:

$$P\left(-1.96 < \frac{(\overline{X}_W - \overline{X}_B) - (\mu_W - \mu_B)}{\sqrt{\frac{0.172^2}{9} + \frac{0.052^2}{7}}} < 1.96\right) = 0.95$$

since 1.96 is the two-tailed 5% critical value for the standard Normal distribution.

The confidence interval is therefore

$$(\bar{x}_W - \bar{x}_B) - 1.96\sqrt{\tfrac{0.172^2}{9} + \tfrac{0.052^2}{7}} < (\mu_W - \mu_B) < (\bar{x}_W - \bar{x}_B) + 1.96\sqrt{\tfrac{0.172^2}{9} + \tfrac{0.052^2}{7}}.$$

With the values $\bar{x}_W = 10.256$ and $\bar{x}_B = 8.307$, this is:

$$1.83 < \mu_W - \mu_B < 2.07.$$

Summary: known variances

The null hypothesis is:

H_0: The difference between the means of the random variable in the two conditions is $(\mu_1 - \mu_2)$.

If

- the random variable, X, has a Normal distribution in each condition
- $\overline{X}_1$ and $\overline{X}_2$ are the means of the samples in the two conditions
- n_1 and n_2 are the sizes of these samples
- σ_1 and σ_2 are the known standard deviations of the random variables X_1 and X_2,

then the test statistic is:

$$\frac{\overline{X}_1 - \overline{X}_2 - (\mu_1 - \mu_2)}{\sqrt{\dfrac{\sigma_1^2}{n_1} + \dfrac{\sigma_2^2}{n_2}}}$$

which has a standard Normal distribution $N(0, 1)$.

In the same situation, a $(100 - a)\%$ confidence interval for the difference of the means in the two conditions is:

$$(\bar{x}_1 - \bar{x}_2) - z_a\sqrt{\frac{\sigma_1^2}{n_1} + \frac{\sigma_2^2}{n_2}} < \mu_1 - \mu_2 < (\bar{x}_1 - \bar{x}_2) + z_a\sqrt{\frac{\sigma_1^2}{n_1} + \frac{\sigma_2^2}{n_2}}$$

where z_a is the two-sided $a\%$ critical value for the standard Normal distribution.

If the variances in the two conditions are known and equal, each distribution having standard deviation σ, then the test statistic simplifies to

$$\frac{(\overline{X}_1 - \overline{X}_2) - (\mu_1 - \mu_2)}{\sigma\sqrt{\dfrac{1}{n_1} + \dfrac{1}{n_2}}}$$

and the confidence interval to

$$(\bar{x}_1 - \bar{x}_2) - z_a\sigma\sqrt{\frac{1}{n_1} + \frac{1}{n_2}} < \mu_1 - \mu_2 < (\bar{x}_1 - \bar{x}_2) + z_a\sigma\sqrt{\frac{1}{n_1} + \frac{1}{n_2}}.$$

Remember you can do the same sort of thing for the paired test, with null hypothesis:

H₀: The difference between the values of the random variable in the two conditions has mean d.

If

- the difference, X, between the pairs of values of the random variable in the two conditions has a Normal distribution
- $\overline{X}$ is the mean of X
- σ is the known standard deviation of X
- n is the size of the sample

then the test statistic is $\dfrac{\overline{X} - d}{\frac{\sigma}{\sqrt{n}}}$ which has a standard Normal distribution, N(0, 1).

In the same situation, a $(100 - a)$% confidence interval for the mean difference between the two conditions is:

$$\overline{X} - z_a \frac{\sigma}{\sqrt{n}} < \mu_1 - \mu_2 < \overline{X} + z_a \frac{\sigma}{\sqrt{n}}$$

where z_a is the two-sided a% critical value for the standard Normal distribution.

Note

This situation – where you know the variance of the difference between the random variables in the two conditions – is very unlikely to arise in practice. Knowing the variance of the random variable in each condition separately is not sufficient, as the point of pairing is that the variable is not independently measured in the two conditions. Thus in a paired test, if X_1 and X_2 represent the random variable in the two conditions, $\text{Var}[X_1 - X_2] \neq \text{Var}[X_1] + \text{Var}[X_2]$.

It may have occurred to you that, in fact, the examples you have considered so far in this chapter were rather contrived, and that is not surprising: it is difficult to think of circumstances where the tests described here actually apply – why should you know the variances of the distributions, but not their means? This does not mean that you have been wasting your time, however: the importance of this technique is seen in the next section.

Tests with large samples

When you used the *t* distribution for testing hypotheses about differences between means and for constructing confidence intervals for the difference between means, you had to make the assumptions

1 the underlying variables are Normally distributed

2 the variables have a common variance.

In many situations where you want to test hypotheses or construct confidence intervals, these assumptions do not hold. Fortunately, provided that a large sample is available, these assumptions are not essential.

1 The Central Limit Theorem says that, for large sample sizes, even when a variable does not have a Normal distribution, its sample mean is approximately Normally distributed.

2 In general, the larger the sample being used, the smaller the error made in assuming that the population has exactly the variance given by its sample estimate.

The tests discussed so far in this chapter, which assume Normally-distributed variables with known variances, will therefore all give sensible results for large samples, even where the underlying variables are not Normally distributed and the variances are not known, but must be estimated from the samples. As a rule of thumb, sample sizes of 50 or so are large enough for this approximation to be reasonable – although this will obviously depend on how non-Normal the underlying distributions are. In many situations the approximation will be justified with substantially smaller samples.

Even where it cannot be assumed that the underlying variables have a common variance, but where large samples are available, separate population variances can be estimated and used as if they were the actual population variances.

EXAMPLE 7.1

Smartos tubes are filled by two different machines. A sample of tubes filled by each machine is taken and the Smartos in each tube are counted. The results are given in the table below.

Number of Smartos per tube	39	40	41	42	43	Total
Frequency in machine A sample	17	23	35	31	27	133
Frequency in machine B sample	21	18	41	39	19	138

Assuming a common variance for the numbers of Smartos per tube produced by the machines, construct a 98% confidence interval for the difference in the mean number of Smartos in the tubes produced by the two machines.

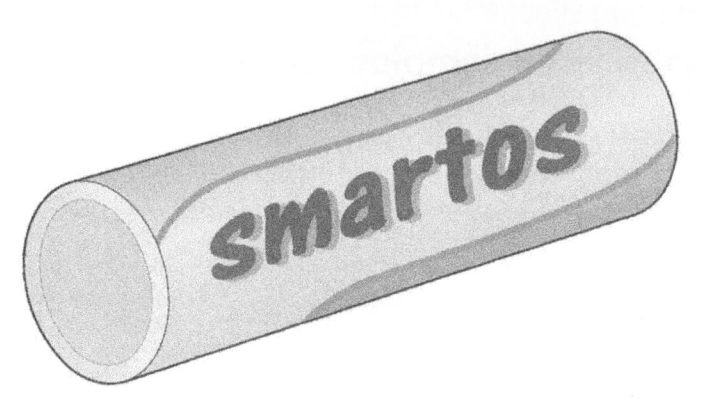

SOLUTION

Here, you certainly cannot assume that the distribution of the number of Smartos per tube is Normal since it is a discrete variable. Nonetheless, because the sample size is large, and you are told that there is a common variance in the two conditions, you can assume that the statistic

$$\frac{(\bar{X}_A - \bar{X}_B) - (\mu_A - \mu_B)}{S\sqrt{\frac{1}{n_A} + \frac{1}{n_B}}}$$

has approximately a standard Normal distribution. ($\bar{X}_A$ and $\bar{X}_B$ are the means of the numbers of Smartos per tube in the sample from each machine, S^2 is the pooled-sample estimator of the common variance, n_A and n_B are the sizes of each sample, and μ_A and μ_B are the true mean numbers of Smartos produced by the two machines.)

The two-tailed 2% critical value for the standard Normal distribution is 2.326, so that for approximately 98% of samples

$$-2.326 < \frac{(\bar{X}_A - \bar{X}_B) - (\mu_A - \mu_B)}{S\sqrt{\frac{1}{n_A} + \frac{1}{n_B}}} < 2.326.$$

That is, an approximate 98% confidence interval for the difference between the true mean numbers is

$$(\bar{x}_A - \bar{x}_B) - 2.326 s\sqrt{\frac{1}{n_A} + \frac{1}{n_B}} < \mu_A - \mu_B < (\bar{x}_A - \bar{x}_B) + 2.326 s\sqrt{\frac{1}{n_A} + \frac{1}{n_B}}.$$

Here

$$n_A = 133, \quad \bar{x}_A = 41.2105, \quad s_A = 1.3030$$
$$n_B = 138, \quad \bar{x}_B = 41.1232, \quad s_B = 1.2525$$

so that

$$s = \sqrt{\frac{132 \times 1.3030^2 + 137 \times 1.2525^2}{133 + 138 - 2}} = 1.2775$$

and so the confidence interval is

$$-0.2738 < \mu_A - \mu_B < 0.4484.$$

General procedure for large samples

Unpaired design

In an experiment with an unpaired design a test of the hypothesis:

H_0: The difference between the means in the two conditions is δ

uses data from two samples, one taken in each condition. These data are summarised by

- $\overline{X}_1$ and $\overline{X}_2$, the means of the samples in the two conditions
- n_1 and n_2, the sizes of these samples
- S_1^2 and S_2^2, the sample estimators of the variances in the two conditions.

The test statistic is

$$\frac{\overline{X}_1 - \overline{X}_2 - \delta}{\sqrt{\dfrac{S_1^2}{n_1} + \dfrac{S_2^2}{n_2}}}$$

which has approximately a standard Normal distribution, if the sample size is large.

In the same situation, a $(100 - a)\%$ confidence interval for the difference of the means in the two conditions is

$$(\overline{x}_1 - \overline{x}_2) - z_a\sqrt{\dfrac{s_1^2}{n_1} + \dfrac{s_2^2}{n_2}} < \mu_1 - \mu_2 < (\overline{x}_1 - \overline{x}_2) + z_a\sqrt{\dfrac{s_1^2}{n_1} + \dfrac{s_2^2}{n_2}}$$

where z_a is the two-sided $a\%$ critical value for the standard Normal distribution.

Special cases

1. If you know that the variances in the two conditions have the values of σ_1^2 and σ_2^2 these values should be used instead of the sample estimates s_1^2 and s_2^2 in the test statistic and the confidence limits.

2. If you believe that the variances are the same in the two conditions you use the statistic

$$\frac{\overline{X}_1 - \overline{X}_2 - \delta}{S\sqrt{\dfrac{1}{n_1} + \dfrac{1}{n_2}}}$$

where $S^2 = \dfrac{(n_1 - 1)S_1^2 + (n_2 - 1)S_2^2}{(n_1 + n_2 - 2)}$ is the pooled sample variance estimate.

Similarly, the confidence interval in this case is

$$(\overline{x}_1 - \overline{x}_2) - z_a s\sqrt{\dfrac{1}{n_1} + \dfrac{1}{n_2}} < \mu_1 - \mu_2 < (\overline{x}_1 - \overline{x}_2) + z_a s\sqrt{\dfrac{1}{n_1} + \dfrac{1}{n_2}}.$$

Paired design

In an experiment with a paired design a test of the hypothesis:

H₀: The mean difference between variables in the two conditions is δ,

uses data summarised by

- $\overline{D}$, the mean of the sample differences between the two conditions
- n, the size of the samples
- S^2, the sample estimator of the variance of the differences between the two conditions.

The test statistic is $\dfrac{\overline{D} - \delta}{\dfrac{S}{\sqrt{n}}}$, which has an approximately standard Normal distribution if the sample size is large.

In the same situation, a $(100 - a)\%$ confidence interval for the difference of the means in the two conditions is

$$\overline{d} - z_a \frac{s}{\sqrt{n}} < \delta < \overline{d} + z_a \frac{s}{\sqrt{n}}$$

where z_a is the two-sided $a\%$ critical value for the standard Normal distribution.

Special case

If you know that the variance of the difference between the two conditions has the value σ^2 this value should be used instead of the sample estimate s^2 in the test statistic and the confidence limits.

EXERCISE 7A

1. There is a misty patch of Irish turf which is supposed to produce multi-leaved clovers with greater regularity than elsewhere. To test this hypothesis, clover stems were collected from this patch of turf, and from a large selection of other locations, and their leaves counted. The frequencies with which each number of leaves arose in the two conditions are shown in the table below.

   Sample from the misty Irish turf

Number of leaves	3	4	5	6
Frequency	227	50	12	2

   Sample from elsewhere

Number of leaves	3	4	5	6
Frequency	433	68	7	3

   (i) Use these data to test the hypothesis that the spot described is special.

   (ii) What assumptions are you making?

2. It has been suggested that, although the number of eggs laid by female hedgesparrows varies widely among birds, individual birds tend to lay more eggs each year that they breed. A sample of 162 female birds have

their nests examined in two successive years, and the change in the number of eggs is recorded. The frequency of each change is recorded in the table below.

Change in number of eggs	−2	−1	0	1	2
Frequency	4	27	77	43	11

Use these data to construct a confidence interval for the mean increase in numbers of eggs per year, stating clearly the assumptions you are making.

3 A bank is deciding whether to introduce a new system for their cashiers. It is only worth the expense if it will reduce the average waiting time by a minute or more. They survey the waiting times for a sample of their customers in a branch and then, after introducing a trial run of the new system in the same branch, resurvey the waiting times. The results of the two surveys are shown in the table below.

Minutes in queue	Frequency With old system	With new system
0	33	49
1	57	58
2	44	44
3	35	24
4	17	12
5	13	2
6	10	4
7	6	1
8	5	0
9	5	0
10	1	1
11	4	1
12	3	0
13	3	0

Test the hypothesis that the waiting times have been reduced by at least one minute, on average, under the new system, stating the assumptions you are making.

4 Two very long shafts fitted to a turbine need to be very accurately the same length, but they cannot be moved to compare them, and are difficult to measure. The engineer whose job it is to check the lengths adopts the following procedure: ten separate measurements are made of each shaft, by a process of which the result is a Normal variable with mean equal to the true length of the shaft and with standard deviation 3 hundredths of a millimetre.

The measurements made in one check are listed in the table below. (Lengths are given as hundredths of a millimetre from the nominal length of the shaft.)

First shaft	+6	+2	+7	−1	+4
Second shaft	−1	+3	+3	+5	−2
First shaft	−3	+3	+2	=7	+7
Second shaft	−4	+4	+2	−3	+0

Test the hypothesis that the two shafts have the same length.

5 The Governor of the Bank of England is attempting to keep the UK discount rate $\frac{1}{4}$% above the Lombard rate. The table below shows the frequency with which different combinations of rates are observed in the market at 12 noon each day over a period of four months.

	UK discount rate (%)								
Lombard rate (%)		5	5.25	5.5	5.75	6	6.25	6.5	6.75	7
	5	1	12	7	1					
	5.25	5	7	9	2					
	5.5		2	2	15	5	4	1		
	5.75				4	4	10			
	6						3	8	2	
	6.25					1		3	4	
	6.5							1	5	4

(i) Use these data to test the hypothesis that the UK rate is on average $\frac{1}{4}$% above the Lombard rate.

(ii) What assumptions are you making? How can this situation be viewed as a random sample from a particular distribution?

6 In an attempt to redesign a combustion chamber, it is necessary to find the difference between the maximum inside and outside temperatures of the casing. The combustion process is rather variable from one ignition to another: in fact the variance of the maximum temperature, in °C, inside the chamber is 3940 and the variance of the temperature of the outer casing is 2710.

Construct a confidence interval for the difference between mean inside and outside temperatures using the data below from a series of experimental ignitions.

Nine ignitions: maximum inside temp (°C)

| 6870 | 6940 | 7010 | 6960 | 6890 |
| 6940 | 6950 | 6920 | 6920 | |

Six ignitions: maximum outside temp (°C)

| 6710 | 6730 | 6680 | 6670 | 6680 |
| 6620 | | | | |

7 A new machine for packing matches into boxes has been delivered. It is supposed to be more accurate – that is, the variation in the number of matches it inserts into each box is less, but the factory manager also wants to check that the new machine is not extravagantly putting a higher average number of matches into each box. She takes a sample of boxes produced by the old and new machines and counts the frequency with which each number of matches arises. The results are given in the table.

Number of matches	40	41	42	43	44
Frequency with old machine	96	42	17	9	2
Frequency with new machine	65	107	19	0	0

Test the hypothesis that the two machines have equal means, stating the assumptions you are using.

8 In an attempt to decide whether a new feeding regime increases the average weight of young salmon in a fish farm, a sample of 165 fish fed in the usual way is weighed. The weights, x_i, in grams, of these fish are summarised by the figures

$$\sum_{i=1}^{165} x_i = 11\,774 \qquad \sum_{i=1}^{165} x_i^2 = 872\,308.$$

A sample of 74 fish is bred with the new feeding regime and their weights, y_i, in grams, are summarised by

$$\sum_{i=1}^{74} y_i = 5491 \qquad \sum_{i=1}^{74} y_i^2 = 409\,272.$$

(i) Test the hypothesis that the average weight of the salmon is higher under the new regime:
 (a) assuming that the variance of their weights is unchanged
 (b) estimating the variance separately in each condition.

(ii) Comment on your results.

9 In an experiment to determine whether presenting a list of words alphabetically or in random order causes them to be remembered more easily, two groups of subjects are given such lists of 30 words to study for one minute. After a distracting task, the subjects are then asked to recall as many words as possible in one minute. The numbers of words recalled in each condition are as follows.

Words recalled	14	15	16	17	18	19	20	21
Frequency: random list	0	0	0	1	10	12	34	78
Frequency: alphabetical list	3	2	23	57	17	21	19	33

Words recalled	22	23	24	25	26	27	28
Frequency: random list	55	22	29	11	2	1	2
Frequency: alphabetical list	48	26	19	4	8	0	0

Note: The bimodal nature of the distribution with an alphabetical list is because subjects use two different strategies for recall in this case.

(i) Test the hypothesis that there is no difference on average in the number of words recalled in the two conditions. State the assumptions that you are making.

(ii) Suggest a paired design for testing this hypothesis.

10 A new golf club is advertised with the claim 'add at least 20 metres to your drive', and a golfers' magazine is testing this claim.

It finds that the new club does enable its sample of golfers to hit further on average: the 120 golfers who used the new club on the test range hit the ball 367 metres on average, while the 142 golfers who used the old club hit only 353 metres on average. The new club was considerably more erratic in its performance, though. The sample estimates of the standard deviation of the length of the drives were 46 metres with the new club, and 27 metres with the old.

(i) Use these data to test the hypotheses

  (a) The new club enables golfers to drive further, on average, than the old.

  (b) The new club enables golfers to drive at least 20 metres further, on average, than the old.

(ii) Construct a confidence interval for the increase in mean distance driven with the new club.

EXERCISE 7B

In this exercise you are expected to choose the appropriate technique for yourself.

1 Two friends, Mary and Susan, are planning to buy a carpet for the living room in their flat. They therefore measure the length and width of their room. The errors in their measurements may be taken as having Normal distributions. Mary's distribution has mean 0 and standard deviation 3, Susan's has mean 0 and standard deviation 2 (all units are cm).

Mary measures the length of the room on four different occasions, obtaining measurements of 425 cm, 427 cm, 422 cm and 426 cm. Susan measures the width of the room once, obtaining a measurement of 366 cm.

Giving your answers in centimetres correct to 1 decimal place, find

(i) a one-sided 95% confidence interval giving a lower bound for the length of the room

(ii) a symmetrical two-sided 99% confidence interval for the width of the room.

One of Susan's friends, calling her calculated interval (l, u), states 'there is probability 99% that the width of the room is between l and u'. Explain why this interpretation is wrong. What is the correct interpretation?

2 For reasons of economy, the manufacturers of an electrical appliance wished to make an adjustment to one of its components. Before finally deciding whether to do so, the effect of the adjustment on the resistance of the component was assessed.

(i) At one factory, the resistances of ten such components selected at random were measured both before and after the adjustment. The results were as follows.

Component	Resistance (ohms) before adjustment	Resistance (ohms) after adjustment
1	37.7	41.0
2	42.1	47.8
3	44.2	44.9
4	35.2	39.6
5	38.6	45.8
6	43.2	45.9
7	47.3	49.6
8	35.9	38.7
9	43.7	44.5
10	42.4	49.1

Test at the 5% significance level whether there is a difference in mean resistance due to the adjustment.

(ii) At another factory, twenty of the components were selected at random and ten of these were chosen at random to receive the adjustment. The resistances of the components were measured, with the following results.

Unadjusted component's resistance (ohms), x	Adjusted component's resistance (ohms), y
42.3	49.2
35.3	44.8
44.3	39.5
42.0	47.7
37.6	39.9
43.6	44.4
35.8	49.3
47.6	38.8
43.1	45.8
38.5	45.7

(For information: $\Sigma x = 410.1$, $\Sigma x^2 = 16\,963.85$, $\Sigma y = 445.1$, $\Sigma y^2 = 19\,948.65$)

Test at the 5% significance level whether there is a difference between the mean resistances in each group, stating carefully the assumption you make about the underlying variances.

(iii) Explain clearly which of the two analyses gives better information and why.

3 Investigations are being made of the time taken to bring water to the boil in a large urn in a cafeteria. It is known that this time varies somewhat and that the variations may be accounted for by taking the boiling time to be Normally distributed.

(i) The boiling times in minutes on ten randomly chosen occasions were 20.2, 17.8, 23.6, 21.1, 19.4, 19.6, 20.9, 20.0, 18.9, 20.3. Find a two-sided symmetrical 95% confidence interval for the true mean boiling time.

(ii) A second urn is acquired, for which the boiling time may again be taken as Normally distributed but with a possibly different mean. A random sample of 20 boiling times for the second urn is found to have mean 19.33 minutes. Information from the manufacturers states that the *true* standard deviation of boiling time is 0.9 minutes for both urns. Assuming this is indeed correct, examine at the 5% level of significance whether the true mean boiling times for the two urns differ.

(iii) Suppose instead that the boiling times for the urns may not be taken as Normally distributed. State the name of, and *briefly* describe, a statistical procedure that could be used to examine whether the two urns have, overall, the same boiling times.

4 Two personal computers are being compared with respect to their performances in running typical jobs. Eight typical jobs selected at random are run on each computer. The table shows the values of a composite unit of performance for each job on each computer.

Job	Computer A	Computer B
1	214	203
2	198	202
3	222	216
4	206	218
5	194	185
6	236	224
7	219	213
8	210	212

It is desired to examine whether the mean performance for typical jobs is the same for each computer.

(i) State formally the null and alternative hypotheses that are being tested.

(ii) State an appropriate assumption concerning the underlying Normality.

(iii) Carry out the test, using a 1% level of significance.

(iv) Provide a symmetrical two-sided 95% confidence interval for the difference between the mean performance times.

5 The central business district of a town is served by two railway stations A and B. Part of a study is to examine whether the mean daily number of passengers arriving at station A during the morning peak period is the same as the corresponding average at station B. Counts were taken at station A for a random sample of 8 working days and at station B for a separate random sample of 12 working days, with the following results for the numbers of passengers arriving during the morning peak period.

Station A

| 1486 | 1529 | 1512 | 1540 | 1506 | 1464 |
| 1495 | 1502 |

Section B

| 1475 | 1497 | 1460 | 1478 | 1520 | 1473 |
| 1449 | 1480 | 1503 | 1462 | 1474 | 1486 |

(i) State formally the null and alternative hypotheses that are to be tested.

(ii) State an appropriate assumption concerning underlying Normality.

(iii) State a further necessary assumption concerning the underlying distributions.

(iv) Carry out the test, using a 5% level of significance.

(v) Suppose that, in a test situation such as this, the *true* variances of the underlying distributions were known. Outline *briefly* how the test would be conducted.

6 A liquid product is sold in containers. The containers are filled by a machine. The volumes of liquid (in millilitres) in a random sample of six containers were found to be

497.8   501.4   500.2   500.8   498.3   500.0.

After an overhaul of the machine, the volumes (in millilitres) in a random sample of 11 containers were found to be

501.1   499.6   500.3   500.9   498.7   502.1
500.4   499.7   501.0   500.1   499.3.

It is desired to examine whether the average volume of liquid delivered to a container by the machine is the same after overhaul as it was before.

(i) State the assumptions that are necessary for the use of the customary t test.

(ii) State formally the null and alternative hypotheses that are to be tested.

(iii) Carry out the t test, using a 5% level of significance.

(iv) Discuss briefly which of the assumptions in part (i) is the least likely to be valid in practice and why.

7 A railway station has a telephone enquiry office. The length of time, in minutes, taken to deal with any caller's enquiry is independent of that for all other callers and is modelled by the continuous random variable X with probability density function

$$f(x) = \frac{1}{4} x e^{-x/2} \qquad 0 \leqslant x < \infty.$$

(i) Show that the mean of X is 4.

Reminder: the limit of $x^m e^{-x}$ as $x \to \infty$ is zero.

(ii) You are now given that the variance of X is 8. State the mean and variance of T, the combined time for dealing with eight callers.

(iii) Explain why a Normal random variable will provide a good approximation to the distribution of T.

(iv) An attempt is made to improve the modelling. The detailed form of the X variable is discarded, though it is still believed appropriate to use a random variable whose variance is twice the mean. Denoting this mean by θ (and therefore the variance by 2θ), write down the parameters of the Normal distribution that is now to be used as an approximation to the distribution of T. Deduce that, according to this distribution,

$$P\left(\frac{T - 8\theta}{4\sqrt{\theta}} < 1.645\right) = 0.95.$$

(v) The combined time for dealing with eight callers is measured once and found to be 25 minutes. Show that, using the distribution in part (iv), the lower limit of a one-sided 95% confidence interval for θ is a solution of the equation

$$64\theta^2 - 443.2964\theta + 625 = 0.$$

What does the other solution of this equation represent?

8 An inspector is examining the lengths of time taken to complete various routine tasks by employees who have been trained in two different ways. He wants to examine whether the two methods lead, overall, to the same times. Ten different tasks have been prepared. Each task is undertaken by a randomly selected employee who has been trained by method A and by a randomly selected employee who has been trained by method B. The times to completion, in minutes, are shown in the table.

Task	Time taken A employee	Time taken B employee
1	33.4	27.1
2	41.0	42.0
3	26.8	23.0
4	37.2	33.9
5	47.4	38.1
6	27.5	27.7
7	34.0	32.7
8	28.4	23.2
9	35.0	35.0
10	20.7	22.7

(i) Explain why these data should be analysed by a paired samples test.

(ii) What underlying distributional assumption is necessary for the paired sample t test to be appropriate? Carry out this test at the 5% level of significance for the data above. Provide a two-sided 90% confidence interval for the true mean difference between times.

(iii) State the name of, and *briefly* describe, a statistical procedure that could be used in circumstances when the assumption in part (ii) is not valid.

9 Steel girders are made by a specialised process which includes a treatment intended to increase the tensile strength of the steel. To check whether this treatment is effective, the tensile strengths of a random sample of seven girders are measured both before and after the treatment. The results (in a suitable unit) are as follows:

Girder	A	B	C	D	E	F	G
Strength before treatment	25.1	23.3	24.7	25.4	24.9	24.0	24.4
Strength after treatment	28.8	25.9	24.5	28.0	24.3	26.3	26.5

Use an appropriate t test to examine, at the 1% level of significance, whether there is evidence that the treatment has been effective. State carefully the necessary distributional assumption.

Provide a one-sided 95% confidence interval giving a lower bound for the mean increase in strength due to the treatment. State carefully the interpretation of this interval.

[MEI]

10 A large university has many academic departments, research institutes and so on, each of which has a general office where supplies (stationery, computer disks, etc.) are kept. At a certain time, the values of these supplies are found for a random sample of nine of the general offices; the values (in thousands of pounds) are:

6.76   8.19   4.28   5.64   7.10
5.88   3.15   7.20   6.52.

Subsequently, the university management introduces new procedures in an effort to reduce the amount of these supplies held in the general offices. Afterwards, the values are found for a random sample of 12 general offices; the values (in thousands of pounds) are

5.06   5.24   6.50   3.85   2.80   7.16
4.88   5.04   4.67   4.50   5.44   5.10.

Use an appropriate t test to examine, at the 5% level of significance, whether there is evidence that the average value of the supplies held in the offices has been reduced.

State carefully the assumptions on which this analysis is based. Provide a two-sided 95% confidence interval for the true difference in mean overall value before and after the introduction of the new procedures. State carefully the interpretation of this interval.

[MEI]

11 A consumer research organisation is comparing prices of food in two large supermarkets. The prices (in pence) of a random sample of items of food sold in both supermarkets are found to be as follows.

Item	1	2	3	4	5
Store A	232	79	188	56	49
Store B	216	74	208	52	42

Item	6	7	8	9	10
Store A	46	19	37	33	19
Store B	49	18	31	38	17

(i) Use a paired t test to examine, at the 5% level of significance, the null hypothesis that the mean difference in prices in the two supermarkets is zero.

(ii) Provide a two-sided 90% confidence interval for the mean difference in prices.

(iii) State the distributional assumption underlying your analysis in parts (i) and (ii).

(iv) Explain why it is appropriate for the research organisation to design the investigation in such a way that a paired, rather than an unpaired, procedure is used for analysis.

[MEI]

12 A test is devised to decide whether eggs in one supermarket are fresher than those in another. In store A, a carton of each of the six grades of egg on sale is examined every day for a month and, from the date code on each carton, the value of random variable X_A, the number of days since packing, is determined. This gives 186 observations of values X_A. In store B, only five grades of egg are on sale: a carton of each is examined every day for a month and the value of random variable X_B, the number of days since packing, is determined. This gives 155 observations of values of X_B.

The hypotheses are

H_0: The mean number of days since packing is the same in both stores.

H_1: The mean number of days since packing is not the same in both stores.

The data are summarised by the values

$\Sigma x_A = 1722$ $\Sigma x_A^2 = 17\,854$ $n_A = 186$

$\Sigma x_B = 1061$ $\Sigma x_B^2 = 8533$ $n_B = 155$

Carry out this test.

KEY POINTS

1. You should now know how to test the hypothesis that the mean value of some random variable differs in two conditions, in a number of contexts. The test statistics used in the different contexts are given in the following table.

Variances	Sample size	Underlying distribution	Paired test	Unpaired test: variances equal	Unpaired test: variances unequal
Known	Any	Normal	$\dfrac{\bar{D}}{\sigma/\sqrt{n}} \sim N(0,1)$	$\dfrac{\bar{X}-\bar{Y}}{\sigma\sqrt{\dfrac{1}{n_X}+\dfrac{1}{n_Y}}} \sim N(0,1)$	$\dfrac{\bar{X}-\bar{Y}}{\sqrt{\dfrac{\sigma_X^2}{n_X}+\dfrac{\sigma_Y^2}{n_Y}}} \sim N(0,1)$
Known	Large	Need not be Normal	$\dfrac{\bar{D}}{\sigma/\sqrt{n}} \approx N(0,1)$	$\dfrac{\bar{X}-\bar{Y}}{\sigma\sqrt{\dfrac{1}{n_X}+\dfrac{1}{n_Y}}} \approx N(0,1)$	$\dfrac{\bar{X}-\bar{Y}}{\sqrt{\dfrac{\sigma_X^2}{n_X}+\dfrac{\sigma_Y^2}{n_Y}}} \sim N(0,1)$
Not known	Any	Normal	$\dfrac{\bar{D}}{S/\sqrt{n}} \sim t_{n-1}$	$\dfrac{\bar{X}-\bar{Y}}{S\sqrt{\dfrac{1}{n_X}+\dfrac{1}{n_Y}}} \sim t_{n_X+n_Y-2}$	No test discussed here is appropriate.
Not known	Large	Need not be Normal	$\dfrac{\bar{D}}{S/\sqrt{n}} \approx N(0,1)$	$\dfrac{\bar{X}-\bar{Y}}{S\sqrt{\dfrac{1}{n_X}+\dfrac{1}{n_Y}}} \approx N(0,1)$	$\dfrac{\bar{X}-\bar{Y}}{\sqrt{\dfrac{S_X^2}{n_X}+\dfrac{S_Y^2}{n_Y}}} \approx N(0,1)$
Known or not	Small		No test discussed here is appropriate		

2. To test the hypothesis that two random variables differ by the amount δ simply replace $\bar{D}$ by $(\bar{D}-\delta)$ or $(\bar{X}-\bar{Y})$ by $(\bar{X}-\bar{Y}-\delta)$ in the numerator of the appropriate statistic.

3. Confidence intervals can be constructed from the test statistic by observing that a confidence interval, in the appropriate situation, for the difference of the means in the two conditions, is given by the interval:
(numerator of statistic) $\pm$ (critical value) $\times$ (denominator of statistic).

4. Note carefully the sections of this table with no appropriate test. It is just as important to know when not to conduct a test as how to do so!

8 The Wilcoxon rank sum test

> She knew only that if she did or said thus-and-so, men would unerringly respond with the complimentary thus-and-so. It was like a mathematical formula and no more difficult.
>
> Margaret Mitchell
> (About Scarlett O'Hara in *Gone With The Wind*)

In December 1994, nine American economists made predictions for the growth rate in American GDP for December 1995. Their predictions are shown below, together with seven British predictions for the growth rate in the British GDP made at the same time.

Predictions for December 1995 growth rate

America	3.5	4.2	2.8	3.2	3.7	2.9	3.4	2.8	3.7
Britain	2.8	3.8	2.6	3.1	3.0	2.6	2.7		

Is there evidence that the American economists are more optimistic than their British counterparts about their respective countries' growth rates?

This is exactly the type of question you have been answering in the Chapters 6 and 7, except that here there is really no reason to assume that the economists' predictions for the growth rate would be Normally distributed. This means that you would not be justified in using a *t* test to compare their predictions. In Chapter 6 of *Statistics 3*, you saw that when the assumptions required for tests based on the Normal distribution are not appropriate, it is possible to use ranking methods to compare the median performance of two groups. There a paired design was used, but the data here are unpaired. In this chapter, you will develop a method, based on ranks, for comparing the medians of two populations which is analogous to the unpaired *t* test in its use of two independent samples.

You can get a feeling for these data visually by ranking all 16 predictions, giving something akin to a back-to-back stem-and-leaf diagram.

This makes it look as though the American predictions are higher on the whole: you can set this up as a hypothesis test.

American predictions	Rank	British predictions
	1.5	2.6, 2.6
	3	2.7
2.8, 2.8	5	2.8
2.9	7	
	8	3.0
	9	3.1
3.2	10	
3.4	11	
3.5	12	
3.7, 3.7	13.5	
	15	3.8
4.2	16	

Figure 8.1

EXAMPLE 8.1

Use the data given on the previous page to test whether the American economists are more optimistic than their British counterparts about their respective countries' growth rates.

SOLUTION

The formal statement is:

H_0: The median difference between American and British economists' predictions is zero.

H_1: The median difference between American and British economists' predictions is positive.

Significance level: 5%
1-tail test

If you add the ranks of the American and British predictions separately you get the Wilcoxon statistics.

$$W_A = 5 + 5 + 7 + 10 + 11 + 12 + 13.5 + 13.5 + 16 = 93$$
$$W_B = 1.5 + 1.5 + 3 + 5 + 8 + 9 + 15 = 43$$

Check: $W_A + W_B = 93 + 43 = 136$

This total should equal the sum of all the ranks,

$$1 + 2 + \ldots + 16 = \tfrac{1}{2} \times 16 \times 17$$
$$= 136,$$

which it does. The tied ranks do not affect the total rank sum.

❓ How have ranks been assigned to data values that are equal (tied ranks)?

The value of W for the smaller set gives the test statistic. In this case B is the smaller set and so the test statistic is 43.

The critical value is found in the table of critical values for the Wilcoxon rank sum test for the relevant sample sizes and significance level (see figure 8.2 overleaf). In this case the sample sizes are 7 and 9, the significance level is 5% and the test is 1-tail.

1–tail	5%	2½%	1%	½%
2–tail	10%	5%	2%	1%
m n				
6 10	35	32	29	27
6 11	37	34	30	28
6 12	38	35	32	30
6 13	40	37	33	31
6 14	42	38	34	32
6 15	44	40	36	33
6 16	46	42	37	34
6 17	47	43	39	36
6 18	49	45	40	37
6 19	51	46	41	38
6 20	53	48	43	39
6 21	55	50	44	40
6 22	57	51	45	42
6 23	58	53	47	43
6 24	60	54	48	44
6 25	62	56	50	45
7 7	39	36	34	32
7 8	41	38	35	34
7 9	43	40	37	35
7 10	45	42	39	37
7 11	47	44	40	38
7 12	49	46	42	40
7 13	52	48	44	41
7 14	54	50	45	

Figure 8.2 Extract from the table of critical values for the Wilcoxon rank sum test

The critical value is also 43.

So the test statistic of 43 lies within the critical region of W.

The null hypothesis is rejected in favour of the alternative hypothesis that the median difference between the American and British economists' predictions is positive.

It is important to understand the range of possible values for W and the relationship of the critical regions to it.

In this example, the smaller sample has size 7 out of a total of 16.

The smallest possible value of W corresponds to ranks 1, 2, 3, ..., 7, totalling $\frac{1}{2} \times 7 \times (7+1) = 28$.

The largest possible value of W corresponds to ranks 10, 11, 12, 13, 14, 15, 16.
In this case $W = \frac{1}{2} \times 16 \times (16 + 1) - \frac{1}{2} \times 9 \times 10 = 91$.

The mean value is $\frac{1}{2}(28 + 91) = 59.5$.

The critical value of 43 given in the tables corresponds to the lower tail. It is $(59.5 - 43) = 16.5$ below the mean. The equivalent value for the upper tail is 16.5 above the mean $59.5 + 16.5 = 76$. You would have used this critical value if the alternative hypothesis had been the other way round, that the difference between the British and American economists' predictions is positive, or if you were carrying out a 2-tail test at the 10% significance level.

```
                                                          W
   28        43        59.5        76        91
              └──── Critical regions ────┘
```

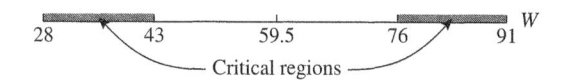

Figure 8.3

This diagram illustrates the range of possible values of W and the critical regions. Notice that the critical regions correspond to extreme values of W.

These results can be generalised. For samples of size m and n, where $m \leqslant n$, the smallest possible value of W is $\frac{1}{2}m(m+1)$ and the largest possible value is $\frac{1}{2}(m+n)(m+n+1) - \frac{1}{2}n(n+1)$. The mean value is $\frac{1}{2}m(m+n+1)$. If the lower critical value is W_c, the corresponding upper tail is $m(m+n+1) - W_c$, that is twice the mean value minus the lower critical value.

The Wilcoxon rank sum test is appropriate for tests of hypotheses similar to those for which the unpaired t tests were used. Note the absence of the special cases that you had to consider there for small or large samples, equal or unequal variances, Normal or non-Normal underlying distributions. This *non-parametric* test is applicable in one form to a wide variety of situations where *difference of location* in two conditions is being tested.

Formal procedure for the Wilcoxon rank sum test

Distributional assumption: That the random variables X and Y have distributions with the same shape, though not necessarily identically located.

H_0: That the two random variables also have the same median.

H_1: **(a)** That the median of X is different from that of Y

or **(b)** That the median of X is larger than that of Y

or **(c)** That the median of Y is larger than that of X.

Note that **(a)** is a two-tailed alternative, while **(b)** and **(c)** are both one-tailed.

Data: The values $x_1, x_2, \ldots, x_m$ of the random variable X in a sample of size m and the values $y_1, y_2, \ldots, y_n$ of the random variable Y in a sample of size n. It is conventional to take $m \leqslant n$ (this affects which random variable is called X and which Y).

Calculation of the test statistic

1. Rank all $(m+n)$ sample values 1 to $(m+n)$, giving the lowest rank to the smallest value. If a set of sample values is equal, each is given the rank which is the average of the ranking positions they occupy together.

2. Calculate the sum, W_X, of the ranks of the x values, and the sum, W_Y of the ranks of the y values.

3. Check that $W_X + W_Y = \frac{1}{2}(m+n)(m+n+1)$.

   This must work because the right-hand side is the formula for the sum of the numbers from 1 to $(m+n)$, i.e. the total of all the ranks.

4. The test statistic is the value of W for the smaller sample, that of size m.

5. The lower tail critical value, W_c, is found from the table of critical values for the Wilcoxon rank sum test.

6. If the upper tail critical value is required, it is given by $m(m+n+1) - W_c$.

Significance of the test statistic

The null hypothesis is then rejected if W is at least as extreme as the appropriate critical value. This critical value is found in the tables according to the two sample sizes, the chosen significance level and whether the test is one- or two-tailed.

The Mann–Whitney test

In the previous example, the larger rank sum for the American economists does not merely reflect their larger predictions, but also the fact that they made more predictions. This effect can be removed by subtracting from each rank sum an amount equal to $\frac{1}{2}N(N+1)$ where N is the respective sample size, to obtain adjusted rank totals known as the *Mann–Whitney T values*.

Justification

If there are m British economists and n American economists, then there are $(m+n)$ economists altogether and so the total of all the ranks, i.e. all the numbers from 1 to $(m+n)$, is $\frac{1}{2}(m+n)(m+n+1)$.

If the ranking of the economists' predictions were random you would expect that the total of the British economists' ranks to be in proportion to their numbers, that is

$$\frac{m}{m+n} \times \frac{1}{2}(m+n)(m+n+1) = \frac{1}{2}m(m+n+1)$$

while for the total of the American economists' ranks you would similarly expect

$$\frac{1}{2}n(m+n+1)$$

These are not equal when m and n are not the same, but the subtraction of the suggested terms

$$\tfrac{1}{2}m(m+n+1) - \tfrac{1}{2}m(m+1) = \tfrac{1}{2}mn$$
$$\tfrac{1}{2}m(m+n+1) - \tfrac{1}{2}n(n+1) = \tfrac{1}{2}mn$$

leaves equal 'adjusted totals', as required.

In this case you get the Mann–Whitney T values

American: $T_A = 93 - \tfrac{1}{2} \times 9 \times 10 = 93 - 45 = 48$

British: $T_B = 43 - \tfrac{1}{2} \times 7 \times 8 = 43 - 28 = 15$

You can now see numerically that, on a comparable basis, the British economists did tend to produce predictions of a lower rank. So, to complete the hypothesis test, all you need to know is whether the value of 15 is small enough to arise only rarely by chance when the underlying distribution of predictions is identical for Britain and America.

The Mann–Whitney tables are used in the same way as the Wilcoxon tables; m is the size of the smaller sample (here 7) and n is the size of the larger (here 9). The Mann–Whitney statistic is the smaller of the two values (here 15) and its critical value (for a 1-tail test) at the 5% level is also shown as 15. So you reject the null hypothesis that there is no difference between the distributions of predictions in America and Britain in favour of the alternative that the American economists are more optimistic.

1-tail	5%	2½%	1%	½%
2-tail	10%	5%	2%	1%

m	n				
6	10	14	11	8	6
6	11	16	13	9	7
6	12	17	14	11	9
6	13	19	16	12	10
6	14	21	17	13	11
6	15	23	19	15	12
6	16	25	21	16	13
6	17	26	22	18	15
6	18	28	24	19	16
6	19	30	25	20	17
6	20	32	27	22	18
6	21	34	29	23	19
6	22	36	30	24	21
6	23	37	32	26	22
6	24	39	33	27	23
6	25	41	35	29	24
7	7	11	8	6	4
7	8	13	10	7	6
7	9	15	12	9	7
7	10	17	14	11	9
7	11	19	16	12	10
7	12	21	18	14	12

Figure 8.4 Extract from the table of critical values for the Mann–Whitney test

The general relationship between the Mann–Whitney and Wilcoxon values is that for sample X with size m and sample Y with size n ($m \leqslant n$),

$$T_X = W_X - \tfrac{1}{2}m(m+1)$$
$$T_Y = W_Y - \tfrac{1}{2}n(n+1)$$

The Mann–Whitney method

While the procedure for converting the Wilcoxon W into the Mann–Whitney T illustrates the relationship between the two, it also raises questions about its usefulness. Why should you take the extra step of converting W into T when you can do the hypothesis test on W?

One possible answer is that you do not have Wilcoxon tables available but do have Mann–Whitney tables, which are rather more common. However, even in that case there is an alternative easier method of calculating T, called the Mann–Whitney method after the statisticians who devised it, independently of Wilcoxon.

Having the two methods can provide a valuable check.

The data for a test consist of two samples. The smaller sample, of size m, is referred to as sample X and the larger, of size n, as sample Y. The statistic, T_X, for the smaller sample is calculated by the Mann–Whitney method as follows.

- For each result in sample X:
  - count the number of results in sample Y which are smaller than it
  - add to this half the number of results in sample Y which are equal to it.
- Add up the numbers obtained in this way for each result in sample Y to obtain T_X.

This is shown in the next sample.

EXAMPLE 8.2

In an experiment on cultural differences in interpreting facial expressions, 16 English children and 23 Japanese children were each shown 40 full-face photographs of American children who had been asked to display particular emotions in their facial expressions.

They were asked to describe the feelings of the children in the photographs and the number of correct responses they made was noted. The results of this experiment, as scores out of 40, are shown below.

English children	34	27	39	29	33	34	39	40
	27	23	34	29	37	37	31	35
Japanese children	32	40	27	25	35	38	27	38
	36	23	28	31	30	37	27	30
	34	40	26	30	35	32	30	

Is there evidence at the 5% level, that English and Japanese children differ in their abilities to identify American facial expressions?

SOLUTION

The formal statement of the hypotheses under test is

H₀: The distributions of English and Japanese scores have the same median.

H₁: The distributions of English and Japanese scores have different medians.

under the assumption that the distributions have the same shape.

Significance level: 5%
2-tail test

The scores are shown below, with their ranks.

Japanese scores	Rank	English scores
23	1.5	23
25	3	
26	4	
27, 27, 27	7	27, 27
28	10	
	11.5	29, 29
30, 30, 30, 30	14.5	
31	17.5	31
32, 32	19.5	
	21	33
34	23.5	34, 34, 34
35, 35	27	35
36	29	
37	31	37, 37
38, 38	33.5	
	35.5	39, 39
40, 40	38	40

Figure 8.5

Here

T_E = the number of Japanese children with scores smaller than 23
    (plus half the number with scores equal to 23)
        + the number of Japanese children with scores smaller than 27
            (plus half the number with scores equal to 27)
            + ...
                + the number of Japanese children with scores smaller than 40
                  (plus half the number with scores equal to 40).

These are easy to read off from the ordered lists: for example, there are 14 Japanese children with scores smaller than 34 and one with a score equal to 34.

This means that each of the three scores of 34 in the 'English' list contributes $\left(14 + 1 \times \frac{1}{2}\right)$ to the value of T_E.

Calculating all the required terms in this way gives

$$T_E = 0.5 + 4.5 + 4.5 + 7 + 7 + 11.5 + 14 + 14.5 + 14.5$$
$$+ 14.5 + 16 + 18.5 + 18.5 + 21 + 21 + 22$$
$$= 209.5.$$

When using this method, it is usual to obtain the other T value from the fact that $T_J + T_E = mn$, so that:

$$T_J = mn - T_E = 16 \times 23 - 209.5 = 158.5.$$

Check

The equivalent Wilcoxon values are $W_E = 345.5$ and $W_J = 434.5$. You can use these values to check the Mann–Whitney values.

$$T_E = W_E - \tfrac{1}{2} m(m+1) \quad : \quad 209.5 = 345.5 - \tfrac{1}{2} \times 16 \times 17$$
$$T_J = W_J - \tfrac{1}{2} n(n+1) \quad : \quad 158.5 = 434.5 - \tfrac{1}{2} \times 23 \times 24.$$

e Critical values for the Wilcoxon rank sum test

In this section you will see how the tables of critical values for this test can be calculated.

Imagine the situation where you have samples of sizes $m = 4$ and $n = 7$. Of the eleven ranks from 1 to 11, four must be assigned to the sample of size 4. The smallest possible value of W_X, the rank sum for the smaller sample, is $1 + 2 + 3 + 4 = 10$. The largest is $8 + 9 + 10 + 11 = 38$. You can list all the ways of obtaining any value of W_X. Some of them are shown below.

10	{1,2,3,4}					
11	{1,2,3,5}					
12	{1,2,3,6}	{1,2,4,5}				
13	{1,2,3,7}	{1,2,4,6}	{1,3,4,5}			
14	{1,2,3,8}	{1,2,4,7}	{1,2,5,6}	{1,3,4,6}	{2,3,4,5}	
15	{1,2,3,9}	{1,2,4,8}	{1,2,5,7}	{1,3,4,7}	{1,3,5,6}	{2,3,4,6}

.... and so on ....

Altogether, there are $\binom{11}{4} = 330$ ways of picking four of the ranks to be in the W_X rank sum, and under the null hypothesis the ranks from 1 to 11 are assigned randomly to the two groups so that each of these possible assignments is equally likely. This means that the probability of each possible rank sum is the number of different ways of making that sum, as a fraction of 330. Thus you can calculate the cumulative probabilities of the smallest possible values of W_X as follows.

$$P(\text{rank sum} = 10) = \frac{1}{330} \qquad\qquad\qquad\qquad = 0.003\,03$$

$$P(\text{rank sum} \leqslant 11) = \frac{1+1}{330} = \frac{2}{330} \qquad\qquad = 0.006\,06$$

$$P(\text{rank sum} \leqslant 12) = \frac{1+1+2}{330} = \frac{4}{330} \qquad\quad = 0.012\,12$$

$$P(\text{rank sum} \leqslant 13) = \frac{1+1+2+3}{330} = \frac{7}{330} \qquad = 0.021\,21$$

$$P(\text{rank sum} \leqslant 14) = \frac{1+1+2+3+5}{330} = \frac{12}{330} \quad = 0.036\,36$$

$$P(\text{rank sum} \leqslant 15) = \frac{1+1+2+3+5+6}{330} = \frac{18}{330} = 0.054\,55$$

The critical value of W_X at the 5% level is therefore 14.

For the W_Y, the rank sum for the larger sample, the smallest values and their corresponding rank sums are:

28	{1,2,3,4,5,6,7}			
29	{1,2,3,4,5,6,8}			
30	{1,2,3,4,5,6,9}	{1,2,3,4,5,7,8}		
31	{1,2,3,4,5,6,10}	{1,2,3,4,5,7,9}	{1,2,3,4,6,7,8}	
32	{1,2,3,4,5,6,11}	{1,2,3,4,5,7,10}	{1,2,3,4,5,8,9}	{1,2,3,4,6,7,9}	{1,2,3,5,6,7,8}
33	{1,2,3,4,5,6,12} {1,2,3,5,6,7,9}	{1,2,3,4,5,7,11}	{1,2,3,4,5,8,10}	{1,2,3,4,6,7,10}	{1,2,3,4,6,8,9}

Because the numbers of sets of ranks giving each of the smallest possible totals are the same as for W_X, the critical value for W_Y at the 5% level will also be the fifth smallest of the possible sums: in this case, 32.

Normal approximation

Tables of critical values of the Wilcoxon rank sum test and of the Mann–Whitney test often only give critical values for sample sizes up to about 25. For larger sample sizes you use the fact that, under the null hypothesis, the test statistics W and T are approximately Normally distributed. W has mean $\frac{1}{2}mn + \frac{1}{2}m(m+n+1)$, variance $\frac{1}{12}mn(m+n+1)$. T has mean $\frac{1}{2}mn$, variance $\frac{1}{12}mn(m+n+1)$.

EXAMPLE 8.3 Determine the 1% one-tailed (2% two-tailed) critical value for the samples of sizes $m = 33$, $n = 58$.

SOLUTION

You want to find the integer t so that

$$P(T \leqslant t) \leqslant 0.01$$

where T has mean $\dfrac{33 \times 58}{2} = 957$

and variance $\dfrac{33 \times 58 \times (33 + 58 + 1)}{12} = 14\,674$.

Note that T is a discrete variable, so that you must make a continuity correction.

$$P(T \leqslant t) \approx P(\text{Normal approximation to } T < t + 0.5)$$

Thus you require

$$\Phi\left(\frac{t + 0.5 - 957}{\sqrt{14\,674}}\right) \leqslant 0.01$$

so

$$t \leqslant 956.5 + \sqrt{14\,674}\,\Phi^{-1}(0.01)$$
$$= 956.5 - \sqrt{14\,674}\,\Phi^{-1}(0.99)$$
$$= 956.5 - \sqrt{14\,674} \times 2.326$$
$$= 674.74.$$

This means that values of T less than or equal to 674 are in the critical region: 674 is the critical value.

EXERCISE 8A

This exercise contains questions about both paired and unpaired samples, to enable you to practise deciding which non-parametric procedure is appropriate.

1. Of the 32 leavers from a school who went on to university, 11 went to Oxford or Cambridge and 21 to other universities. Three years later, when these 32 got jobs, their starting salaries, in £, were as listed below.

Oxford and Cambridge students

9 012	10 760	11 405	11 617	12 030
13 040	13 772	14 200	16 430	17 500
21 650				

Students from other universities

7 860	9 540	10 300	10 340	10 980
11 040	11 650	11 790	11 995	12 000
12 545	12 800	12 950	13 270	13 280
14 350	14 608	14 980	15 200	15 330
18 750				

(i) Test, at the 5% level, the hypothesis that the starting salaries of Oxford and Cambridge graduates are higher than those of graduates from other universities.

(ii) Criticise the sampling procedure adopted in collecting these data.

2 The blood cholesterol levels of 46 men and 28 women are measured. These data are shown below.

Men	621	237	92	745
	301	550	182	723
	1301	56	104	428
	209	478	119	303
	417	869	384	1058
	939	1080	1104	829
	1061	145	382	919
	813	770	312	205
	610	139	206	174
	67	258	333	1203
	407	826	810	922
	717	106		
Women	208	529	104	72
	377	482	50	620
	1003	162	94	391
	149	371	208	194
	901	205	370	871
	710	973	304	189
	683	191	233	127

Is there evidence at the 5% level that the blood cholesterol levels of men and women differ?

Do the data suggest that the assumptions of the test are justified?

3 Given two rock samples A and B, geologists say that A is harder than B if, when the two samples are rubbed together, A scratches B. Eleven rock samples from stratum X and seven from stratum Y are tested in this way to determine the order of hardness. The list below shows 18 samples in order of hardness and which stratum they came from. The hardest is on the right.

X X X X X Y X Y X X Y X Y Y X X Y Y

Is there evidence at the 5% level that the rock in stratum Y is harder than that in stratum X?

4 Check the claim in the tables that the critical value for the Mann–Whitney test, at the 2.5% level, for samples of sizes $m = 5$, $n = 8$, is 6.

5 An aggregate material used for road surfacing contains some small stones of various types. A highway engineer is examining the composition of this material as delivered from two separate suppliers. The stones are broadly classified into two types, rounded and non-rounded, and the percentage of the rounded type is found in each of several samples. It is desired to examine whether the two suppliers are similar in respect of this percentage.

(i) In an initial investigation, histograms are drawn of the proportions of rounded stones in samples from the two suppliers. Discuss briefly what these histograms should indicate about the shape of the underlying distribution so that the comparison may reasonably be made using

(a) t test
(b) a Wilcoxon rank sum test.

(ii) It is decided that a Wilcoxon rank sum test must be used. Detailed data of the percentage of the rounded type of stone for 15 samples, 9 from one supplier and 6 from the other, are as follows.

Supplier 1	46 52 34 17 21 63 55 48 25
Supplier 2	59 53 71 39 66 58

Test at the 5% level of significance whether it is reasonable to assume that the true median percentages for the suppliers are the same.

6 The canteen in a factory is some distance from the building where the actual work takes place. The company believes that its employees take longer walking back to work after breaks in the canteen than they do in walking there. They time ten people walking to the canteen and ten walking back from it. Their times, in seconds, are as follows.

Time to canteen	50	46	57	72	33	84
	104	77	39	63		
Time from canteen	55	72	56	88	33	109
	127	75	40	75		

(i) Use these data to carry out a test of the company's belief at the 5% significance level.

After the test has been carried out, the person who collected the data points out that they refer to just ten individuals. Their times are given in the same order.

(ii) Carry out a new hypothesis test in the light of this information.

(iii) Compare and comment on the results of the two tests.

7 Random samples $x_1, x_2, \ldots, x_m$ and $y_1, y_2, \ldots, y_n$ are taken from two independent populations. The Wilcoxon rank sum test is to be used to test the hypotheses:

H_0: The two populations have identical distributions.

H_1: The two populations have identical distributions except that their location parameters differ.

Accordingly, the complete set of $m + n$ observations is ranked in ascending order (it may be assumed that no two observations are exactly equal). S denotes the sum of the ranks corresponding to $x_1, x_2, \ldots, x_m$.

(i) Consider the case $m = 4$, $n = 5$.

(a) Show that, if all the xs are less than all the ys, the value of S is 10.

(b) List all possible sets of ranks of the xs that give rise to a value of S such that $S \leq 12$.

(c) What is the total number of ways of assigning four ranks from the available nine to the xs?

(d) Deduce from your answers to parts (b) and (c) that the probability that $S \leq 12$ if H_0 is true is $\frac{4}{126}$.

(e) Compute the value of this probability as given by the Normal approximation $N(\frac{1}{2}m(m+n+1), \frac{1}{12}mn(m+n+1))$ to the distribution of S if H_0 is true.

(ii) The following are the numerical values of the data for a case with $m = 6$, $n = 8$.

Sample 1	4.6	6.6	6.0	5.2
$(x_1, x_2, \ldots, x_m)$	8.1	9.5		
Sample 2	5.5	7.9	7.1	6.3
$(y_1, y_2, \ldots, y_n)$	8.4	6.8	10.2	9.0

Test H_0 against H_1 at the 5% level of significance, using the normal approximation given in part (e) above to the distribution of S under H_0 or otherwise.

8 As part of the procedure for interviewing job applicants, a firm uses aptitude tests. Each applicant takes a test and receives a score. Two different tests, A and B, are used. The distributions of scores for each test, over the whole population of applicants, are understood to be similar in shape, approximately symmetrical, but not Normal. However, the location parameters of these distributions may differ. The personnel manager is investigating this by considering the medians of the distributions, with the null hypothesis H_0 that these medians are equal. It is thought that test B might lead to consistently lower scores, so the alternative hypothesis H_1 is that the median for test B is *less than* that for test A.

The scores from test A for a random sample of seven applicants for a particular job are as follows.

37.6   34.3   38.5   38.8   35.8   38.0   38.2

The scores from test B for a separate random sample of seven applicants for this job are as follows

37.3   33.0   33.9   32.1   37.0   35.0   36.2

(i) Calculate the value of the Wilcoxon rank sum test statistic for these data.

(ii) State the critical value for a one-sided 5% test of H_0 against H_1.

(iii) State whether values *less than* this critical value would lead to the acceptance or rejection of H_0.

(iv) Carry out the test.

Now suppose, instead, that the two distributions can be taken as Normal (with the same variance), and that the test is to be conducted in terms of the means. Describe briefly a procedure based on the t distribution for carrying out this test using these data.

9 Random samples $x_1, x_2, \ldots, x_m$ and $y_1, y_2, \ldots, y_n$ are taken from two independent populations. It is understood that these two populations have identical distributions except possibly for a difference in location parameter. The null hypothesis H_0 that they have the same location parameter is to be tested against the alternative hypothesis H_1 that their location parameters differ, using the Wilcoxon rank sum test. The complete set of all $m+n$ observations is ranked in ascending order (it may be assumed that no two observations are exactly equal); W denotes the sum of the ranks corresponding to $x_1, x_2, \ldots, x_m$.

(i) Show that the minimum value W can take is $\frac{1}{2}m(m+1)$.

(ii) Find the maximum value W can take.

(iii) The sample data are as follows:

Sample A $(x_1, x_2, \ldots, x_m)$	10.2 13.5 15.2 15.4 10.8 17.7 12.1 13.8
Sample B $(y_1, y_2, \ldots, y_n)$	14.6 19.3 11.6 12.9 18.4 16.9 18.2 18.7 16.1 19.0

Calculate the value of W and hence carry out a two-sided 5% test.

(iv) Show that if H_0 is true the expected value of W is $\frac{1}{2}m(m+n+1)$. Given that the variance of W if H_0 is true is $\frac{1}{12}m(m+1)$, repeat the test in part (iii) using a Normal approximation to the distribution of W under H_0.

10 While at a summer camp, children are given healthy food and take plenty of exercise. In their publicity, the camp's organisers claim that after a stay the children are 'leaner and fitter'.

An advertising watchdog body decide to check this claim. They weigh 12 children at the start of their stay and when they leave, three weeks later. The 12 children are also required to run 1 mile at the start and end of their stay; on both occasions, the times of the 1st, 2nd, ..., 12th to complete are recorded. The data are given below.

Weights (pounds)

Name	Start	End
Dwight	98	101
Floyd	114	108
Peaches	89	88
Barbie	45	47
Randy	87	84
Mary-Jo	112	106
Marilyn	78	77
Hank	87	85
Cindy	48	48
Leroy	67	66
Billy-Jo	78	73
Chuck	99	96

Place	Start	End
1	7m 55s	7m 39s
2	7m 56s	7m 52s
3	8m 12s	8m 05s
4	8m 13s	8m 12s
5	8m 46s	8m 30s
6	9m 35s	8m 55s
7	9m 56s	8m 56s
8	10m 34s	8m 56s
9	11m 22s	10m 01s
10	15m 15s	15m 12s
11	15m 38s	15m 12s
12	19m 22s	15m 12s

Times (minutes and seconds)

(i) Explain why it is not appropriate to use tests based on the Normal distribution or the t distribution.

(ii) Use appropriate tests at the 5% significance level on these data to investigate the camp's organisers claim that after a stay the children are 'leaner and fitter'.

(iii) Do the camp's organisers have grounds to criticise the experiment?

11 Random samples of size 4 are taken from each of two independent populations. The Wilcoxon rank sum test is to be used to test the hypotheses:

H_0: The two populations have identical distributions.

H_1: The two populations have identical distributions except that their location parameters differ.

The usual procedure of ranking the complete set of eight observations in ascending order is followed (it may be assumed that no two observations are exactly equal). The sum of the ranks corresponding to the observations from one of the populations is denoted by W.

(i) State the minimum and maximum possible values of W.

(ii) State the total number of ways of assigning four ranks from the eight available to the observations from which W is calculated.

(iii) Deduce that the probability that W equals 10 or 26 if H_0 is true is $\frac{2}{70}$.

(iv) Hence *write down* the level of significance of the test that rejects H_0 if the value of W is 10 or 26.

(v) Find the level of significance of the test that rejects H_0 if the value of W is 10, 11, 25 or 26.

(vi) Repeat part (v) using the Normal approximation to the distribution of W under H_0, making appropriate use of a continuity correction. You are reminded that the parameters of this Normal approximation are $\mu = \frac{1}{2}m(m+n+1)$ and $\sigma^2 = \frac{1}{12}mn(m+n+1)$.

(vii) In a particular experiment, the numerical values of the data are as follows.

Sample 1:   11.4   13.6   10.8   11.9
Sample 2:   12.1   14.4   15.7   14.1

Test H_0 against H_1 at the *six* percent level of significance.

[MEI]

KEY POINTS

1. The Wilcoxon rank sum test is used for testing the null hypothesis that two random variables, X and Y, have the same median under the assumption that their distributions have the same shape.

2. To calculate the test statistic from a sample of m values of X and n values of Y, with $m < n$:
   - Rank the sample values from 1 to $(m+n)$, giving the lowest rank to the smallest value.
   - W_X and W_Y are the sums of ranks of X values and Y values respectively.
   - The test statistic W is the value of W_X or W_Y derived from the smaller sample, i.e. that of size m.

3. The null hypothesis is then rejected if W is less than or equal to the appropriate critical value.

4. For larger values of m and n, W is approximately Normally distributed as
$$N\left(\frac{mn}{2} + \frac{1}{2}m(m+n+1),\ \frac{mn(m+n+1)}{12}\right)$$

The Mann–Whitney test

5. The Mann–Whitney test statistic T may be deduced from the Wilcoxon statistic by using

   Sample X, size m $\qquad T_X = W_X - \frac{1}{2}m(m+1)$

   Sample Y, size n $\qquad T_Y = W_Y - \frac{1}{2}n(n+1)$

   (Check: $T_X + T_Y = mn$)

   The statistic T is T_X.

6. T is often calculated using the alternative method of counting the number of times an X exceeds a Y.

7. For larger values of m and n, T is approximately Normally distributed as
$$N\left(\frac{mn}{2},\ \frac{mn(m+n+1)}{12}\right)$$

9 Errors in hypothesis testing

Errors using inadequate data are much less than those using no data at all.

Charles Babbage

When the Chartbusters video chain decides to stock a title, it orders about four hundred copies of the video to send out to its many shops from a distributor who mass-produces copies under licence from the movie company. Before accepting the delivery and paying the distributor, the Chartbuster quality control department views a small number of the videos to make sure that the copying has been carried out to an acceptable standard. How should this testing be carried out?

Chartbuster's contract with the distributor states that no more than 3% of the video copies may be blemished on delivery and so the company has decided on the following procedures.

- Select 12 copies of the title at random from the batch.
- View each of the 12 copies, counting those which have a serious blemish.
- Reject the batch if more than one copy in the sample is blemished.

In this chapter you are going to look at how effective different statistical testing procedures are, and how this effectiveness depends on the sample size used and the criterion adopted for making the decision involved.

Types of errors in hypothesis testing

Ideally, Chartbuster would like this procedure to produce the results:

- if 3% (or fewer) of the copies are seriously blemished, the batch will be accepted
- if more than 3% of the copies are seriously blemished, the batch will be rejected. However, as their procedure involves testing only a small sample of the batch, they cannot hope to discriminate so precisely.

(I) One possible error is that Chartbuster will reject a perfectly acceptable batch. The probability of this happening can be calculated using the binomial distribution, as the sample is small compared to the entire batch and you assume 12 copies are chosen at random.

In the worst case where the batch is still acceptable, 3% of the copies will be seriously blemished and so

P(batch is erroneously rejected)
$$= \text{P(more than one copy in the sample is blemished)}$$
$$= 1 - \text{P(zero or one copy is blemished)}$$
$$= 1 - \left((1 - 0.03)^{12} + \binom{12}{1} 0.03 \times (1 - 0.03)^{11}\right)$$
$$= 0.048\,65 \approx 5\%.$$

Of course, if fewer than 3% of the copies are seriously blemished – that is, the batch is better than just acceptable – the probability that the batch is erroneously rejected will be less than this.

(II) Another possible error is that Chartbuster will accept a poorly copied batch: if as many as 10% of the copies were blemished, for instance, you would have:

P(batch is erroneously accepted)
$$= \text{P(at most one copy in the sample is blemished)}$$
$$= (1 - 0.1)^{12} + \binom{12}{1} 0.1 \times (1 - 0.1)^{11}$$
$$= 0.659 \approx 66\%$$

This seems rather high so you could reverse this question and ask what proportion, p, of the copies would have to be blemished before there was at most, say, 5% chance of erroneously accepting them.

$$\text{P(batch is erroneously accepted)} = 5\%$$

i.e. $\text{P(at most one copy in the sample is blemished)} = 5\%$

i.e. $(1-p)^{12} + \binom{12}{1} p(1-p)^{11} = 0.05$

i.e. $(1-p)^{11}(1 + 11p) = 0.05$

This equation needs to be solved numerically (for instance, by the Newton–Raphson method) to give

$$p = 0.3387 \approx 34\% \text{ of copies blemished.}$$

This means that, following Chartbuster's procedure, 34% or more of the copies in a batch would have to be seriously blemished to bring the chance of erroneously accepting it below 5%.

You can rephrase Chartbuster's quality control procedure as a hypothesis test. They are setting up the hypothesis:

H_0: 3% of the copies are blemished
H_1: more than 3% of the copies are blemished

and conducting a one-tailed binomial test with critical region $\{r > 1\}$.

Note that, as usual with a one-tailed hypothesis test, the parameter value of the null hypothesis is quoted as 'proportion blemished $= 3\%$, not as the full null range 'proportion blemished $\leq 3\%$'. You do this following the general principle that the null hypothesis is accepted unless there is good evidence that it is false: that is, that none of the values in the full null range is acceptable. Because the most extreme of the null range of parameter values, 'proportion blemished = 3%', will be accepted if any proportion blemished in the null range is, you need quote only this single value. An alternative convention, which is not used here is to quote the hypotheses:

H_0: 3% or fewer of the copies are blemished
H_1: more than 3% of the copies are blemished

but, nonetheless, to calculate the distribution of the test statistic under the null hypothesis using 'proportion blemished = 3%'.

The error calculation carried out in (I) above determined the probability of a *type I error*, that is, *rejecting the null hypothesis when it is true*. This probability is given the symbol α and is identical to what you have, so far, called the *significance level* of the test.

You are able to calculate α because you took the null hypothesis to be a *simple hypothesis*. That is, knowing that H_0 is true gives, as explained above, an exact value (of 3%) for the population parameter, p, rather than a range and hence the sampling distribution of the test statistic under H_0 can be calculated.

The error calculation carried out in (II) above determined the probability of a *type II error*, that is, *accepting the null hypothesis when the alternative hypothesis is true*.

Because H_1 is a *composite hypothesis* which states that the population parameter lies in a range of values (here, $0.03 < p \leq 1$) you cannot calculate the probability of accepting the null hypothesis merely by knowing that one of the range of alternatives is true. You are able to make this calculation only by picking a specific, simple alternative hypothesis (here $p = 0.1$); different values of p would have given different probabilities.

Operating characteristic

You have seen that the probability of a type II error is not a single value, but a function of the population parameter, p. The function which gives the probability, for each p, of accepting the null hypothesis is called the *operating characteristic of the test*. If p lies within the region specified by the alternative hypothesis, the probability of a type II error is given by the operating characteristic.

For Chartbuster's test, the operating characteristic (OC) is the probability that a batch is accepted when the true value of the proportion of blemished copies is p.

$$OC(p) = P(\text{at most one copy in the sample is blemished})$$
$$= (1-p)^{12} + \binom{12}{1} p(1-p)^{11} = (1-p)^{11}((1-p) + 12p)$$
$$= (1 + 11p)(1-p)^{11}$$

This function is tabulated below and illustrated in figure 9.1

p	0.00	0.05	0.10	0.15	0.20	0.25	0.30	0.35	0.40	0.45
OC(p)	1.00	0.88	0.66	0.44	0.27	0.16	0.09	0.04	0.02	0.01

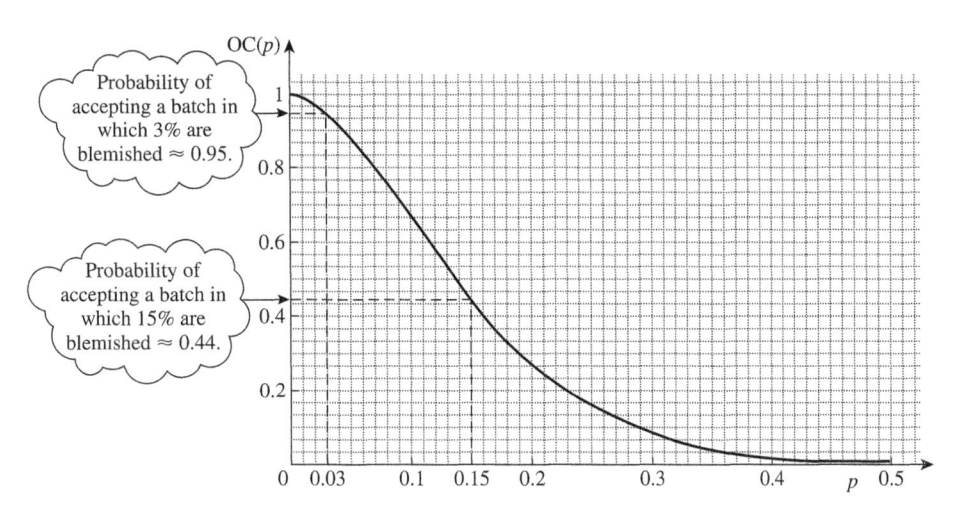

Figure 9.1

The graph shows that if p is above, but close to, the value 0.03 given by the null hypothesis then there is a very high probability that the null hypothesis will be erroneously accepted, that is, that a type II error will be made. This is neither surprising nor particularly worrying for Chartbuster. What might well be a problem for them, however, is that even with 15% of the videos blemished, the quality control will fail to pick this up 44% of the time.

? How can the company improve their test?

The effect of changing the significance level of the test

Suppose you change the quality control department's rule so that they accept a batch only if it has no blemished videos in the sample of 12 tested. The value of α, the probability of a type I error, is now

$$\begin{aligned}
&P(\text{reject null hypothesis if it is true}) \\
&= P(\text{reject batch when 3\% are blemished}) \\
&= P(\text{at least one copy in the sample is blemished}) \\
&= 1 - P(\text{zero copies are blemished}) \\
&= 0.3062 \approx 31\%.
\end{aligned}$$

The operating characteristic, which gives the probability of a type II error, is again a function of the proportion, p, of the batch which is blemished.

$$\mathrm{OC}(p) = \mathrm{P}(\text{accept batch when proportion } p \text{ is blemished})$$
$$= \mathrm{P}(\text{no copies in the sample are blemished})$$
$$= (1-p)^{12}$$

This function is tabulated below and illustrated in figure 9.2. The operating characteristic for the original test is shown by a dashed line for comparison.

p	0.00	0.05	0.10	0.15	0.20	0.25	0.30	0.35	0.40	0.45
OC(p)	1.00	0.54	0.28	0.14	0.07	0.03	0.01	0.01	0.00	0.00

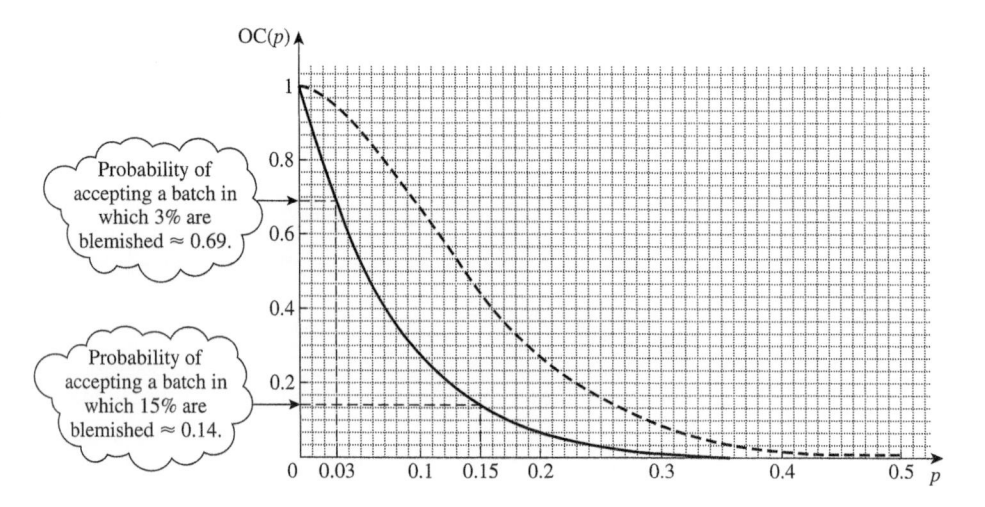

Figure 9.2

This graph shows the test's much reduced probability of accepting batches with high proportions of blemished copies – but this improvement has been bought at a price: the test is rejecting 31% of the perfectly acceptable batches with only 3% blemished copies.

The effect of changing the sample size

Suppose instead that the quality control department takes larger samples, of 27 videos, and rejects the batch if the sample contains three or more blemished copies. The value of α, the probability of a type I error, is now

$$\mathrm{P}(\text{reject null hypothesis if it is true})$$
$$= \mathrm{P}(\text{reject batch when 3\% are blemished})$$
$$= \mathrm{P}(\text{at least three copies in the sample are blemished})$$
$$= 1 - \left((1-0.03)^{27} + \binom{27}{1}(1-0.03)^{26} 0.03 \right.$$
$$\left. + \binom{27}{2}(1-0.03)^{25}(0.03)^{2} \right)$$
$$= 0.0462.$$

This significance level for the test, 4.62%, is very similar to the original value of 5%. So it is still true that only about 5% of batches with the acceptable proportion, 3%, of blemished copies are being rejected.

The operating characteristic, which gives the probability of a type II error, is, as a function of the proportion, p, of the batch which is blemished

$$\begin{aligned}\text{OC}(p) &= \text{P}(\text{accept batch}) \\ &= \text{P}(0 \text{ or } 1 \text{ or } 2 \text{ copies in the sample are blemished}) \\ &= (1-p)^{27} + \binom{27}{1}(1-p)^{26}p + \binom{27}{2}(1-p)^{25}p^2 \\ &= (1-p)^{25}(1 + 25p + 35p^2).\end{aligned}$$

This function is tabulated below and illustrated in figure 9.3. The operating characteristic of the original test is shown by a dashed line for comparison.

p	0.00	0.05	0.10	0.15	0.20	0.25	0.30	0.35	0.40	0.45
OC(p)	1.00	0.85	0.48	0.21	0.07	0.02	0.01	0.00	0.00	0.00

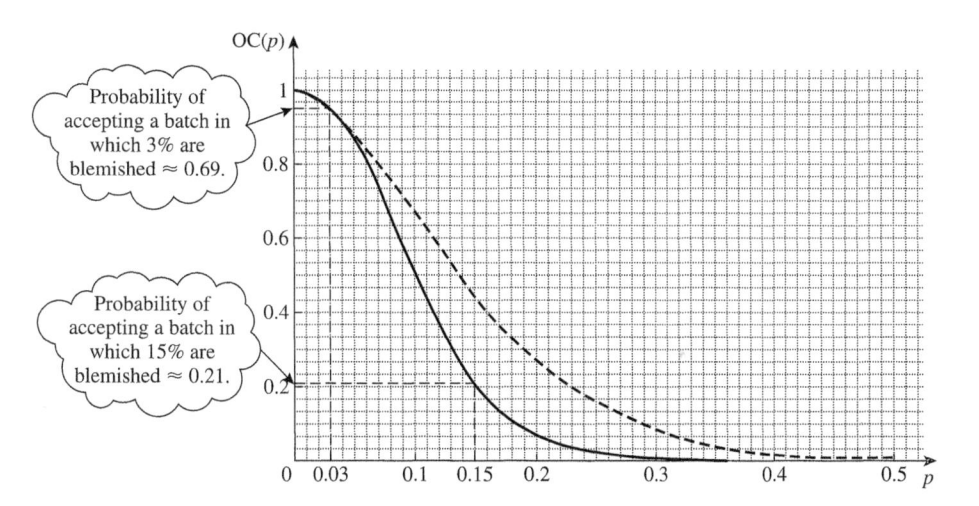

Figure 9.3

The graph shows that this test also greatly reduces the probability of accepting batches with high proportions of blemished copies – but again the improvement only comes at a price: this time, literally, as the cost of paying someone to watch more than twice as many copies in the search for blemishes.

Suppose that two tests, A and B, have the same significance level, but A has a smaller operating characteristic than B for all values of the relevant parameter in the range specified by the alternative hypothesis. In this situation, test A is better than test B in the sense that it is more likely to discriminate accurately between situations where the null hypothesis is and is not true in the population as a whole. However, A may not be a better test to use: it may be more difficult or expensive to carry out.

A related concept used by statisticians is the *power* of a test. This is the function

$$\text{power} = (1 - \text{operating characteristic})$$

so the power of a test is the probability that the null hypothesis is rejected for a given value of the relevant population parameter. In the situation described in the previous paragraph, test A is *more powerful* than test B.

It is important to note a difference in the status of the probabilities of type I and type II errors. When hypothesis testing, the null hypothesis will usually refer explicitly to the value of a parameter – for instance stating that the probability of some event is 0.3. However, there is generally also an underlying assumption being made about the distribution of the population – for instance, that the binomial model is appropriate. The probability of a type I error, which is the probability of rejecting the null hypothesis when it is true, can be calculated on the basis of the underlying assumption which forms part of the null hypothesis, and so is an exact theoretical value. The probability of a type II error, on the other hand, is the probability of accepting the null hypothesis when it is false. As you have seen, this probability can only be calculated as a function of the true parameter value, but the calculation also relies on the underlying assumption about the distribution being true. If the null hypothesis is false, for instance, because successive events are not independent with a constant probability of occurrence so that the binomial model is not appropriate, it is impossible to work out the probability of accepting the null hypothesis. This should always be borne in mine when interpreting claims about operating characteristics of tests: if the distributional assumption being made is inappropriate, these will not tell you anything very useful.

Normal hypothesis testing

Intelligence tests are designed (by testing on a very large sample) so that scores on the test have a Normal distribution with a mean of 100 and a standard deviation of 15 in the population as a whole. Such tests have sometimes been used to try to test whether a particular subset of the population has a higher or lower average intelligence that the population as a whole.

The hypothesis being tested might be:

H_0: the mean intelligence of the subset is 100

H_1: the mean intelligence of the subset is different from 100

on the assumption that the intelligence of the subset will have a standard deviation of 15.

Suppose a scientist wishing to test this hypothesis took 50 people and decided to test at the 10% significance level. This means that the probability, α, of a type I error should be 0.1.

You know that if the sample of 50 is chosen randomly from the subset, and H_0 is true then the sample mean has distribution

$$\overline{X}_{50} \sim N\left(100, \frac{15^2}{50}\right) = N(100, 4.5)$$

so that

$$\frac{\overline{X}_{50} - 100}{\sqrt{4.5}} \sim N(0, 1).$$

You need to choose a critical value, c, for rejection so that

$$0.1 = P(\text{reject null hypothesis when it is true}).$$

As this is a two-tailed test, you want to determine the two-tailed critical value for a standard Normal distribution at the 10% significance level. This is found from Normal tables to be

$$c = \phi^{-1}(0.95) = 1.645.$$

The null hypothesis will be rejected if the test statistic is in either tail, that is

$$\frac{\overline{X}_{50} - 100}{\sqrt{4.5}} > 1.645 \text{ or } \frac{\overline{X}_{50} - 100}{\sqrt{45}} < -1.645.$$

Rearranging these inequalities gives

$$\overline{X}_{50} > 100 + 1.645\sqrt{4.5} = 103.49 \text{ or } \overline{X}_{50} < 100 - 1,645\sqrt{4.5} = 96.51.$$

Thus, finally, the null hypothesis will be rejected if the sample mean is greater than 103.49 or less than 96.51.

The operating characteristic of this test depends on the true mean intelligence of the subset, μ, and is given by

$$OC(\mu) = P(\text{accept null hypothesis when true mean} = \mu).$$

That is

$$OC(\mu) = P(96.51 < \overline{X}_{50} < 103.49)$$

where the distribution of $\overline{X}_{50}$ is $\overline{X}_{50} \sim N(\mu, 4.5)$.

So

$$OC(\mu) = P\left(\frac{96.51 - \mu}{\sqrt{4.5}} < Z < \frac{103.49 - \mu}{\sqrt{4.5}}\right) \quad \text{where } z \text{ is a standard Normal variable}$$

$$= \Phi\left(\frac{103.49 - \mu}{\sqrt{4.5}}\right) - \Phi\left(\frac{96.51 - \mu}{\sqrt{4.5}}\right)$$

For instance

$$OC(102) = P(\text{accept null hypothesis when true mean intelligence} = 102)$$
$$= \Phi\left(\frac{103.49 - 102}{\sqrt{4.5}}\right) - \Phi\left(\frac{96.51 - 102}{\sqrt{4.5}}\right)$$
$$= \Phi(0.7024) - \Phi(-2.5880)$$
$$= 0.7587 - 0.0048 = 0.7539.$$

The values in the following table can be calculated in the same way.

μ	90	92	94	96	98	100	102	104	106	108	110
$OC(\mu)$	0.001	0.017	0.118	0.405	0.754	0.900	0.754	0.405	0.118	0.017	0.001

A graph of the operating characteristic against μ is shown in figure 9.4

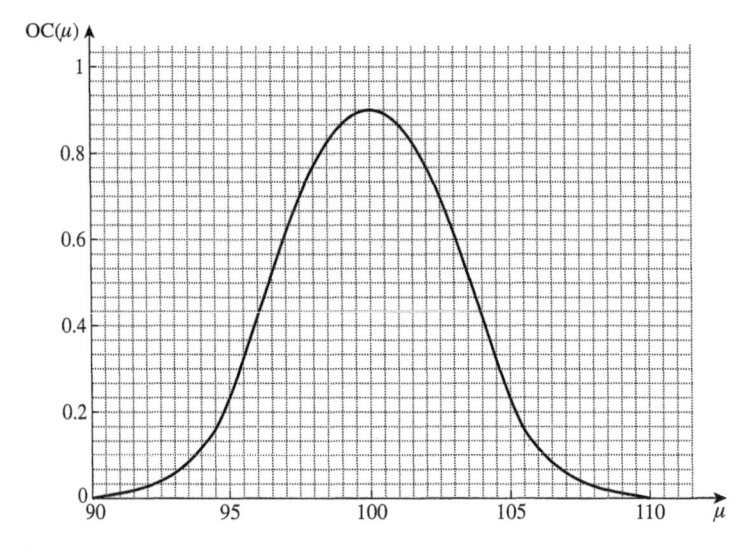

Figure 9.4

It is straightforward (although it involves a considerable amount of work) to repeat the calculation above for the operating characteristic in two other cases (the original is shown as a dashed line in figures 9.5 and 9.6).

The significance level is changed to 1%, but the sample size remains at 50

μ	90	92	94	96	98	100	102	104	106	108	110
$OC(\mu)$	0.16	0.116	0.400	0.755	0.949	0.990	0.949	0.755	0.400	0.116	0.016

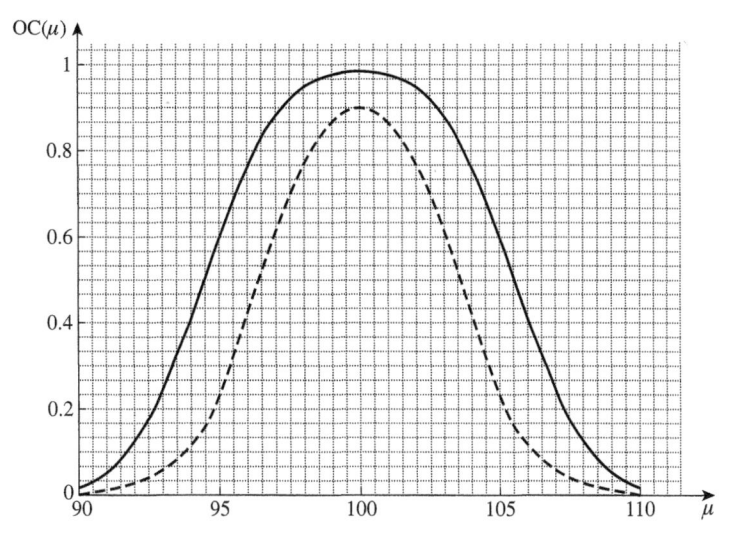

Figure 9.5

The probability of a type I error is now only 0.01, but the operating characteristic shows that the probability of a type II error is greater at every possible true value of μ.

The significance level remains at 10%, but the sample size is raised to 200

μ	90	92	94	96	98	100	102	104	106	108	110
$OC(\mu)$	0.000	0.000	0.000	0.017	0.405	0.900	0.405	0.017	0.000	0.000	0.000

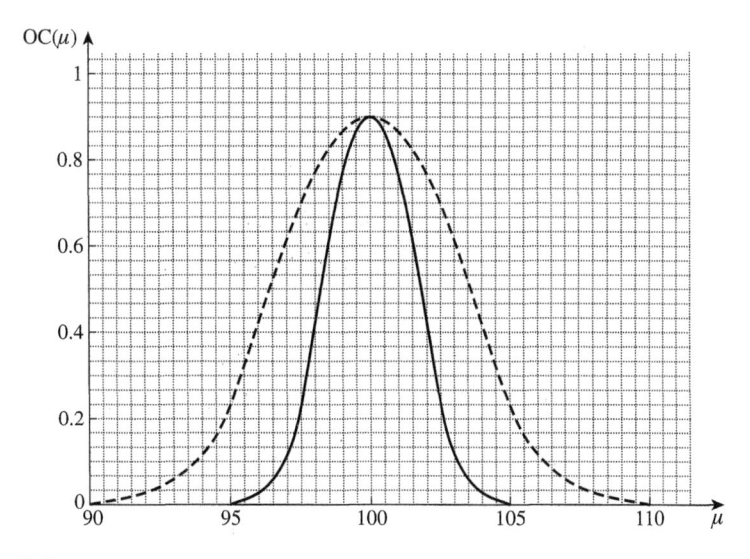

Figure 9.6

The probability of a type I error is unchanged at 0.1, but the operating characteristic shows that the probability of a type II error is less at every possible true value of μ.

INVESTIGATION

Suppose that the scientist's alternative hypothesis is that the mean intelligence of his subset is greater, so that he is working with a one-tailed test. Construct the operating characteristics using one of the combinations of significance level and sample size given above, and compare your graph with the one given in the text.

A simple alternative hypothesis

So far, you have met only composite alternative hypothesis – that is, those giving a range of parameter values. However, it is possible for both null and alternative hypotheses to be simple – that is, giving only a single parameter value. For instance, the scientist above may be trying to support, or challenge, the work of another group of researchers who have claimed, on the basis of a substantial sample, that a particular subset has a mean intelligence of 102. His hypothesis would be:

H_0: the mean intelligence of the subset is 100

H_A: the mean intelligence of the subset is 102

on the assumption that the intelligence of the subset will have a standard deviation of 15.

As usual, α is the significance level, i.e.

$$\begin{aligned}\alpha &= \text{probability of a type I error} \\ &= \text{probability of accepting } H_A \text{ when } H_0 \text{ is true} \\ &= 1 - OC(100).\end{aligned}$$

In the case of a simple alternative hypothesis, it is usual also to define

$$\begin{aligned}\beta &= \text{probability of a type II error} \\ &= \text{probability of accepting } H_0 \text{ when } H_A \text{ is true} \\ &= OC(102).\end{aligned}$$

Note the symmetry of these definitions: when both null and alternative hypothesis are simple, there is little difference in the status of the two.

Ideally, you would like $\alpha = \beta = 0$, but you already know that this cannot be achieved: in fact choosing a critical value for the test fixes α and β simultaneously so that if you choose a critical value to produce a given α, then a value for β follows automatically.

If you choose the critical value c and a sample size of n, then

$$\alpha = P(\text{sample mean greater than } c \text{ when population mean is } 100)$$
$$= 1 - \Phi\left(\frac{c - 100}{\frac{15}{\sqrt{n}}}\right)$$

and

$$\beta = P(\text{sample mean less than } c \text{ when population mean is } 102)$$
$$= \Phi\left(\frac{c - 102}{\frac{15}{\sqrt{n}}}\right) = 1 - \Phi\left(\frac{102 - c}{\frac{15}{\sqrt{n}}}\right)$$

The graph in figure 9.7 shows how α and β vary with c, in the case of $n = 400$.

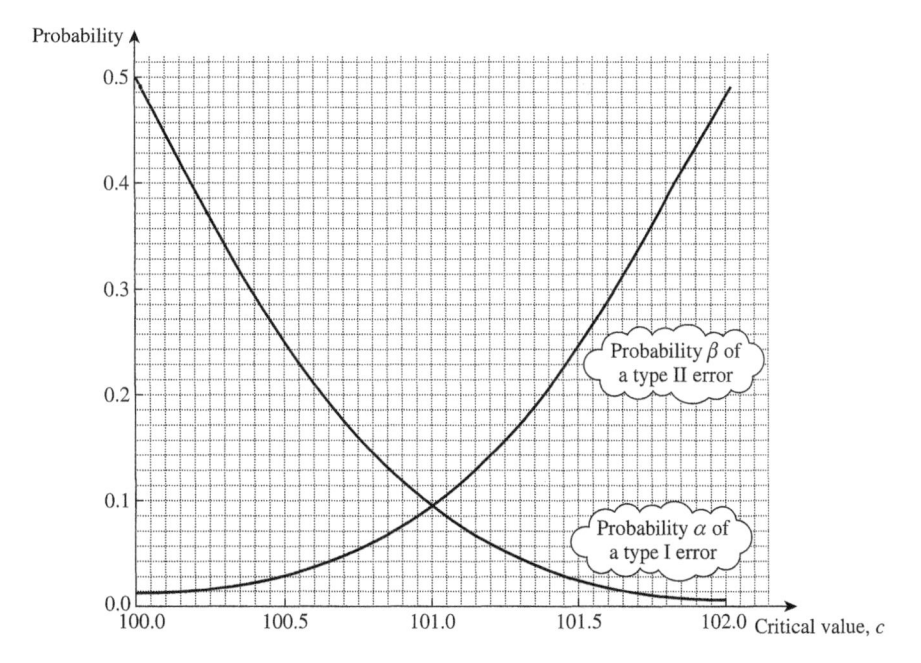

Figure 9.7

The essential point to note is that, with a fixed sample size, reducing α inevitably increases β. You cannot, for instance, with this sample size, have both α and β less than 0.05.

It may seem obvious in this situation that 101 should be chosen as the critical value because it makes errors in either direction equally likely. However, depending on why the work is being done, it may be that errors one way or the other are more important. Any critical value between 100 and 102 could be a sensible choice in the appropriate circumstances.

The graph in figure 9.8 shows the pairs of α, β values which can be achieved by choosing the critical value appropriately for a range of values of n.

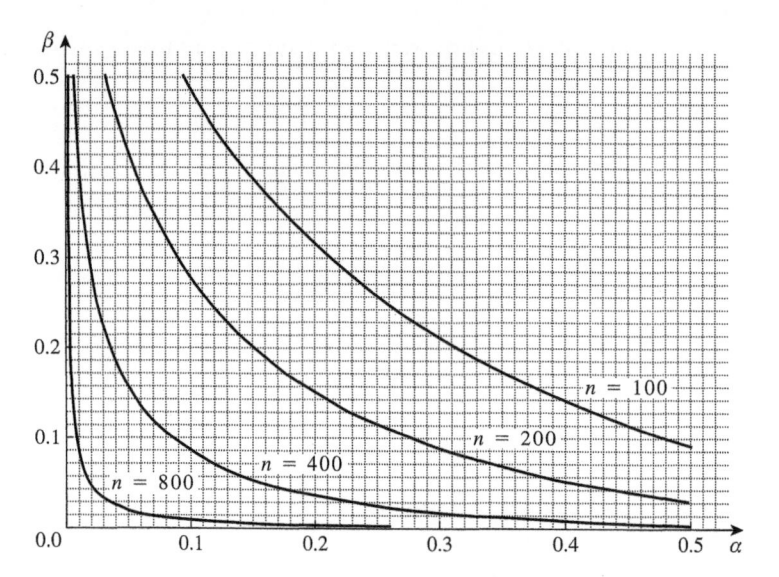

Figure 9.8

A scientist in this situation might well start from what he considers appropriate significance levels and deduce from these the parameters of the experiment he needs to perform. For instance, suppose the scientist wants to ensure that $\alpha = 0.01$ and $\beta = 0.05$. What size of sample should he set and what should the critical value be?

Using the results above, the desired values of α and β mean that

$$= 1 - \theta\left(\frac{c - 100}{\frac{15}{\sqrt{n}}}\right) = 0.01$$

and

$$= 1 - \theta\left(\frac{102 - c}{\frac{15}{\sqrt{n}}}\right) = 0.05$$

Using the Normal tables, these become

$$\frac{c - 100}{\frac{15}{\sqrt{n}}} = \Phi^{-1}(0.99) = 2.326$$

and

$$\frac{102 - c}{\frac{15}{\sqrt{n}}} = \Phi^{-1}(0.95) = 1.645.$$

Adding these two equations gives

$$\frac{2}{\frac{15}{\sqrt{n}}} = 3.971 \text{ or } \sqrt{n} = 29.7825$$

so the sample size required is $n = 887$.

Substitution back into one of the simultaneous equations then gives $c = 101.17$.

EXERCISE 9A

1 A two-tailed test of the fairness of a coin is being conducted, in which the coin is tossed 20 times and the number of heads noted.

(i) If the test is to be conducted at the 5% level, use cumulative binomial tables to find the critical region for the test. What is the exact value of α, the probability of a type I error?

(ii) Use the tables to find the probability of accepting the null hypothesis of no bias if, in fact, the probability of a head is 0.00, 0.05, 0.10, ..., 0.90, 0.95, 1.00, and thus plot the operating characteristic of the test.

2 A one-tailed test is being undertaken to investigate a die which is supposed to show a six too frequently. The die is to be rolled seven times and the null hypothesis of no bias will be rejected if the die shows six more than twice.

(i) Show that the probability of a type I error for this test is just under 10%.

(ii) Show that the operating characteristic of this test is given by the expression
$$(1-p)^5(1 + 5p + 15p^2)$$
where p is the probability of the die showing a six, and sketch the graph of this function.

(iii) For which values of p is the probability of a type II error below 10%?

3 Hugo is buying a tank of tropical fish. There are 16 fish in the tank, and the pet-shop owner claims that half are male and half are female. As sexing this species of fish requires close examination, Hugo decides to test this hypothesis by removing four fish from the tank at random, without replacement. He will reject the pet-shop owner's claim unless his sample of four contains at least one male and at least one female fish.

(i) Find the significance level for this test.

(ii) For each possible number of male fish in the tank (from 0 to 16) determine the probability of a type II error, and thus sketch the operating characteristic of the test.

(iii) Would the significance level and operating characteristic be very different if Hugo had sampled with replacement?

4 In radio-carbon dating, the number of beta particles emitted per minute by a sample of carbon from a charred bone is given by a Poisson distribution whose mean, λ, depends on the age of the sample.

A charred bone is found which, because of the deposits with which it is associated, is known to be either 1800 years old, in which case $\lambda = 7.2$, or 2600 years old, in which case $\lambda = 3.8$.

An archaeologist's strategy for deciding between these hypotheses is to count the number, B, of beta particles emitted by the sample in m minutes, accepting that $\lambda = 7.2$ if $B > c$ and that $\lambda = 3.8$ if $B < c$.

Define $\alpha = $ P(accepting $\lambda = 3.8$ when $\lambda = 7.2$) and $\beta = $ P(accepting $\lambda = 7.2$ when $\lambda = 3.8$).

(i) If $m = 1$ and $c = 5.5$, determine the values of α and β.

(ii) If $m = 8$ and $c = 40$, use a Normal approximation to the Poisson distribution to find α and β.

(iii) Why might an archaeologist choose c so that α and β were not equal?

5 In a test on extra-sensory perception, a supposed clairvoyant is asked to predict the suit of 12 cards selected randomly, with replacement, from a reshuffled pack. The hypothesis testing strategy is to count the number, C, of cards for which the suit is predicted correctly and then:

if $C > 6$, reject the null hypothesis of no clairvoyance

if $C < 6$, accept the null hypothesis of no clairvoyance

if $C = 6$, draw a random number uniformly distributed on [0, 1] from a calculator, accepting the null hypothesis if this is less than r and rejecting if this is greater than r.

(i) Find the value of r which gives this test an exact significance level of 0.05.

(ii) For this value of r, what is the probability of a type II error if the clairvoyant in fact has a probability of 0.5 of correctly predicting the suit of a card?

6 The random variable, X, is distributed uniformly on the range $[0, m]$, where m is claimed to have the value m_0, but is suspected to have a smaller value than this. In order to test the null hypothesis, $m = m_0$, against the alternative, $m < m_0$, a sample of n values of X is drawn and the largest of the n values is recorded as the value of the random variable L. The null hypothesis will be rejected if this largest value is less than some critical value.

(i) Explain why
P(largest of the n values is less than I)
$= \left(\dfrac{I}{m}\right)^n$.

(ii) Hence determine

(a) the critical value of I in terms of α, the significance level of the test, m_0 and n

(b) the operating characteristic for the test as a function of m.

(iii) If $\alpha = 0.0625$ and $m_0 = 100$, sketch the operating characteristic in the cases $n = 1, 2, 4$.

(iv) Explain why, if you are free to choose n, then, for any simple alternative hypothesis for m, you can have $\beta = 0$, with α as small as you wish. In what sense does this mean that you can actually 'find out' what m is?

7 It is thought that people are likely to perform better on an endurance test, which measures the time for which a weight can be supported with an outstretched arm, if they are in a group than individually. The differences in times (group – individual) are modelled by the random variable D, with distribution $D \sim N(\mu, \sigma^2)$.

Eighty subjects are asked to perform the test individually and in a group and the differences in times are recorded. The results are summarised by the mean difference $\bar{d}$ and the unbiased variance estimate s^2.

(i) State suitable null and alternative hypotheses.

(ii) If α is to equal 0.01, determine the critical value of $\bar{d}$ above which the null hypothesis will be rejected, in terms of s.

You should assume that a sample size of 80 is sufficiently large that you can take the standard deviation of D to equal and use the Normal rather than the t distribution for your calculation.

(iii) If $\sigma = 22$ seconds, construct a graph of the operating characteristic of this test.

8 Define the following terms with reference to hypothesis testing.

(i) type I error

(ii) type II error

(iii) operating characteristic

The random variable X is distributed as $N(\mu, 9)$. A test is required of the null hypothesis
H_0: $\mu = 20$ against the alternative hypothesis
H_1: $\mu \neq 20$, using the customary procedure based on the sample mean $\bar{X}$, with a sample of size 25; thus the test statistic to be used is
$\dfrac{(\bar{X} - 20)}{\left(\tfrac{3}{5}\right)}$.

The probability of a type I error is to be 1%.

(iv) Show that H_0 is to be accepted if
$18.45 < \bar{x} < 21.55$.

(v) Show that an expression for the operating characteristic of the test is

$$P\left(\frac{18.45 - \mu}{0.6} < Z < \frac{21.55 - \mu}{0.6}\right)$$

where $Z \sim N(0, 1)$. Evaluate this expression for $\mu = 17, 18, 19, 20, 21, 22, 23$ and hence draw a sketch of the operating characteristic.

9 Independent observations $x_1, x_2, \ldots, x_n$ are taken from the Normally distributed population $N(\mu, \sigma^2)$ where the value of σ^2 is known to be 4. The null hypothesis value of μ is 1 and the only other possible value of μ is 2.

α denotes the probability that the null hypothesis is rejected when, in fact, it is true. β denotes the probability that the null hypothesis is accepted when, in fact, it is false.

(i) Suppose that $n = 25$ and it is decided to reject the null hypothesis if the observed sample mean $\bar{x}$ exceeds 1.4. Determine α and β.

(ii) Suppose $n = 4$ and it is required that $\alpha = 0.05$. Determine the constant k for which observed values of $\bar{x}$ exceeding k lead to rejection of the null hypothesis. Also find β.

(iii) Suppose it is required that $\alpha = \beta = 0.025$. Determine the required sample size n and the constant k for which observed values of $\bar{x}$ exceeding k lead to rejection of the null hypothesis.

10 (i) Define the following terms in connection with hypothesis testing: type I error, type II error, operating characteristic.

(ii) A test is to be made concerning a parameter θ. The null hypothesis is that θ has the particular value θ_0; this is to be tested against the two-sided alternative $\theta \neq \theta_0$.

(a) Draw a quick sketch of the operating characteristic for a *perfect* test that *never* makes an error.

(b) Draw a quick sketch showing the operating characteristics of two hypothesis tests, one of which is 'better' than the other in the sense that it is less likely to accept the null hypothesis whenever it is false. Explain how this is demonstrated by the operating characteristics.

(iii) The random variable X is distributed as $N(\mu, 16)$. A random sample of size 25 is available. The null hypothesis $\mu = 0$ is to be tested against the alternative hypothesis $\mu \neq 0$. The null hypothesis will be accepted if $-1.5 < \bar{x} < 1.5$, where $\bar{x}$ is the value of the sample mean, otherwise it will be rejected. Calculate the probability of a type I error. Calculate the probability of a type II error if, in fact, $\mu = 0.5$; comment on the value of this probability.

KEY POINTS

When analysing a hypothesis test the following notations are used.

1 Rejecting the null hypothesis when it is true is called a *type 1 error*. The probability of a type I error is the significance level of the test.

2 Accepting the null hypothesis when it is false is called a *type II error*.

3 With a compound alternative hypothesis, the probability of a type II error, viewed as a function of the parameter whose value is being tested, is called the *operating characteristic* of the test.

4 The *power* of a test is (1 − the operating characteristic of the test).

10 Analysis of variance

The control of large numbers is possible, and like unto that of small numbers, if we subdivide them.

Sun Tse Ping Fa

The ABC Engineering Company produces many fittings for DIY stores. In one of their workshops, three machines are all producing spacing rods, which ought to be the same length (though it does not matter exactly what this length is). A quality control manager suspects that the machines are producing rods of different lengths so, from each machine, he takes five rods at random, all produced during the same shift. The lengths of the rods in millimetres, in the samples from the three machines were as follows.

> The terms *sample* and *group* are both commonly used in analysis of variance, but not always consistently. In the rest of this chapter, the complete set of observations is referred to as the sample and this consists of a number of groups (e.g. the observations from different machines).

	Machine	
1	2	3
32.1	28.0	28.7
28.8	26.9	27.6
30.2	26.8	28.9
30.7	28.5	29.6
27.7	30.2	29.2

This may be illustrated diagramatically.

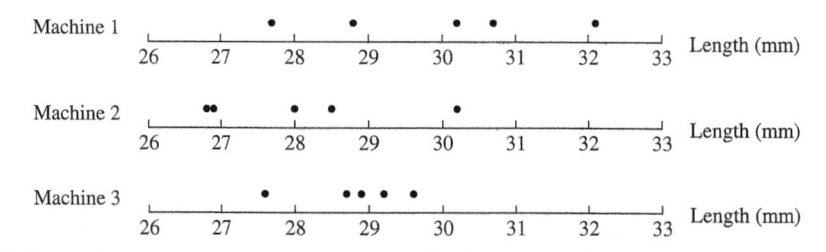

Figure 10.1

There is evidently some variation in the measurements. How much of it can be attributed to unpredictable fluctuations in the production of each machine, the *within groups variation*, and how much to consistent differences in the average performance of the machines, the *between groups variation*?

If you assume that the populations from which the manager is sampling, the outputs of the three machines, have a common variance, then the within groups variation enables you to estimate this common variance. If the mean length of the rods from the three machines is also the same, the only reason for differences between the group means is chance differences in the samples – and the common variance will determine how much variation between the group means you should expect. If the mean lengths of the rods in the populations from which the rods are drawn are different, however, you would expect this to increase the variation between the group means. The usual hypothesis testing methodology then suggests that unequal means in the populations can be detected by looking for variation between group means that is significantly greater than would be expected on the assumption of equal population means.

The method outlined above is called *analysis of variance* (ANOVA for short). ANOVA uses the within groups variation and the between groups variation to produce two figures, which will be unbiased estimates of the common population variance *if the three populations have the same mean*. If, on the other hand, the three populations have significantly different means, then the estimate of the common variance from the between groups variation will be too large. When the estimate is made, the relatively large differences in length caused by measuring the output of different machines, will be mistaken for random fluctuations in the performances of machines producing rods with the same mean lengths.

The best way of explaining the method in detail is to work through an example.

The notation used here and in subsequent work is as follows.

k = the number of groups $\qquad$ x_{ij} = the jth member of the ith group

n_i = the number of observations in $\qquad$ n = the total sample size
the ith group

$\bar{x}_i$ = the mean of ith group $\qquad$ $\bar{x}$ = the overall sample mean

s_i^2 = the variance of the ith group $\qquad$ s^2 = the overall sample variance

As there are three groups, $k = 3$. The remaining statistics are summarised below.

Machine	1	2	3	Overall sample
Group size	$n_1 = 5$	$n_2 = 5$	$n_3 = 5$	$n = 15$
Group mean	$\bar{x}_1 = 29.90$	$\bar{x}_2 = 28.08$	$\bar{x}_3 = 28.80$	$\bar{x} = 28.93$
Group variance	$s_1^2 = 2.905$	$s_2^2 = 1.927$	$s_3^2 = 0.565$	$s^2 = 2.142$

Note

All of the statistics in the table can found by entering the data (the three groups separately followed by the overall sample) into a scientific calculator in statistics mode. The group sizes and group means are self-explanatory. The sample variance is the *unbiased* estimate of the population variance.

ACTIVITY   Enter the data yourself and confirm that the results obtained are correct.

The *within groups* estimate s_w^2

Whether or not the null hypothesis is true, an unbiased estimate of the population variance is given by pooling the three group variances.

$$s_w^2 = \frac{(n_1 - 1)s_1^2 + (n_2 - 1)s_2^2 + (n_3 - 1)s_3^2}{n_1 + n_2 + n_3 - 3}$$

$$= \frac{4 \times 2.905 + 4 \times 1.927 + 4 \times 0.565}{5 + 5 + 5 - 3} = \frac{21.59}{12} = 1.799$$

Note that this can also be given by

$$s_w^2 = \frac{\sum_j (x_{1j} - \bar{x}_1)^2 + \sum_j (x_{2j} - \bar{x}_2)^2 + \sum_j (x_{3j} - \bar{x}_3)^2}{n_1 + n_2 + n_3 - 3}.$$

In general

$$s_w^2 = \frac{\sum_i \sum_j (x_{ij} - \bar{x}_i)^2}{n - k}.$$

The numerator is known as the *within groups sum of squares* (of deviations from the group means) and the denominator is the *degrees of freedom*.

The within groups sum of squares is also known as the *residual sum of squares*.

The *between groups* estimate s_b^2

Provided the null hypothesis is true, an unbiased estimate of the population variance is also given by replacing every item in a group by the group mean and considering the variance of the deviations of the group means from the overall mean.

$$s_b^2 = \frac{n_1(\bar{x}_1 - \bar{x})^2 + n_2(\bar{x}_2 - \bar{x})^2 + n_3(\bar{x}_3 - \bar{x})^2}{k - 1}$$

$$= \frac{5 \times (0.97)^2 + 5 \times (-0.85)^2 + 5 \times (-0.13)^2}{3 - 1} = \frac{8.401}{2} = 4.201$$

Note that this can also be given by

$$s_b^2 = \frac{\sum_i n_i(\bar{x}_i - \bar{x})^2}{k - 1} = \frac{\sum_i n_i(\bar{x}_i - \bar{x})^2}{k - 1}.$$

The numerator is known as the *between groups sum of squares* (of deviations of the group means from the overall mean) and the denominator is the *degrees of freedom*. A proof that s_b^2 is an unbiased estimate of σ^2 is given in the appendix.

Summary

The results obtained so far can be summarised in the following table:

Source of variation	Sum of squares	Degrees of freedom	Variance estimate
Between groups	8.401	2	$s_b^2 = 4.201$
Within groups	21.59	12	$s_w^2 = 1.799$

Carrying out the hypothesis test

Formally, you set up a hypothesis test as follows. Let μ_1, μ_2, μ_3 represent the mean lengths of the rods in the three populations from which the groups are drawn. The null and alternative hypotheses are given by

$H_0: \mu_1 = \mu_2 = \mu_3 = \mu$

H_1: Not all the population means are the same.

To compare the estimates s_w^2 and s_b^2 you use a test called the F test. For this test to be appropriate, it is essential that the three populations have a common variance and that the lengths of the rods in each population are Normally distributed. This is a strong assumption, of course, but it does not seem unreasonable in the present example.

The F test statistic is

$$F = \frac{s_b^2}{s_w^2}$$

$$= \frac{4.201}{1.799} = 2.335.$$

If H_0 is true, then you would expect F to have a value around 1, whereas if H_0 is false you would expect s_b^2 to overestimate, so F will be greater than 1. As usual, tables are available to tell you which values of F are unlikely to occur by chance in a group if the null hypothesis of equal means is true of the populations. This critical value depends on v_1 the degrees of freedom in the numerator, and on v_2 the degrees of freedom in the denominator of the F statistic, as well as on the significance level. Here the numerator has 2 degrees of freedom and the denominator has 12 degrees of freedom. Selecting, as an example, a significance level of 5%, the tables give a critical value of 3.89, as shown on the next page.

Figure 10.2 5% points of the F distribution

v_2\v_1	1	2	3	4	5	6	7	8	10	12	24	∞
1	161.4	199.5	215.7	224.6	230.2	234.0	236.8	238.9	241.9	243.9	249.0	254.3
2	18.5	19.0	19.2	19.2	19.3	19.3	19.4	19.4	19.4	19.4	19.5	19.5
3	10.13	9.55	9.28	9.12	9.01	8.94	8.89	8.85	8.79	8.74	8.64	8.53
4	7.71	6.94	6.59	6.39	6.26	6.16	6.09	6.04	5.96	5.91	5.77	5.63
5	6.61	5.79	5.41	5.19	5.05	4.95	4.88	4.82	4.74	4.68	4.53	4.36
6	5.99	5.14	4.76	4.53	4.39	4.28	4.21	4.15	4.06	4.00	3.84	3.67
7	5.59	4.74	4.35	4.12	3.97	3.87	3.79	3.73	3.64	3.57	3.41	3.23
8	5.32	4.46	4.07	3.84	3.69	3.58	3.50	3.44	3.35	3.28	3.12	2.93
9	5.12	4.26	3.86	3.63	3.48	3.37	3.29	3.23	3.14	3.07	2.90	2.71
10	4.96	4.10	3.71	3.48	3.33	3.22	3.14	3.07	2.98	2.91	2.74	2.54
11	4.84	3.98	3.59	3.36	3.20	3.09	3.01	2.95	2.85	2.79	2.61	2.40
12	4.75	3.89	3.49	3.26	3.11	3.00	2.91	2.85	2.75	2.69	2.51	2.30
13	4.67	3.81	3.41	3.18	3.03	2.92	2.83	2.77	2.67	2.60	2.42	2.21
14	4.60	3.74	3.34	3.11	2.96	2.85	2.76	2.70	2.60	2.53	2.35	2.13

($v_1 = 2$, $v_2 = 12$ highlighted; value 3.89 circled)

As the calculated value is less than the critical value, the result is not significant and you would accept the null hypothesis H_0 and conclude that all 15 observations might well have come from the same Normal population with common mean as well as common variance. The evidence suggests that there is no significant difference between the measurements obtained from the three groups.

Extending the example

Suppose that it is found that the measurement of 27.7 mm from machine 1 was, in fact, from machine 2. Does this information affect your conclusion?

The data now read as shown in the following table.

Machine 1	Machine 2	Machine 3
32.1	28.0	28.7
28.8	26.9	27.6
30.2	26.8	28.9
30.7	28.5	29.6
	30.2	29.2
	27.7	

The summary statistics for the newly grouped data are shown in the table below.

Machine	1	2	3	Overall sample
Group size	$n_1 = 4$	$n_2 = 6$	$n_3 = 5$	$n = 15$
Group mean	$\bar{x}_1 = 30.45$	$\bar{x}_2 = 28.02$	$\bar{x}_3 = 28.80$	$\bar{x} = 28.93$
Group variance	$s_1^2 = 1.857$	$s_2^2 = 1.566$	$s_3^2 = 0.565$	$s^2 = 2.142$

The *within groups* estimate is

$$s_w^2 = \frac{(n_1 - 1)s_1^2 + (n_2 - 1)s_2^2 + (n_3 - 1)s_3^2}{n_1 + n_2 + n_3 - 3}$$

$$= \frac{3 \times 1.857 + 5 \times 1.566 + 4 \times 0.565}{4 + 6 + 5 - 3} = \frac{15.66}{12} = 1.305$$

The *between groups* estimates is

$$s_b^2 = \frac{n_1(\bar{x}_1 - \bar{x})^2 + n_2(\bar{x}_2 - \bar{x})^2 + n_3(\bar{x}_3 - \bar{x})^2}{k - 1}$$

$$= \frac{4 \times (1.52)^2 + 6 \times (-0.91)^2 + 5 \times (-0.13)^2}{3 - 1} = \frac{14.33}{2} = 7.166$$

The results obtained so far can again be summarised in a table.

Source of variation	Sum of squares	Degrees of freedom	Variance estimate
Between groups	14.33	2	$s_b^2 = 7.166$
Within groups	15.66	12	$s_w^2 = 1.305$

Finally, calculate the *F* test statistic:

$$F = \frac{s_b^2}{s_w^2}$$

$$= \frac{7.166}{1.305} = 5.491.$$

As the degrees of freedom are once again $v_1 = 2$ and $v_2 = 12$, the critical value for a 5% level of significance is again 3.89. As the calculated value is greater than the critical value, the result is significant and you would reject the null hypothesis, H_0, in favour of the alternative hypothesis, H_1. You would conclude that there is sufficient evidence to suggest that the differences between the means as reflected in the between groups estimate of the population variance are too large to be accounted for by chance fluctuations, i.e. not all of the population means are the same.

EXERCISE 10A

1 Tests were carried out by a chemist to measure the percentage of impurity in a chemical solution, using five different methods on groups of four. The percentage of impurity was recorded as follows.

Method	% impurity			
1	25	19	20	21
2	27	28	24	28
3	21	18	21	17
4	20	21	21	17
5	24	27	21	24

The chemist wishes to test, at the 5% significance level, if there is any significant difference between the mean percentages obtained by the different methods.

(i) State suitable null and alternative hypotheses for an analysis of variance test.

(ii) Construct a summary table of the group sizes, group means and group variances of the five groups and the overall values.

(iii) Construct a summary table of sums of squares, degrees of freedom and variance estimates for within groups and between groups variation.

(iv) Calculate the F statistic and compare it with the critical value obtained from tables.

(v) State your conclusions.

2 The times, to the nearest minute, taken by Alex, Bobby and Carol to complete a random sample of crosswords were as follows.

Alex	77	81	71	76	80
Bobby	72	58	74	66	70
Carol	76	85	82	80	77

At the 5% level, test whether the differences in times they take to do crosswords are significant.

[MEI]

3 Four machines, each dispensing sugar in nominal quantities of 1 kg, produce the following quantities when five measures are taken from each.

Dispenser	Mass of sugar (g)
1	998 1002 1000 1011 1003
2	1006 1010 1014 997 1005
3	991 1001 999 998 993
4	1006 984 993 1001 998

Test whether the quantities produced by the machines are significantly different

(i) at the 5% level

(ii) at the 1% level.

4 Samples of four different varieties of wheat, planted in similar ground, gave the following yields in kilograms.

Variety	Yield (kg)			
A	40	42	44	
B	46	44	46	46
C	35	38		
D	37	49	37	

Are the mean yields significantly different at the 5% level?

5 A catering firm wished to buy a meat tenderiser, but was concerned with the effect on the weight loss of meat during cooking. The following results were obtained for the weight loss of steaks of the same pre-cooked weight when three different tenderisers were used.

Tenderiser	Weight loss in grams				
A	36	28	42	58	
B	17	59	33		
C	36	74	29	55	48

Carry out an analysis of variance to test, at the 5% level of significance, whether there is a difference in weight loss between tenderisers.

[AEB]

6 An experiment was conducted to study the effects of various diets on pigs. A total of 24 similar pigs were selected and randomly allocated to one of the five groups so that the control group, which was fed a normal diet, contained eight pigs and each of the other groups, to which the new diets were given, contained four pigs each. After a fixed time the gains in mass, in kilograms, of the pigs were measured. Unfortunately, by this time two pigs had died, one of which was on diet A and the other on diet C. The gains in mass of the remaining pigs are recorded in the table.

Test for differences between the diets

(i) at the 5% level of significance
(ii) at the 1% level of significance.

[AEB]

Diet	Gains in mass (kg)			
Normal	23.1	9.8	15.5	22.6
	14.6	11.2	15.7	10.5
A	21.9	13.2	19.7	
B	16.5	22.8	18.3	31.0
C	30.9	21.9	29.8	
D	21.0	25.4	21.5	21.2

The *total* estimate s^2

Although you compare s_w^2 and s_b^2 using the F test, a third method of estimating the common population variance is to regard all the observations as one sample, and calculate the usual variance estimate s^2.

Provided the null hypothesis is true, that the populations from which the groups are drawn all have the same mean, μ, then s^2 also gives an unbiased estimate of σ^2.

Returning to the first example, the table of results gives $s^2 = 2.142$.

Note that s^2 is given by

$$s^2 = \frac{\sum_i \sum_j (x_{ij} - \bar{x})^2}{n - 1}.$$

The numerator is known as the *total sum of squares* (of deviations from the overall mean) and the denominator is the *degrees of freedom*.

In the example,

$$\sum_i \sum_j (x_{ij} - \bar{x})^2 = (32.1 - 28.93)^2 + (28.8 - 28.93)^2 + \ldots$$
$$+ (29.2 - 28.93)^2$$
$$= 29.99$$

and $n - 1 = 14$, which gives the quoted figure, $s^2 = 2.142$.

You have now seen three ways of estimating the population variance, σ^2, all of which produce unbiased estimates, given that the null hypothesis is true. The results now obtained can be summarised in a table.

Source of variation	Sum of squares	Degrees of freedom	Variance estimate
Between groups	8.401	2	$s_b^2 = 4.201$
Within groups	21.59	12	$s_w^2 = 1.799$
Total	29.99	14	$s^2 = 2.142$

Two very important properties are illustrated here.

$$\text{Total sum of squares} =$$
$$\text{within groups sum of squares} + \text{between groups sum of squares.}$$

$$\text{Total degrees of freedom} =$$
$$\text{within groups degrees of freedom} + \text{between groups degrees of freedom.}$$

The second equation is easy to follow as, using the generalised form for the degrees of freedom,

$$n - 1 = (n - k) + (k - 1)$$

The first equation in generalised form gives

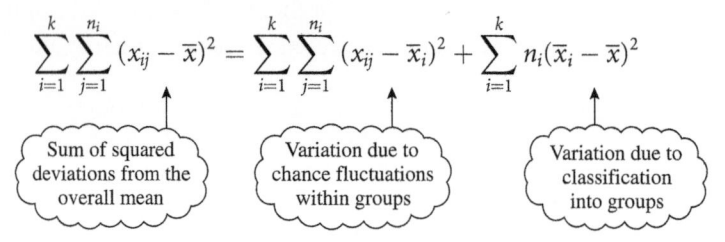

$$\sum_{i=1}^{k}\sum_{j=1}^{n_i}(x_{ij} - \overline{x})^2 = \sum_{i=1}^{k}\sum_{j=1}^{n_i}(x_{ij} - \overline{x}_i)^2 + \sum_{i=1}^{k}n_i(\overline{x}_i - \overline{x})^2$$

- Sum of squared deviations from the overall mean
- Variation due to chance fluctuations within groups
- Variation due to classification into groups

These formulae can be awkward to evaluate directly if the population mean is, for example, a recurring decimal. Alternative versions for the formulae for the *total* sum of squares and the *between groups* sum of squares, involving group and grand totals, can be derived by simple algebraic manipulation.

Let S_i represent the total of the *i*th group and let S represent the overall sample total, i.e.

$$S_i = \sum_j x_{ij} \quad \Rightarrow \quad \overline{x}_i = \frac{S_i}{n_i}$$

and

$$S = \sum_i \sum_j x_{ij} \quad \Rightarrow \quad \overline{x} = \frac{S}{n}.$$

Between groups sum of squares

$$\sum_i n_i(\bar{x}_i - \bar{x})^2 = \sum_i n_i(\bar{x}_i - \bar{x})(\bar{x}_i - \bar{x})$$

$$= \sum_i n_i(\bar{x}_i^2 - 2\bar{x}\bar{x}_i + \bar{x}^2)$$

$$= \sum_i n_i \bar{x}_i^2 - 2\bar{x}\sum_i n_i \bar{x}_i + \bar{x}^2 \sum_i n_i$$

$$= \sum_i \frac{S_i^2}{n_i} - \frac{2S^2}{n} + \frac{S^2}{n}$$

$$= \sum_i \frac{S_i^2}{n_i} - \frac{S^2}{n}$$

Total sum of squares

$$\sum_i \sum_j (x_{ij} - \bar{x})^2 = \sum_i \sum_j (x_{ij} - \bar{x})(x_{ij} - \bar{x})$$

$$= \sum_i \sum_j (x_{ij}^2 - 2\bar{x}x_{ij} + \bar{x}^2)$$

$$= \sum_i \sum_j x_{ij}^2 - 2\bar{x}\sum_i \sum_j x_{ij} + n\bar{x}^2$$

$$= \sum_i \sum_j x_{ij}^2 - \frac{2S^2}{n} + \frac{S^2}{n}$$

$$= \sum_i \sum_j x_{ij}^2 - \frac{S^2}{n}$$

Within groups sum of squares

This may now be obtained by subtraction.

Within groups sum of squares =
total sum of squares − between groups sum of squares

$$= \sum_i \sum_j x_{ij}^2 - \frac{S^2}{n} - \left(\sum_i \frac{S_i^2}{n_i} - \frac{S^2}{n}\right) = \sum_i \sum_j x_{ij}^2 - \sum_i \frac{S_i^2}{n_i}$$

Returning to the extended example on page 196, the alternative sum of squares formulae can be used to produce the variance estimates s_b^2 and s_w^2.

The summary statistics for the grouped data are shown in the table below.

Machine	1	2	3	Overall sample
Group size	$n_1 = 4$	$n_2 = 6$	$n_3 = 5$	$n = 15$
Group total	$S_1 = 121.8$	$S_2 = 168.1$	$S_3 = 144.0$	$S = 433.9$

$$\sum_i \sum_j x_{ij}^2 = 32.1^2 + 28.8^2 + \ldots + 29.6^2 + 29.2^2 = 12\,581.3$$

The *between groups* estimate is

$$s_b^2 = \frac{\sum_i \frac{S_i^2}{n_i} - \frac{S^2}{n}}{k-1} = \frac{\frac{121.8^2}{4} + \frac{168.1^2}{6} + \frac{144.0^2}{5} - \frac{433.9^2}{15}}{3-1}$$

$$= 7.166.$$

The *within groups* estimate is

$$s_w^2 = \frac{\sum_i \sum_j x_{ij}^2 - \sum_i \frac{S_i^2}{n_i}}{n-k} = \frac{12\,581.3 - \left(\frac{121.8^2}{4} + \frac{168.1^2}{6} + \frac{144.0^2}{5}\right)}{15-3}$$

$$= 1.305$$

The ANOVA model

The general form of the hypothesis for the analysis of variance is

$H_0: \mu_1 = \mu_2 = \ldots = \mu_k = \mu$
H_1: Not all population means are the same.

where $x_{ij} \sim N(\mu_i, \sigma^2)$.

Each observation may be written in the form $x_{ij} = \mu_i + e_{ij}$ where e_{ij} represents the *experimental error*, i.e. the measure of the deviation of the *j*th observation of the *i*th group (x_{ij}) from the corresponding population mean μ_1. It is also assumed that $e_{ij} \sim N(0, \sigma^2)$.

An alternative and preferred form of this equation is obtained by substituting $\mu_i = \mu + \alpha_i$, where μ is defined to be the mean of all the μ_i; i.e. $\mu = \frac{1}{k}\sum_i \mu_i$.

Therefore you may write $x_{ij} = \mu + \alpha_i + e_{ij}$ subject to the restriction that $\sum_i \alpha_i = 0$. It is customary to refer to α_i as the *treatment effect* of the *i*th population. The null hypothesis, that the *k* population means are equal against the alternative that at least two of the means are unequal, may now be replaced by the equivalent statements

$H_0: \alpha_1 = \alpha_2 = \ldots = \alpha_k = 0$
H_1: Not all the α_1 are zero.

The *t* test for the difference between population means

The analysis of variance tests whether there are any overall differences among the population means. To see whether two particular means, μ_i and μ_j, are the same, you may, of course, use an ordinary two-sample *t* test.

$H_0: \mu_i = \mu_j$

$H_1: \mu_i \neq \mu_j$

As $\text{Var}(\overline{X}_i) = \dfrac{\sigma^2}{n_i}$ and $\text{Var}(\overline{X}_j) = \dfrac{\sigma^2}{n_j}$, then

$$\text{Var}(\overline{X}_i - \overline{X}_j) = \frac{\sigma^2}{n_i} + \frac{\sigma^2}{n_j} = \sigma^2\left(\frac{1}{n_i} + \frac{1}{n_j}\right)$$

so if you knew σ^2 you could take as the test statistic

$$\frac{\overline{x}_i - \overline{x}_j}{\sigma\sqrt{\dfrac{1}{n_i} + \dfrac{1}{n_j}}}$$

and refer this to N(0, 1). However, the population variance σ^2 is unknown. An unbiased estimator for σ^2 is given by s_w^2, regardless of any hypothesis about the population means, so you use the test statistic

$$\frac{\overline{x}_i - \overline{x}_j}{s_w\sqrt{\dfrac{1}{n_i} + \dfrac{1}{n_j}}}$$

and refer to t_{n-k}.

There is, however, the difficulty that there will usually be many pairs of means and you could well find one pair (or more) to give a significant result by chance (a type I error). With k groups there are $^kC_2$ possible *t* tests, and by considering every one, the probability of such an occurrence at the 5% level is given by

$$P(\text{at least one type I error}) = 1 - P(\text{no type I error in } ^kC_2 \text{ tests})$$

$$= 1 - (0.95)^{^kC_2}$$

$$\approx 0.4 \text{ when } k = 5, \text{ for example.}$$

In the extension of the original example, it would seem sensible to compare machine 1 with machines 2 or 3. For example, consider machines 1 and 2. The test statistic is

$$\frac{\bar{x}_1 - \bar{x}_2}{s_W\sqrt{\frac{1}{n_1} + \frac{1}{n_2}}} = \frac{30.45 - 28.02}{\sqrt{1.305}\sqrt{\frac{1}{4} + \frac{1}{6}}} = 3.300$$

which you compare with t_{12}. The result is significant, even at the 1% level, for which the critical value is 3.055. By rejecting the null hypothesis for the F test you came to the conclusion that there was sufficient evidence to suggest that not all population means, μ_i, were equal. By rejecting the null hypothesis for the t test you come to the conclusion that there is sufficient evidence to suggest that $\mu_1 \neq \mu_2$.

A similar t test applied to machines 1 and 3 produces a t statistic of 2.24. By comparison with the critical value, you would not reject the null hypothesis at the 1% level. That is, there is not enough evidence to reject the null hypothesis that $\mu_1 = \mu_3$.

Note

The analysis of variance method covered in this chapter involves one source of variation and so is called one-way analysis of variance. Similar techniques for two sources of variation are called two-way analysis of variance, and so on.

EXERCISE 10B

1 As part of a project to improve the steerability of trucks, a manufacturer took three trucks of the same model and fitted them with soft, standard and hard front springs respectively. The turning radius (the radius of the circle in which the truck could turn full circle) was measured for each truck using a variety of drivers, speeds and conditions. The following results are available.

Source of variation	Sum of squares	Degrees of freedom
Between springs	37.9	2
Within springs	75.6	18
Total	113.5	20

(i) How many observations were made altogether?

(ii) Assuming that each truck underwent the same number of tests, how many was this?

(iii) Carry out a one-way analysis of variance at the 5% significance level to test for a difference in the springs.

[AEB]

2 A batch of bricks was randomly divided into three parts and each part was stored by a different method. After a week the percentage water content of a number of bricks stored by each method was measured.

Method of storage	% water content					
1	7.4	8.5	7.1	6.2	7.8	
2	5.5	7.1	5.6			
3	4.8	5.1	6.2	4.9	6.1	7.1

(i) Construct a summary table of the group sizes, group means and group variances of the three groups and the overall values.

(ii) Construct a summary table of sums of squares, degrees of freedom and variance estimates for within groups and between groups variation.

(iii) Use the analysis of variance to test, at the 5% level of significance, for differences between methods of storage.

[AEB]

3 Eastside Area Health Authority has a policy whereby any patient admitted to a hospital with a suspected heart attack is automatically placed in the intensive care unit. The table below gives the number of hours spent in intensive care by such patients at five hospitals in the area:

Hospital

A	B	C	D	E
30	42	65	67	70
25	57	46	58	63
12	47	55	81	80
23	30	27		
16				

(i) Use a one-way analysis of variance to test, at the 1% level of significance, for differences between hospitals.

(ii) Write down an estimate, with its standard error, of the mean time spent in intensive care by this type of patient in hospital C.

[AEB]

4 A commuter in a large city can travel to work by car, bicycle or bus. She times four journeys by each method, with the following results (in minutes).

Car	Bicycle	Bus
27	34	26
45	38	41
33	43	35
31	42	46

(i) Carry out an analysis of variance at the 5% significance level to find whether there are differences in the mean journey times for the three methods of transport.

(ii) The time of day at which she travels to work varies. Bearing in mind that this is likely to affect the time taken for the journey, suggest a better design for her experiment and explain briefly why you believe it to be better.

(iii) Suggest a factor, other than leaving time, which is likely to affect the journey time and two factors, other than journey time, which might be considered when choosing the method of transport.

[AEB]

5 An archaeological team unearthed human skulls at three different locations. It was known that certain different subspecies of 'early man' differed in the length of their skulls, so it was decided to examine whether or not the average skull lengths of the underlying population of 'early man' at these three locations could be assumed to be the same. The lengths in millimetres of the skulls found at the locations were as follows.

Location	Length of skull
1	188 179 183 171 187 172 176 174
2	176 193 181 191 178
3	180 159 175 170 169 166

(i) Carry out a one-way analysis of variance using a 5% significance level, carefully displaying your working.

(ii) State carefully the null and alternative hypotheses and the critical value of your test statistic.

(iii) Discuss briefly your conclusions. What are the assumptions underlying your analysis?

[MEI]

6 (i) In a one-way analysis of variance, k treatments are being compared. There are n_i observations on the ith treatment, and x_{ij} represents the jth observation on the ith treatment ($i = 1, 2, \ldots, k$; $j = 1, 2, \ldots, n_i$). A suitable statistical model is

$$x_{ij} = \mu + \alpha_i + e_{ij}$$
$$i = 1, 2, \ldots, k; \quad j = 1, 2, \ldots, n_i$$

where μ represents the overall population mean for the whole situation, α_i represents the population mean amount by which the ith treatment differs from the overall mean, and e_{ij} represents the 'experimental error'.

(a) State carefully the statistical properties that the e_{ij} need to possess for the usual analysis of variance to be applicable.

(b) Explain why the null hypothesis customarily tested can be written as $\alpha_1 = \alpha_2 = \ldots = \alpha_k = 0$.

(ii) At an agricultural research station, four different fertilisers are being compared. Each is applied to a number of similar plots of soil and a standard variety of wheat is grown under carefully controlled conditions. The yields of wheat, measured in a convenient unit, from the plots are as follows.

Fertiliser 1	23.7	24.2	24.9	24.6	
Fertiliser 2	22.9	23.7	23.6	24.4	23.4
Fertiliser 3	22.9	23.6	22.4		
Fertiliser 4	24.3	24.9	24.5	24.0	

(a) Carry out the customary one-way analysis of variance using a 5% significance level, carefully displaying your working and stating the critical value of your test statistic.

(b) Discuss briefly your conclusions.

[MEI]

7 At a chemical plant, trials are being conducted concerning the production of a particular chemical. Four processes for making this chemical are being compared in terms of the purity of the product. The following data show the percentages of impurity in the product in a number of experimental runs using each process.

Process A	6.21	5.64	7.47	7.36	
Process B	11.55	10.63	5.62	7.57	8.13
Process C	9.31	7.46	11.13	10.22	
Process D	9.06	5.59	5.72	3.60	7.23

Note: $(6.21)^2 + (5.64)^2 + \ldots + (7.23)^2 = 1163.6658$.

(i) State the conditions that are necessary for it to be appropriate to analyse these data using the customary one-way analysis of variance.

(ii) Assuming these conditions are satisfied, carry out the analysis of variance using a 5% significance level, stating the null and alternative hypothesis and the critical value of the test statistic.

(iii) Process A is the standard process and process C the cheapest. Use a t test to examine, at the 5% significance level, whether the mean percentage impurities for these two processes differ.

[MEI]

8 (i) In a one-way analysis of variance situation, k treatments are being compared. There are n_i observations on the ith treatment; the jth observation on the ith treatment is denoted by x_{ij} ($i = 1, 2, \ldots, k$; $j = 1, 2, \ldots, n_i$). A statistical model commonly used for this situation is

$$x_{ij} = \mu + \alpha_i + e_{ij}$$

where e_{ij} represents the experimental error.

(a) State carefully the statistical properties that the e_{ij} need to possess for the usual analysis of variance to be applicable. Interpret the parameters μ and α_i in the model.

(b) State, in terms of the α_i, the null hypothesis that is customarily tested.

(ii) In an engineering development laboratory, prototypes of a casting are being made by three processes. A critical dimension is measured for each casting and the results (in centimetres), for a random sample of four castings made by each process, are as follows.

Process A	9.681	9.54	9.95	9.83
Process B	10.12	9.78	10.02	9.94
Process C	9.63	9.68	9.51	9.48

Carry out the customary one-way analysis of variance using a 1% significance level, stating the critical value of the test statistic.

[MEI]

9 A food manufacturer has been attempting to improve a breakfast cereal. Four new recipes (A, B, C, D) have been developed. Members of a tasting panel have assigned 'scores' to random samples produced by the four recipes as follows.

A	28.7	29.4	30.5	29.0
B	31.1	30.4	30.2	31.5
C	27.7	33.6	32.2	32.8
D	33.0	33.6	32.2	32.8

Note: The sum of these scores is 484.2 and the sum of their squares is 14 711.22.

(i) Carry out the customary one-way analysis of variance to examine whether or not it may be assumed that there are differences between the recipes.

Use a 0.1% significance level, display your results carefully and state the critical value of your test statistic.

(ii) Let x_{ij} denote the jth observation on the ith treatment in a one-way analysis of variance situation (such as that in part (i)), where, in general, $i = 1, 2, \ldots, k$ and $j = 1, 2, \ldots, n_i$. State a suitable statistical model on which the one-way analysis of variance can be based. Interpret the parameters of your model and state the statistical properties of any terms representing experimental error. State, in terms of the parameters of your model, the null hypothesis that is customarily used.

[MEI]

10 At an agricultural research station, a trial of four varieties of carrot is being carried out under carefully controlled conditions. The yields, in kilograms per plot, at the end of the trial are as follows.

Variety A	44.2	43.8	45.6	42.2
Variety B	46.7	45.0	45.8	43.6
Variety C	50.2	48.8	46.4	48.6
Variety D	41.3	39.9	42.6	

Note: $(44.2)^2 + (43.8)^2 + \cdots + (42.6)^2 = 30\,465.63$.

(i) Carry out the customary one-way analysis of variance to examine whether it may be assumed that there are differences between the varieties. Use a 1% significance level. Display your working carefully.

(ii) Let x_{ij} denote the jth observation on the ith treatment in a general one-way analysis of variance situation ($i = 1, 2, \ldots, k$; $j = 1, 2, \ldots, n_i$) and let σ^2 denote the common population variance underlying all the observations. Denote the within groups sum of squares by SS_R and the group variance for the ith group by s_i^2, so that

$$SS_R = \sum_{i=1}^{k} \sum_{j=1}^{n_i} (x_{ij} - \bar{x}_I)^2$$

and

$$s_i^2 = \frac{1}{n_i - 1} \sum_{j=1}^{n_i} (x_{ij} - \bar{x}_i)^2$$

where: $\bar{x}_i = \frac{1}{n_i} \sum_{j=1}^{n_i} x_{ij}$.

Use the result that the underlying distribution of s_i^2 is $\dfrac{\sigma^2}{n_i - 1}\chi^2_{n_i-1}$ to deduce that $\sum_{j=1}^{n_i}(x_{ij} - \bar{x}_i)^2$ has the underlying distribution $\sigma^2 \chi^2_{n_i-1}$.

(iii) The additive property of χ^2 states that the random variable, which is the sum of independent random variables each having χ^2 distributions, has itself a χ^2 distribution; and further, its degrees of freedom is the sum of the degrees of freedom of the random variables in the sum. Use this result to deduce that the distribution underlying SS_R is $\sigma^2 \chi^2_{n-k}$ where $n = \sum_{i=1}^{k} n_i$.

KEY POINTS

1. The general form of the hypothesis for the analysis of variance is
$H_0: \mu_1 = \mu_2 = \cdots = \mu_k = \mu$
H_1: Not all population means are the same
where $x_{ij} \sim N(\mu_i, \sigma^2)$.

2. Each observation may be written in the form $x_{ij} = \mu_i + e_{ij}$, where e_{ij} measures the experimental error, i.e. the deviation of the *j*th observation of the *i*th group (x_{ij}) from the corresponding population mean μ_i. It is also assumed that $e_{ij} \sim N(0, \sigma^2)$.

3. The test statistic is $F = \dfrac{s_b^2}{s_w^2}$.

Source of variation	Sum of squares	Degree of freedom	Variance estimate
Between groups	$\sum_{i=1}^{k} n_i(\bar{x}_i - \bar{x})^2$	$k - 1$	$s_b^2 = \dfrac{\sum_{i=1}^{k} n_i(\bar{x}_i - \bar{x})^2}{k - 1}$
Within groups	$\sum_{i=1}^{k}\sum_{j=1}^{n_i}(x_{ij} - \bar{x}_i)^2$	$n - k$	$s_w^2 = \dfrac{\sum_{i=1}^{k}\sum_{j=1}^{n_i}(x_{ij} - \bar{x}_i)^2}{n - k}$

where
k = the number of groups
n_i = the size of the *i*th group
$\bar{x}_i$ = the mean of the *i*th group
s_i^2 = the variance of the *i*th group

x_{ij} = the *j*th member of the *i*th group
n = the total sample size
$\bar{x}$ = the overall sample mean
s^2 = the overall sample variance.

11 Design of experiments

Have you noticed that the astronomers and mathematicians are the most cheerful people of the lot? I suppose that perpetually contemplating things on so vast a scale makes them feel that it doesn't matter a hoot anyway, or that anything so large and elaborate must have some sense in it somewhere.

Dorothy Sayers

A horticulturist has developed a new variety of potato which he claims gives higher yields than a standard variety with a similar taste. How could you test this claim?

The best way to test the claim is to undertake an *experiment*: to grow the two varieties and measure the yields. However, you need to design the experiment carefully. If you grow the standard variety in one field and the new variety in another, any difference in the yield per hectare may be due to differences in the soil quality, drainage or aspect of the fields. Even if you choose two plots of land which are identical as far as you can tell, and plant two sets of potatoes that are as alike as possible in terms of size and number, you do not expect to get exactly the same yield from each of them: there is some variability inherent in the situation.

In an experiment, some aspect of a situation is altered, and the effect of the alteration is measured. In this example, you (the experimenter) choose the plots, plant the varieties of potato and measure the yield. This is in contrast to a survey (such as an opinion poll), where the aim is simply to record the situation that exists without altering any aspect of it.

Often, organisations spend millions of pounds on the strength of experimental findings. The horticulturist may undertake a huge expansion of operations if your experiment confirms his claim. It is important that you are as certain as possible that the decision reached is the correct one. However, experiments themselves cost money: they need to be designed well so that

- the information obtained is reliable

- the maximum information is obtained for a specified cost (or the cost is minimised while obtaining the required information).

This chapter begins to look at the fundamental principles that should be followed when designing experiments. Some of them are analogous to principles used to design surveys.

Principles of experimental design

Comparing like with like

In the potato example, it is clearly not satisfactory to plant one variety in one field and the other variety in another field: you are not then *comparing like with like*. A higher yield from the new variety might be due to differences in the fields rather than to the type of potato. The aim is to grow the two types of potato in situations that are as similar as possible. Ideally, the only thing that should differ is the type of potato.

> There are many psychological experiments in which identical twins have been studied. Why do you think twins are of such interest to psychologists?

In any experiment there are sources of variability: it is virtually impossible to get exactly the same result from two successive experiments, even when the materials used and the conditions of the experiment are kept as constant as possible. Possible sources of variability are

- materials
- methods
- machines
- ambient conditions
- measuring instruments
- people.

Replication

> If you had planted one half of a field with standard potatoes and the other half with the new variety, and the new variety produced the higher yield, would you accept that it was indeed better?

Again you should be wary. Even though using the same field means that you are trying to compare like with like, the higher yield might just be due to the inherent variability of the situation. It might not signify any real difference.

You need to know something about the variability of the yields from the two varieties in order to be able to make a valid comparison. To achieve this, you need to repeat or *replicate* the experiment several times. For example you might decide to divide the field into several plots, and allocate each variety to half of the plots. This would tell you something about the variability of each of the varieties under these conditions and so give you a much better idea of whether the two varieties were giving significantly different yields. Replication also allows you to estimate the variance of any statistical model that you develop from your results.

Randomisation

> You have divided the field into ten equal-sized plots in order to perform five replicate experiments. You suspect that some plots are more fertile than others because they are nearer to a stream or more sheltered from the wind. How will you decide which variety is to be sown in which plot?

Clearly there is a danger of introducing bias in a situation like this. Depending on your (possibility sub-conscious) prejudices, you might be tempted to put the new variety in the plots which you suspect to be more fertile, or perhaps to do exactly the opposite. The best solution is to randomise the allocation of the varieties to the plots. You could number the plots 0, 1, 2, ..., 9 and then write these numbers on identical pieces of paper, put them in a hat, shake it and then pull out five pieces of paper. The numbers written on the paper would be the plots in which you plant the new variety.

One real experiment that failed because the samples were not randomly chosen was a study into the benefits of free school milk. Initially the children who were to receive the free milk were chosen by some random method. Subsequently, teachers were told that they could move children from one group to another if the groups did not appear to be balanced in terms of social background. When it came to the analysis of the results, it was found that teachers had tended to move children from poorer backgrounds into the group that would receive free milk. As a result it was impossible to say whether differences between the two groups were due to the free milk or to social background. The two factors are said to have been *confounded* – their effects could not be separated.

Randomisation also makes it less likely that unknown factors will affect experimental results. In an experiment to see how the yield from a chemical reaction depends upon the concentration of one of the reagents, the experiments should not be performed in order of increasing concentration. It may be that some other effect, of which the experimenters are not aware, is going on at the same time. For example, the temperature of the room might be increasing. In this case, an increase in the yield might be due to the increasing temperature rather than to the change in the concentration of the reagent. (Of course, if temperature were known to be a problem, steps could be taken to control it.)

Randomisation requires the use of some kind of objective method for selecting a sample or choosing the sequence of tests. The choice of the sample must not be left to a human being, as it is easy to show that human beings frequently choose samples which are biased in some way, even when they are trying very hard to be fair. There are some experiments in which randomisation is quite obviously necessary, and others in which it does not appear to be required. However, it has been said that randomisation is analogous to insurance: the cost is usually relatively low, but it provides a safeguard against unforeseen disasters.

Pilot experiment

Unless you have previous experience of the proposed experiment, and know the possible problems and the sorts of measurements that are likely, it is wise to undertake a *pilot experiment*. This is a smaller version of the proposed experiment. It may identify problems that you have not envisaged, allowing you to improve the experimental design. It also enables you to estimate the amount of variability that should be expected in the response variable, so that you can decide how many replicates will produce a specified level of certainty in your conclusions.

Terminology

The standard term for a variable whose values are chosen by the experimenter is a *treatment* or *factor*. The value of this variable is called its *level*. In some cases the level will be a number, such as the amount of fertiliser per square metre, and in others it will be a qualitative description. In the potato example, the 'treatment' is potatoes and the 'level' is the type of potato. The variable to be measured (the yield per hectare in the potato example) is called the *response variable*. The substance on which the treatment is used is called the *experimental material*: in the potato example, the field is the experimental material. An *experimental unit* is the smallest section of the experimental material which may receive a specific treatment. If the field were divided into plots in order to compare the yields from the potatoes, the plots would be the experimental units.

Blocks are sections of the experimental material which are assumed to differ from one another, but which are expected to be reasonably homogeneous within themselves. The fields could differ from each other in their location, in the amount and type of fertiliser applied in recent years, and/or in the effect of the crops grown in them in previous years. The variability within each block would generally be expected to be small compared with the variability between the blocks. There may, of course, be only one block, for example if all the plots were in the same field. Blocking is usually used when there is reason to expect variability between different sections of the experimental material. Randomisation, by contrast, should always be used, to minimise the effect of any unknown variability.

In the potato experiment, the aim is to make a comparison between two different treatments (the two varieties of potato). Sometimes you might wish instead to compare the effect of a treatment with the effect of no treatment. For example, you might wish to try out a fertiliser on a wheat crop. In order to see if it had any effect, you would need to leave some of the wheat unfertilised. The unfertilised wheat is called a *control*. It is actually common practice to include a control even when comparing several different treatments: an experiment to compare the effect of several different fuel additives on the fuel consumption of a car might well include a control run with no additive.

> A manufacturer of noise-reducing screens for separating motorways from housing estates claims that her screen will reduce the noise level by 25%. She has chosen a motorway site were she can raise and lower a long section of screen fairly quickly. It takes about 5 minutes to raise or lower the screen and she leaves it in each position for about 10 minutes.
>
> How would you run an experiment to test the claim? Identify which technical terms apply.

Dealing with subjective measurements

In the examples considered so far, the response variable can be measured. To measure the yield from the potatoes, the crop from each of the plots is simply weighed.

However, in an experiment to compare the durability of several kinds of paint exposed to severe weather conditions, the results may be in the form of an expert's assessment, by eye, of the finish of each paint at the end of the test period. If the expert has been involved in the development of the paints and already has ideas about which paint is best, this could lead to bias in the assessment. To avoid such bias, the experiment can be set up in such a way that the assessor does not know which paint is on which test square. This is one version of a *blind* experiment.

Another version of a blind experiment would be required to test a drug to prevent migraine headaches. If there are 30 migraine sufferers available for the test, 15 of these could be chosen at random and given the new treatment, whilst the remaining 15 could be given the standard treatment. Each person could be asked to record the number of migraine attacks that they had over a period of (say) 3 months. The migraine sufferers should be kept unaware of which treatment they are receiving, because there might be a tendency for those receiving the new treatment to feel better, just because they are receiving something which they perceive to be special.

An experiment is blind when the treatment used is unknown either to the subjects (experimental unit), or to the person making the assessment. In some cases, particularly in medical trials, a *double blind* experiment is used. In this case, both the patient receiving the treatment (the subject) and the person assessing the treatment are kept unaware of which treatment has been given to which patient.

It is well known that some patients get better just because they believe in the treatment. In medical trials, if a treatment is to be tested and no other treatment is available for comparison, a *placebo* may be given to the control group. A placebo is just a substance which has no healing effect, but which looks like the treatment which is being tested, so that patients cannot tell whether they are receiving treatment or not.

EXERCISE 11A

1. What are the advantages and disadvantages of each of the following methods for comparing two treatments for glandular fever?

   (i) Ask several doctors to record for a year which of the treatments they give to glandular fever patients, and how quickly the patients recover.

   (ii) Ask the doctors to allocate patients to one or other of the treatments by spinning a coin (if it is heads, give treatment A, and if it is tails, give treatment B), and record how quickly they recover.

   (iii) Examine the records to find which patients had suffered from glandular fever during the last year, see which treatment they had been given and then ask the patients how long it took them to recover.

2. In each of the following cases, explain why the experiment does not compare like with like and suggest a better design for the experiment.

   (i) A hi-fi salesman wishes to compare people's perception of the sound quality of a new system and a standard popular system. In order to do this, he asks 20 customers to listen first to the standard system and then to the new system, and to say which they prefer.

   (ii) A haulage firm is about to buy some new lorries and wishes to compare their performance. One aspect in which they are interested is the fuel consumption. To test this, they put one gallon of fuel into each of the lorries. Each lorry is then driven around a test track by a representative of the relevant manufacturer until the fuel is used up.

3. You are to design an experiment to test the effectiveness of two different toothpastes in reducing plaque. The assessment of the patients is to be done visually by a dentist, rather than using a measuring instrument. How would you organise the experiment?

4. A new formulation for relieving headaches is to be tested on a group of volunteers who suffer from frequent and severe headaches. The volunteers are to note down the severity of their headache and the time until they feel the relief from the medicine. The volunteers have been chosen partly on the basis that they all currently use the same dissolving tablet for relief from their headaches. How would you organise the experiment?

5. A precision engineering firm is deciding which of three suppliers to use for the carbide cutting inserts for one of their lathes. The lathe is used to produce pistons for a manufacturer of lorries. There is no difference in price between the three types of insert, so the criterion is to be the 'cutting edge life', defined as the number of pistons that can be produced before the surface of the pistons being produced becomes unsatisfactory. The cutting edge life of a single insert is expected to be about 200 pistons. A batch of material sufficient to test five inserts from each manufacturer is available.

(i) Why might it not be satisfactory to test all five inserts from manufacturer A, then all five from manufacturer B, then all five from manufacturer C?

(ii) Why might it not be satisfactory to test one insert from manufacturer A, then one from manufacturer B, then one from manufacturer C, and so on?

(iii) How would you decide on the order in which the inserts should be tested?

6 For each of the following experiments, identify (where relevant) the treatments, levels, experimental material, experimental units, response variable, blocks and control.

(i) An additive has just been developed to strengthen steel. One batch of molten steel is to be divided into ten portions and the additive is to be put into five of them, which will be chosen at random.

(ii) A grower of soft fruit wishes to decide how much fertiliser she should use on her gooseberries to maximise their yield. There are three separate plots of gooseberries, and six rows in each plot. She wants to know whether to use a 'small' amount, a 'medium' amount or a 'large' amount of fertiliser, so she treats two rows in each plot with each of these amounts.

(iii) The Ministry of Defence wishes to compare two different tanks that might be purchased for the British Army. It is concerned about the reliability of the tanks and, in particular, wants to find out how much continuous use the army can expect from the tanks before any kind of repair is required. Tank teams are allocated at random to the tanks, and they are driven continuously around a large course, including firing at targets, until forced to stop for a repair.

(iv) An engineering firm needs a new drilling machine. It wishes to compare three types of machine. It has been decided that the machines will be judged on the number of holes that can be drilled in 10 minutes. There are two drills of each type, and workers are assigned at random to the drills. The material to be drilled comprises similar castings produced in one batch.

Fitting and checking models

Sometimes, the results of an experiment tell you immediately what you want to know. On other occasions, you might need to draw some simple plots and calculate the measures of location and spread. The *exploratory*, or *initial*, *data analysis* (*EDA* or *IDA*) is a very important part of the process of analysing experimental results, and may be all that is required. However, if the answer is not obvious, you may need to conduct a formal statistical hypothesis test in order to reach a decision. To conduct a hypothesis test it is often necessary to assume that the data may be satisfactorily modelled by a particular probability distribution, such as a Normal distribution.

> Which model (binomial, Normal or Poisson) might you assume to be appropriate for each of these situations?
>
> (i) The number of defective switches in a batch of 20.
>
> (ii) The lengths of pistons for a car engine.
>
> (iii) The number of accidents per month in a factory.
>
> (iv) The mean weight of samples of five bags of cement.
>
> (v) The number of times per week that the drill bit breaks on a single machine.

Completely randomised design

Returning to the potato experiment, there would almost certainly be some variability in the fertility from one plot to another even if they were all in the same field. If you could measure this in some way, you could try to take it into account in the experimental design or in the model. However, if the fertility variations in the land were unknown, random allocation of the treatments would be the best you could do. An experiment in which there is only one block of experimental material, divided into units, and in which treatments are assigned to the units by some random method, is said to have a *completely randomised design*.

Suppose that the field could be divided into ten plots and that five of them are chosen by some random method. The standard variety could be planted in these five plots, and the new variety could be planted in the remaining five plots.

Analysis of data from completely randomised experiments

Suppose that the potato experiment has now been done, using a completely randomised design. The arrangement of plots in the field and the yields per unit area, in suitable units, are as shown in figure 11.1.

S	S	N	S	N
(32)	(38)	(41)	(29)	(43)
N	S	N	N	S
(37)	(37)	(39)	(40)	(40)

S = standard variety
H = new variety

Yields per unit area giving in brackets.

Figure 11.1

The results are summarised in the table and figure 11.2

Yields of standard variety	Yields of new variety
29	37
32	39
37	40
38	41
40	43

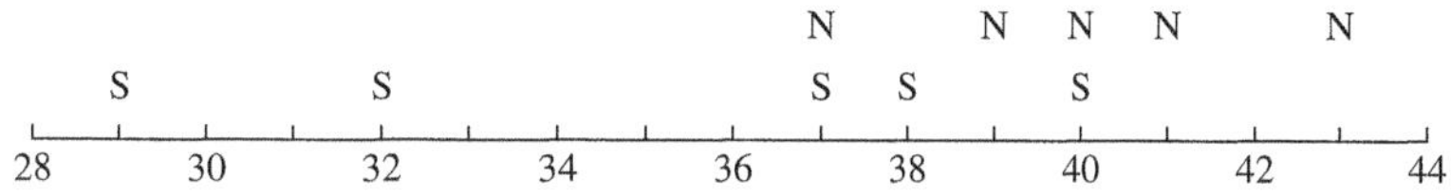

```
                                      N    N N  N        N
       S          S            S  S      S
   |----|----|----|----|----|----|----|----|
   28   30   32   34   36   38   40   42   44
```

Figure 11.2

It does appear that the new variety tends to give higher yields, and possibly that its yields are more consistent. It would be worth carrying out further trials using the above results as a pilot experiment to decide how many replicates to use.

With more data, a box-and-whisker plot or a back-to-back stem-and-leaf diagram could be used to display the results. For a very large data set, a back-to-back histogram could be used (like a population pyramid). If more than two treatments are being compared, box-and-whisker plots are still useful, but back-to-back stem-and-leaf diagram and histograms are not. Instead of back-to-back histograms, *comparative frequency polygons* can be used as in the next example. These are obtained by joining the mid-points of the tops of the columns in the histograms.

In many cases, these visual representations may be all that is required to make a decision.

EXAMPLE 11.1

In the hemming section of a clothing factory, the supervisor is interested in the effect of the material on the time which it takes one of the workers to perform his task. She arranges for the two materials of interest to be arranged in random order as they come to the machinist. The times taken for the task, in seconds, are given in the table below. The supervisor would have preferred to have used equal numbers of the two kinds of material, but this was not possible.

Material A	22.1	23.3	22.1	22.0	22.4	21.1	22.8	23.2	23.6
	26.2	20.7	21.1	22.3	21.6	20.6	22.2	23.1	
Material B	21.0	21.7	25.6	27.2	23.9	24.2	22.6	22.0	24.7
	26.4	21.9	23.3	22.0	22.9	22.4			

(i) Draw a back-to-back stem-and-leaf diagram, a box-and-whisker plot, a back-to-back histogram and frequency polygons for the data.

(ii) What conclusions can you draw?

SOLUTION

(i) Material A   Material B

          | 26 | 2 means 26.2

```
              7 6 | 20 |
              6 1 1 | 21 | 0 7 9
      8 4 3 2 1 1 0 | 22 | 0 0 4 6 9
            6 3 2 1 | 23 | 3 9
                    | 24 | 2 7
                    | 25 | 6
                  2 | 26 | 4
                    | 27 | 2
                    | 28 |
```

Figure 11.3 Back-to-back stem-and-leaf diagram

Material A

20.6   21.6 22.2   23.1   26.2

Material B

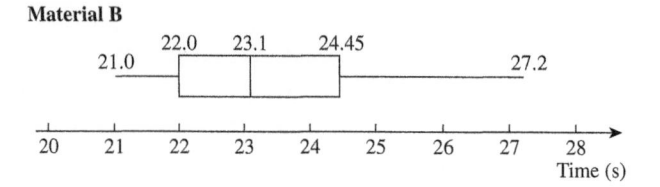

       22.0   23.1   24.45
21.0   27.2

20   21   22   23   24   25   26   27   28
                                        Time (s)

Figure 11.4 Box-and-whisker plots

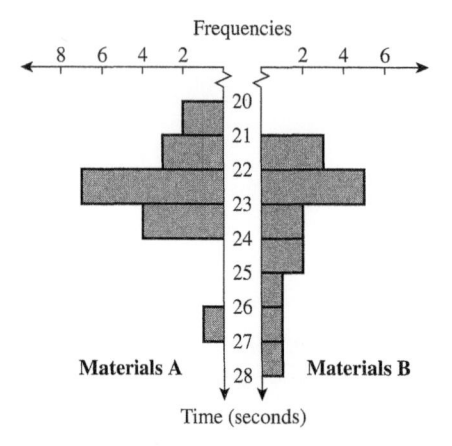

Frequencies

8   6   4   2   2   4   6

20
21
22
23
24
25
26
27
Materials A   28   Materials B

Time (seconds)

Figure 11.5 Back-to-back histogram

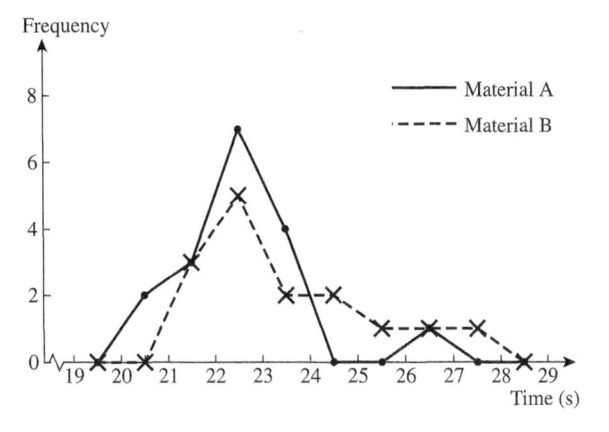

Frequency polygon showing Material A (solid) and Material B (dashed) over Time (s) from 19 to 29.

Figure 11.6 Frequency polygon

(ii) The machinist completes the task more quickly when working with material A, and there is also more variability with material B.

Sweeping by means

Sweeping by means is a very simple method of taking the investigation of data a little further. It may also be used in analysing more sophisticated experimental designs, as you will see later in this chapter.

The first step is to find the mean of each sample, and to use this as a summary of that sample. You then calculate the residual (observed value minus the mean) for each experimental unit. For the potato yield data, the results are as follows.

	Residuals Standard variety	New variety
	−6.2	−3
	−3.2	−1
	+1.8	0
	+2.8	+1
	+4.8	+3
Mean	35.2	40

You can see from this that the new variety has a mean yield that is 4.8 units more than that of the standard variety. Whether this is a sufficiently large difference to convince you that the new variety really is better depends on the size of the residuals. In this case, the residuals are similar in size to the difference in the means, so the results are not particularly convincing.

In this situation the best thing to do would be to ask for further experiments to be done, using more replicates. The information from this first experiment could be used to estimate the variability expected in the results, and from this to suggest how many replicates to use. This initial experiment would effectively have been used as a pilot experiment.

With a large number of replicates (i.e. a large number of plots), you could use a z test (because of the Central Limit Theorem – see *Statistics 3*) to look for evidence of a real difference between the yields. With small data sets it might be appropriate to use the Wilcoxon rank sum test (see Chapter 8) or possibly a two sample t test (see Chapter 6).

Plots of the data will often be enough to indicate whether there is a difference between the treatments. Hypothesis tests may just be used to confirm the conclusions.

Note

There is a danger, especially when using a large number of replicates, that a hypothesis test will show a 'significant' difference even when that difference is too small to be of any practical importance. *Statistically significant* is not necessarily the same as *practically important*.

In many situations, the number of replicates used is limited by practical considerations such as time and cost. For example, a farmer wishing to use only one field for the comparison of three types of wheat will want to use normal farm equipment to plant the crop. This will make very small plots impractical, and so limit the number of plots into which the fields may be divided. If an experiment involves using precious metals, or other expensive materials, the cost of a large number of replicates might be prohibitive. Some experiments in the chemical industry last for a week: if there is only one plant, it may only be possible to run one experiment at a time, so only a few replications of the experiment would be possible. In this case, time is the limiting factor.

EXERCISE 11B

1. A paint manufacturer wishes to test the durability of four different formulations for white paint. The plan is to apply the paints to 0.5 m square pieces of wood and to fix these along an outside wall of the factory. After one year the quality of the paint surface will be assessed by an expert. There are to be 7 replications for each formulation, so 28 squares of wood are required.

    (i) Write a set of simple instructions so that a completely randomised design may be used to carry out this experiment.

    (ii) Explain the purpose of the design in this context.

2 In an experiment to assess the efficacy of a noise screen beside a motorway, five measurements were taken when the screen was up and another five were taken when the screen was down. The experiment was performed over a period when the traffic level was fairly constant and the times when the screen was up and down were chosen by random allocation.

The following values were obtained.

Screen up	45	58	31	49	55
Screen down	83	71	76	65	74

On the basis of the values above, would you accept the sales representative's claim that this type of screen reduced the noise level by at least 25%?

3 The product development team at a paint factory has proposed that it would be better to use a bought-in resin in the paint than to use the resin produced in-house. In order to investigate whether the cost of this would be justified, an experiment is performed to test the resistance of the paint to a solvent. Paints containing the two different resins are randomly allocated to a total of 30 different surfaces, allowed to dry and then rubbed with solvent. The number of strokes required to disrupt the paint surface is taken as a measure of the solvent resistance of each paint. The results are given in the table below.

In-house	182 151 263 193 145 239 163 141
	112 177 122 117 157 160 135
Bought in	82 177 143 86 100 154 89 134
	112 80 104 120 90 118 107

Analyse these results and summarise your conclusions in a brief report.

4 A firm manufacturing light bulbs wishes to compare the effect of two gases (X and Y) which could be used to fill the bulbs, on the number of hours for which the bulbs may be used. In case there is some systematic variability in the quality of the bulbs being produced, a completely randomised design is used to assign each gas to 100 bulbs as they come from the production line. According to the Central Limit Theorem, the mean lifetimes should be approximately Normally distributed, and so should the difference in the means. The test statistic is

$$\frac{\bar{x} - \bar{y}}{\sqrt{\frac{S_x^2}{50} + \frac{S_y^2}{50}}}$$

The results of a completely randomised experiment are given in the table.

Unfortunately, the original results are not available, only the summary statistics. Does there appear to be a significant difference between the effects of using the different gases? Can you say anything further?

Gas	Sample size	$\sum_{i=1}^{50}$	$\sum_{i=1}^{50}(x_i - \bar{x})^2$
X	50	50 116	497 378
Y	50	52 062	280 794

5 In order to compare the yields from four varieties of wheat a completely randomised design is used with five replicates of each variety.

The resulting yields in kilograms per hectare are shown in the table below.

Haven	Hereward	Hunter	Riband
7500	8300	7100	7500
8100	8000	7400	7500
7900	7800	7600	7700
7600	7900	7500	7400
7300	7400	7000	7100

(i) Assuming that the seeds for all the varieties cost the same amount, decide whether this experiment provides evidence of a significant difference between the varieties.

(ii) If the seed costs were not the same for each variety how would you modify your analysis to take this into account?

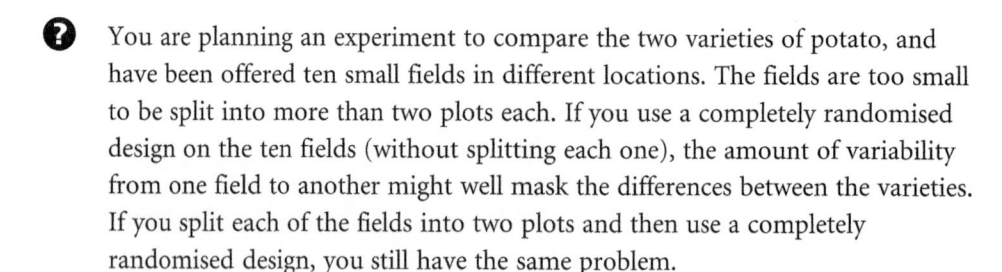

Paired design

> You are planning an experiment to compare the two varieties of potato, and have been offered ten small fields in different locations. The fields are too small to be split into more than two plots each. If you use a completely randomised design on the ten fields (without splitting each one), the amount of variability from one field to another might well mask the differences between the varieties. If you split each of the fields into two plots and then use a completely randomised design, you still have the same problem.
> How can you best organise the planting?

In this situation a *paired design* is appropriate. Each field is split into two plots, and then one plot in each field is randomly allocated to the new variety. The standard variety is planted in the other plot. The two plots in each field are likely to be similar, and so the differences in the yields should be due mainly to differences in the varieties. Since you have used random allocation to decide which plot in each field is planted with the new variety, you have avoided the problem of bias.

You can see that this is effectively a block design, but that in this case each block (field) contains only two experimental units (plots).

Manufacturers of soaps and detergents often use a paired design when they wish to compare the effect on customer's hands of a new product with that of a current product, They simply ask some volunteers to sit with one hand immersed in water containing the current product and the other hand in water containing the new product. The assumption is that the effect of the product on a person's right hand will be similar to the effect on the left hand, but it will probably be different from the effect on someone else's hands. As usual, the choice of which hand should be put in the new product should be done by a random method.

Analysis of data from paired experiments

In the experiment to compare the two varieties of potato, the results of the paired design are given in the following table.

Field	A	B	C	D	E	F	G	H	I	J
Yield from new variety	472	457	485	451	453	420	457	450	415	435
Yield from standard variety	470	451	483	450	452	418	452	451	416	437
Difference in yield (new − standard)	+2	+6	+2	+1	+1	+2	+5	−1	−1	−2

Since the experiment has a paired design, it is useful to look at the differences in the yields for each field.

From this it looks as if the new variety does give a larger yield. To analyse these results formally, you could use

- a sign test (see *Statistics 3* and below),
- a Wilcoxon paired sample test (see *Statistics 3*), or
- a paired sample *t* test (see *Statistics 3*).

Your choice of test will depend on the assumptions you have made about the distribution of the yields.

The null hypothesis is that there is no difference between the varieties. The alternative hypothesis is that the new variety has a higher yield, so the test is one-tailed. A significance level of 5% is fairly standard.

For the sign test, the null hypothesis is that any differences between the yields are due to chance, so the probability that the new variety gives a higher yield than the standard variety is 0.5. The test statistic is the number of fields in which the new variety gives a higher yield than the standard variety. You model this by the random variable R, where

$$R \sim B(10, 0.5).$$

As the distribution of R is binomial, which is discrete, it is not possible to have a significance level of exactly 5%. From statistical tables you can obtain the following values.

$$P(R \geq 8) = 0.0547 \quad P(R \geq 9) = 0.0107 \quad P(R = 10) = 0.0010$$

If you define the critical region as [9, 10], the significance level is 0.0107 or 1.07%. If you define it as [8, 9, 10] the significance level is 0.0547 or 5.47%, which is close to the usual value of 5%. The critical region of [8, 9, 10] is clearly the best choice in this case.

In this case the test statistic, r, is 7. It does not fall in the critical region, so there is insufficient evidence to conclude that the new variety has a higher yield.

If the conditions for their application were satisfied, the Wilcoxon single sample rank sum test or the paired sample *t* test could be used here. In this particular case, all three tests reach the same conclusion, however, it is certainly possible to reach different conclusions by using different tests.

Sweeping by means in a paired experiment

You may use a version of the method of sweeping by means to find out more about the data obtained from the paired experiment on the two potato varieties.

The overall mean of the 20 yields is 448.75. Subtracting this from each of the yields in the table on the previous page gives a table of residuals.

Field	A	B	C	D	E	F	G	H	I	J
New variety residuals	23.25	8.25	36.25	2.25	4.25	−28.75	8.25	1.25	−33.75	−13.75
Standard variety residuals	21.25	2.25	34.25	1.25	3.25	−30.75	3.25	2.25	−32.75	−11.75
Column means	22.25	5.25	35.25	1.75	3.75	−29.75	5.75	1.75	−33.25	−12.75

The residuals tell you by how much the yield of each plot is above or below average. The mean of each column tells you how much the yield of each field is above or below average. For example, the mean yield from Field A is 22.25 units above the overall average, with the new variety yielding 1 unit more than this and the standard variety yielding 1 unit less. You can rewrite the table to show the figures in this form.

Field	A	B	C	D	E	F	G	H	I	J
New variety	+1	+3	+1	+0.5	+0.5	+1	+2.5	−0.5	−0.5	−1
Standard variety	−1	−3	−1	−0.5	−0.5	−1	−2.5	+0.5	+0.5	+1
Field effects	22.25	5.25	35.25	1.75	3.75	−29.75	5.75	1.75	−33.25	−12.75

This table shows clearly how the various fields compare, and how the two varieties of potato compare within each field. Fields A and C give the highest yields and F and I give the lowest. The main feature of interest, however, is that in seven of the ten fields the new variety produced a higher yield than the standard variety. Further, in the three fields in which the standard variety produced the higher yield, the differences were relatively small.

Sweeping by means has taken more time and effort than simply looking at the differences between the yields of the two varieties for each field, but it has also provided some extra information. In practical situations this extra information could well be worth the extra work. In some circumstances it provides sufficient information, and no further analysis is required. Usually, though, sweeping by means is used as a form of exploratory data analysis, to investigate data informally before going on to apply a formal hypothesis test.

Comparing several treatments

Whether you wish to compare 2 treatments or 22, you should always aim to follow the design principles of comparing like with like, randomisation and replication. Graphical methods of presenting the results are useful however many treatments are being compared. What may become less easy as the number of treatments increases is choosing a suitable hypothesis test.

You can use various tests to compare the treatments two at a time. The sign test, the t test and the Wilcoxon test are all possibilities for paired data; for unpaired data the two sample t test or Wilcoxon rank sum test can be used. However, there is a problem concerning the significance level.

Suppose that you wish to compare just three treatments, P, Q and R. The null hypothesis is that all of the treatments are equivalent. To test this by comparing the treatments in pairs (P and Q, Q and R, P and R) using a significance level of 5%, you must perform three separate tests.

When the null hypothesis is correct,

$$\begin{aligned}P(\text{reject the null hypothesis}) &= P(\text{at least one of the tests gives a significant result}) \\ &= 1 - P(\text{none of the tests gives a significant result}) \\ &= 1 - 0.95^3 \\ &= 0.142\,625.\end{aligned}$$

This means that the probability of a *type I error* – rejecting the null hypothesis when it is correct – is about 14%. If you were comparing 22 treatments by testing them in pairs, the number of tests would be

$$^{22}C_2 = 231.$$

The overall significance level would be

$$1 - 0.95^{231} = 0.999\,992\,852.$$

In other words, you would almost certainly obtain some 'significant' results even if there were no differences between the treatments. If you try to compensate for this by reducing the significance level of the individual tests, the probability of a *type II error* – accepting the null hypothesis when it is false – is increased.

A way round this problem is to use the one-way analysis of variance (ANOVA) test (see Chapter 10). The test is really just an extension of sweeping by means. For the test to be valid, each of the samples must be Normally distributed with the same variance. Inspection of the residuals reveals whether this is a reasonable assumption, and a probability plot can be used if required. If the assumptions required for ANOVA are not valid, then it may be appropriate to use a non-parametric (distribution-free) test instead.

EXERCISE 11C

1 A firm is about to update its computing facilities by buying a considerable number of new computers. Two models are being considered, and it is decided to compare these by seeing how long they take to carry out some standard spreadsheet and database operations. A paired design is used: each machine is made to perform the same operation on the same data using the same software. The times taken, in seconds, by each machine are shown in the following table.

Operation	A	B	C	D	E	F	G	H	I
Machine X	42.7	7.4	84.5	24.2	39.4	56.1	47.3	63.2	12.4
Machine Y	51.3	7.1	85.3	26.1	38.7	59.3	46.1	66.3	15.2

(i) Display these results on suitable charts and comment on them.

(ii) Carry out
   (a) a sign test
   (b) a Wilcoxon paired sample test
   (c) a paired sample t test.

   Identify your assumptions in each case, and indicate whether they appear to be valid.

(iii) State your conclusions and recommendations in a form suitable for the managers of the firm, who are not statisticians.

2 A laboratory needs to compare two methods for measuring the level of cholesterol in a person's blood. In order to do this a paired design is used: a sample of blood is taken from 20 people and the cholesterol level in each sample is measured using the two different methods. The results are shown in the table below.

Subject	Method A	Method B
1	36.6	36.7
2	36.5	36.9
3	36.8	34.7
4	36.2	35.5
5	37.0	37.9
6	37.5	36.6
7	37.9	36.8
8	37.2	35.3
9	36.6	36.3
10	36.3	37.1
11	36.4	36.1
12	37.3	36.3
13	38.0	38.3
14	36.9	37.5
15	36.9	38.2
16	38.2	38.0
17	37.3	37.3
18	36.5	36.1
19	37.3	37.4
20	38.3	38.9

Analyse these results to see if there is any difference between the two methods.

3 The resistance to solvents of a paint can be tested by rubbing the paint surface with a solvent-soaked pad, and counting the number of strokes required to disrupt the surface coating. A paint manufacturer is considering changing the type of resin it puts into its paints, and wants to compare the solvent-resistance of the resulting paint to that of the current formula.

Since the results may depend upon the surface to which the paint is applied, 15 different surfaces are prepared and each paint is applied to half of each surface, random allocation being used to specify which half is used for which paint. The results are given in the table below.

Surface	Resin A	Resin B
A	182	173
B	151	154
C	263	255
D	193	186
E	145	147
F	239	221
G	163	161
H	141	145
I	112	118
J	177	153
K	122	122
L	117	114
M	157	149
N	160	155
O	135	128

Use a graphical method to analyse the differences between the two kinds of paint. What conclusion do you reach and what would be your recommendation to the management?

The technical director asks you to confirm your assessment with a hypothesis test. Use a non-parametric test and explain briefly why a t test would not be appropriate in this case.

(The situation here is similar to that in question 3 in Exercise 11B, but notice that the experimental design is different.)

4 Researchers at a detergent factory are developing new products for the washing of protective clothing badly soiled by industrial waste. Five products have reached the stage of comparative trials and an experiment is to be designed for this purpose. Typical washing loads will be washed by the new products and assessed for cleanliness.

(i) (a) What is the purpose of replication?
(b) How could the principle of replication be applied in this experiment?

(ii) (a) What is the purpose of randomisation?
(b) How could the principle of randomisation be applied in this experiment?

(iii) What practical problems might arise in organising this experiment?

Randomised block design

A grower of soft fruit wishes to compare four different fertilisers (W, X, Y, Z) to see which gives the highest yields. She has three small fields (A, B, C) available for the experiment. She knows from past experience that the fields differ in fertility, but she does not have any records to quantify this. The fertiliser sprayer is sufficiently small that each field can be divided into 12 sections and a different fertiliser applied to each. The fertilisers are allocated to the sections using random allocation, and the resulting layout is shown in figure 11.7. This is an example of a randomised block.

Field A

W	W	Y
X	Z	X
Z	Y	Y
X	Z	W

Field B

X	W	Z
Y	W	X
Y	Z	Z
W	X	Y

Field C

Y	X	W
W	Z	Y
Z	W	X
X	Y	Z

Figure 11.7

Using each fertiliser within each field enables the grower to separate the effects of the field fertilities from the effects of the fertilisers. A randomised block design is actually an extension of a paired design: in this case the fields are blocks and, instead of two treatments (as in a paired experiment), each field receives four different treatments. As for paired designs, the allocation of the treatments (the fertilisers) within each block is done using random numbers.

Each fertiliser is used on three sections of each field. There are therefore three replicates of each treatment within each block, and so it is possible to assess the variability within the blocks for each fertiliser. In this example, each block has the same number of replicates of each treatment: the design is said to be *balanced*. If the number of replicates varies from block to block, the design is said to be *unbalanced*.

Balanced designs are generally preferred, since the analysis turns out to be a little simpler. However, in some situations unbalanced designs are unavoidable because of the nature of the blocks. For example, suppose that you wish to try out three different treatments on the salmon tanks on a fish farm. Each tank is already divided into 8 separate sections. Taking the tanks as the blocks, you can either use only two replicates of each treatment per block (leaving two sections in each block unused) or use an unbalanced design.

Analysis of data from randomised block experiments

A good first step in analysing the results of a randomised block experiment is to look at simple data displays. The conclusion might be obvious from this initial data analysis. It might be helpful to calculate the means and, possibly, some measure of spread. However, a more formal analysis is quite complicated when there are several replicates per block. The formal analysis usually involves the method of *analysis of variance* (see Chapter 10) which requires that the response variable should be Normally distributed and that the variance should be the same within each block.

When each treatment is used exactly once in each block, the situation is simpler, and can be analysed in several straightforward ways.

Another fruit farmer wishing to compare the effects of the four fertilisers has seven fields (A, B, C, D, E, F and G) available for his experiment. In this case, however, it is only possible to divide each field into four plots. The arrangement is shown in figure 11.8.

Field A			Field B			Field C			Field D	
X	W		W	X		X	W		Y	Z
Z	Y		Z	Y		Y	Z		X	W

Field E			Field F			Field G	
Y	Z		X	W		Z	Y
W	X		Y	Z		X	W

Figure 11.8

The resulting yields are given in the table below.

	Treatment (Fertiliser)			
Field	W	X	Y	Z
A	53	54	56	60
B	59	62	68	71
C	36	39	39	41
D	49	51	58	59
E	53	58	69	75
F	35	35	36	39
G	66	67	69	76

It is clear without further analysis in this case that the yields increase from W to X to Y to Z in each field, and so this is the order of effectiveness of the fertilisers. Sometimes the effects of the treatments may not be as clear as this, and you need to investigate the results a little further. The technique of sweeping by means may be helpful.

Sweeping by means in a randomised block experiment

As before, you start by calculating the mean yield for each field, then subtract this from each of the observed yields. For example, the mean yield for field A is

$$\frac{1}{4}(53 + 54 + 56 + 60) = 55.75.$$

When fertiliser W is applied the yield for field A is 53: this is 2.75 units less than the average for Field A.

$$53 - 55.75 = -2.75$$

Subtracting the field mean from each individual result in this way gives the following table.

| | Treatment (Fertiliser) | | | | |
Block (fields)	W	X	Y	Z	Block effect
A	−2.75	−1.75	+0.25	+4.25	55.75
B	−6.00	−3.00	+3.00	+6.00	65.00
C	−2.75	+0.25	+0.25	+2.25	38.75
D	−5.25	−3.25	+3.75	+4.75	54.25
E	−10.75	−5.75	+5.25	+11.25	63.75
F	−1.25	−1.25	−0.25	+2.75	36.25
G	−3.50	−2.50	−0.50	+6.50	69.50

This table shows how much each yield was above or below the average for the field. You can see, for example, that the yields from plots treated with fertiliser W are always below average, and those from plots treated with fertiliser Z are always above average.

It is possible to go one stage further, by applying a similar process to the columns, including the 'block effect' column, giving the table below. (The figures are all given correct to 2 decimal places.)

The mean of this column for W is −4.61: you put this at the bottom of the column and change the first entry in the column to +1.86, since −2.75 is 1.86 above this column mean.

| | Treatment (Fertiliser) | | | | |
Block	W	X	Y	Z	Block effect
A	+1.86	+0.71	−1.43	−1.14	+1.00
B	−1.39	−0.54	+1.32	+0.61	+10.25
C	+1.86	+2.71	−1.43	−3.14	−16.00
D	−0.64	−0.79	+2.07	−0.64	−0.50
E	−6.14	−3.29	+3.57	+5.86	+9.00
F	+3.36	+1.21	−1.93	−2.64	−18.50
G	+1.11	−0.04	−2.18	+1.11	+14.75
Treatment effect	−4.61	−2.46	+1.68	+5.39	+54.75

The effect of this process is to decompose each of the original values into the sum of four components. For example, the top left entry in the table can be broken down as follows.

observed value = overall mean + block effect + treatment effect + residual
53 = 54.75 + 1 + −4.61 + 1.86

By using this process you are effectively fitting an *additive model* to the data. The assumption is that the actual yield is the sum of

- an overall mean
- a block (field) effect
- a treatment (fertiliser) effect and
- a residual

The residual should be the result of random elements. If there is some pattern in the residuals, the validity of this assumption should be checked. In this example, there is no noticeable pattern.

? Why would the existence of some pattern in the residuals make you doubt the suitability of an additive model?

The size of the residuals is the standard against which the differences between the treatments are measured. If the differences between the treatment effects are large compared to the residuals, it seems likely that there is a real difference between the treatments. If the differences between the treatment effects are similar to (or smaller than) the residuals, they could just be a result of the variability of the situation.

You can use various types of plot to look at the residuals. A dot-plot can be used when the samples are very small. A stem-and-leaf diagram is helpful for larger samples. A box-and-whisker plot is more useful for very large samples.

For the fruit-growing example, the stem-and-leaf diagram is given in figure 11.9. Note that the numbers in a stem-and-leaf diagram are usually cut rather than rounded: the 1.86 in the table is entered as 1.8 and not as 1.9. (This makes it easier to find the corresponding value in a data list when you wish to query a particular entry on a stem-and-leaf diagram.) However, as this is only an exploratory data analysis it doesn't really matter whether you cut or round.

Figure 11.10 shows the *five letter summary* of the residuals. The summary contains the five values that are required to draw the box-and-whisker plot. The *hinge spread* (*interquartile range*) and the range have been shown to the right of the summary.

⚠ There are different conventions for finding upper and lower quartiles and these can result in different values, particularly when you are working with small samples. The term 'hinge' is used for a quartile defined in a particular way so there is no ambiguity about the values of the hinges for any given data set. For an odd data set, the median is included in each of the two subsets whose medians give the hinges (or 'quartiles'). For an even data set, there is no ambiguity.

The box-and-whisker plot of the residuals is shown in figure 11.11. The 'whiskers' of the box-and-whisker plot extend only as far as observations which are not outliers. (When working with the median and the hinges, an outlier is usually defined as an observation which is more than $1\frac{1}{2}$ times the hinge spread beyond one of the hinges. An extreme outlier is an observation which is more than 3 times the hinge spread beyond one of the hinges.)

To find the depth, simply count in from either end until you get to the class including the median, where you give in brackets the number of items in that class.

```
28 items          1 | 2  represents 1.2
Depths
 1          5 | 8
            4 |
 3          3 | 3 5
 5          2 | 0 7
11          1 | 1 1 2 3 8 8
13         +0 | 6 7
(5)        −0 | 7 6 6 5 0
10         −1 | 9 4 4 3 1
 5         −2 | 6 1
 3         −3 | 2 1
           −4 |
           −5 |
 1         −6 | 1
```

The median is in this row.

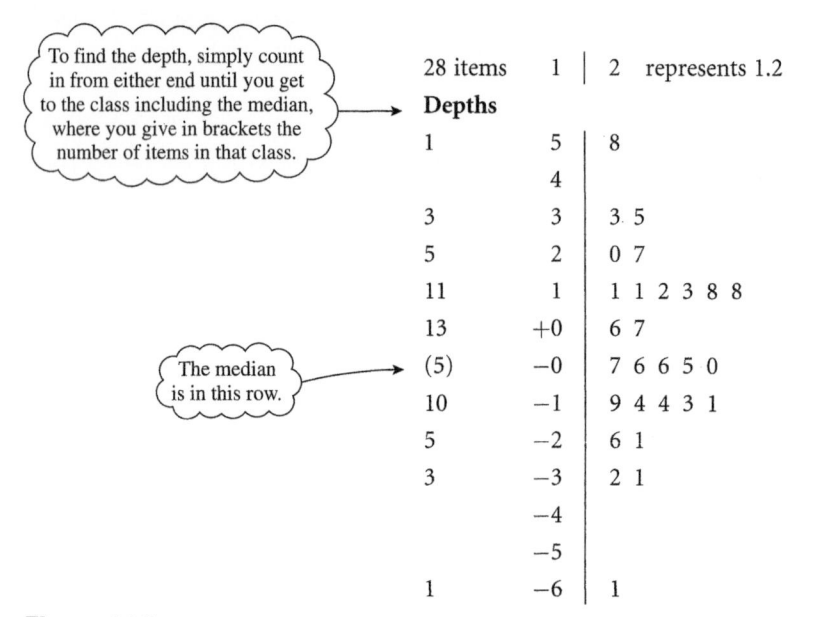

Figure 11.9

28 items	Depths				Spreads
Median	14.5		−0.25		
Hinges	7.5	−1.4		1.55	2.95
Extrema	1	−6.1		5.8	11.9

Figure 11.10

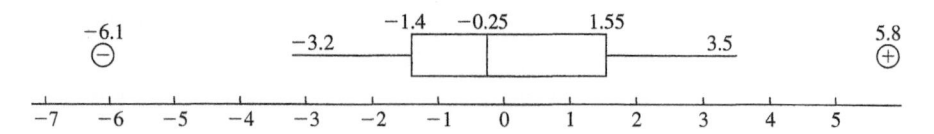

Figure 11.11

The reason for looking at the residuals was to see whether the differences between the fertilisers, found using the method of sweeping by means, represented real differences or whether they might just be due to random variability. If the additive model is appropriate, the random variation is given by the residuals. The shape of the stem-and-leaf diagram suggests that a Normal distribution may be appropriate to model the residuals. Most of the residuals lie between −3.2 and +3.5, a range of 6.7. Therefore it is reasonable to accept that differences greater than 6.7 represent real differences. Using this criterion, it appears that fertiliser Z really is better than both W and X since the difference between the treatment effects for Z and W is 10(5.39 + 4.61) and the difference between the treatment effects for Z and X is 7.85 (5.39 + 2.46). The other differences may just be due to experimental variability.

The standard method of analysis for randomised block designs is *two-way ANOVA* (analysis of variance). This is an extension of the technique of sweeping by means. For the hypothesis tests in two-way ANOVA to be valid, the additive model should fit the data and the residuals should be Normally distributed with the same variance. This can be checked by looking at the tables obtained by sweeping by means, and using a probability plot if necessary.

ACTIVITY

Show that the same decomposition of the data above is obtained by the following alternative method.

1   Calculate the overall mean and subtract this from all of the values in the table.
2   Calculate the means of each row and column to obtain the row and column effects.
3   Subtract the row and column effects from the values in the table obtained at step 1 to find the residuals.

(This method is slightly quicker than sweeping by means, but sweeping by means leads on more naturally to median polish, covered below.)

Median polish

Resistant statistics

In a small sample, the presence of one exceptionally large value will have a considerable effect on both the mean and the standard deviation. If the exceptional value can be shown to be an error, then it may be discarded. Otherwise, you should be very wary of discarding it. One sensible approach is to do the analysis twice: once including the value and once excluding it. If the conclusion is unchanged, then there is no need to worry. If the conclusions are different, it may be necessary to obtain more data.

Because of this problem, it is sometimes better to work with *resistant statistics*. These are measures of location and spread which are affected little, if at all, by extreme values in the data. The median and the interquartile range are examples of resistant statistics.

Suppose that the five measurements taken in an experiment were

12.3   13.8   15.7   15.9   16.5,

but that by mistake, they were recorded as

12.3   13.8   15.7   15.9   **165**.

Mean 14.84, median 15.7
$s = 1.74$, IQR $= 2.1$

Mean 44.54, median 15.7
$s = 67.36$, IQR $= 2.1$

You can see that the mean and the standard deviation are significantly affected by the error, whereas the median and the interquartile range are unaffected. In this case the error might easily be detected and the value corrected or discarded. However, in other cases an extreme value might be correct or it might not be detected. In such cases, the use of the median gives a measure of location which is much more stable and, arguably, much more representative of the data set. The median and the interquartile range are called resistant statistics because they are resistant to the effects of outliers, or extreme values.

Median polish is a method similar to sweeping by means. It is resistant to outliers, and is easier to perform by hand. The aim is the same: to fit an additive model to the data.

To see how the method works, look again at the data from the comparison of four different fertiliser used on seven different fields (below).

The first step is to find the row (block) medians.

Block	Treatment (Fertiliser)				Block median
	W	X	Y	Z	
A	53	54	56	60	55
B	59	62	68	71	65
C	36	39	39	41	39
D	49	51	58	59	54.5
E	53	58	69	75	63.5
F	35	35	36	39	35.5
G	66	67	69	76	68

This tells you that field G gave the best overall yields and that field F was the worst overall.

The next step is to subtract the row medians from the values in the rows.

Block	Treatment (Fertiliser)				Block median
	W	X	Y	Z	
A	−2	−1	+1	+5	55
B	−6	−3	+3	+6	65
C	−3	0	0	+2	39
D	−5.5	−3.5	+3.5	+4.5	54.5
E	−10.5	−5.5	+5.5	+11.5	63.5
F	−0.5	−0.5	+0.5	+3.5	35.5
G	−2	−1	+1	+8	68

At this stage you can easily compare the performances of the different fertilisers within each field. As before, the yields obtained using fertiliser W are always below average (the median in this case) and those obtained using fertiliser Z are always above average.

You now find each of the column medians. In the fertiliser columns this is the average amount by which the yield is above or below the median value for the field. In the final column, it is the overall average (median) yield.

Block	Treatment (Fertiliser)				Block median
	W	X	Y	Z	
A	−2	−1	+1	+5	55
B	−6	−3	+3	+6	65
C	−3	0	0	+2	39
D	−5.5	−3.5	+3.5	+4.5	54.5
E	−10.5	−5.5	+5.5	+11.5	63.5
F	−0.5	−0.5	+0.5	+3.5	35.5
G	−2	−1	+1	+8	68
Column median	−3	−1	+1	+5	+55

You can now see clearly that fertiliser Z gives the highest yields overall – on average it is 4 units better than Y, 6 units better than X and 8 units better than W.

Finally, you subtract each column median from each value in the corresponding column.

Block	Treatment (Fertiliser)				Block median
	W	X	Y	Z	
A	+1	0	0	0	0
B	−3	−2	+2	+1	+10
C	0	+1	−1	−3	−16
D	−2.5	−2.5	+2.5	−0.5	−0.5
E	−7.5	−4.5	+4.5	+6.5	+8.5
F	+2.5	+0.5	−0.5	−1.5	−19.5
G	+1	0	0	+3	+13
Column median	−3	−1	+1	+5	+55

The significance of the results depends how they compare with the residuals in the table. If the differences between the treatment medians are large compared with the residuals then the differences are probably important. If the residuals are large compared with the differences between the treatment medians, the differences are probability are probably not significant.

A dot-plot, or a stem-and-leaf diagram, of the residuals enables you to look at their distribution (see figure 11.12).

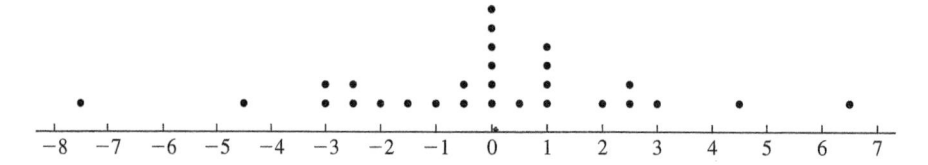

Figure 11.12

Most of the residuals lie between −3 and +2.5, which is a range of 5.5. This means that fertiliser Z does seem to be significantly better than W and X because its effect is greater by 8 units (5 + 3) and 6 units (5 + 1), respectively. The other treatment differences are of the same magnitude as the residuals and could therefore be due to the natural variability of the situation.

Note

Unlike sweeping by means, median polish gives different results if you start with the columns rather than the rows. It makes sense to start with the blocks, to remove their effect, and then move on to the treatments, as in the example above. If the median of the row medians or the column medians is not zero, the whole process may be repeated.

EXERCISE 11D

1 The table below shows the results for a different set of fertilisers. Use either version of sweeping by means to analyse them. Summarise your findings in a brief report.

Block	Treatment (Fertiliser)			
	P	Q	R	T
A	48	58	65	75
B	54	62	75	83
C	58	70	78	93
D	68	73	83	102
E	68	83	97	108
F	74	88	101	116
G	77	94	104	122

2 In an experiment to compare the yields from different varieties of wheat, a randomised block design was used. The results are given in the table below. Analyse the results and write a short report summarising any differences between the yields of the varieties.

Block	Variety			
	Haven	Hereward	Hunter	Riband
1	7500	8300	7100	7500
2	8100	8000	7400	7500
3	7900	7800	7600	7700
4	7600	7900	7500	7400
5	7300	7400	7000	7100

3 A company is about to buy some new machines for making widgets on a production line. It is considering three different types of machine (A, B and C), all costing approximately the same amount. In order to help in the decision process, five operators (P, Q, R, S and T) from the production line are asked to try out each of the three machines. The operators are allocated to the machines in a random order, and then given time to familiarise themselves with the machine before seeing how many widgets they can produce in one hour.

Case 1
One possible set of results is given in the table below.

Operator	Machine		
	A	B	C
P	72	74	79
Q	77	84	88
R	59	59	67
S	44	51	61
T	41	49	58

Case 2
Another possible set of results is shown below.

Operator	Machine		
	A	B	C
P	82	74	73
Q	77	91	78
R	62	50	67
S	34	51	64
T	35	49	68

(i) Look at both tables. Do you feel confident to make a decision straight away in either of the cases?

(ii) Analyse both sets of results using median polish.

(iii) State in each case which machine should be purchased on the basis of these results (assuming that no further tests can be done). In each case say how certain you feel about your conclusion.

4 Wheat responds well to applications of nitrogen fertiliser. Because of environmental concerns, this is applied in a number of separate applications (*top dressings*). Even when the total amount of fertiliser is kept constant, changing the timing of the top dressings can affect the growth of the crop. In an experiment to compare the effect of different top-dressing patterns on one particular variety of wheat (Hereward), a randomised block design was used. The yields in kilograms per hectare are given in the table below.

Block	Pattern of application		
	X	Y	Z
1	8300	8500	8800
2	8000	8400	8700
3	7800	8200	8000
4	7900	7900	8500
5	7400	8400	8000

(i) Use median polish to analyse these results.

(ii) Report your conclusions.

The following year the experiment was repeated using a different variety of wheat (Hunter). The yields in kilograms per hectare were as follows.

Block	Pattern of application		
	X	Y	Z
1	7100	7400	7900
2	7400	7900	8200
3	7600	7500	8100
4	7500	7500	7900
5	7000	8000	7300

(iii) Use median polish again to analyse these results. Are your conclusions the same as for the Hereward?

5 In an experiment to compare the effects of different forms of lighting on the number of eggs laid by hens, a randomised block design was used. Each block consisted of a pen of six hens. One of the three treatments was natural light, and the other two involved extending 'daylight' hours using low intensity and high intensity light respectively. The yields (number of eggs in twelve weeks) are given in the table below.

Use a suitable method to analyse these results and report your conclusions.

Block	Treatment		
	Natural	High	Low
1	330	372	359
2	288	340	337
3	295	343	373
4	313	341	302

6 Researchers at a detergent factory are developing five experimental products for the washing of protective clothing badly soiled by industrial waste. The products have reached the stage of comparative trials and an experiment is to be designed for this purpose. Typical loads will be washed using each of the products, and assessed for cleanliness.

(i) High capacity washing machines suitable for heavy-duty washing are made by five manufacturers. The researchers can carry out 50 experimental washes. Explain why a randomised block design, with the machines as the blocks, would be more sensible than a completely randomised design.

(ii) In a preliminary investigation each product was used once in each machine. The results are shown in the table in the form of a standard cleanliness measure determined for each wash. Use two complete steps of median polish to analyse these data.

Product	Machine				
	1	2	3	4	5
A	31	23	45	25	27
B	21	14	36	16	19
C	17	17	27	31	35
D	18	21	27	32	38
E	26	21	36	31	32

(iii) Use the results of the median polish to explain the advantages of using the randomised block design in the full experiment.

Latin squares

The rate at which hemming can be done depends upon the sewing machine used, the type of fabric being sewn and the skill of the operator.

A textile company needs to compare the speed of four types of sewing machine in order to decide which type to purchase. The fabric sewn at the factory falls into four clear categories. The company has arranged to borrow one machine of each type for the first week in March. All the necessary information must be gathered in that week.

How should the experiment be conducted?

The response variable in this situation is the number of items hemmed in one day. The treatments are the four sewing machines. If enough information could be gathered during the week using only one operator, a randomised block design could be used, with each type of fabric constituting a block of experimental material.

However, since an operator can only work on one machine at a time, this would mean that three machines would be lying idle. In order to gather as much information as possible, it would be better to use four operators, so that all four machines could be in use all week. If there were only one type of fabric, a randomised block design could then be used, with each operator constituting a block.

The problem is that in this situation (and in many others) the experimental material is classified in two different ways – in this case the operators and the types of material. You need a new type of experimental design: a *Latin square* design.

The organisation of the Latin square for the hemming experiment is shown in the following table. The operators are called A, B, C and D; the fabric types are called P, Q, R and S; the machines are called 1, 2, 3 and 4. The essential feature is that each machine is used once by each operator and once on each type of fabric.

		Operator			
		A	B	C	D
Fabric type	P	1	2	3	4
	Q	4	1	2	3
	R	3	4	1	2
	S	2	3	4	1

To use a Latin square design, you need the number of blocks under each classification (the number of operators and the number of fabric types in this case) to be the same as the number of treatments. Because there are four machines to be tested, the company must use four operators and four types of fabric.

Latin squares are used in situations like this where there are three variables. The analysis will give information about the differences between the machines, the differences between the operators and also the effects of the different fabrics. The company may be interested in all of this information, or just in the differences between the machines.

ACTIVITY

Use your calculator or random number tables to choose four pairs of numbers, each number between 1 and 4. Starting with the Latin square above, exchange the two rows identified by your first pair of numbers, then the two columns given by your second pair of numbers, then the two rows given by your third pair of numbers, and, finally, the two columns identified by your final pair of numbers.

Check that the arrangement which remains is still a Latin square.

This method may be used to produce new Latin Square designs from the basic design.

Analysis of data from Latin square experiments

The number of items hemmed are given in the following table.

Operator

		A	B	C	D
Fabric type	P	910	980	1100	1310
	Q	1180	870	1040	1160
	R	1150	1280	970	1130
	S	1100	1150	1300	990

To see which result goes with which machine you need to refer back to the original table.

The Latin square has provided a way of organising the experiment. Now a version of sweeping by means (the version used in the Activity on page 233) will be used to investigate these data. The first step is to find the *overall* (or *grand*) mean and to subtract it from all of the values in the table. The results of this are shown below.

Operator

		A	B	C	D
Fabric type	P	−191.25	−121.25	−1.25	+208.75
	Q	+78.75	−231.25	−61.25	+58.75
	R	+48.75	+178.75	−131.25	+28.75
	S	−1.25	+48.75	+198.75	−111.25

1101.25

This is the overall mean.

The next step is to estimate the operator effects, by finding the mean of each column; the fabric effects, by finding the mean of each row; and the machine effects, by finding the mean of the entries for each machine.

In this case, the entries for machine 1 all appear on the 'leading diagonal' of the original square. The mean effect of machine 1 is therefore

$$\frac{1}{4}(-191.25 - 231.25 - 131.25 - 111.25) = -\frac{665}{4} = -166.25$$

Performing all of these sets of calculations gives the tables below.

		Operator A	B	C	D	Fabric effects
Fabric type	P	−191.25	−121.25	−1.25	+208.75	−26.25
	Q	+78.75	−231.25	−61.25	+58.75	−38.75
	R	+48.75	+178.75	−131.25	+28.75	+31.25
	S	−1.25	+48.75	+198.75	−111.25	+33.75
Operator effects		−16.25	−31.25	+1.25	+46.25	1101.25

Machine	1	2	3	4
Effect	−166.25	−38.75	+38.75	+166.25

Notice that the sum of each set of effects is zero (a useful check).

Sweeping by means has decomposed each of the original entries by assuming an additive model. For the top left entry, which applies to operator A working on machine 1 with fabric type P,

observed value = overall mean + operator effect + fabric effect + machine effect + residual.

910 = 1101.25 + (−16.25) + (−26.25) + (−166.25) + +17.5

As usual when using the method of sweeping by means, the size of the residuals indicates whether the differences between the machines are likely to be real or just part of the natural variability in the situation. To find the residuals you subtract the operator effect, the fabric effect and the machine effect from each value in the table, giving the results overleaf.

		Operator				Fabric effects
		A	B	C	D	
Fabric type	P	+17.5	−25.0	−15.0	+22.5	−26.25
	Q	−32.5	+5.0	+15.0	+12.5	−38.75
	R	−5.0	+12.5	+2.5	−10.0	+31.25
	S	+20.0	+7.5	−2.5	−25.0	+33.75
Operator effects		−16.25	−31.25	+1.25	+46.25	1101.25

A stem-and-leaf diagram of the residuals is given in figure 11.13.

```
1 | 2   represents 12

+2 | 0 2
+1 | 2 2 5 7
+0 | 2 5 7
-0 | 5 2
-1 | 5 0
-2 | 5 5
-3 | 2
```

Figure 11.13

The range of the residuals is 55 (or 54 using the cut values). The machine effects are reproduced in the table below.

Machine	1	2	3	4
Effect	−166.25	−38.75	+38.75	+166.25

Since the difference between any pair of machines is greater than 55, it seems that the four sewing machines really differ in the speeds at which they may be used, with machine 4 the fastest and machine 1 the slowest.

With a Latin square design you can compare several different treatments when the experimental units fall into blocks under two different criteria. In the hemming example, the four sewing machines are the treatments, and their rate of operation is the response variable. The rate of operation of the machines is expected to depend on both the fabric type and the operator of the machine (these are the two blocking criteria).

Using sweeping by means to analyse Latin squares means your are trying to fit an additive (linear) model to the data. If there is a pattern in the residuals, this suggests, as usual, that the additive model is not appropriate. If the additive model is appropriate, and the treatment effects are larger than the residuals, you can reasonably conclude that there is a real difference between the treatments.

EXERCISE 11E

1 The Latin square and the numbers of items hemmed in one day in another hemming experiment are shown in the table below.

		\multicolumn{4}{c}{Operator}
		A	B	C	D
Fabric type	P	900	1020	1150	1290
	Q	1210	930	1060	1200
	R	1150	1270	1000	1140
	S	1040	1160	1290	1030

		\multicolumn{4}{c}{Operator}
		A	B	C	D
Fabric type	P	1	2	3	4
	Q	4	1	2	3
	R	3	4	1	2
	S	2	3	4	1

Which type of machine should be purchased?

2 An experiment to compare the effects on the milk yield of four different diets fed to cows during the winter uses a Latin Square design. The diets are referred to as A, B, C and D, and the cows are referred to as P, Q, R and S. The diets were allocated to the cows as shown in the Latin square below, over four different three-week periods referred to as 1, 2, 3 and 4. Each cow was fed the appropriate diet for the full three weeks, and the milk yield in litres was recorded in the final week. (The yields in the first two weeks were not recorded as part of the experimental data because they might include some carry-over effects from the previous diet. The details of the experimental design and the milk yields are given below. (Table entries show diet followed by milk yield in litres.)

		\multicolumn{4}{c}{Cow}
		P	Q	R	S
Period	1	A:109	B:111	C:166	D:141
	2	B:108	D:115	A:124	C:119
	3	C:122	A: 79	D:139	B: 93
	4	D:126	C: 86	B:116	A: 76

Analyse these results and report on them.

3 Three different timings of application of a top dressing of nitrogen fertiliser are to be compared in their effects on the yields of three varieties of wheat. Three fields are available and so a Latin square design is used. The patterns of application and the resulting yields in kilograms per hectare are shown in the table.

		\multicolumn{3}{c}{Variety}
		Haven	Hereward	Riband
Field	1	Y:7400	Z:7900	X:7500
	2	X:8100	Y:7900	Z:7300
	3	Z:7300	X:7600	Y:7700

(i) Are you able to reach any firm conclusion concerning the effectiveness of the different timing patterns for applying the fertiliser?
(ii) Do your conclusions depend upon the variety of wheat being grown?
(iii) Do any patterns of application appear to be especially effective for any particular variety or varieties?

KEY POINTS

1. The two key principles in designing experiments are *replication* and *randomisation*.
   - Replication means repeating the experiment several times with everything under your control being held the same. This enables you to assess the variability inherent in the situation.
   - Randomisation means using random numbers to choose the order in which the experiments are carried out, which treatments are applied to which experimental units, etc. This removes the bias which could result from a subjective choice in these matters, and the possibility of confounding.

2. The *treatments* or *factors* are the things which you are deliberately changing. They could be continuous, discrete or categorical variables.

3. The *response variable* is the variable whose value you expect to change as a result of applying the different treatments or factors. It is the variable which you measure.

4. The *experimental material* is the material to which the treatments or factors are applied. It is divided into the experimental units which receive the different treatments. For example, in an experiment comparing different types of carrot, the experimental material could be a field, and the experimental units would be plots of the field.

5. A *block* is a section of experimental material which is treated as though it were homogeneous. In the analysis of the results of the experiment, you make allowance for the blocks being different from each other.

6. A *control* is effectively no treatment. A control is especially important if there is only one real treatment, as it is essential to have a comparison of some sort.

7. When experiments are done on humans, there is often a powerful psychological effect. The patient can feel better, and show real improvement, just because they believe that the treatment is doing them good. To allow for this, experiments often include a *placebo* as a control – the patient is given something which appears to be a treatment but which has no active component.

8. When experiments are done on humans, the patient is often not allowed to know which treatment they are receiving, possibly a placebo, so as to remove psychological effects. Also, when there is a possibility that the person assessing the effects of the treatment may be biased if they know which treatment the patient is receiving, this information may be kept from the assessor. Either of these situations may be referred to as a *blind experiment*. If neither the patient nor the assessor knows which treatment is being used, it is called a double blind experiment.

9 *Resistant statistics* are statistics which are not influenced by a small number of extreme values. The median and the inter-quartile range are resistant statistics, the mean and the standard deviation are not resistant statistics.

10 In a *completely randomised design*, the experimental material consists of a single block and the treatments are randomly allocated to the experimental units.

11 In a *randomised block design*, the experimental material consists of blocks and the treatments are randomly allocated to the experimental units within the blocks.

12 In a *Latin square design*, each treatment is applied exactly once in each row and each column.

13 *Median polish* and *sweeping by means* are methods of fitting an additive model of the form

Yield = Overall average + Treatment effect + Block effect + Residual

to a randomised block design where each treatment is used only once in each block.

14 *Paired designs* are used whenever possible because two treatments are applied to the same piece of experimental material, or to two (almost) identical pieces. This means that the differences in the response variable should be caused by the differences between the treatments and not by differences in the experimental material, as could be the case if the different treatments were used on different people.

Appendix

A proof that s_b^2 is an unbiased estimate of σ^2

A proof that s_b^2 is an unbiased estimate of σ^2, on the assumption that all the samples come from populations with the same mean, μ, is as follows.

Let $\overline{X}_i$ be the sample mean of the ith sample and $\overline{X}$ be the overall sample mean. Then

$$\overline{X} = \frac{1}{n}(n_1\overline{X}_1 + n_2\overline{X}_2 + \ldots + n_k\overline{X}_k).$$

Since the samples are all independent,

$$\mathrm{E}[\overline{X}_1\overline{X}_2] = \mathrm{E}[\overline{X}_1\overline{X}_3] = \ldots = \mathrm{E}[\overline{X}_1\overline{X}_k] = \mu^2$$

and so

$$\mathrm{E}[\overline{X}_1\overline{X}] = \frac{n_1}{n}\mathrm{E}[\overline{X}_1^2] + \frac{n_2}{n}\mathrm{E}[\overline{X}_1\overline{X}_2] + \ldots + \frac{n_k}{n}\mathrm{E}[\overline{X}_1\overline{X}_k]$$

$$= \frac{n_1}{n}\mathrm{E}[\overline{X}_1^2] + \frac{n - n_1}{n}\mu^2$$

$$= \frac{n_1}{n}\left(\mu^2 + \frac{\sigma^2}{n_1}\right) + \frac{n - n_1}{n}\mu^2 \quad \text{Since } \mathrm{E}[\overline{X}_1^2] - \mu^2 = \mathrm{Var}[\overline{X}_1] = \frac{\sigma^2}{n_1}$$

$$= \mu^2 + \frac{\sigma^2}{n}.$$

This means that

$$\mathrm{E}\left[n_1(\overline{X}_1 - \overline{X})^2\right] = n_1\mathrm{E}[\overline{X}_1^2] - 2n_1\mathrm{E}[\overline{X}_1\overline{X}] + n_1\mathrm{E}[\overline{X}^2]$$

$$= n_1\left(\mu^2 + \frac{\sigma^2}{n_1}\right) - 2n_1\left(\mu^2 + \frac{\sigma^2}{n}\right) + n_1\left(\mu^2 + \frac{\sigma^2}{n}\right)$$

This is where the assumption $\mathrm{E}[\overline{X}_1] = \mathrm{E}[\overline{X}]$ is used.

$$= \left(1 - \frac{n_1}{n}\right)\sigma^2$$

Similar results hold for $\mathrm{E}\left[n_2(\overline{X}_2 - \overline{X})^2\right]$ and so on; thus

$$\mathrm{E}\left[n_1(\overline{X}_1 - \overline{X})^2 + n_2(\overline{X}_2 - \overline{X})^2 + \ldots + n_k(\overline{X}_k - \overline{X})^2\right]$$
$$= \left(1 - \frac{n_1}{n}\right)\sigma^2 + \left(1 - \frac{n_2}{n}\right)\sigma^2 + \ldots + \left(1 - \frac{n_k}{n}\right)\sigma^2$$
$$= (k-1)\sigma^2.$$

That is, $\dfrac{n_1(\overline{X}_1 - \overline{X})^2 + n_2(\overline{X}_2 - \overline{X})^2 + \ldots + n_k(\overline{X}_k - \overline{X})^2}{k-1}$ is an unbiased estimate of σ^2, as required.

Answers

Chapter 1

Activity (Page 15)

1 If S is the least of $X_1, X_2, \ldots, X_n$, where $X_1, X_2, \ldots, X_n$ have distribution with the cumulative distribution function $F_X(x)$, then

$$F_S(x) = P(\text{least value in sample} \leq x)$$
$$= 1 - P(\text{least value in sample} > x)$$
$$= 1 - P(\text{all values in sample} > x)$$
$$= 1 - [1 - P(\text{a value of } X \leq x)]^n$$
$$= 1 - [1 - F_X(x)]^n$$

In Example 1.3, $f_S(x) = \frac{3}{8}e^{-3x/8}$ and $E[S] = \frac{8}{3}$; in Example 1.4 $E[S] = 0.151$; in Example 1.5

$$P(S = s) = \left(1 - \left(\frac{11}{12}\right)^3\right)\left(\left(\frac{11}{12}\right)^3\right)^{s-1} \text{ and }$$

$E[S] = 4.35$.

Exercise 1A (Page 16)

1 (i) $E(P) = \pi$, $\text{Var}(P) = 0.7971$
   (ii) $E(\bar{P}) = \pi$, $\text{Var}(\bar{P}) = \dfrac{0.7971}{n}$
   (iii) n of the order of 10 million

2 mean $= 1.390$, variance $= 0.0668$

3 mean $= 0.6677$, variance $= 0.1259$

mean $\to \dfrac{2}{3}$ as $L \to \infty$

4 (i) $f(x) = \dfrac{(1-u^2)(2+3u-u^3)}{8}$ where $u = \dfrac{(x-20)}{3}$ mean of $L = 20.77$

   (ii) mean of $H = 20.09$, variance $= 7.209$
   (iii) mean of $M = 20.09$, variance $= 1.442$

5 (i) expectation $= 2.5$, variance $= 1.25$
   (ii) $P(r) = \dfrac{3r^2 - 3r + 1}{64}$, expectation $= \dfrac{55}{16}$,

   variance $= \dfrac{143}{256}$

   (iii) Distribution of sum

r	3	4	5	6	7
P(r)	$\frac{1}{64}$	$\frac{3}{64}$	$\frac{6}{64}$	$\frac{10}{64}$	$\frac{12}{64}$

r	8	9	10	11	12
P(r)	$\frac{12}{64}$	$\frac{10}{64}$	$\frac{6}{64}$	$\frac{3}{64}$	$\frac{1}{64}$

So the mean of three scores has expectation 2.5, variance $\dfrac{5}{12} = \dfrac{1.25}{3}$ as expected.

6 (i) $T = 60 \times \left(0.8 \times \dfrac{W}{70} + 0.2 \times \dfrac{C}{14}\right)$
   (ii) $E(T) = 39.26$, $\text{Var}(T) = 25.98$
   $P(\max 47 \text{ or more}) = 0.0777$

7 (i) $\dfrac{1}{1296}$
   (ii) $P(X \leq 2) = \dfrac{1}{81}$;
   $P(X = 2) = P(X \leq 2) - P(X = 1) = \dfrac{5}{432}$
   (iii) $\dfrac{65}{1296}$
   (iv) $\dfrac{671}{1296}$; greater than $\dfrac{1}{2}$

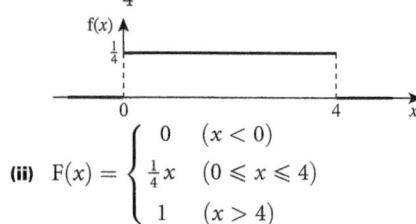

8 (i) $f(x) = \dfrac{1}{4}$ $(0 \leq x \leq 4)$

   (ii) $F(x) = \begin{cases} 0 & (x < 0) \\ \frac{1}{4}x & (0 \leq x \leq 4) \\ 1 & (x > 4) \end{cases}$

   (iii) p.d.f. of Y is $f(y) = \dfrac{1}{2}y$ $(0 \leq y \leq 2)$

9 (i) $N(9.9, (0.6)^2)$
   (ii) (a) 0.2523
       (b) 0.0334
       (c) 0.7143
   (iv) not independent

10 (ii) variance
   (iii) 0
   (v) $\mu_2 = \dfrac{3}{80}$, $\mu_3 = -\dfrac{1}{160}$. Not symmetrical
   (vi) $\mu_3 = 0$. Not symmetrical

Chapter 2

❓ (Page 21)

See text that follows.

❓ (Page 24)

See text that follows.

Exercise 2A (Page 29)

1 (ii) $\dfrac{n}{n-1} V$ is unbiased

3 (i) (a) L: $P(3) = \dfrac{1}{20}$, $P(4) = \dfrac{3}{20}$, $P(5) = \dfrac{6}{20}$, $P(6) = \dfrac{10}{20}$

M: $P(2) = \frac{4}{20}$, $P(3) = \frac{6}{20}$, $P(4) = \frac{6}{20}$,
$P(5) = \frac{4}{20}$

(b) $E[L] = \frac{21}{4}$, $E[M] = \frac{7}{2}$

(c) $E[2M-1] = 6$, $E[L] \neq 6$

(ii) (a) L: $P(1) = \frac{1}{56}$, $P(2) = \frac{3}{56}$, $P(3) = \frac{6}{56}$,
$P(4) = \frac{10}{56}$, $P(5) = \frac{15}{56}$, $P(6) = \frac{21}{56}$
M: $P(1) = \frac{6}{56}$, $P(2) = \frac{10}{56}$, $P(3) = \frac{12}{56}$,
$P(4) = \frac{12}{56}$, $P(5) = \frac{10}{56}$, $P(6) = \frac{6}{56}$

(b) $E[L] = \frac{119}{24}$, $E[M] = \frac{7}{2}$

(c) $E[2M-1] = 6$, $E[L] \neq 6$

4 (i) $P(\Pi = \frac{1}{3}) = 9p^2$; $P(\Pi = \frac{1}{6}) = 6p(1-3p)$;
$P(\Pi = 0) = (1-3p)^2$

(ii) $9p^2 \times \frac{1}{3} + 6p(1-3p) \times \frac{1}{6} +$
$(1-3p)^2 \times 0 = p$

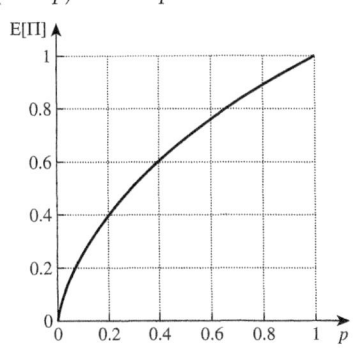

5 (iv) [Graph of $E[\Pi]$ vs p]

The estimate is biased for all values of p except 0 and 1.

(v) If $p = 0$ then the experiment will never end so no value of N will be determined; if $p = 1$ then $N = 1$, $\Pi = 1$ and so Π is unbiased.

8 (iii) T_3 has a smaller variance than the other two estimators, so is less likely to give an estimate far from the true value of μ – see the work on mean square error later in this chapter.

9 (i) $E[T] = k(n-1)\sigma^2$, $Var[T] = 4k^2(n-1)^2\sigma^4$

10 (iii) $Z = 3$ or 5, $E[Z] = 4$, $Var[Z] = 1$

(iv) Y is biased, but has a small variance; Z is unbiased but has a larger variance for $n = 4$ or 5.

11 (iv) $E[Y] = \frac{n}{n+1}\theta$, $Var[Y] = \frac{n\theta^2}{(n+2)(n+1)^2}$

(iv) $Var[Z] = \frac{\theta^2}{n(n+2)}$

(vi) Both unbiased, but Z seems preferable as it has a smaller variance than $2\overline{X}$ (for $n > 1$).

12 (ii) $Var[T] = c_1^2\sigma_1^2 + (1-c_1)^2\sigma_2^2$

Minimum when $c_1 = \frac{\sigma_2^2}{\sigma_1^2 + \sigma_2^2}$, $c_2 = \frac{\sigma_1^2}{\sigma_1^2 + \sigma_2^2}$,

$Var[T] = \frac{2\sigma_1^2\sigma_2^2}{\sigma_1^2 + \sigma_2^2}$

(iii) T is a minimum variance unbiased estimator – it estimates correctly on average and is rarely far from the true mean – but it cannot be determined without knowing the variances of X_1 and X_2 which is unlikely in practice if μ is unknown.

13 (iv) $k = \frac{1}{n-1}$

14 Y has mean θ, variance θ, $E[Y^2] = \theta + \theta^2$. $\overline{Y}$ has variance $\frac{\theta}{n}$.

$\frac{1}{n}\sum Y_i^2$ unbiased estimator for $\theta + \theta^2$.

$a = 4$, $b = 2$

15 (vi) $E\left[\frac{1}{X}\right] = -\frac{p\ln p}{q}$ so biased

(v) $E[X^2] = \frac{2}{p^2} - \frac{1}{p}$; $a = \frac{1}{2}$, $b = -\frac{1}{2}$

Exercise 2B (Page 39)

1 (i) (a) 13.79
  (b) 145.5
 (ii) (a) 7.346
  (b) 19.60
  (c) 20.60

2 0.003 916

3 First 5, second 11

4 (ii) $s^2 = \dfrac{(n_1-1)s_x^2 + (n_2-1)s_y^2 + \dfrac{n_1 n_2}{n_1+n_2}(\overline{y}-\overline{x})^2}{n_1+n_2-1}$

(iii) Here, both samples are drawn from a single population, so a pooled estimate of the mean is made; in the text it was assumed that the samples were drawn from two populations and that only the variance was a common value to be estimated, so separate estimates of the mean were made.

5 (ii) $n\sigma^2$

(iii) $Var[\overline{X}] = \frac{\sigma^2}{n}$ so $E[n(\overline{X}-\mu)^2] = \sigma^2$

(v) 95% Normal confidence interval has bounds:

mean $\pm 1.96 \times \sqrt{Var} = \sigma^2 \pm 1.96 \times \sqrt{\dfrac{2\sigma^4}{n-1}}$

and if n is large s can be used to approximate σ.

6 (iii) $E[X^2] = v(v+1) + 2\theta v + \theta^2$

(v) $E[\overline{X}] = $ mean of distribution $= \theta + v$;
$E[S^2] = $ variance of distribution $= v$, so S^2 is an unbiased estimator of v and $\overline{X} - S^2$ is an unbiased estimator of θ, since
$E[\overline{X} - S^2] = E[\overline{X}] - E[S^2] = \theta$.

7 (iii) $E[X^2] = \sigma^2 + \mu^2$

(v) $E[\overline{X}^2] = \frac{\sigma^2}{n} + \mu^2$

(vii) $E[T] = \frac{n-1}{n}\sigma^2$

Exercise 2C (Page 49)

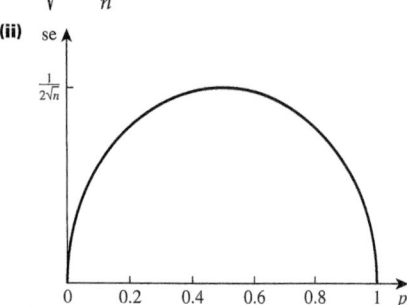

1 (i) $\sqrt{\dfrac{p(1-p)}{n}}$

(ii) se

[graph showing a semicircular curve from $p=0$ to $p=1$, peaking at $\frac{1}{2\sqrt{n}}$ around $p=0.5$; horizontal axis labelled 0, 0.2, 0.4, 0.6, 0.8, 1]

(iii) About a million

2 (i) se $= \sqrt{\dfrac{r}{t}}$

(ii) $E[T] = \dfrac{n}{r}$, $Var[T] = \dfrac{n}{r^2}$

$\dfrac{n-1}{n} R_2$ is unbiased with mse $\dfrac{r^2}{n-2}$;

mse $R_2 = \dfrac{(n+2)r^2}{(n-1)(n-2)}$

3 (i) $E[W] = \dfrac{t}{2}$, $Var[W] = \dfrac{t^2}{12}$

(ii) $E[T] = t$, $Var[T] = \dfrac{t^2}{18}$, $se(T) = \dfrac{t}{\sqrt{18}}$

(iii) $f(s) = \dfrac{6s^5}{t^6}$, $(0 \leq s \leq t)$

(iv) $E[S] = \dfrac{6t}{7}$, $Var[S] = \dfrac{3t^2}{196}$

(v) $E[T_a] = \dfrac{6at}{7}$, $Var[T_a] = \dfrac{3a^2 t^2}{196}$

(vi) $a = \dfrac{7}{6}$, mse $= \dfrac{t^2}{48}$

(vii) mse $= \dfrac{t^2}{28}(21a^2 - 48a + 28)$ so $a = \dfrac{8}{7}$ gives

minimum mse $= \dfrac{t^2}{49}$.

(viii) Very little difference in mse so might as well use unbiased estimator.

4 (i) Factorial expression gives number of ways of picking r elements of a sample to be below and r elements to be above the median value x; $(F(x))^r$ is the probability that the r elements picked are below x; $(1 - F(x))^r$ is the probability that the r elements picked are above x; and $f(x)$ is the density for the median value x itself.

(ii) (a) $E[\text{median}] = \dfrac{a}{2}$, $Var[\text{median}] = \dfrac{a^2}{20}$

(b) $E[\text{mean}] = \dfrac{a}{2}$, $Var[\text{mean}] = \dfrac{a^2}{36}$

(iv) (a) $E[L_k] = \dfrac{3ka}{4}$, $Var[L_k] = \dfrac{3k^2 a^2}{80}$

$\text{mse}(L_k) = \dfrac{12k^2 - 15k + 5}{20} a^2$

(b) L_k unbiased if $k = \dfrac{2}{3}$

(c) minimum mse at $k = \dfrac{5}{8}$ is $\dfrac{a^2}{64}$

5 (i) $\text{mse}(\Pi_2) = \dfrac{np(1-p) + (0.5 - p)^2}{(n+1)^2}$

Π_2 is consistent: mse tends to zero as n tends to infinity.

(ii) Π_2 has a smaller mse if p is near to 0.5, though only significantly so for small values of n.

(iii) No: smaller mse is not a criterion for an estimator to be discriminating; Π_2 will actually tend to disguise bias compared with Π_1.

(iv) Π_3 is not consistent (unless $p = 0.5$): mse $= (p - 0.5)^2$ for all n. It might be the most sensible estimator for small n if the coin is only slightly biased.

6 (i) $E[T] = 2\lambda$, $Var[T] = 2\lambda^2$

(ii) $E[S_c] = 2cn\lambda$, $Var[S_c] = 2c^2 n\lambda^2$

bias $(S_c) = (2cn - 1)\lambda$

$\text{mse}(S_c) = \lambda^2 \{2n(2n+1)c^2 - 4nc + 1\}$

(iii) unbiased when $c = \dfrac{1}{2n}$

(iv) minimum mse when $c = \dfrac{1}{1 + 2n}$

(v) consistent in both cases

7 (i) $N(0, 2\sigma^2)$

(ii) T is unbiased.

(iii) $Var[T] = 2\sigma^4$

(v) $\dfrac{Var[T]}{Var[S^2]} = n - 1$ so S^2 is more efficient than T and more so for larger n.

(vi) Gives an early rough estimate if sampling is slow or expensive.

Chapter 3

Exercise 3A (Page 64)

1 (i) $\lambda = \dfrac{a + b + c}{20}$

(ii) Because, assuming the same number of cars travel east and west, it is the overall mean number of cars travelling east (or west) per minute.

2 $\hat{p} = \dfrac{2a + b}{2n}$

3 $\hat{p} = \dfrac{1}{4}$

4 (i) $L = \dfrac{(a + b + c)!}{a! b! c!} p^{4a+3b}(1-p)^{b+2c} \times$

$(1 + 2p + 3p^2)^c$

(ii) $12(a+b+c)p^3 = (4a+b)p^2 + (4a+2b)p + (4a+3b)$

5 (i) ${}^mC_a(\hat{p}^4)^a(1-\hat{p}^4)^{m-a} \times {}^nC_b(\hat{p}^8)^b(1-\hat{p}^8)^{n-b}$;
$(m+2n)\hat{p}^8 + (m-a)\hat{p}^4 - (a+2b) = 0$

(ii) $\hat{p} = 0.9474$

6 (i) **(a)** $6\hat{\mu}^3 + (1320-(a+b+c))\hat{\mu}^2 + 20(4320-(5a+8b+9c))\hat{\mu} + 2400(720-(a+2b+3c)) = 0$

(b) $120(3\hat{\lambda}^3 + 2\hat{\lambda}^2 + \hat{\lambda}) - (a+2b+3c) = 0$

(ii) (a) $\hat{\mu} = 47.41$
(b) $\hat{\lambda} = 1.314$

7 $\dfrac{1}{2\beta\sqrt{t_1}}e^{-\left(\frac{\sqrt{t_1}}{\beta}\right)} \times \dfrac{1}{2\beta\sqrt{t_2}}e^{-\left(\frac{\sqrt{t_2}}{\beta}\right)} \times \ldots$
$\times \dfrac{1}{2\beta\sqrt{t_r}}e^{-\left(\frac{\sqrt{t_r}}{\beta}\right)} \times \left(e^{-\left(\frac{\sqrt{\tau}}{\beta}\right)}\right)^{n-r}$;
$\hat{\beta} = \dfrac{\sqrt{t_1}+\sqrt{t_2}+\ldots+\sqrt{t_r}+(n-r)\sqrt{\tau}}{r}$

8 (i) $f(x) = \dfrac{\delta}{\pi(\delta^2+x^2)}$

(ii) $\sum_{i=1}^{n} \dfrac{2}{\hat{\delta}^2+x_i^2} = \dfrac{n}{\hat{\delta}^2}$

(iii) $f(x) = \dfrac{\delta}{2\alpha(\delta)(\delta^2+x^2)}$,
$\sum_{i=1}^{n} \dfrac{2}{\hat{\delta}^2+x_i^2} = \dfrac{n}{\hat{\delta}^2} + \dfrac{nH}{\hat{\delta}\alpha(\hat{\delta})(H^2+\hat{\delta}^2)}$, where
$\alpha(\delta) = \arctan\left(\dfrac{H}{\delta}\right)$

(iv) $\sum_{i=1}^{n} \dfrac{2(x_i-\hat{\xi})}{\hat{\delta}^2+(x-\hat{\xi})^2} = 0$

9 (i) $\hat{\beta} = 31$
(ii) $\hat{\alpha} = \frac{7}{64}$

10 (i) $\ln(x_1 x_2 \ldots x_n)\hat{\kappa}^2 + (2n+\ln(x_1 x_2 \ldots x_n))\hat{\kappa} + n = 0$

(ii) $\hat{\kappa} = \dfrac{(2-s)+\sqrt{4+s^2}}{2s}$

(iii) $\hat{\kappa} = 4.375$

Chapter 4

Exercise 4A (Page 71)

1 $G(t) = \frac{1}{36}t^2 + \frac{2}{36}t^3 + \frac{3}{36}t^4 + \frac{4}{36}t^5 + \frac{5}{36}t^6 + \frac{6}{36}t^7 + \frac{5}{36}t^8 + \frac{4}{36}t^9 + \frac{3}{36}t^{10} + \frac{2}{36}t^{11} + \frac{1}{36}t^{12}$

2 $G(t) = \frac{1}{6} + \frac{5}{18}t + \frac{2}{9}t^2 + \frac{1}{6}t^3 + \frac{1}{9}t^4 + \frac{1}{18}t^5$

3 $G(t) = \frac{1}{8} + \frac{3}{8}t + \frac{3}{8}t^2 + \frac{1}{8}t^3$

4 $G(t) = \frac{3}{5}t + \frac{3}{10}t^2 + \frac{1}{10}t^3$

5 $G(t) = \frac{3}{5}t + \frac{2}{5} \times \frac{3}{5}t^2 + \left(\frac{2}{5}\right)^2 \times \frac{3}{5}t^3 \times \frac{3}{5}t^4 + \ldots + \left(\frac{2}{5}\right)^{n-1} \times \frac{3}{5}t^n + \ldots = \dfrac{3t}{5-2t}$

6 $k = \frac{1}{153}$; $G(t) = \frac{1}{153}t + \frac{2}{153}t^2 + \frac{6}{153}t^3 + \frac{24}{153}t^4 + \frac{120}{153}t^5$

7 $G(t) = \frac{1}{3} + \frac{1}{2}t + \frac{1}{6}t^3$

8 $G(t) = \frac{12}{35} + \frac{18}{35}t + \frac{1}{7}t^2$

Exercise 4B (Page 75)

1 $E(X) = 2\frac{1}{6}$; $Var(X) = 2\frac{23}{36}$
2 $E(X) = 2\frac{2}{3}$; $Var(X) = \frac{8}{9}$
3 $E(X) = 3\frac{1}{2}$; $Var(X) = 2\frac{11}{12}$
4 $E(X) = 1\frac{1}{2}$; $Var(X) = \frac{3}{4}$
5 $Var(X) = na(1-a)$
6 $G(t) = \left(\frac{12}{13} + \frac{1}{13}t\right)^4$; $E(X) = \frac{4}{13}$; $Var(X) = \frac{48}{169}$
8 $a = \frac{1}{3}, b = \frac{1}{6}, c = \frac{1}{2}$
9 $G(t) = \frac{1}{36}t + \frac{3}{36}t^2 + \frac{5}{36}t^3 + \frac{7}{36}t^4 + \frac{9}{36}t^5 + \frac{11}{36}t^6$;
$E(X) = 4\frac{17}{36}$; $Var(X) = 1.97$

Exercise 4C (Page 84)

1 (ii) $G(t) = \left(\dfrac{t}{6-5t}\right)^2$

(iii) $E(X) = 12$; $Var(X) = 60$

2 (i) $G_X(t) = t(0.6+0.4t)$;
$G_Y(t) = t(0.2+0.5t+0.3t^2)$;
$G(t) = G_X(t) \times G_Y(t)$
$= t(0.6+0.4t) \times t(0.2+0.5t+0.3t^2)$

(ii) $E(X+Y) = E(X)+E(Y) = 3.5$;
$Var(X+Y) = Var(X)+Var(Y) = 0.73$

3 (i) The p.g.f. for constant c is $G_c(t) = t^c$.
Since X and c are independent:
$G_Y(t) = G_{X+c}(t) = G_X(t) \times G_c(t) = t^c G_X(t)$.

(ii) $E(c) = c$ and $Var(c) = 0$; the results follow from the independence of X and c.

4 (i) $G_X(t) = e^{3.4(t-1)}$, $G_Y(t) = e^{4.8(t-1)}$

(iii) $G_{X+Y}(t) = e^{12.2(t-1)}$

5 (i) $\frac{1}{6}t + \frac{1}{3}t^2 + \frac{1}{2}t^3$; $G_X = \left(\frac{1}{6}t + \frac{1}{3}t^2 + \frac{1}{2}t^3\right)^5$

(ii) $E(X) = 11\frac{2}{3}$, $Var(X) = 2\frac{7}{9}$

6 $G_Z(t) = G_X(t) \times G_Y(t) = \dfrac{t(1-t^6)}{6(1-t)} \times \dfrac{t(1-t^4)}{4(1-t)}$

Exercise 4D (Page 87)

1 (i) *Hint*: Let $G(t) = p_1 t + p_2 t^2 + p_3 t + \ldots$ and find $G(1) + G(-1)$.

(ii) (a) $G(t) = \frac{1}{36}(t^2 + 2t^3 + 3t^4 + 4t^5 + 5t^6 + 6t^7 + 5t^8 + 4t^9 + 3t^{10} + 2t^{11} + t^{12})$; 0.5

(b) $G(t) = \dfrac{2t}{3-t}$; 0.25

2 (i) $\frac{1}{6}$ **(ii)** $\frac{1}{6}$ **(iii)** $\frac{2}{3}$

(iv) $E(R) = 3\frac{1}{3}$

3 (i) $P(X=r) = e^{-\lambda}\dfrac{\lambda^r}{r!}$; $G_X(t) = e^{\lambda(t-1)}$

(ii) $k = \dfrac{1}{1-e^{-\lambda}}$

(iv) $E(Y) = \dfrac{\lambda e^\lambda}{e^\lambda - 1}$

4 $3\frac{6}{7}$

5 (i) $P(X = x) = pq^{x-1}, x \geq 1$

  (ii) $E(X) = \frac{1}{p}; \text{Var}(X) = \frac{q}{p^2}$

  (iii) $G_Y(t) = [G(t)]^k = \left(\frac{pt}{1-qt}\right)^k = \frac{p^k t^k}{(1-qt)^k}$

6 (i) $P(X = x) = e^{-\theta_1}\frac{\theta_1^x}{x!}; P(Y = y) = e^{-\theta_1}\frac{\theta_2^y}{y!}$

  $P(X + Y = z) = e^{-(\theta_1+\theta_2)}\frac{(\theta_1 + \theta_2)^z}{z!}$.

  (ii) $G_X(t) = e^{\theta_1(t-1)}; G_Y(t) = e^{\theta_2(t-1)};$
  $G_{X+Y}(t) = e^{(\theta_1+\theta_2)(t-1)}$

  (iii) (a) $P(X + Y = z) = e^{-(\theta_1+\theta_2)}\frac{(\theta_1 + \theta_2)^z}{z!}$

  (b) $\theta_1 + \theta_2$
  (c) $\theta_1 + \theta_2$

7 $k = e^{-2}$

  (i) $e^{-2}, e^{-2}, \frac{3}{2}e^{-2}, \frac{7}{6}e^{-2}, \frac{25}{24}e^{-2}$
  (ii) 3
  (iii) 5
  (iv) 3

8 (iii) $P_n = (2p-1)^{n-1}(\theta - 0.5) + 0.5$

9 (i) $q_j = \frac{j-1}{N}, p_j = \frac{N-j+1}{N}$

  (ii) $G(t) = \frac{p_j t}{1 - q_j t}, E(X_j) = \frac{N}{N-j+1}$

  (iv) $\text{Var}(X) = N\left(N - 1 + \frac{N-2}{2^2} + \frac{N-3}{3^2} + \ldots + \frac{1}{(N-1)^2}\right)$

10 (i) $G_X(t) = \frac{2}{3} + \frac{1}{3}t$
  (ii) $G_Y(t) = \frac{1}{2} + \frac{1}{2}t$
  (iii) $E(S) = \frac{11}{6}, \text{Var}(S) = \frac{17}{36}$

Chapter 5

Exercise 5A (Page 96)

1 $\mu_3 = 0$

3 (i)

  (ii) $\mu_3 = -\frac{1}{160}$

4 (i)

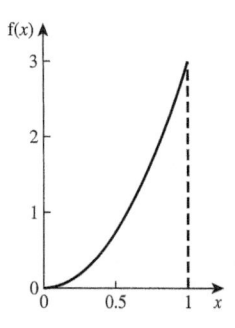

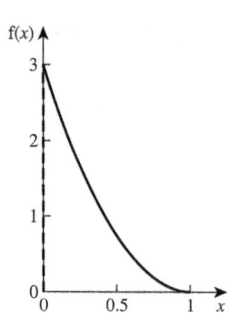

  (ii) $\mu_3 = \frac{1}{160}$

Exercise 5B (Page 109)

1 The m.g.f. of $B(n, p)$ is $(q + pe^\theta)^n$
  (i) $(q + pe^\theta)^{n_1+n_2+\ldots+n_k}$

2 The m.g.f. of Poisson (m) is $e^{-m}e^{me^\theta}$.
  (i) $e^{-M}e^{Me^\theta}$ where $M = m_1 + m_2 + \ldots + m_n$
  (ii) The distribution of Y is Poisson (M).

3 mean $= np$, variance $= npq$

4 (i) The integral diverges at the upper limit if $u = (\lambda - t)x$ is negative, i.e. if $\lambda < t$. In the case $\lambda = t$ the integrand is infinite.

  (ii) The m.g.f. of Y is $\left(\frac{\lambda}{\lambda - t}\right)^{nk+n}$

  mean $= \frac{nk+n}{\lambda}$, variance $= \frac{nk+n}{\lambda^2}$

  (iii) The p.d.f. of Y is $\frac{\lambda^{nk+n} y^{nk+n-1} e^{-\lambda y}}{(nk+n-1)!}$.

5 (ii) $e^{t^2/2}$
  (iii) $e^{\mu t + \sigma^2 t^2/2}$
  (iv) means are $2\mu, 0$; variances are $2\sigma^2, 2\sigma^2$

6 (iii) $\mu, \mu, \mu + 3\mu^2$
  (iv) 3

7 (i) $M(\theta) = (1 = 2\theta)^{-n/2}$

8 (i) X has the distribution function $1 - e^{-0.001x}$ and p.d.f. $0.001e^{-0.001x}$
  (iv) Option 2

9 (ii) $\frac{\alpha}{\alpha - \theta} \times \frac{\beta}{\beta - \theta}$

  (iii) The m.g.f. of Z is $\frac{\alpha}{\alpha - \theta} \times \frac{\beta}{\beta - \theta}$

  (iv) $\frac{1}{\alpha} + \frac{1}{\beta}$

10 (i) The m.g.f. is $\frac{\lambda}{\lambda - \theta}$, mean $= \frac{1}{\lambda}$, variance $= \frac{1}{\lambda^2}$

  (ii) S_n is the time to the arrival of the nth car; the m.g.f. is $\frac{\lambda^n}{(\lambda - \theta)^n}$

  (iii) $\frac{\lambda^n}{(\lambda - \theta)^n}$

(iv) The p.d.f of S_n is the same as that of Y. S_n and Y have the same m.g.f., so they must be the same random variable and thus have the same p.d.f.

Chapter 6

❓ (Page 114)

An advantage is that the after-lunch group have not done the experiment before so on both occasions the subjects are not 'in practice'. A disadvantage is that there may be differences between the two groups, particularly if they are small in number.

❓ (Page 119)

- Did you take two independent random samples of the appropriate population in the two conditions?
- Is the variable Normally distributed in each condition? The differences should be continuous rather than discrete and you could also look at a stem-and-leaf diagram for each condition – they should be unimodal and roughly symmetrical if the assumption of Normality in the population is plausible.
- Does the variable have the same variance in each condition? You could look at a stem-and-leaf diagram for each condition – they should have roughly the same spread if the assumption of equal variances in the population is plausible.

Exercise 6A (Page 123)

1 (i) $s = 2.646$, $t = 1.192$, $v = 17$, 1-tailed test
Accept H_0 even at 5% level: not heavier

(ii) Assumptions: independent random samples on the two islands – it is hard to sample animal populations randomly – some individuals are more catchable than others; Normally distributed weights on each island – seems reasonable; same variance of weights on each island – at first glance the Daphne Major variance seems larger but the samples are small.

2 (i) $s = 5.146$, $t = 0.304$, $v = 43$, 2-tailed test
Accept H_0 even at 10% level: same yield

(ii)
```
            9 0 8 9
      0 4 2 4 1 2 4 3 4
  9 8 5 9 8 5 1 8 5 7 5 7 6 8 8
3 2 1 0 1 1 2 0 0 4 0 0 3 0 3 3
            7 7 6 2 6 9
```

Assumptions: independent random samples of plots for the two varieties – you cannot tell how this selection was made; Normally distributed yield with same variance in each variety – the stem-and-leaf diagram suggests this is not unreasonable.

(iii) Select plots; plant some of each variety on half of each plot. An improvement since small average differences in yield are more likely to show up when the differences attributable to the plots are eliminated.

3 (i) $s = 1.568$, $t = 1.989$, $v = 40$, 1-tailed test
Accept H_0 at $2\frac{1}{2}$% level, reject at 5% level

(ii) Assumptions: independent random samples for the two groups – volunteer samples can be biased; Normally distributed ratings with the same variance in each group – probably not a reasonable assumption with data taking only a small number of discrete values.

(iii) Difficult because it is hard to pay two different rewards to the same person without alerting them to the point of the experiment.

4 (i) $s = 5.675$, $t = 2.085$, $v = 32$, 1-tailed test
Critical value at 5% level is less than 1.697
Assumptions: independent random samples of introverts and extroverts – you cannot tell how this selection was made; Normally distributed heights with the same variance in each group – nothing in the data to suggest this is unreasonable.

(ii) No: causal conclusion is not justified – a confounding factor (e.g. features of childhood nurture) may produce both taller and more extrovert people.

5 (i) $s = 25.27$, $t = 1.264$, $v = 63$, 1-tailed test
Critical value at 5% level is more than 1.660
Assumptions: independent random samples for the two groups – hard to tell, but seems unlikely; Normally distributed incomes with the same variance in each group – not reasonable, as income distribution is likely to be skewed and the variance to be different in the two groups.

(ii) Those who have stayed on will have had fewer years in work. It would be better to investigate income eight years after completing education or income over time from age 24 to 30, say.

6 (i) $s = 3.453$, $t = 1.792$, $v = 23$, 1-tailed test
Accept H_0 at $2\frac{1}{2}$% level, reject at 5% level

(ii) Assumptions: independent random samples for the two floors – 'last year' is not a random sample of person-days and not independent for the two floors; Normally distributed numbers of days absence with the same variance on each floor – probably not a reasonable assumption with data taking only a small number of discrete values.

Exercise 6B (Page 127)

1 $t = -1.166$, $v = 22$, 1-tailed
Accept H_0 even at 5% level: not less
Assumptions: independent random samples of males and females; normally distributed lengths with the same variance in each group.

2 (i) $t = 2.35$, $v = 11$, 1-tailed
Reject H_0 at $1\frac{1}{2}$% level and above: less
(ii) Assumptions: random sample of pairs; Normally distributed differences between male and female lengths in mantis pairs.
(iii) The paired test is better able to discriminate the difference due to sex in mantis size when other effects (e.g. age, diet, habitat) which affect male and female lengths similarly are eliminated by pairing.

3 $t = 1.005$, $v = 22$, 1-tailed
Accept H_0 even at 5% level: not more
Assumptions: independent random samples of patients for treatment or non-treatment; Normally distributed post-operative stays with the same variance in each group.

4 (i) $t = 0.953$, $v = 6$, 2-tailed
Accept H_0 even at 10% level: 2° rise
(ii) Assumptions: random sample of locations; Normally distributed changes in temperature.

5 $t = 0.115$, $v = 9$, 1-tailed
Accept H_0 even at 5% level: 10.3 less
Assumptions: random sample of dyslexic adults; Normally distributed differences in real and nonsense words learnt.

6 (i) $t = -1.243$, $v = 67$, 2-tailed
Reject H_0 even at 1% level: not 5.1 less
(ii) Assumptions: independent random samples of dyslexic and non-dyslexic adults; Normally distributed numbers of nonsense words recalled with the same variance in each group.
In this question the assumptions are about two groups and the actual numbers of words they recall in one condition; in question 5, about one group and the difference in the number of words recalled in two conditions.
(iii) The hypotheses are related. If D_r, D_n, N_r, N_n are the mean numbers of words recalled, respectively, by dyslexic adults recalling real words, dyslexic adults recalling nonsense words, non-dyslexic adults recalling real words and non-dyslexic adults recalling nonsense words, then the known information is that $N_r - N_n = 10.3$ and $N_r - D_r = 5.1$. Thus if the null hypothesis of question 5 is true, so that $D_r - D_n = 10.3$, this implies that $(N_r - N_n) - (D_r - D_n) = 0$ or $N_n - D_n = N_r - D_r = 5.1$ which is the null hypothesis of question 6.

Exercise 6C (Page 132)

1 (i) $\bar{x} = 23.182$, $s = 4.708$, $v = 10$, $\tau = 2.228$
upper limit 26.34
(ii) Assumptions: independent random samples of hen and duck eggs; Normally distributed masses with the same variance for each type of egg.

2 (i) mean difference $= 2.632$, $s = 7.783$, $v = 18$, $\tau = 1.736$ (interpolation)
interval 2.632 ± 3.100
(ii) Assumptions: random sample of twins; Normally distributed differences in salary.

3 mean difference $= 13.615$, $s = 10.31$, $v = 12$, $\tau = 2.681$, interval 13.615 ± 7.665

4 mean difference $= 17.111$, $s = 12.186$, $v = 14$, $\tau = 1.761$, upper limit 27.93

5 mean difference $= 241.48$, $s = 136.13$, $v = 31$, $\tau = 1.696$ (interpolation)
interval 241.48 ± 81.31

Chapter 7

Exercise 7A (Page 150)

1 (i) $z = 1.5997$, 1-tailed test
Accept H_0 at 5% level, reject at 10% level
(ii) Assumptions: independent random samples from the appropriate populations of clover; appropriate to use the Central Limit Theorem to justify a Normal approximation to the distributions of sample means; variances of populations well approximated by their sample estimators.

2 $0.1852 \pm 0.0691\tau$; $\tau = 1.96$ for 95% interval
Assumptions: random sample of birds; appropriate to use the Central Limit Theorem to justify a Normal approximation to the distribution of sample means; variance of population well approximated by its sample estimator.

3 $z = 1.2869$, 1-tailed test
Accept H_0 at 5% level, reject at 10% level
Assumptions: independent random samples of

waiting times; appropriate to use the Central Limit Theorem to justify a Normal approximation to the distributions of sample means; variances of populations well approximated by their sample estimators.

4 $z = 1.819$, 2-tailed test
Reject H_0 at 5% level, accept at 2% level

5 (i) $z = 2.379$, 2-tailed test
Reject H_0 at 2% level, accept at 1%

(ii) Assumptions: random sample of rate-differences; appropriate to use the Central Limit Theorem to justify a Normal approximation to the distribution of sample mean differences; variance of differences well approximated by its sample estimator.
The data could be seen as a random sample of targeting errors made at random by the Bank in their systematic attempt to shadow the Lombard rate, but it is hard to see how the values on 40 successive days could be seen as a random sample – each day's errors are likely to be correlated with the previous day's level of success.

6 $251.67 \pm 29.82\tau$
$\tau = 1.96$ for 95% interval

7 $z = 1.049$
Accept H_0 even at 10% level
Assumptions: independent random samples of boxes from the two machines; appropriate to use the Central Limit Theorem to justify a Normal approximation to the distributions of sample mean contents; variances of contents well approximated by their sample estimators.

8 (i) (a) $z = 1.6986$, 1-tailed test
Accept H_0 even at 2% level
(b) $z = 2.3034$, 1-tailed test
Reject H_0 even at 2% level

(ii) Either the variances in the two populations are, approximately, the same in which case this is an erratic pair of samples (since the sample variances differ) possibly leading to a type II error in conclusion (a); or the variances are significantly different in the two populations and conclusion (a) is using an incorrect assumption and is hence unreliable.

9 (i) $z = 7.9847$, Reject H_0
Assumptions: independent random samples of subjects; appropriate to use the Central Limit Theorem to justify a Normal approximation to the distributions of mean numbers of words recalled; variances of numbers of words recalled well approximated by their sample estimators.

(ii) Prepare two lists of words A and B: select a single set of subjects, divided into four equal subsets and have each subset learn and recall one of: list A randomly followed by list B alphabetically, list B randomly followed by list A alphabetically, list A alphabetically followed by list B randomly, list B alphabetically followed by list A randomly.

10 (i) (a) $z = 2.934$, 1-tailed test
Reject H_0 at 1% level
(b) $z = 1.257$, 1-tailed test
Accept H_0 at 10% level

(ii) Interval is $14 \pm 4.77\tau$; $\tau = 1.96$ for 95% interval

Exercise 7B (Page 153)

1 (i) Lower bound 422.5
(ii) Interval 366 ± 5.15
Correct interpretation: this procedure leads to an interval including the true mean with probability 0.99.

2 (i) $\tau = 5.061$, $\nu = 9$, 2-tailed test: critical value 2.262
Reject H_0
(ii) $\tau = 1.974$, $\nu = 18$, 2-tailed test: critical value 2.104
Accept H_0
(iii) The first is a more discriminating analysis – a type II error is less likely because the paired design eliminates variation due to differences in resistance amongst components which might swamp the effect of the adjustment.

3 (i) 20.18 ± 1.10; 2-tailed test: critical value 2.262
(ii) $z = 2.439$, 2-tailed test: critical value 1.96
(iii) Use a Wilcoxon rank sum test – see page 163.

4 (i) H_0: Mean performance difference $= 0$.
H_1: Mean performance difference $\neq 0$.
(ii) Over the population of jobs, performance differences are Normally distributed.
(iii) $t = 1.090$, $\nu = 7$, 2-tailed test: critical value 3.499
Accept H_0
(iv) 3.25 ± 7.05

5 (i) H_0: Mean arrivals at the two stations are equal.
H_1: Mean arrivals at the two stations are not equal.
(ii) Over the population of days, arrival numbers are independently and Normally distributed at each station.
(iii) The variance of the arrival numbers is the same for each station.

(iv) $t = 2.507, v = 18$, 2-tailed test: critical value 2.104
Reject H_0
(v) Use a Normal test (see pages 143–146)
6 (i) Filling volumes before and after overhaul are Normally distributed with a common variance.
(ii) H_0: Mean volumes delivered before and after overhaul are equal.
H_1: Mean volumes delivered before and after overhaul are not equal.
(iii) $t = 0.9424, v = 15$, 2-tailed test: critical value 2.131
Reject H_0
(iv) No reason why an overhaul should not affect the variance of the volume delivered, so common variance assumption doubtful.
7 (ii) $E[T] = 32, \text{Var}[T] = 64$
(iii) The Central Limit Theorem states that distribution of the sum of many identical random variables is Normal even if the underlying distribution is not: $n = 8$ is not large, but the underlying distribution is continuous and unimodal so you can expect a reasonable approximation.
(iv) $T \approx N(8\theta, 16\theta)$
(v) The other solution represents the upper limit of a one-sided 95% confidence interval.
8 (i) A single sample of tasks has been taken and the times taken by the two employees are not therefore independent samples as required by an unpaired design.
(ii) Differences in times on population of tasks is normally distributed.
$t = 2.274, v = 9$, 2-tailed test: critical value 2.262
Reject H_0
Confidence interval: 2.6 ± 2.1
(iii) Wilcoxon paired sample test – see *Statistics 3* Chapter 6.
9 $\bar{d} = 1.8, s^2 = 2.527, t = 2.996$
c.v. = 3.143 so accept H_0: treatment seems ineffective Assumption: differences Normally distributed. Confidence interval: $(0.633, \infty)$
Interpretation: intervals determined in this way include the true mean difference in 95% of samples.
10 Means: 6.08, 5.02; $s^2 = 1.746$
$t = 1.8192$, c.v. = 1.731 so reject H_0: seems to be improvement
Assumptions: Normal populations with the same variance.
Confidence interval: $(-0.16, 2.28)$
Interpretation: intervals determined in this way include the true difference of means in 95% of samples.

11 (i) $\bar{d} = 1.3, s^2 = 89.34, t = 0.4349$
c.v.=2.262 so accept H_0: seems mean price the same.
(ii) $(-4.18, 6.78)$
(iii) Differences Normally distributed
(iv) The paired test compares the prices of the same item in both supermarkets and so eliminates variation, common to both supermarkets, in price between items.
12 Means 9.258, 6.845; variances = 10.334, 8.251
Test statistic = 7.316, 2-tailed test: c.v. at the 5% level = 1.96 so reject H_0 and conclude that the eggs at one supermarket are fresher than those in the other.

Chapter 8

? (Page 162)
They have been given the mean value of the ranks they would have had if they had been slightly different.

Exercise 8A (Page 170)

1 (i) $T = 100$, critical value = 73
or $W = 197$, critical value = 224
Accept H_0: no difference
(ii) Taking all the leavers from one school who went to university does not give a random sample of graduates.
2 $T = 490$, critical value = 467
or $W = 896$, critical value = 873
Accept H_0: no difference
A stem-and-leaf diagram of the data suggests that the men's data are much more strongly bimodal than the women's so the distributions differ not only in their location but also in their shape.
3 $T = 18$, critical value = 19
or $W = 87$, critical value = 86
Reject H_0: harder
5 (i) (a) Both histograms show approximate Normality.
(b) The histograms are approximately the same shape.
(ii) $T = 9$, critical value = 10
or $W = 66$, critical value = 65
Reject H_0: different
6 (i) Calling the first sample X and the second Y, $W_X = 95$ and $W_Y = 115$.
The critical value for a 1-tail Wilcoxon (2-sample) rank sum test at the 5% significance level, for $m = n = 10$, is 82.
Since $95 > 82$, H_0 is accepted.

(ii) It is now appropriate to do a Wilcoxon (paired sample) signed rank test on the differences.
The signed rank sums are $W_- = (-)4.5$, $W_+ = 40.5$.
The critical value for $n = 9$ is 8.
Since $4.5 < 8$, the null hypothesis is rejected.

(iii) The two tests give different results illustrating that the paired test, when you can do it, is more sensitive than the 2-sample test.

7 (i) (a) $\{1,2,3,4\}, \{1,2,3,5\}, \{1,2,3,6\}, \{1,2,4,5\}$
(c) $^9C_4 = 126$
(e) 0.0331

(ii) $W = 36$, critical value $= 29$
Accept H_0

8 (i) $W = 35$
(ii) $W = 39$
(iii) Rejection
(iv) Reject H_0
Calculate $\dfrac{\bar{x}_A - \bar{x}_B}{s\sqrt{\dfrac{1}{7} + \dfrac{1}{7}}}$, where $\bar{x}_A, \bar{x}_B$ are the sample means and s^2 is the unbiased pooled-sample estimate of the population variance; compare this with the one-tailed 5% critical value for the t distribution with 12 degrees of freedom.

9 (ii) $\frac{1}{2}m(m+1) + mn$
(iii) $W = 52$, critical value $= 53$
Reject H_0

10 (i) Standard deviations are not known so Normal tests should not be used.
No reason to suppose the underlying distributions are Normal, so t tests should not be used.

(ii) **Leaner**
Wilcoxon (paired sample) rank sum test on the difference in the weights.
One-tail test, $n = 11$, critical value $= 13$
$W_- = (-)11.5$, $W_+ = 54.5$
Since $11.5 < 13$, H_0 (that there is no weight loss) is rejected. The claim that they are leaner is justified.

Fitter
Wilcoxon (two-sample) rank sum test
Critical value for 1-tail test at 5% significance level with $m = n = 12$ is 120.
$W_S = 164.5$, $W_E = 135.5$
Since $135.5 > 120$, the H_0 is accepted and so the organiser's claim that the children leave fitter is not accepted.

(iii) Yes, individual times should have been recorded for the fitness test so that a paired sample test could have been used. This might well have given a different result.

11 (i) Min 10, max 26
(ii) 70
(iv) $\frac{2}{70} \approx 0.02857$
(v) $\frac{4}{70} \approx 0.05714$
(vi) $p = 0.0606$
(vii) $W = 11$; significant at 6% level

Chapter 9

? (Page 179)

The possibilities of changing the significance level of the test and changing the sample size are discussed in the text that follows.

Exercise 9A (Page 189)

1 (i) Critical region is $\{x \leq 5\} \cup \{x \geq 15\}$; $\alpha = 0.0414$
(ii) OC(p) graph

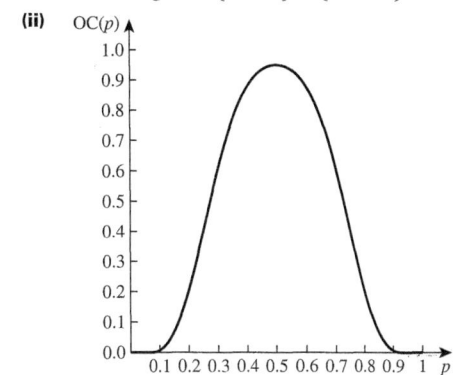

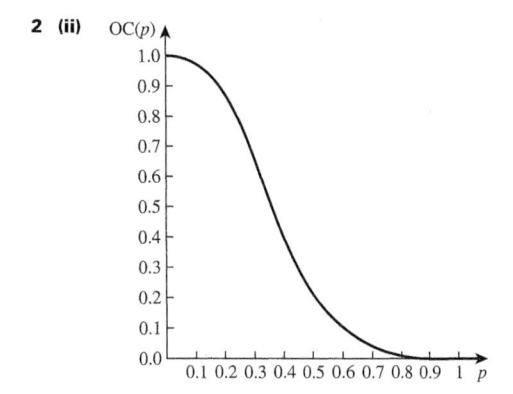

2 (ii) OC(p) graph
(iii) $p \geq 0.596$

3 (i) $\frac{1}{13}$

(ii)

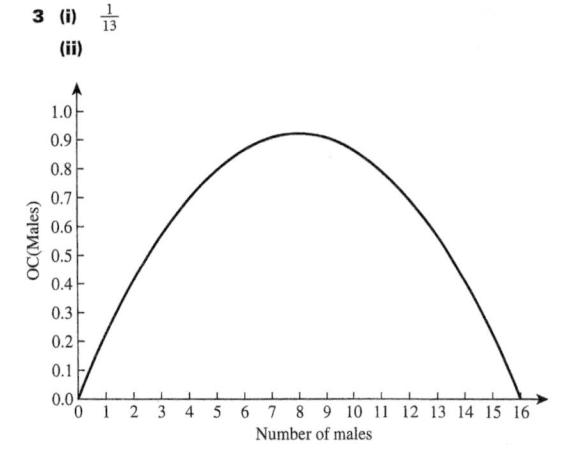

(iii) Significance level $= \frac{1}{8}$
The operating characteristic is similar but not identical, see graph.

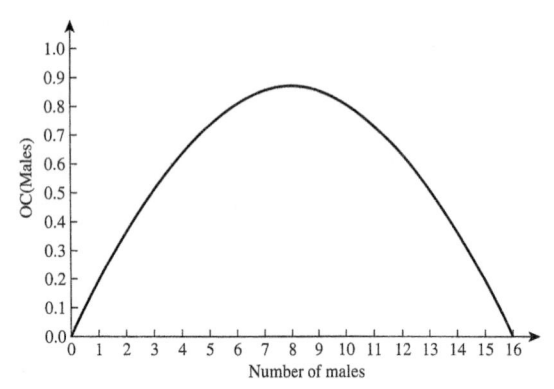

4 (i) $\alpha = 0.2759, \beta = 0.1844$
(ii) $\alpha = 0.0086, \beta = 0.0335$
(iii) It may be better to underestimate the age of the bone, rather than overestimate it.

5 (i) $R = 0.11$
(ii) probability of type II error $= 0.412$

6 (i) The probability of picking a value less than I is $\frac{I}{m}$. The probability of picking n values less than I is $\left(\frac{I}{m}\right)^n$.
(ii) (a) $I_{\text{crit}} = m_0 \alpha^{1/n}$
(b) $\text{OC}(m) = 1 - \alpha \left(\frac{m_0}{m}\right)^n$

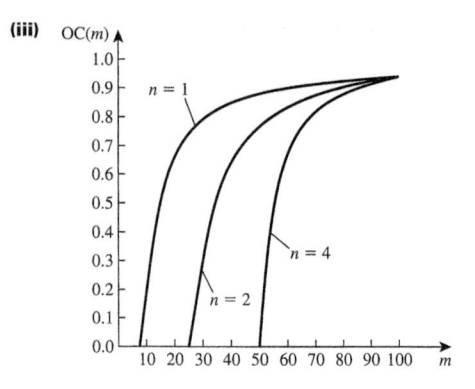

(iii)

(iv) You need to choose n to be large enough so that $\text{OC}(m) = 0$ for the value of m in the alternative hypothesis. Keep changing the value of m in the alternative hypothesis until you find the smallest value for which H_0 is rejected.

7 (i) $H_0: \mu = 0;\ H_1: \mu > 0$
(ii) $\overline{d} > 0.26s$
(iii)

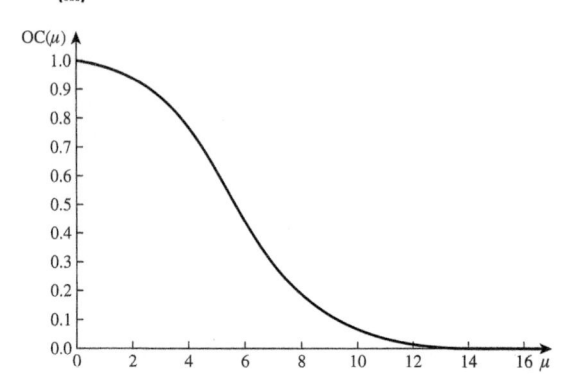

8 (i) Rejecting the null hypothesis when it is true.
(ii) Accepting the null hypothesis when it is false.
(iii) With a compound alternative hypothesis, the probability of a type II error, viewed as a function of the parameter whose value is being tested.
(v) 0.0078, 0.2266, 0.8203, 0.9902, 0.8203, 0.2266, 0.0078

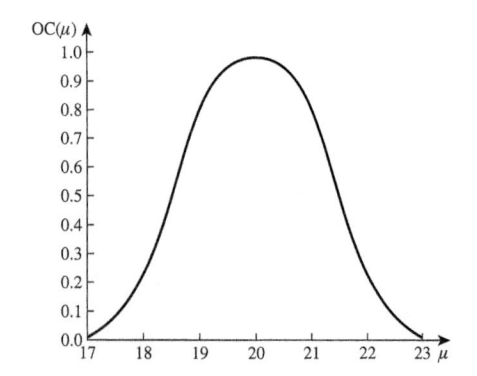

9 (i) $\alpha = 0.1587, \beta = 0.0668$
  (ii) $k = 2.645, \beta = 0.7405$
  (iii) $k = 1.5, n = 61$
10 (i) See the answer to question 8.
  (ii) (a)

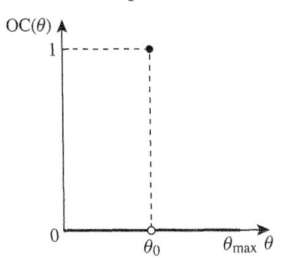

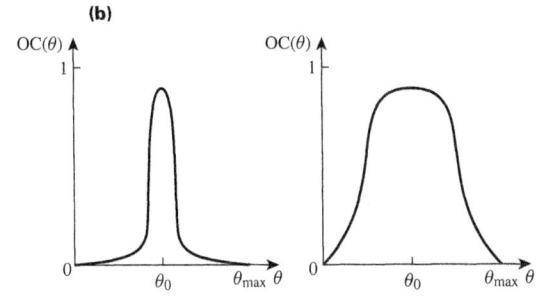

  (b)

  The first graph shows a 'better' test as it more closely approximates the graph in part (a).
  (iii) P(type I error) = 0.0608
  P(type II error) = 0.8881
  There is a high probability of a type II error.

Chapter 10

Exercise 10A (Page 197)

1 (i) $H_0: \mu_1 = \mu_2 = \mu_3 = \mu_4 = \mu_5$, H_1: Not all μ_i equal.
  (ii)

Method	1	2	3	4	5	Overall
Group size	4	4	4	4	4	20.00
Group mean	21.25	26.75	19.25	19.75	24.00	22.20
Group variance	6.92	3.58	4.25	3.58	6.00	12.17

  (iii)

Source of variation	SS	DF	VE
Between groups	158.2	4	39.55
Within groups	73.0	15	4.87

  (iv) $F = 8.13$
  (v) Reject H_0
2 $s_b^2 = 195; s_w^2 = 23; F = 8.48;$ C.V. $= 3.89$; reject H_0
3 $s_b^2 = 122.9; s_w^2 = 23; F = 3.21$
  (i) C.V. $= 3.24$; accept H_0
  (ii) C.V. $= 5.29$; accept H_0
4 $s_b^2 = 37.5; s_w^2 = 13.94, F = 2.69;$ C.V. $= 4.07$; accept H_0
5 $s_b^2 = 147.5; s_w^2 = 290.2; F = 0.51;$ C.V. $= 4.26$; accept H_0
6 $s_b^2 = 97.4; s_w^2 = 24.3; F = 4.01$
  (i) C.V. $= 2.96$; reject H_0
  (ii) C.V. $= 4.67$; accept H_0

Exercise 10B (Page 204)

1 (i) 21
  (ii) 7
  (iii) $s_b^2 = 18.95; s_w^2 = 4.2; F = 4.51;$ C.V. $= 3.55$; reject H_0
2 (i)

Method of storage	1	2	3	Overall
Group size	5	3	6	14
Group mean	7.4	6.067	5.7	6.386
Group variance	0.58	0.536	0.697	1.211

  (ii)

Source of variation	SS	DF	VE
Between groups	8.27	2	4.14
Within groups	8.69	11	0.79

  (iii) $F = 5.234;$ C.V. $= 3.98$; reject H_0
3 (i) $s_b^2 = 1626.7; s_w^2 = 127.3; F = 12.8;$
  C.V. $= 5.04$; reject H_0
  (ii) mean $= 48.25$ hours;
  standard error $= 5.64$ hours.
4 (i) $s_b^2 = 27.75; s_w^2 = 50.31; F = 0.55;$
  C.V. $= 4.26$; accept H_0
  (ii) She could classify journey times as 'rush hour' and 'not rush hour' and time four journeys for each mode of transport in each category. Carrying out an analysis of variance for each category would allow her to choose the quickest mode of transport for rush hour and for other times.
  (iii) e.g. day of week, comfort, cost
5 (i) $s_b^2 = 281.3; s_w^2 = 50.6; F = 5.56$
  (ii) $H_0; \mu_1 = \mu_2 = \mu_3$, H_1: Not all μ_i equal;
  C.V. $= 3.63$
  (iii) Reject H_0.
  It is assumed that the lengths of the skulls at the three locations have the same variance and that the lengths are Normally distributed.
6 (i) (a) $e_{ij} \sim N(0, \sigma^2)$
  (b) $\mu_1 = \mu_2 = \ldots = \mu_k = \mu$
  Substituting $\mu_i = \mu + \alpha_i$:
  $\mu + \alpha_1 = \mu + \alpha_2 = \ldots = \mu + \alpha_k = \mu$
  $\Rightarrow \alpha_1 = \alpha_2 = \ldots = \alpha_k = 0$
  (ii) (a) $s_b^2 = 1.655; s_w^2 = 0.262; F = 6.32;$
  C.V. $= 3.49$
  (b) reject H_0

7 (i) The variances of the percentages of impurity in the product produced by each of the processes must be the same. The percentages of impurity in the product produced by each of the processes must be Normally distributed.

(ii) $s_b^2 = 11.08$; $s_w^2 = 3.52$; $F = 3.15$;
$H_0: \mu_1 = \mu_2 = \mu_3 = \mu_4$
$H_1:$ Not all μ_i equal; C.V. $= 3.35$; accept H_0

(iii) $t = -2.156$; C.V. $= -2.145$; just significant

8 (i) $e_{ij} \sim N(0, \sigma^2)$
μ is the mean of all μ_i.
α_i is the treatment effect of the ith population.

(ii) $s_b^2 = 0.153$; $s_w^2 = 0.0205$; $F = 7.44$;
C.V. $= 8.02$; accept H_0

9 (i) $s_b^2 = 17.78$; $s_w^2 = 0.3975$; $F = 44.7$;
C.V. $= 10.8$; accept H_0

(ii) $x_{ij} = \mu + \alpha_i + e_{ij}$
$\sum \alpha_i = 0$, $x_{ij} \sim N(\mu_i, \sigma^2)$,
$e_{ij} \sim N(0, \sigma^2)$
$H_0: \alpha_1 = \alpha_2 = \ldots = \alpha_k = 0$

10 (i) $s_b^2 = 31.84$; $s_w^2 = 2.01$; $F = 15.8$;
C.V. $= 6.22$; reject H_0

Chapter 11

❓ (Page 210)

Identical twins have the same genetic make-up so any differences between them can be attributed to external effects. When psychologists apply a different treatment to each of the twins in a pair and compare the results they are comparing like with like.

❓ (Page 210)

This discussion point is designed to bring out the need for replication. You need to know about the variability of the yields from the two varieties in order to determine whether any differences you observe are due to the variety or to the inherent variability in the situation. This is discussed in the text that follows.

❓ (Page 211)

You need to allocate the varieties to the plots randomly so as not to introduce bias into the situation. This is discussed in the text that follows.

❓ (Page 213)

The amount of time which can be given to the experiment will probably be determined by financial considerations. Suppose it is just one day, which is thought to be typical. Suppose that several hours are available, covering periods of expected high traffic flow and low traffic flow, and hopefully other variables such as types of vehicles.

Divide the time period into 15-minute slots, to allow for raising or lowering the screen and 10 minutes for recording relevant data. Then randomly allocate half of the slots to having the screen up and the remainder to having it lowered.

Randomisation has then been used in allocating the periods. Replication is being used because there are several slots with the screen raised and several with it lowered.

Exercise 11A (Page 214)

1 (i) This is a very subjective method. The doctors choose which treatment to give to which patient and so they may give the treatment which they believe to be the best to those patients whom they consider to be suffering the most. As the doctors assess when the patient has recovered they may tend to give a slightly earlier date to those who have used the treatment which they consider to be the best. Also, the doctors may not be able to visit the patients, or have them call at the surgery, to find out exactly when they have recovered.

(ii) This method is better than the method in part (i) since the treatments are allocated by a random method. However, there is still the disadvantage that the doctors who are assessing the effectiveness of the treatments know which one the patient has been allocated.

(iii) The method is quicker as there is no need to wait a year for the results. However, the treatments were not allocated in a random manner in the first place so this introduces bias. Also the patients may not remember very accurately when they recovered.

2 (i) The method would be better if the order in which the customers listened to the systems was randomised. If each customer compared the systems several times that would test whether they could really distinguish between them.

(ii) Any differences in the fuel consumption of the lorries could be due to the different skills of the drivers rather than to the differences in the lorries and so it would be better to use the same 'neutral' driver for each of the lorries. The differences could also be due to random effects and so it would be better if each truck were driven several times or, better still, if several trucks were available from each manufacturer.

3 Use a double blind experiment. Randomly allocate the two toothpastes to equal numbers of patients.

4 Use a single blind experiment, randomly allocating the volunteers into two equal-sized groups.

5 (i) There might be a systematic change in the lathe as it is used. If it deteriorates over time the later carbide cutting inserts might have a shorter life because of the change in the lathe rather than because they are inferior.

(ii) If the inserts of type A affected the lathe in some way, loosening some bolts for example, then the type B inserts might wear out sooner than they should.

(iii) The order in which the inserts are used should be randomised. Also, the order in which the material on which they are being tested should be randomised if this is appropriate.

6 (i) The treatments are the additive and no additive. The experimental material is the batch of molten steel and the experimental units are the ten portions into which it is divided. The control is the no additive treatment. The response variable is the strength of the steel.

(ii) The treatment is the fertiliser and the three levels are small, medium and large amounts. The gooseberry bushes are the experimental material and the blocks are the three plots. The experimental units are the individual rows. The response variable is the yield.

(iii) The treatments are the two types of tank. The response variable is the time to failure.

(iv) The treatments are the three types of drill. The experimental material is the casting. The experimental units are the six pieces of material to be drilled. The response variable is the number of holes drilled in ten minutes.

❓ (Page 216)

(i) Binomial
(ii) Normal
(iii) Poisson
(iv) Normal
(v) Poisson

Exercise 11B (Page 220)

1 Place the squares of wood in order and number them 1, ..., 28. Randomly allocate the different types of paint to the squares (to cope with any systematic changes in the wood). Have the same person paint each of the squares (to compare like with like, in case there are differences between the people doing the painting) in the order in which they are numbered (to cope with any systematic changes in the painting style, the weather conditions, the paint brushes, etc.).

Have the assessment done by someone who does not know which paint is which (to overcome bias on the part of the assessor).

2 The data support the claim of a 25% reduction in the noise level.

3 The five letter summary is as follows.

	In-house			Bought in	
	157		Median	8	107
138		179.5	Quartiles	4.5 89.5	127
112		263	Extrema	1 80	177

The box-and-whisker plots are given below.

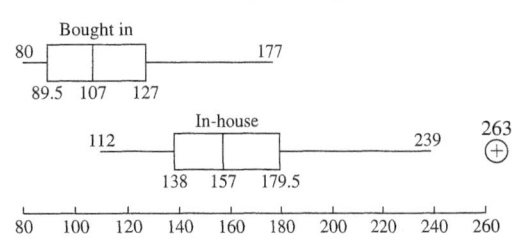

The evidence is very strong that the in-house resin produces paint which is more resistant to the solvent. There is no reason to pay the extra money to buy in the resin.

4 Let μ_X and μ_Y be the mean lifetimes, in hours, of the populations of bulbs filled with gases X and Y respectively.

Let the corresponding standard deviations, in hours, be σ_X and σ_Y.

H_0: $\mu_X = \mu_Y = \mu$
H_0: $\mu_X \neq \mu_Y$
Two-tailed test
Significance level: 5%

Under H_0 $\overline{X} \sim N\left(\mu, \frac{\sigma_X^2}{50}\right)$ and $\overline{Y} \sim N\left(\mu, \frac{\sigma_Y^2}{50}\right)$.

So $\overline{X} - \overline{Y} \sim N\left(0, \frac{\sigma_X^2}{50} + \frac{\sigma_Y^2}{50}\right)$.

So $\dfrac{\overline{X} - \overline{Y}}{\sqrt{\dfrac{\sigma_X^2}{50} + \dfrac{\sigma_Y^2}{50}}} \approx N(0, 1)$.

Since the samples are large you may estimate the population variances by the sample variances,

giving $\dfrac{\overline{X} - \overline{Y}}{\sqrt{\dfrac{\hat{\sigma}_X^2}{50} + \dfrac{\hat{\sigma}_Y^2}{50}}} \approx N(0, 1)$

which is equivalent to the result given in the question.

Substituting in the values gives

$$\frac{\frac{50\,116}{50} - \frac{52\,062}{50}}{\sqrt{\frac{497\,378}{\frac{49}{50}} + \frac{280\,794}{\frac{49}{50}}}} = -2.1838\ldots$$

This is lower than the critical value of -1.96 so the result is significant and you reject H_0.

Conclusion: The data suggest that the different gases do result in different mean lifetimes for the bulbs. In fact, it seems that filling with gas Y gives the longer lifetimes.

The variance estimate for bulbs filled with gas X is almost double that for bulbs filled with gas Y, so it seems that there is more variability for the bulbs filled with gas X.

5 (i) No, the differences may be due to chance.
(ii) Use profit rather than yield as the response variable.

❓ (page 222)

Use a paired design: divide each field into two and randomly allocate one variety to each part. You expect the differences between the ten fields to be greater than the differences between the two plots within a field. This is discussed in the text that follows.

Exercise 11C (Page 226)

1 (i)

Operation	A	B	C	D	E	F	G	H	I
Machine X	42.7	7.4	84.5	24.2	39.4	56.1	47.3	63.2	12.4
Machine Y	51.3	7.1	85.3	26.1	38.7	59.3	46.1	66.3	15.2
Difference	−8.6	0.3	−0.8	−1.9	0.7	−3.2	1.2	−3.1	−2.8

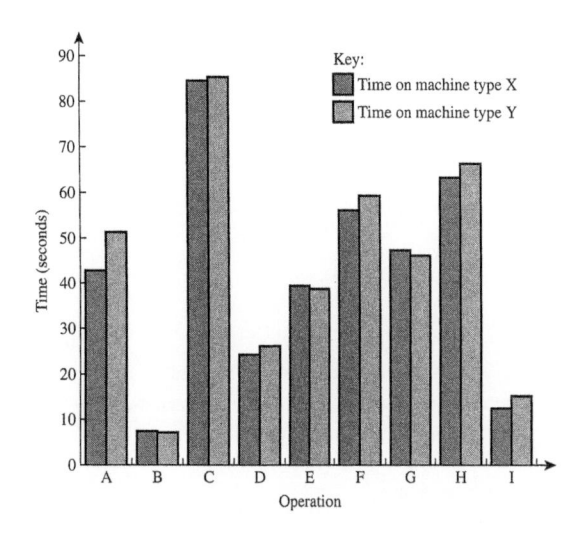

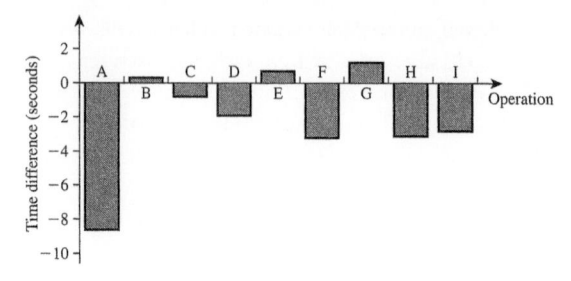

The table and charts show that the time taken on a machine of type X is usually less than that taken on a machine of type Y. The biggest difference is when they are used for operation A.

(ii) In each hypothesis test, the null hypothesis is that there is no difference between the machines and the alternative hypothesis is that there is a difference, so it is a two-tailed test. The significance level used is 5%.

(a) The number of operations on which the machine of type X is slower than the machine of type Y, is modelled by $R \sim B(9, 0.5)$ under the null hypothesis. For a two-tailed test the critical region is $r = 0, 1, 8$ or 9.

The test statistic (the number of differences which are positive) for these data is 3. This is not significant, so you accept H_0.

The sign test has no distributional assumptions.

(b)

Operation	Time on machine type X	Time on machine type Y	Difference	Rank
A	42.7	51.3	−8.6	9
B	7.4	7.1	0.3	1
C	84.5	85.3	−0.8	3
D	24.2	26.1	−1.9	5
E	39.4	38.7	0.7	2
F	56.1	59.3	−3.2	8
G	47.3	46.1	1.2	4
H	63.2	66.3	−3.1	7
I	12.4	15.2	−2.8	6

The sum of the ranks of the positive differences, W_+, is 7.

The critical value from tables is 5, so again the result is not significant.

This test assumes that the distribution of the differences is symmetrical, which is doubtful because of the extreme value, −8.6.

(c) The model of the differences here is
$D_1, \ldots, D_9 \sim N(\mu, \sigma^2)$ so
$\bar{D} \sim N\left(\mu, \dfrac{\sigma^2}{9}\right)$ so $\dfrac{\bar{D} - \mu}{\frac{\sigma}{\sqrt{9}}} \sim N(0, 1)$ and

$\dfrac{\bar{D} - \mu}{\frac{\sigma}{\sqrt{9}}} \sim t_8$ where $\hat{\sigma}^2 = \dfrac{\sum_i (D_i - \bar{D})^2}{8}$.

Under H_0, $\mu = 0$ so $\dfrac{\bar{D} - \mu}{\frac{\sigma}{\sqrt{9}}} \sim t_8$.

For the given data set $\bar{d} = -2.022$ and $\hat{\sigma} = 2.982$ so the test statistic is

$\dfrac{\bar{d}}{\frac{\hat{\sigma}}{\sqrt{9}}} = \dfrac{-2.022}{\frac{2.982}{\sqrt{9}}}$ which is -2.035.

The critical values are ± 2.306 so the result is not significant and, again, you accept H_0. This test assumes that the differences are Normally distributed, and this would not appear to be a valid assumption.

2 The two methods seem to be giving similar values, but results given by method A may have a tendency to be higher than those given by method B.

Using a significance level of 5%, the critical values for the sign test are 5 and 15. The test statistic is 10, which is not significant.

The critical values for the Wilcoxon rank sum test are 46 and 125 ($n = 19$ since the results are the same for subject 17). The test statistic is 113, which is not significant.

The critical values for the t test are ± 2.093 (with 19 degrees of freedom). The test statistic is
$\dfrac{0.19}{\frac{0.897\,892}{\sqrt{20}}} = 0.946\ldots$, which is not significant so, again, you accept H_0.

All of the tests confirm that the two methods are consistent with each other.

3

The graph suggests that resin A has more resistance to rubbing with the solvent than does the resin B.

The differences do not appear to be Normally distributed and so a t test would not be appropriate.

For a Wilcoxon rank test, the critical values are 21 and $(14 \times \frac{15}{2} - 21 =)\ 84$. The test statistic for the given data is 88* which is significant, so the data suggest that there is a difference between the two resins, with resin A being better.

4 (i) (a) The purpose of replication is to assess the variability of the situation to see whether apparent differences are due to the products or could be due to random variation.

(b) Each product is used several times.

(ii) (a) Randomisation is used to overcome problems from systematic effects. For example, the 'typical' washing loads might be getting progressively more, or less, difficult to clean. Alternatively, the washing machine(s) being used might be less and less effective as the experiment progresses.

(b) Random allocation should be used to specify which product should be applied to each washing load and the order in which the loads are washed.

(iii) One practical problem might be the time involved. If loads are held until all are washed they might get soiled. If the assessment is made immediately after the wash, it might be difficult for assessments to be consistent. If more machines are used to speed things up, a more complex design is required.

❓ (Page 231)

If the additive model is valid, the residuals should be random. A pattern in the residuals suggests that they are not random, so there is some other component in the situation which should be incorporated in the model. If you can identify and model this feature, the model should be better, but it will be more complicated.

Exercise 11D (Page 237)

1 The values in the table below are given to 2 decimal places. Your values might differ slightly.

| | | Fertiliser | | | |
Field (Block)	P	Q	R	T	Field effects
A	3.96	2.39	−1.32	−5.04	−19.82
B	2.96	−0.61	1.68	−4.04	−12.82
C	0.71	1.14	−1.57	−0.29	−6.57
D	3.96	−2.61	−3.32	1.96	0.18
E	−3.54	−0.11	3.18	0.46	7.68
F	−3.29	−0.86	1.43	2.71	13.43
G	−4.79	0.64	−0.07	4.21	17.93
Treatment effect	−17.46	−5.89	4.82	18.54	81.32

All the treatment effects seem to represent real effects.

2

| | | Variety | | | |
Block	Haven	Hereward	Hunter	Riband	Block effects
1	−200	400	−240	40	20
2	250	−50	−90	−110	170
3	50	−250	110	90	170
4	−100	0	160	−60	20
5	0	−100	60	40	−380
Variety effect	100	300	−260	−140	7580

The differences between the varieties seem to be real effects apart from the differences between Hunter and Riband.

3 Case 1

| | | Machine | | |
Operator	A	B	C	Operator effect
P	5	0	−3	15
Q	0	0	−4	25
R	7	0	0	0
S	0	0	2	−8
T	−1	0	1	−10
Machine effect	−7	0	8	59

It appears that about eight more widgets per hour can be produced on machine C than on machine B and about seven more widgets per hour can be produced on machine B than on machine A, so machine C appears to be the best. The residuals range from −4 to 7 so the differences between machine A and machine B, and between machine B and machine C, could be due to chance, but about half of the residuals are zero so it seems more likely that the differences are real.

Case 2

| | | Machine | | |
Operator	A	B	C	Operator effect
P	9	0	−6	12
Q	0	13	−5	16
R	1	−12	0	0
S	−16	0	8	−11
T	−13	0	14	−13
Machine effect	−1	0	5	62

The residuals are much larger. They are generally bigger than the machine effects and so the differences between the machines could well be due to chance. On the basis of these results you would choose machine C but you could not be very confident about your choice.

4 (i)

| | Pattern of application | | | |
Block	X	Y	Z	Block effect
1	0	0	0	500
2	−200	0	0	400
3	0	200	−300	0
4	200	0	300	−100
5	−400	400	−300	0
Application effect	−200	0	300	8000

(ii) The differences between the patterns could have occurred by chance.

(iii)

| | Pattern of application | | | |
Block	X	Y	Z	Block effect
1	0	0	100	−100
2	−200	0	−100	400
3	300	−100	100	100
4	300	0	0	0
5	0	700	−400	−200
Application effect	−300	0	400	7500

Again, all the differences could be due to chance.

5 Sweeping by means gives the following results.

Block	Natural	High	Low	Block effect
1	2.58	2.08	−4.67	20.92
2	−7.42	2.08	5.33	−11.08
3	−15.75	−10.25	26.00	4.25
4	20.58	6.08	−26.67	−14.08
Treatment effect	−26.25	16.25	10.00	332.75

When compared with the size of the residuals, there seems to be a fairly clear increase in the number of eggs laid when using the extensions to the natural day. However, the difference between the two forms of lighting for extending the day could well be due to chance variation.

6 (i) The machines may well differ from each other and a randomised block allows for this, whereas a completely randomised design could end up with, say, product A just being used on machine 1 which would result in the two 'effects' being confounded as it would not be possible to distinguish the effect of product A from the effect of machine 1.

(ii) After first application of median polish:

Product	Machine 1	2	3	4	5	Product effect
A	8	0	7	−8	−7	2
B	7	0	7	−8	−6	−7
C	0	0	−5	4	7	−4
D	−3	0	−9	1	6	0
E	5	0	0	0	0	0
Machine effect	−10	−10	5	0	1	31

After second application of median polish:

Product	Machine 1	2	3	4	5	Product effect
A	3	0	7	−8	−7	2
B	2	0	7	−8	−6	−7
C	−5	0	−5	4	7	−4
D	−8	0	−9	1	6	0
E	0	0	0	0	0	0
Machine effect	−5	−10	5	0	1	31

The medians of the row medians and the column medians are now both zero, so the process terminates.

The residuals range from −9 to +7, which is more than the differences between the product medians, so there is insufficient evidence to conclude that there is a real difference between the products.

(iii) The differing values of the column medians in the final table suggest that there might be real differences between the machines. Using a randomised block design in the full experiment will help remove the variability due to using different machines.

Exercise 11E (Page 243)

1

Fabric type	Operator A	B	C	D	Fabric effect
P	3.50	2.75	−0.50	−5.75	−25.00
Q	−0.75	−2.00	−1.75	4.50	−14.25
R	−1.00	2.25	−2.00	0.75	24.00
S	−1.75	−3.00	4.25	0.50	15.25
Operator effect	−40.75	−18.00	8.75	50.00	1114.75

Machine	1	2	3	4
Effect	−148.5	−51.5	49	151

From the size of the residuals, the differences between the machines are probably real. The machines improve from 1 to 4.

2 Finding the means gives the following results.

Period	Cow P	Q	R	S	Period effect
1	−7.250	3.250	3.500	0.500	17.375
2	−3.000	−0.750	3.000	0.750	2.125
3	3.000	4.750	−7.000	−0.750	−6.125
4	7.250	−7.250	0.500	0.500	−13.375
Cow effect	1.875	−16.625	21.875	−7.125	114.375

Diet	A	B	C	D
Diet effect	−17.375	−7.375	8.875	15.875

The diet appears to increase in effect from A to D. Both C and D are better than A and B but the other differences could be due to chance.

3 (i) Sweeping by means gives the following results.

		Variety		
Field	Haven	Hereward	Riband	Field effect
1	−200.0	266.7	−66.7	−33.3
2	266.7	−66.7	−200.0	133.3
3	−66.7	−200.0	266.7	−100.0
Variety effect	−33.3	166.7	−133.3	7633.3

Pattern	X	Y	Z
Effect	100	33.333 33	−133.333

The residuals are large compared with the pattern effects after attempting to fit the additive model, so it looks as though the differences could just be due to chance variation. If, instead, you use median polish, you obtain the same results (with different numbers in the table).

(ii) Removing the field effects suggests that timing X is good for Haven, Z for Hereward, and Y for Riband.

(iii) The possibly good combinations are
Haven + Field 2 + Timing X
Hereward + Field 1 + Timing Z
Riband + Field 3 + Timing Y.

Index

additive model 231, 241
alternative hypothesis 120, 161, 177, 186
analysis of variance 192, 226, 229
ANOVA model 202
assumptions underlying the t test 118

balanced design 228
between groups estimate 194
between groups sum of squares 194, 200
between groups variation 192
bias *see also* unbiased estimators 25, 26, 43
binomial distribution 9, 13, 70, 74, 85, 86, 98, 176
blind experiment 213
block 212, 228

Cauchy distribution 52, 102
Central Limit Theorem 109, 141, 147
characteristic function 97
χ^2 (chi-squared) test 1, 4, 68
combinations of random variables 10
comparative frequency polygon 217
comparing estimators 41
comparison between paired and unpaired tests 121
completely randomised design 216
composite hypothesis 178
conditions 114
confidence intervals 128, 141, 144, 149, 150
　and hypothesis tests 134
　for the difference of two means 129, 150
confounding 1, 211
consistency 48
continuous distribution 61, 91
continuous random variable 8, 62, 97
control treatment 212
convolution theorem 79, 105
critical region 117, 142, 162, 163

critical values
　for Mann–Whitney test 165, 170
　for Wilcoxon rank sum test 161, 163, 168
cumulative distribution function 7, 12, 13, 14, 22, 42, 140

data generating process 2
degrees of freedom 36, 38, 116, 129, 131, 194, 199
discrete distribution 8, 91
discrete random variable 69, 73, 79, 97
distributions of combinations of random variables 10
distributions of functions of random variables 5, 137
double blind experiment 213

efficiency 47
errors in hypothesis testing 176
estimation 20
estimators
　as random variables 21
　for mean and variance 34, 43, 149
expectation 6, 72, 135
experiment 209
experimental design 210
experimental error 202
experimental unit 212
exploratory data analysis 215
exponential distribution 12, 94, 101

factor 212
frequency polygon 219
F statistic 195
F test 195
functions of random variables 5

generation of moments 106
geometric distribution 14, 70, 74, 87
good estimators 24
goodness of fit testing 4

hinge 232

hinge spread 231, 232
hypothesis testing
　for difference of means 113
　in statistical modelling 4
　underlying logic of, 119
　when variance is known 141
　when variance is unknown 116, 119
hypothesis tests and confidence intervals 128

independent random sample 4, 118
independent random variables 10, 77

kurtosis 93

large samples 134, 147, 149
large sample tests 134
Latin square 239
levels 212
likelihood 55
linear combinations of random variables 10
linear transformation 80, 104
location 163
logarithmic differentiation 57

Mann–Whitney method 166
Mann–Whitney test 164
maximum and minimum values in a sample 11
maximum likelihood
　criterion 57
　estimation 54, 61
　estimator 59, 60
　　properties of, 60
　method 56
mean 72, 73, 92
　of distribution 3
mean absolute error 45
mean square error 45
median 161
median polish 233, 234
modelling 1, 215
moment generating functions 91, 97
　linear transformation result 104
　properties of, 103
moments 91, 92

negative binomial distribution   83
non-parametric tests   163
Normal approximation   141, 149, 169
Normal distribution   100, 104, 108
Normal hypothesis testing   182
Normality assumption   147

operating characteristic   178
outcome probabilities, assigning   2, 3

paired design   114, 121, 150, 222
paired sample *t* test   121, 223
parameter estimation   4
pilot experiment   212
placebo   213
Poisson distribution   68, 86, 99
pooled samples   36, 149
population distribution   21, 27
population variance in large samples   147
power   182
probability density function   3, 6, 8, 12, 22, 23, 42
probability distribution   5, 15, 69, 134
probability generating functions   67
  basic properties   69
  expectation and variance   72
  for three or more variables   82
  of standard distributions   85

randomisation   211
randomised block design   228
randomness   2
random sampling without replacement   4
random variable   3

ranking   161
rank sum test   160
real world, modelling   2
replication   210
residual   226, 231, 236, 242
residual sum of squares   194
resistant statistics   233, 234
response variable   212

sample
  maximum and minimum   11
  mean   11
  randomness   118
  size   180
  statistics   4
sampling distribution   115
  of estimators   22, 41
sampling process   3
significance level   120, 161, 164, 179, 181, 184
sign test   223
simple hypothesis   178
skewness   93
standard deviation of estimators   44
standard error   43
statistical model, construction of   3
stem-and-leaf diagram   218, 231
subjects   114
sum of independent random variables   77
sweeping by means   219, 224, 229

tail probabilities   139
test for difference between population means   125, 203
tests of location   163
test statistic   115, 121, 142, 145, 149, 150, 161, 164, 169, 195

tied ranks   161
total estimate   199
total sum of squares   199
treatment   212
triangular distribution   26
T value   165
twin studies   123
two-way analysis of variance   233
type 1 and type 2 errors   178, 225

unbalanced design   228
unbiased estimators   25, 28, 34, 37, 43, 47, 116, 193, 246
uniform distribution   69
uniform (rectangular) distribution   21, 41, 96
unpaired design   114, 160
unpaired sample *t* test   117, 118, 121, 122, 125
unpaired tests   113, 121, 122, 149

variance *see also* population variance   72, 79, 93, 135
  of combinations of random variables   10
  of differences between two conditions   149
  known   141, 159
  not known   34, 116, 119, 147, 159

Wilcoxon paired sample test   223
Wilcoxon rank sum test   160
within groups estimate   194
within groups sum of squares   194, 200
within groups variation   192
W value   161